IDEOLOGIES,
GOALS,
AND VALUES

Recent Titles in Contributions in Sociology
Series Editor: Don Martindale

Politics, Character, and Culture: Perspectives from Hans Gerth
Joseph Bensman, Arthur J. Vidich, and Nobuko Gerth, editors

Ethnicity, Pluralism, and Race: Race Relations Theory in America Before Myrdal
R. Fred Wacker

Civil Religion and Moral Order: Theoretical and Historical Dimensions
Michael W. Hughey

Countercultural Communes
Gilbert Zicklin

Max Weber's Political Sociology: A Pessimistic Vision of a Rationalized World
Ronald M. Glassman and Vatro Murvar, editors

The Adventure of Reason: The Uses of Philosophy in Sociology
H. P. Rickman

Social Hierarchies: Essays Toward a Sociophysiological Perspective
Patricia R. Barchas, editor

Social Cohesion: Essays Toward a Sociophysiological Perspective
Patricia R. Barchas, editor

Family and Work: Comparative Convergences
Merlin B. Brinkerhoff, editor

Work, Organizations, and Society: Comparative Convergences
Merlin B. Brinkerhoff, editor

No Place to Hide: Crisis and Future of American Habitats
Manuel Marti, Jr.

Systems of Discourse: Structures and Semiotics in the Social Sciences
George V. Zito

IDEOLOGIES, GOALS, AND VALUES

Feliks Gross

Foreword by Don Martindale

Contributions in Sociology, Number 52

Greenwood Press
Westport, Connecticut • London, England

Library of Congress Cataloging in Publication Data

Gross, Feliks.
  Ideologies, goals, and values.

(Contributions in sociology, ISSN 0084-9278 ; no. 52)
  Bibliography: p.
  Includes index.
  1. Ideology—Addresses, essays, lectures.
2. Values—Addresses, essays, lectures.   3. Goal
(Philosophy)—Addresses, essays, lectures.   I. Title.
II. Series.
B823.3.G76   1984   303.3'72   84-3754
ISBN 0-8371-6377-3 (lib. bdg.)

Library of Congress Catalog Card Number: 84-3754
ISBN: 0-8371-6377-3
ISSN: 0084-9278

First published in 1985

Greenwood Press
A division of Congressional Information Service, Inc.
88 Post Road West
Westport, Connecticut 06881

Printed in the United States of America

10 9 8 7 6 5 4 3 2 1

Contents

Figures and Tables   vii

Foreword by Don Martindale   ix

Introduction   xxi

Acknowledgments   xxxiii

Part I   Ideologies   **1**

1. The Directive and Regulatory System   3

2. Ideologies—The World Outlook and Values   26

3. The Structure of Ideologies   44

4. The Appeal and Function of Values   58

5. Definition of Values: Structure of Goals   71

Part II   Goals   **75**

6. Types of Goals: Elementary Goal Structure   77

7. Formation of Goals: Needs and Stimuli   91

8. Horizontal Sequence of Goals:
   Goals and Incentives   103

9. Strategies   119

10. Social Planning and Ethics   128

11. The Logic of Planning   145

12. Distant Goals   156

13. Social Rhythm and Cyclical Goals:
    Time and Goals   183

Part III   Values   **209**

14. Hierarchies of Values: Vertical Structure   211

15. Multiple Sets of Values: Parallel Hierarchies   237

16. In Search of Universal Values   273

17. Toleration and Pluralism   300

    Bibliography   321

    Index   337

Figures and Tables

Figures

Fig.	1.1	Idea Systems and Values	13
Fig.	2.1	The Base Affects the Superstructure	31
Fig.	3.1	Perception and Thoughtways	45
Fig.	3.2	Structure of a Belief System	46
Fig.	3.3	Structure of a Political Ideology	49
Fig.	4.1	Sign	60
Fig.	6.1	Goal and Parameters	86
Fig.	6.2	Decision Making: Selection of Preferred Actions (Options)	89
Fig.	8.1	Horizontal Goal Structure	104
Fig.	9.1	Strategy and Tactics	120
Fig.	11.1	Situation and Planning	147
Fig.	11.2	Planning	149
Fig.	12.1	Time Range of Major Architectural Projects, 2000 BC – 2000 AD	170
Fig.	13.1	Spatialization of Time	200
Fig.	14.1	Hierarchy of Values or a Vertical Structure of Values	213
Fig.	14.2	A Vertical Approach to Values	232
Fig.	15.1	National and Multiple Value Subsystems	251
Fig.	17.1	Types of Multicultural States	307

Tables

Tab. 12.1   Range of Major Projects, 2700 BC – 1970 AD   163

Tab. 12.2   Means (in Years) of Goal Range and
            Historical Attention Span of Major Religious
            Architectural Construction Projects,
            c. 20th Century BC – 19th century AD   169

Tab. 12.3   Means (in Years) of Goal Range of Major
            Secular Architectural Construction Projects in
            Europe and the United States, 2d century BC
            – 20th Century AD   169

Tab. 16.1   Boat People Admitted to Various Countries
            as of September 1978   288

Foreword

Don Martindale

In the beginning was experience.

Man is conscious before he becomes self-conscious. As self-consciousness fitfully dawns, the individual is already *there*: sleeping and waking; growing hungry and seeking ways to satisfy himself; responding to cold and heat, pain and pleasure; growing bored and restless and seeking diversion or fatigued and seeking rest. As he becomes self-conscious, he finds his life entwined with those of others, many of whom have power to satisfy or frustrate him. He discovers himself seeking ways to win them to his causes; he basks in their approval; he shivers in the cloud-cold of their disapproval. The day may even come when he generalizes this: *Socialization is a transformation that individuals largely carry out upon themselves.*

Experience, the primary reality, always comes in particulars: this moment; this occasion; this person; this face; this smile or frown; this pain or pleasure. Fortunately one particular experience is often very like another, so an individual is able in some measure to anticipate and grow more effective in time. But in the procession of incidents from day to day, however similar, one is never quite identical to another and there are always breaks and discordances. Success in the many enterprises an individual discovers himself engaged in as he becomes self-conscious, depends largely upon ability to extract similarities from differences, generalizing them into tools for the mastery of new experience. In fact, self-consciousness and the process of extracting generalizations from particular cases often come together. And some persons with more knowledge and experience and with a special relationship to the individual, often prove to have at hand a store of generalizations. Particularly when experience collapses and falls in on the individual, parents, relatives, older friends, or teachers quote sayings or proverbs that apply to experience like his own or they tell him stories that suggest strategies for outwitting disaster.

The individual will not be long in discovering that in the wider ongoing world of men vital information may be found on almost anything if only he will take the trouble to acquire it; in his childhood he, in some measure, recapitulates the childhood of humankind, and in proverbs and fairy tales he receives some of man's first generalizations about life and information on ancient strategies for survival—forms of intelligence that have still not lost their anchorage in natural history. As the individual grows up, he is expected to turn his back upon these childish things, consulting for orientation, rather, learned disciplines such as philosophy and social science. The social wisdom of proverb and fairy tale belong to the archaic world of the sage and the storyteller. In sublimated form they lived on for a time in philosophy, only to have their foundation in natural history disappear with the rise of social science.

With this observation one touches, for the first time, the paradox of Feliks Gross. Though prominent in the highest ranks of contemporary social science, he moves in the aura of a more archaic form of social intelligence—one, in contrast to the *knowledge* of the social sciences, that belongs to the *wisdom* of the past. He has not lost contact with the sage and the storyteller and, in his own writing and research, draws sustenance from a tap root in natural history.

Sketch for a Portrait

While this is not the place to undertake the biography of Feliks Gross and space is not available here to do it justice, a few biographical notes and a sketch for a portrait are essential to locate *Ideologies, Goals, and Values* in his life and work.

Even the basic statistics on his activities reveal Feliks Gross as a formidable adversary. In addition to teaching as a sociologist and political scientist at New York University and Brooklyn College from 1946 until his retirement from active teaching, he has been visiting professor at numbers of other colleges and universities (see chronology), written many books and articles and published in a number of languages. In tabular form the record is as follows.

Feliks Gross: Some Professional Statistics

Accomplishment	Number
Universities served at	7*
Books	23**
Major articles	49**
Languages in which books and articles appear	9
Countries in which articles appear	10
Major field researches	6

* These represent only universities with major terms of service. Shorter terms of service were served at twelve to eighteen more.
** This does not include reprints and translations into languages other than those in which the original book or article appeared.

And when one adds to this formidable record the fact that in addition to authoring or editing some twenty-three books of his own, he has contributed to at least eight volumes by others; that he was a syndicated columnist for Asian and Latin American Newspapers Foreign News Service, that he has been a member of the research council of the Foreign Policy Research Institution of Philadelphia, Pennsylvania, that he has been president of the Taraknath Das Foundation, a member of the Board of Directors of the International League of Human Rights and a consultant of the National Committee for Prevention and Causes of Violence, it is evident that Feliks Gross is a natural phenomenon.

Definitive answers to the inevitable questions that arise whenever one seeks to take his measure will have to wait on Feliks Gross's memoirs and his biography. However, the questions are clear: How did this contemporary social scientist manage to retain an archaic aura? From what sources did he generate his astonishing energy? Some provisional suggestions follow.

At the time this sketch was undertaken, the only materials publicly available on Feliks Gross apart from his books, which report his researches and his theories about other things, but not about himself, were the schematic items in biographical reference books. Nevertheless, some salient facts stood out: He was the son of a lawyer; he derived from the Jewish minority of Poland; he had earned his doctoral degree from the University of Cracow; he had had an extraordinarily productive career in teaching and research, ranging from anthropology to international relations; he was sympathetic to democratic socialism; he had a love of high culture. He fitted one of the personality types that was outlined in a classic of American sociology and seems to have been primarily a contribution of Florian Znaniecki, himself a Pole.

Thomas and Znaniecki in *The Polish Peasant* had observed that individuals who find themselves in marginal situations between minority and majority cultures have three ideal-typical ways of resolving conflicts their situations may generate: the *Philistine*, who clings to traditional formulas and stereotypes; the *Bohemian* who responds situationally to influence from now one, now another culture with no attempt at self-consistency, often drifting between worlds with a deteriorating sense of self-esteem; the *Creative*, who walks a tightrope between both cultural worlds, seeking to make the best of both and being forced to invent new solutions to make it possible. By the nature of his situation as scion of a sophisticated legal family and destined from the start for a professional education, Feliks Gross was predestined for the life formula of a Creative man. By virtue of his occupation an attorney has a ringside seat on problems of politics and power, crime and punishment, conflict and its resolution. An interest in conflicts of value, power, and legitimate forms of conflict resolution extends to Feliks Gross's earliest childhood.

While Feliks Gross's life formula was of a creative type that could, in part, have had its origins in minority status—though it should be noted that it does not necessarily require minority status to generate a life formula of creativity—this in no way accounts for the substantive forms assumed by his creativity. One possible way to determine the parameters of his ideas and interests is to review them in the social milieu of his adolescence and young manhood (the times when most individuals depart from the shelter of their families, make adjustments to the adult outside world, and found families of their own), triangulating to him from the landmarks of the intellectual life of his time and place. While there are risks in such a procedure, it offers some possibility of locating an individual in his time and among his contemporaries.

Feliks Gross was twelve years old when World War I ended, by which time the Bolshevik phase of the Russian Revolution had been carried through. Poland, in the aftermath of Versailles, was in a position where it could undertake reconstruction for a time without interference from either Germany or Russia. Socialism was popular in student and labor circles in Central and Eastern Europe. For example, Paul Felix Lazarsfeld, who was born in Vienna five years before Feliks Gross, but who was also completing his education in the 1920s, noted in his memoir, *An Episode in the History of Social Research: A Memoir*, that he was active in the student socialist movement. Moreover, when Lazarsfeld was taken on as an assistant in the Psychological Institute of Charlotte and Karl Bühler and empowered to set up projects of his own, he chose to make a study of Marienthal, a village south of Vienna whose population was almost entirely unemployed. As a student in Cracow in the 1920s Feliks Gross was involved in a workers' adult education movement, was making his first field studies of coal and salt miners and construction workers, and was writing his first book (jointly with his brother Zygmunt) on *The Sociology of Political Parties*.

Marxism, which had become institutionalized in the German labor movement, was in these circles turning into a rhetorical ideology to which lip service was paid while in practice it was being subjected to strong pressures to make it pragmatically responsive to the day-to-day needs of the workers. The Marxism of the Russian radicals had first been converted into an instrument for carrying out a seizure of power on the basis of the dissatisfaction of the peasants and once the Bolsheviks acceded to power, was being turned into the secular theology of a new oriental despotism.

One group of radical students in Germany in the 1920s, a group that was eventually to become known as the Frankfurt School and who led by Max Horkheimer and Theodor Adorno, sought to dissociate an academic form of revolutionary Marxism from both the Leninist-Stalinist and German Social Democratic varieties and to combine it with cultural elitism.

The period of the 1920s in Central and Eastern Europe—the time and place where Feliks Gross was coming of age—was a time for the diffusion of nationalism, of socialism of pre-Marxist forms, of Zionism, and of Marxism in a number of versions. Possibly because of its institutionalization as the official ideology of the German labor movement and by the prestige it acquired by becoming the official ideology of the USSR, Marxism was claiming a virtual monopoly of socialism (that is, its spokesmen were making this claim in its name). It has been said of the Jewish minority of Central and Eastern Europe at the time that it had only two viable options: Zionism or Marxism. However, Marxism was by no means a single unified tradition, and the circumstances of the economic classes varied considerably between West, Central, and Eastern Europe. Neither the German or the Russian versions of Marxism fitted the circumstances of Poland very well.

Hence, when one undertakes to triangulate to Feliks Gross's point of view in this milieu and from these points, he does not fit very well in the spaces where it would be necessary to place him: He was sympathetic to Zionism, but gave no evidence of envisioning it as a major solution for himself; he was deeply critical of many features of Marxism, though clearly in sympathy with the humanistic dimension of Marx's thought; he had a deep appreciation of the higher forms of culture, but displayed no inclination to prefer the avant garde cultural elitism of the Frankfurt school. This left no possibility, in completing the remainder of this sketch, other than appealing directly to Gross himself.

Feliks Gross was born June 17, 1906, in Cracow, Poland, to the family of a prominent attorney. His father was elected to the Austrian Parliament as deputy of Cracow. His relatives were mixed Jewish and Catholic. While his father and mother were Jewish, his mother's (Augusta Alexander's) sisters, his aunts, were married to Catholics. Later one of his uncles was a senator in the Polish *Sejm* (parliament) from the Polish Socialist party. From childhood Feliks had a room in the home next door of a Catholic uncle, Arthur Zabielski. His uncle prepared candles so his aunt could light them on the Day of Atonement, and the Grosses celebrated Christmas and other Christian holidays with him.

The ambience of the parental household was humanistic and socially responsible, characterized by the drive for achievement. As a liberal lawyer and politician, Adolf Gross was interested in housing cooperatives and had sponsored the most advanced legislation on housing in Europe at the time. His older brother, Ludwik, was the discoverer of the leukemia virus (the Gross virus).

Feliks was raised in an atmosphere where it was taken for granted that cultural preferences must be respected without prejudice, and he experienced no conflicts between his Jewish and Polish loyalties.

Among his oldest childhood memories was a story by Kipling that translated into Polish as "The Cat Who Walked Alone." Possibly because it represented one of those occasions when for the first time he encounters himself though he may not realize it at the time, Feliks found in the story an identification: He was like the cat that must, in the end, walk alone, see for himself, and make his own choices in a search for truth, decency, and a good society.

In *World Politics and Tension Areas*, Feliks Gross has described the formation of the Jewish minority in Cracow and its character at the time of his young manhood. Jews had been present in Poland for a millennium, usually protected by the state, which valued their business, financial, and intellectual skills; sporadically persecuted by the Church and right-wing political movements for ideological reasons, generally getting along with the local population with which it in part mixed and with which it sometimes came into competition, conflict, and discrimination as when non-Jewish Poles developed business and financial skills of their own. In Gross's summary:

The City of Cracow was inhabited at the time by Roman Catholic and Jewish populations and by a small Protestant community, with the Jewish population forming a complex subculture of many degrees of acculturation. Ethnic and religious divisions in Cracow were complicated by the class structure, and a variety of political orientations that contributed to their diversity.
Orthodox Jewish groups, which preserved their own specific culture, combined a pattern of strong self-segregation with neutrality toward outsiders. A minor group of Polish Catholic nationalists joined self-segregation with hostility toward other groups that increased in times of tension. Between these two extremes there were many Polish-Catholics and Jews who were de facto integrated. Furthermore, there were other Polish and Jewish groups which favored a pluralistic solution (cultural autonomy).[1]

Feliks Gross straddled those groups that he described as de facto integrated and favoring pluralistic solutions to intercultural relations.

While still in high school he responded sensitively to the miseries produced by war. He became a pacifist, convinced that the federation for Europe and the development of a world community were the only answers to war. Woodrow Wilson and the League of Nations were popular in his school. With a group of friends he organized a student European federalist, pacifist and League of Nations Association. Peace and European federalism was a lifelong interest. He met later the founder of the European federalist movement (author of *Paneropa*) R. N. Coudenhove Kalergi and the German pacifist and liberal philosopher Wilhelm Friedrich Förster. Their friendly, at times close, association and cooperation continued especially during the crucial war years.

A consequence of an impulse that had been developing from childhood and was epitomized by the tale of the cat who walked alone became manifest upon Feliks Gross's graduation from the gymnasium. He had been turning in his mind the prospect of becoming a technical student and decided to become acquainted firsthand with mechanics and the world of manual workers. He spent six months in a railroad yard learning about locomotives and developing a deep and abiding respect for those who work with their hands. A pattern was emerging: to read everything on a subject and to test it against firsthand experience.

Feliks Gross's student career at the University of Cracow can be described as brilliant. He read widely. As one of those rare persons who derive energy from what they do, he involved himself deeply in student affairs and politics. He carried out extensive firsthand researches on coal and salt miners, craftsmen, construction workers, even small peddlers, studying their interests, education, home furnishings, books, and reading habits. He listened to the stories, songs, and legends of the workers in sections of Cracow, being perhaps the first to make the discovery of the existence of urban folklore. Even before finishing the university, he was elected to a mediation commission headed up by the labor inspector to arbitrate economic conflicts between farmhands and landowners.

He became convinced that adult education was a major resource for improving the lot of workingmen. He joined and became active in the Workers University Association, an adult education movement. He began writing even before completing his university studies, publishing his first book before completing his degree. He became Magister Juris in 1929 and Dr. of Juris prudence in 1930.

Among persons who Feliks Gross indicates had formative influence on him, he cites Bronislaw Malinowski as his mentor. Malinowski's practice of reading and digesting everything available on the field he expected to study, translating this matter into hypotheses and problems, then exploring every facet of the reality firsthand in utmost detail, confirming, rejecting, or modifying ideas as a result—a methodological procedure that raised the level of theorizing and the precision of fieldwork in anthropology to a higher plane—became his own basic ideal. Malinowski confirmed the trend that had been present in his own thought from the beginning. Feliks Gross and Malinowski became friends. Malinowski arranged an appointment for Gross as occasional lecturer in the London School of Economics, though the outbreak of World War II prevented him from honoring it. Malinowski and Gross had a joint book underway in 1942 at the time of Malinowski's death.

Also among his mentors, Gross counts Stanislaw Estreicher, rector of the University of Cracow, who was his teacher and the father of his closest friend from childhood, Karol Estreicher, later professor of arts history at the University of Cracow. Feliks Gross met his wife-to-be, Priva Baidaff, when she was an arts history student. Rector Estreicher taught law and legal history, and from his lectures Gross learned much about the history of human rights. A man of great courage, Estreicher died in a Saxenhausen concentration camp after the German occupation.

Feliks Gross also learned much from Jan S. Bystron, a fine ethnographer and professor of sociology, the first to be appointed at the University of Cracow. In times of the rise of Fascism, Bystron wrote a slashing, witty analysis of nationalism: *The National Megalomania*. For some years Gross was enriched by the ideas and friendship of humanistic Polish socialists. He especially appreciated Zygmunt Zulawski, a humane, courageous trade union leader and member and deputy-speaker (Vice Marshall) of the *Sejm* (parliament) who early recognized the primacy of political power and structure to the economic. Gross also became friends with Zygmunt Zaremba, an editor, author, and theoretician, and a prominent leader of the democratic socialist underground during the war.

For more than forty years, Feliks Gross was close to Adam Ciolkosz, a talented political writer and historian, and a major spokesman for Polish democracy and socialism. Gross worked closely with Ciolkosz when he was editor of a democratic socialist daily in Cracow, admiring his skill as an editor and writer. Ciolkosz, in turn, always displayed critical as well as friendly and helpful interest in Gross's writings. This relationship continued to the last days of Ciolkosz's life.

Among Gross's friends in the Workers Educational Society, mention must be made of Stefan Rzeznik, a tobacco factory worker who later became a leader in the underground. His friendship with historian of the Holocaust, Michael Borwicz, has continued for a half century since their student years.

In the United States Feliks Gross developed numerous close friendships and acquaintanceships with colleagues discussed in the Acknowledgments and with Arnold Zurcher, Henry Banford Parkes, Ludwik Krzyzanowski, Roman Michalowski, Rex Hopper, Robert Erich, Hans Trefousse, John Gange, and Joseph S. Roucek. With Karl August Wittfogel, of Columbia University, and his wife, Esther Goldfrank, Feliks Gross developed a friendship that grew closer with every passing year.

Finally, Feliks Gross formed a new cultural community of friends in Italy which included the statistician Vittorio Castellano, Franco Ferrarotti, Francesco Cerase, Eugenio del Monte, Renato Treves, and Luciano Pellicani.

Feliks Gross's education was primarily Polish. In 1931 he won a Carnegie Fellowship which permitted him to continue his studies in Paris. His postgraduate education for short periods in Geneva, Paris, Berlin, and London was not aimed at attaining additional degrees, but at learning from library research, lectures and seminars. American experience and scholarship strongly influenced his work.

Scholarly and academic work had most appeal to him as a profession. He passed the Cracow bar exam in 1935, practicing, for a time, as a trial lawyer, defending in political cases and learning firsthand the difference between justice and the language of the courts. His appointment as ''docent'' (lecturer) at the University of Cracow faced difficulties because of his background and views.

Feliks Gross was a member of the Polish Socialist Party and viewed himself as a socialist, but it was of an older form of democratic and ethical socialism, endemic to Poland long before Marx had begun to formulate his theories. He read Marx and appreciated his humanism, but resisted Marx's ideological simplifications, perceiving that Marx was addressing himself to conditions different from those in Poland. The realities of Polish experience belied the notion that creativity came only from the economic base and that culture and its institutions (the state, law, and ideologies) were epiphenomenal. He was not prepared to permit the Marxist claim to a monopoly on democratic and ethical socialism to go unchallenged, but noted that historically Polish, Italian, French, and English versions of socialism all developed as early or earlier than the Marxian forms and that many of the pre-Marxian forms of socialism were more responsive to the empirical needs of laboring groups than was Marxism with its elaborate metaphysics taken over from Hegel and the German idealists.

In 1934 Feliks Gross organized and served as director of the Labor Social Science School of the Workers University Association (TUR) of Cracow, until 1938. He traveled to Norway, England, and Denmark, studying their adult education methods for possible application to Polish problems. The school was a product of these travels and research.

As a member of the Polish Socialist party, he spoke at public meetings of the Socialist Poale Zionists. He visited their kibbutzim in the city. While he did not opt for their solution to the problems of the Jewish minority, he recognized their right to it. In the late 1930s he received an invitation to lecture at the University of Jerusalem.

The Jews, in Feliks Gross's view, had made a substantial contribution to the renascence of European culture, science, and industry. They had inhabited the continent as long and, in some cases, longer than many European nations which arrived with the great migrations. They were and are Europeans, and their equal and human rights should never be surrendered, but restated and defended.

By the age of 30 Feliks Gross had already written or edited four books. The next year, 1937, he married Priva Baidaff, later a professor of art history at the City University of New York. In the United States he did not abandon his Polish heritage, but has been active in Polish American associations, lecturing to Polish workers as far west as Detroit, serving as vice president of the Polish Institute of the Arts and Sciences in America, an organization of elite of the Polish-American professional, academic, and cultural community.

In the Holocaust Feliks and Priva lost many of their friends and family members. The time also brought deeper appreciation of non-Jewish Polish friends who, at risk of their own lives, for the Germans employed the death penalty for hiding Jews, hid his brothers, sister, and mother. His mother died in a slave labor camp in Germany. His older brother Otto was killed during the war when he was a physician for the partisans, together with his wife Sofia. Sofia could easily have saved her life and those of her children; she was a Catholic and also a physician, but preferred to share the perils of her husband. His sister and her husband were deported to Soviet labor camps, but survived. Priva lost her entire family. Feliks and Priva, with only their knapsacks, managed later to escape by way of Russia, Siberia, and Japan.

Making his way with Priva to the United States, Feliks was active in the movement for European federalism, and Feliks became secretary-general of the Central East European Planning Board (for Czechoslovakia, Greece, Yugoslavia, and Poland) serving until 1945. In 1945 he was appointed as visiting professor for New York University, continuing to serve until 1968. In 1946 he was appointed professor of sociology and anthropology at Brooklyn College, serving until his retirement.

By this time the foundation had been laid for one of the most astonishingly rich careers in social science in the United States since World War II. He retained a deep interest in Poland and Poles both in Europe and America, serving as an advisor to the Polish government in exile, giving a series of lectures on the "Voice of America," participating in panel discussions and interviews, making contact with Polish workers in America, lecturing to Polish groups, and participating in the affairs of the Polish cultural community.

In addition to his early field work on Polish coal and salt miners and on construction workers, his researches include: studies of the Arapaho and Shoshone of the Wind River Reservation; studies of the Italian villages of Fumone and Lazio; studies of tensions on the Italian-Yugoslavian border; studies of the

Apache of the Mescalero Reservation of New Mexico; and studies of the values of fishermen on the islands of northeast Maine. Also for more than ten years, as chairman of the Early Childhood Study Center of Brooklyn College (which had French, Chinese, and Spanish speaking children from three to five years old), he had the opportunity to study child behavior and made a beginning of the study of the acquisition of a second language.

How did he do it all? In his teaching alone at New York University and Brooklyn College he was putting in twenty to twenty-two hours weekly while commuting by plane and rail for research, lectures elsewhere, and public service projects. It will do no good to dwell upon it—the mystery only deepens. It is time to turn from this provisional sketch for a portrait to *Ideologies, Goals, and Values*, which represents one of the most full and lucid statements to date of a quest upon which Feliks Gross has been embarked from the beginning. For he has indeed, like Thoreau, been a man with a quest. Thoreau had put the matter this way:

I long ago lost a hound, a bay horse, and a turtledove, and am still on their trail. Many are the travelers I have spoken concerning them, describing their tracks and what calls they answer to. I have met one or two who had heard the hound, and the tramp of the horse, and even seen the dove disappear behind a cloud, and they seemed as anxious to recover them as if they had lost them themselves.[2]

Feliks Gross describes himself as a human, an American, a Pole, *and* a "unitarian" Jew (he connects these characteristics with *and* not *or*) and identifies his Jewishness as belonging to the Essenic tradition, from which, as the ancient Jewish historian Josephus insisted and as the Dead Sea Scrolls have confirmed, Christianity derived, and he dreams of peace, unity, and the self-realization of man. And while we await his memoirs and his biography, there is only one additional comment to be made: One never knows what to expect next from a cat who walks alone and who must see for himself and make his own choices in his search for truth, decency, and the good society.

The Place of *Ideologies, Goals and Values* in Gross's Work

Ideologies, Goals, and Values formulates the basic analytical ideas Feliks Gross has been developing for his entire professional career. In a manner suggestive of Spencer, he views sociocultural activity as integrated into three great systems: a directing system - a regulating system - and a sustaining system, though he is not concerned with the third. As he phrases the matter, so far as the terminology of Marxism is retained, Gross maintains that he is concerned with the superstructure (the directing and regulating systems) rather than the base.

At the level of basic needs—determined by biology and the environment—there is, in Gross's view, a fundamental unity of mankind. Experience of the world in terms of these needs unfolds itself in the form of facts and values and is realized in terms of means (instrumental values) and ends (consummatory values).

However, in contrast to other creatures, man's fulfillment of his needs, is not biologically pre-programmed, but is left largely to his free choice. He must learn from others or invent himself his solutions to problems. Hence an unusual role is played by culture, socially shared and transmitted ideas, notions, sentiments, and suppositions, for man has neither the time nor the energy to invent more than a tiny fraction of the things needed to get along in the interpersonal world. Moreover, in the process of acquiring culture, needs are transformed into new forms. And under no circumstances can ideas be dismissed as mere superstructural phenomena affected by but not affecting the base. They may be good or bad, comprehensive or limited, but no human social life is possible without them. Nor can the analysis of ideologies be reduced merely to the unmasking of forms of false consciousness. In their most comprehensive sense ideologies are coextensive with the idea systems of civilization.

Following his examination of the various pragmatic and normative components of ideologies in their manifestations in directing and controlling or regulating systems, Gross carries out an analysis of goals, the objectives pursued in individual and social life. In this rich central portion of his manuscript Gross differentiates goal-oriented or telic behavior from institutional and aleatory types, explores further the difference between instrumental and consummatory goals and pragmatic and normative systems, describes elementary goal structures and the transformations and reconstructions that occur when need systems become more complex. Socially reconstructed patterns are seen as organized into strategies and subject to social planning of limited or comprehensive scope and for relatively immediate or remote time periods. The discussion of goals concludes with an interesting review of the problems of social rhythm, cyclical goals, and various time spans, illustrated by religious and temple architecture.

The concluding section of *Ideologies, Goals, and Values* is primarily confined to the analysis of vertical structures of value—that is, the formation of value hierarchies. In contrast to horizontal structures of values—which are discussed in part II which in Gross's view are fundamentally dynamic, vertical structures of value—hierarchies are static or behavior limiting. Ideologies, goals, and values can be explored at various levels: micro—the level of the peasant village or tribe; macro—the level of the social movement or large political party; mega—the level of the nation, culture, or civilization. At whatever level, vertical structures of value tend to be behavior limiting and static. It is from this perspective that Feliks Gross analyzes social hierarchies, the possibilities of authoritarian, totalitarian and antitotalitarian regimes. He closes this section and the volume with a luminous discussion of toleration and pluralism. In his view pluralistic systems of social life offer the fullest possibility of both realization of the basic unity of mankind and access to the rich forms of cultural diversity that can rise on this foundation.

Ideologies, Goals, and Values can, perhaps, best be described as the conceptual synthesis toward which Feliks Gross has been working all his life. Too many contemporary scholars close their careers, in the words of T. S. Eliot, with a whimper. Feliks Gross belongs to an older tradition and is determined to wind his up with a bang.

Postscript

Having so quickly come to the end of this brief statement, it is useful to return for a final look at the question formulated in the opening pages: Where, for all his contemporaneity, did Gross acquire the aura of an older time? How did he generate such Homeric energies?

The answer in some measure is to be found in the fact that while developing a rare mastery of contemporary social science, he has also managed to retain a lifelong involvement in the ongoing affairs of the times and has repeatedly found renewal in the common people—even carrying out research among Maine fishermen, Italian peasants, and such American Indian tribes as the Arapaho and Shoshone. He has managed to clasp the world of international politics and the on-going life of simple people in a single embrace. He has won a reputation as an inspired teacher. He is one of those rare persons who give everything they know away and can afford to do so only because they cannot give themselves away, since they find renewal in the very act. As one of Feliks Gross's former students said: "Professor Gross is extraordinary. When he speaks, it is as if Marco Polo had entered the classroom. He seems to have been everywhere and known everyone worth knowing."

While winning recognition as a major contemporary social scientist, Feliks Gross has kept faith with those first social interpreters, the sage and the storyteller. In his lectures to his students it is reported that his formulations often assume quasi-proverbial form. He recalls Walter Benjamin's observation that a proverb is "an ideogram of a story. A proverb . . . is a ruin which stands on the site of an old story and in which a moral twines about a happening like ivy around a wall." Feliks Gross is a storyteller, and it could be said of him, as Benjamin said of Nikolai Leskov, that his gift "is the ability to tell his entire life. The storyteller . . . is the man who could let the wick of his life be consumed completely by the gentle flame of his story. . . . The storyteller is the figure in which the righteous man encounters himself."

Introduction

La dernière chose qu'on trouve en faisant un ouvrage, est de savoir celle qu'il faut mettre la première. (The last thing one finds—while working on a book—is what should be put at the very beginning.)

Pascal, *Pensées*

By the end of 1940, respect for the dignity of man and human rights disappeared from the entire, immense continent. Totalitarian states covered the old world from Gibraltar to Vladivostock. Two and a half thousand years earlier, whenever Greeks and their culture moved, they built theaters and agoras, symbols of intellectual freedom and dialogue. In 1940 this immense stretch of earth was dotted with concentration camps. Slavery made a comeback.

Back in November 1936, historian, Elie Halévy, argued at the French Philosophical Society that a new era of tyrannies began in 1914. It began—I suppose—later. But by 1940—this, at time slow, at time violent, change came to its fruition.

Hardly any territory free from totalitarian tyranny was left on the Continent. Somewhere, on the outskirts of Europe, isolated islands of free men survived for a price of humiliation. Then the network of concentration and forced labor camps stretched for thousands of miles, from the Atlantic to the Pacific. There were of course symbols, there was the Right and the Left and different flags. The line was drawn through the middle of Europe—West was on the Right, East with its symbols of liberation was on the Left, but concentration camps were on both sides of this dividing line.

Nationalism and socialism, the two ideologies which met here originated once as the great hope of nineteenth-century mankind. Nationalism was an ideology of liberation of the peoples; socialism was a vision of a society free of exploitation, of an emancipated working class.

Ideologies serve also as a legitimacy of power. The same, or similar, political ideology which once carried the trends of liberation and emancipation of mankind, in a different historical period, used by different parties, may serve and result in oppression. Centuries back, the case of religion was similar. Benedictines built hospitals and hospices; bishops erected schools and cathedrals; but inquisitioners allied with kings and princes practiced a cruel and oppressive tyranny. The same religion, the same symbols served different objectives.

In their extremes and in our time, both ideologies led to their very negation, to the enslavement of nations and to dictatorship and forced labor. Nationalism fused with a vulgarized socialist appeal, the German national socialism, led to tyranny unprecedented in European history. But nationalism from the beginning harbored the dangers of tribal and racist resurgence and of hostility toward those who are different. With communism, it was different. Here, the choice of means, means contrary to ethical goals, corrupted the ends.

The two promising visions of a better, even perfect, mankind were then defeated by their inner contradictions. What did survive, with strength and vigor, were the very values, which initially guided the ideologies: the promise of freedom, social justice, respect for dignity of man, equality of all, the goals of liberation of man.

The values were stronger than the ideologies. They remained, while doubt and revision set in among the partisans of various orientations of socialism and nationalism. The values formed the core and set the directions for actions, they harbored goals, and the reconstruction of human ideologies began from ethical imperatives, testing the latter critically against reality and applying the basic principles in search of new directions. Here was the new beginning. The relevance of ideologies and values was again clear and convincing, tested against facts and data of their effects and function.

Not all political philosophies and ideologies shared this fate. Democratic societies, which advanced working political institutions, successfully countered the powerful totalitarian tide. Variations of socialism continued uncorrupted as instruments of advancement of the working men when associated closely with values of freedom and democratic institutions.

A theory may lead to self-deception and the negation of reality, to the rejection of hard facts for the sake of logical consistency of the cherished doctrine. In interpreting a theory which they advanced as a scientific method, orthodox marxists—in that critical inter war time—suggested theories, that fascism and nazism are nothing else than the last stage of capitalism, after which the great era of liberation will come and a utopian society, a perfect one on the Soviet model, will prevail.

This political development was interpreted by many as a simple consequence of economic development. Ideologies were only a superstructure; it was the change in the base, in the economic base, which resulted into success of those extreme ideas and movements.

The economic conditions, have of course affected the entire development of events at that time, but is such interpretation a sufficient one? These economic changes had their impact on ideas and institutions, but was this the only source of change?

Those events, tragic as they were for most of the mankind, were at the same time a major historical experience, relevant beyond their own uniqueness. They pointed toward general causes, suggested also general and relevant findings for understanding future processes and events. They could not, or should not have, left unaffected our perception and understanding of social reality and historical processes. For in history and social sciences observation is an instrument of inquiry: It is what experimentation is for hard sciences. And here were facts and data obvious and observable, recorded. They had to affect our thinking and understanding of man and society.

Let us suggest some tentative inferences:

1. Ideologies, political ideologies appeared in our century—even more so than in the past—as a powerful instrument in the integration and manipulation of groups, collectives, in the motivation of individuals as well as groups and crowds, moreover in setting the direction of social actions, in setting goals and in determining the processes of development. Political ideologies displaced in their intensity, influence, and relevance, religious orientations of the medieval times. Their relevance can be compared with the religious motivation of early and middle Medieval Christianity (ninth to fourteenth century) and the fanaticism it generated.

History does not move on a single, but on several, tracks. Furthermore, the same idea systems are perceived and interpreted differently by different groups and individuals. Difference in culture and personality as well as class affects the perception and interpretation of ideas.

Christianity humanized a brutal and cruel society. It generated art and philosophy. But it also generated religious fanaticism and hostility against difference.

The political idea system repeated this history. National and socialist ideology humanized politics and especially, labor, social-economic conditions. But, they also generated or propelled fanaticism and hostility.

2. Similar or largely identical economic systems of production were then associated with entirely diverse political ideologies. Idea systems were not necessarily a simple consequence of the economic base. The economic base produced not a single superstructure but many different ones. Contrary to orthodox marxist views, this superstructure of ideas, institutions, and values was at times far stronger than the economic base; moreover the superstructure was decisive for the direction of economic production and the uses of the product. It was the ideology and the values which determined the purpose of production—for war and conquest, or for peace. This superstructure, contrary to dogmatic theories, was powerful by itself and not a simple consequence of means and modes of production, although the relevance and effects of the latter is by no means denied.

Ideas emerged as a "social force"—as a cause motivating man. Economic needs and goals—yes, of course they are and always were a powerful cause of human actions and social process. But the strength of ideas, long recognized primarily by French historians sociologists, philosophers, psychologists (Fustel de Coulanges, Durkheim, Tarde, Fouillè, Halévy) also by the Germans (Dilthey, Weber, Sombart) was largely underestimated by many theoreticiains.

3. Ideologists and ideologies may become victims of their own logic and contradictions. Idea systems lend themselves to many logical and ideological interpretations which may generate policies and lead to developments neither wished nor anticipated by those who fathered those hopeful and promising visions and idea systems. This inner logic of ideas, or interpretation of those ideas and their inner contradictions, may lead to a self-defeat of the very values and objectives which were initially desired and advanced by the authors and partisants of the ideologies which affected the political movements. In this self-defeating process the idea systems break down since they do not fulfill the promise such as the advancement of social and economic wellbeing of the working class, freedom, social justice. On the other hand, fascism and nazism, successful in their goals of conquest and oppression of the weaker, were in permanent conflict with the very core values, the moral principles and ideas which created modern society and guided generations. Their actions were hostile to the very basic values generations had already sensed and acquired.

4. While idea systems broke down, the basic dominant values survived undefeated, constant if not permanent, in this changing world of ideas. When the realization of those ideologies reduced man to servitude, the guiding principles, the values survived. The ideological and social reconstruction of the same ideologies began again, appealing to those values of political freedom, human rights, social justice and equality, and the reestablishment of ethics—with its Hellenic and Christian Judaic roots.

5. Our culture is built on dialogue, but also on criticism, opposition, and protest. The protest, a creative protest is prophetic, Judaic in its tradition as dialogue is Hellenic in its origins. The prophet carried both protest and religious renovation. His right to protest was recognized by the ancient Israelites. Morally right, independent views were stronger than the might of the princes. His moral message was a source of legitimacy.

In our times, both protest and opposition against the violation of the basic principles, carried by individuals as at one time by prophets, had a legitimacy of its own, and it was the beginning of a renovation. The nucleus of renaissance formed the dominant values. This prophetic protest and renewal supplied the elements of the continuation of values and the reconstruction of our civilization.

6. Totalitarian strategy and tactics were effective in defeating democratic movements and conquering societies which at one time cherished ideas of political freedom and respect for an individual. The strength of those strategies was at least in part a consequence of a clear sense of direction as well as the will to move toward the once established goals. Hence the sense of direction and clarity of goals contributed to their successes and victory. The effectiveness

of their strategy and constancy to purpose, to strategic direction toward major objectives, depended not solely on means and resources, but also on organization of their partisans, moreover on organization and structure of goals.

The goal structure of the totalitarian movements applied a pattern developed long before in military strategy. A logical, rational goal structure directed toward breaking the will of the opponent has been historically developed in military theory. We have learned that even insane goals, born in a morbid phantasy of a fanatic, can be achieved by a logical and rational structure of means and goals projected toward the achievement of the latter. Here belongs the case of genocide, processed by modern, industrial means.

7. Since the capture of power by communists and fascists, our experience suggests the primacy of political power. Throughout the nineteenth century, the development of political economy as a scholarly discipline suggested the primacy of economic power; control of economic power, it was argued, secures control of political power, of instruments of government.

The totalitarian conqueror of states and continents first captured political power and used political power over the state and army—to establish economic control, to capture other instruments of power, especially the economic ones, to begin with the financial, monetary. Experience of the last half century indicates the primacy of political power in capturing and consolidating the control over states and society.

8. Neither social, political, or even scientific progress is a historical necessity determined by the development of the economic forces. The movement toward an improvement of social and political conditions calls for continuous effort, an effort clearly oriented toward desired values. It calls also for the selection of proper, humane means. Neither social justice nor human dignity are a consequence of historical necessity determined solely by the development of the economic forces, the economic base. A modern industrial technology has been used by totalitarian powers as much as by democratic. Fascist Italy, Communist Russia, Democratic America, almost feudal Japan, and Social Democratic Sweden produced ships and automobiles of similar design and quality.

The origin of man's desire for justice and freedom and his movement toward those goals, at least in what is called Western Civilization, is not a sole consequence of the development of economic forces. It can be gained, lost and recovered or lost forever. It is up to us, to maintain and continue it.

This is a distant experience indeed. A general overall image of the historical past is slowly emerging.

Those of us, quite young at that time, who learned to look at facts first and then at theory or doctrine and test the theory against the facts, against developments that we witnessed, began with those comments and considerations, perhaps only reflexions. When in 1941, only a few months before Pearl Harbor, I put some of my comments into a notebook, it was already a kind of a balance of ideas on the past, as well as an outlook toward the future.

The notebook had an attractive silk binding and rough, dark paper. Purchased in Yokohama it testified to the type of scarcity which affected Japan. I wrote my comments on board of one of those end-of-the-century steamships, a boat of a past era. Crossing the immense Pacific, from its Far Eastern shores, the once disconnected fragments of Occidental history appeared as fitting and interconnected details of an epoch moving toward decisive events which might set the course of mankind for a century or centuries to come.

The cruel and destructive war was man made. It is so easy to blame the historical forces, this anonymous and irresponsible process, and expiate man's folly and cruelty set in motion by false prophets.

The subject matter of this volume touches only slightly on those historical events. But the theoretical theme, distant as it may seem has such connections.

I know the weakness of this volume, it is no more than an attempt. Nonetheless, the beginnings are somewhere there, in a nascent catastrophic past and in a critical view toward established doctrines, but also in the faith in humanity, in ethical commitment of the prophetic tradition and in our roots of freedom of the Hellenic dialogue.

This book is concerned with the directive and regulatory nature of idea systems, values, and goals. The images of a future society, the goals—immediate and distant—move humankind and set the path of history. Values and norms regulate our behavior; they are the yardsticks of right and wrong and of what "ought to be."

Ideas and values have a major relevance in shaping and initiating our history and cannot be reduced solely to a sequence of changes in the means and modes of production. To the contrary, at times ideas and values determine such changes. The relevance of the economic base is obvious. Historians and scholars knew this long before the terms were coined. But the use of the economic forces and the direction are affected by values and ideas. The concepts of economic base and a superstructure of ideas and values are of a theoretical merit. If we keep the terms, then the study is concerned with the superstructure. Yet we shall deal with the economic base when the nature of the problem calls for us to do so. We will trace the origins of ideas and values when doing so contributes to a main theme of the book: a study of the structure and working of an idea system's goals and values.

Values are either yardsticks of our behavior, norms of conduct, or goals, goal-oriented symbols. Later, a more comprehensive definition will be suggested. Values can be considered in terms of their static structure, their "anatomy," or in terms of their dynamic aspect, the actions and processes that they generate.

Furthermore, we shall deal with the unity and difference of values, with values considered as universal, even absolute, and those which are relative. This brings us to the final section and to the discussion of patterns of coexistence and the domination of groups of differing value orientation. Pluralism is discussed, and the workability of pluralistic systems is seen as depending on the strength of shared values as well as on skills in the resolution or reduction of conflicts.

A large section of this book is devoted to goals. Moreover, an attempt has been made to suggest a theory of goals and of the relationship between goals and norms of conduct. Various goal structures are discussed in part II; nonetheless, I am inclined to believe that the basic goal structure, the elementary one, is always the same and can be discovered in various strategies. There are of course variations in organizing, setting strategies and tactics, but the same elements are always there, that is, goals and actions related to the latter; stages in long-range goals; intermediary or stage goals, related to a terminal or strategic goal. In all goal structures there is a causal connection between need or stimulus and goal or actions.

The relevance of goals in daily life and human destiny, their quality, which lends itself both to an analysis of the past and to future projections, makes the interest in a study of goals more than an academic one. Man is goal oriented—this is a major motivating force. Or let us put it somewhat differently: Goals reflect our needs, desires, intentions, sentiments. Goals are indeed concentrations of our will and needs.

Goals are our driving force: the very sense of our life is reflected in them. The breakdown of goals—of individual goals—is tantamount to personal, psychological stress, to a depressed mood, to the change from an active person into a passive one. I have observed this sudden breakdown of goals in Maine fishermen, who at an advanced age decided to sell their boats and did not have adequate different skills or interests and found that all their activities and life-goals were tied to their boats.

Indeed, too many goals, confused and conflicting ones, may be as oppressive for an individual as in a different way is the absence of goals. Reconstruction of individual goals may suggest a therapy, a way out of psychological stress or emotional unhappiness.

Goals and their structure are central for understanding man and society, for our understanding history and our activities. Theories focused the theme on actions, theories of actions were of course related to goals. Actions, however, are only consequences of our goals and intentions, of our will. It is the nature of goals and their structure that is essential, that reflects our own energy and will.

The structure and nature of goals lend themselves to a special field of inquiry. In fact, military theoreticians were perhaps first to develop such a discipline: strategy. Theories of goals and action that man has advanced in the art of aggression and defense are not yet advanced in the art of peace or in major areas of our constructive and productive efforts. Yes, it is true that today the term *strategy* has wider application. Perhaps a discipline called simply a theory of goals may call for more interest and work in the future.

This study is focused on ideologies, goals, and values. But idea systems and goals are discussed on various levels. We may suggest at this point three levels: a microsociological level, of village communities or tribes; the macrosociological or middle level, of social movements and large political parties; and on a more general, broader level, a megasociological level, which embraces an entire nation or culture, integrating in time and space groupings of several nations or otherwise distinct societies. This last level, integrated by institutions and values, we may call civilizations. Alfred Weber in his *Prinzipien der Geschichts und Kultur-soziologie* (1951) called historical units of epochs of similar social structures and values *Geschichtskörper* a historical corpus.

Data concerning communities and microsociological studies are of a different nature than those concerning larger groupings—social political movements, crowd and mass phenomena—and are still different from the last group, concerned with a long range of time and wider societies.

We may postulate at this point that these three different approaches, different levels in terms of groups, involve also different levels of abstractions. On the second or third level, theoretical findings or postulates can be developed solely as logical constructs, or such an approach may be advanced with a strong support of data. Empirical data of the first microsociological level were largely derived from this writer's own field work.

In terms of methods, a hypothesis is an a priori device, a result of some experience or imagination, even inventiveness at times. However, in our cases some of the hypotheses emerged during the field research and were advanced later, as observations and interviews, or some conversations suggested further generalization. Hence structuring of goals on a horizontal line was a consequence of field research in an Italian village community where such structures were easily observable. Parallel value structures appeared clearly in a Maine lobster-men's community. Here the norms of conduct in business and trade were not only different but clearly separate from those generally followed in community life, among friends and neighbors. The hierarchy of values in turn could be perceived among the Arapahoes on the Wind River Reservation. Some of the values were strong and resisted change, while others were more flexible or weaker. Of course the interest and bias of the observer affect the direction of observation, the way things are perceived. Nonetheless, some of the concepts emerged during research. The initial hypothesis was limited solely to an assumption that values are structured, and my objective was to find out the way they were structured and how they worked. All three field studies were published separately (see below).

Slowly the three structures emerged—horizontal, vertical, and parallel—as a consequence of those field studies. They did correspond, of course, to my earlier readings and findings and above all to some very ancient models of means and ends, value hierarchies, and more recent theories of multiple values.

Let us comment here that the facts were gathered in a variety of ways and are also of a different quality. But social sciences deal with a different universe than what are called today "hard sciences." The nature of facts and data is different, and the validation, the verification of our findings, is not identical. We deal here with approximation, with tentative findings, frequently with personal impressions, and we move carefully within the boundaries of probabilities, not certainties, with a humble admission of the limitations of our efforts.

Models or graphs have been used, perhaps even extensively in our discussions. I believe, that their use is seminal, that they are helpful in clarifying theories, hypotheses, and findings and in reporting and presenting social processes, structures and relations, hierarchies of values, as well as, in illustrating and replicating the relationship of empirical data. Graphs, which have been more recently called models, are now in general use in social sciences. One may sense, however, certain reservations, expressed sometimes in discussions and conversations by distinguished scholars in the field of humanities, whether this type of illustration is advisable or useful. It may be argued, that such a reduction of social reality to a visual presentation may on one hand simplify the complex reality, on the other reify abstract constructs, equate definitions or abstract, verbal concepts with real, observable objects. Furthermore, social phenomena reduced to models and statistical data, to numbers and graphs, may deprive the social drama of its human quality, ideas, sentiments, and human values. It may be further argued that visual models supply an element of a scientific decorum to disciplines which are not necessarily a part of science and that extensive use of graphic, abstract presentations is an unnecessary attempt to make humanities scientific, applying devices which belong to other disciplines.

We do not intend to begin or continue here a useless and unending debate, whether sociology and social sciences are "sciences," whether their methods are indeed scientific or not. Sociology and social sciences use methods which are appropriate, scientific in terms of their disciplines and in terms of the nature of data with which they are concerned. They belong also, at least in certain areas, to humanities.

In this case, there is, however, a single question to be answered: Whether the designing of models is a useful device in our field or not, or whether it is only an ancillary or even a temporary fad? We deal with empirical or historical data, or abstract concepts, and the question is can we visualize such abstractions or observed empirical related data?

In mathematics, however, translation of abstract and intellectual constructs into visual forms was of unusual significance. Of course, mathematics is a different field and analogy is a risky device.

Interestingly enough, the early use of graphic abstractions in political essays can be traced a century before Descartes, (who applied graphic replicas in mathematics), to Niccolo Machiavelli's study *Dell'Arte Della Guerra (The Art of War)* which appeared in Florence in 1521. The Florentine writer, was at the same time a scholar and man of politics. He used the graphs in an ingenious way, he plotted them by means of columns of identical letters.

Since the turn of the century models and graphs have been used routinely in social and related sciences. Another Italian political and social scientist at the turn of our century, Vilfredo Pareto, used models profusely in his voluminous and basic work. Models were used far earlier in logic and more than sixty years ago by Ferdinand de Saussure in his classic work in linguistics.

There is, however, more to it. After all, the fact that others have used such a device before, others whom we consider as masters, great masters indeed, does not make the method or techniques efficient or correct. The method has to be justified by its own merit, by the fact that it works, produces results.

In this sense, visual presentation of theories or relationships of empirical data, of facts has its own merits. It seems, that theories and findings in sociology and social sciences in general, lend themselves well to visual presentation. It is not accidental that Machiavelli and almost four hundred years later Pareto used a similar device. Graphic presentation has its proper application with certain type of data and materials. Machiavelli discussed definite and logically organized social groups (by definite, we mean here, clear, easy to grasp and to understand in terms of purpose, function). Where conduct is logical and rationally organized (and a part of our behavior is rational and logical, otherwise we could not survive), the simple sequence of steps or actions can be plotted as a model. The same is true about realities, relationship of empirical data, phenomena, which we, in our thinking wrongly or rightly perceive in terms of a logical sequence, e.g. causation. Models replicate our images, our thinking.

We may postulate that logically and rationally organized data can be as a rule presented graphically, translated into or reduced to graphic models. Models could be roughly divided into synchronic and diachronic, or static and dynamic categories. For instance, social structure as well as a sequence of actions and goals can be presented that way—the former in a static, the latter in a dynamic model. But what is the purpose of such presentation?

First of all, a major function of scientific thinking is its economy. Selection and relating of data, is focused and narrowed down to relevant facts, relevant in terms of their relationship and functions. Models are such abstractions reduced to the essentials, and in consequence they are instruments of such an intellectual economy. Furthermore, they supply a visual imagination of a theory or findings, in addition to verbal and mental abstractions.

Findings and theories, relationships of data reduced to models, permit further a use of the latter, for the next stages of an inquiry permit the identification similar, analogous structures and sequences.

The literature of our subject is extensive. If we consider related fields, "extensive" is not the proper word. The literature is immense.

Where are the beginnings? Values, ideas, and goals have been discussed for more than two and a half millennia. Beginnings could be traced to the pre-Socratic times, and the discussion of values, norms, ideas was already well established in the writings of Plato and Aristotle. Aristotle suggested a theory of means and ends, of goals and actions. A. W. H. Adkins in his illuminating volume, *Moral Values and Political Behaviour in Ancient Greece*, traced his analysis of such norms or standards as *agathos* and *arete* (good and virtue, excellence) to more distant times, to Homer and Hesiod, and interpreted this meaning in terms of their historical context and of behavior.

But this goes, of course, farther back. Ethics is concerned with conduct, with values and discussion of the nature of our norms. In their religious context, it appears in major monotheistic religions. In polytheistic religions ethics is not necessarily a part of the religious system. Throughout the medieval times what we call today values and ethics are a major theme of theology and later of philosophy.

But our theme and approach are primarily sociological; we are concerned with values, goals, and ideologies as observers, not as actors. Our guiding purpose is to understand and describe their structures and working, not to judge and evaluate. However, we are also concerned with the relationship of various normative orders, especially relationships and conflicts of normative and pragmatic orders—simply, conflicts between ethical imperatives and those of efficiency in politics or economic planning. Here, lines are crossed. Moreover, fields cannot be tightly separated, nor was it our intention to do so. To the contrary, lines between the disciplines were crossed.

We shall not discuss further the extensive literature of this field. To begin with, it is not the major theme of this volume, nor does space permit an adequate bibliographical essay. A selected bibliography, however, has been added for orientation, and it suggests the wealth of writings and work on values and ideologies in various disciplines. Solely for orientation, we have included a very general survey, reduced to a broad outline, in chapter 1, note 7.

The major themes of this volume were the subject of this writer's lectures and seminars at Brooklyn College and the Graduate School of the City University of New York and in seminars and lectures at the University of Rome in 1957 and especially in 1964 and 1972, also at Columbia University.

Some chapters are based on earlier attempts and articles. The boundaries between normative and scientific approaches and on different valuations in differing orders have been discussed in "Soziologie und Ethik" (*Kolner Zeitschrift fur Soziologie*, vol. 6, no. 2 1953/54, also in *Revista Mexicana de Sociologia*, vol. 15, no. 2, 1953). The structure of idea systems is in *European Ideologies* (New York: Philosophical Library, 1948); and infinite values are the topic of "Infinite Values and Social Change" (*Transactions of the New York Academy of Sciences*, ser. II. vol. 26, no. 6, 1964) and "Enfoque Valorativo del Cambio Social" (*Revista Mexicana de Sociologia*, vol. 20, no. 1, 1958). On causal quality of ideas see "Materialismo Storico in la Luce dell Esperienza" (Critica D'Oggi, no. 14–15, 1962).

The three field studies appeared separately; on values of the Arapaho Indians, to which some reference has been made in this text, see *Ethnos*, (no. 2–4, 1949) and *University of Wyoming Publications* (vol. 15, no. 3 1950); on the goal structure in an Italian village community see *La Revue Internationale de So-*

ciologie (vol. 6, no. 13, 1970); on the value structure of the Maine fishermen see *La Revue Internationale de Sociologie* (vol. 10, no. 1, 1974). The value structure in Bonagente appeared in a far more extensive volume, *Il Paese* (New York and Rome: New York University Press and the University of Rome, 1973), which also appeared as a publication of the University of Rome, in Italian.

Some of the comments on goal-oriented behavior, their predictive nature, and foreign policy appeared in *Il Politico* of the University of Pavia, vol. 46, no. 4, 1982). These short comments are also a part of lectures given at a seminar at the University of Florence and at the Diplomatic Institute of the Italian Foreign Office in 1975 and 1977. Some of the other discussions were also published in other journals in a rather initial form.

A collection of studies on values appeared also in Italian in a volume entitled *Saggi Sv Valori e Struttura* (Rome; Istituto di Statistica C. Gini, Università di Roma, 1966) with an introduction by Professor Vittorio Castellano.

This volume, however, represents a new attempt but includes, of course, past work and experience. For editorial reasons the text has been reduced, and two field studies of the original (on the goal-value structure of Italian peasants in Lazio and pattern of values of a fishermen community on the islands of Maine) have been deleted and reduced to a short digest.

Acknowledgments

An attempt to encompass ideologies, goals, and values in a single study, within the same frame of reference, was for me a difficult attempt. At the beginning, it seemed that there was not a single, organizing principle and that a better way, if not the only one, was to present this theme in a number of independent, separate papers, essays bound together in one collection rather than a systematic study. The frame of reference was, however, a workable one. Here was the problem of organization of the material gathered over years of study and research.

Dr. James T. Sabin of the Greenwood Press, was indeed very helpful and encouraging in those discussions on integrating and reducing the subject matter. I appreciate his interest in this project, his tactful patience (the manuscript took several years), and above all his penetrating insight into the difficult issues of the major theme and clear comments. Thanks are given also to Mary Walker and Mildred Vasan at Greenwood for careful editing and unusual attention to detail.

Don Martindale's personal qualities, his literary talent, and broad, as well as subtle, humanistic approach and philosophy of social sciences were well expressed not only in his witty and brilliant comments but also in his sharp and at the same time friendly and constructive criticism. I appreciate his careful reading; his comments were very helpful in reducing and at the same time integrating and focusing this volume.

Since the beginning of my work on this subject, I found a friendly interest and criticism among my colleagues at Brooklyn College and later at the Graduate School of the City University of New York, beginning with my friends Walter Dyke, who was noted for his work on the Navajos, and Robert Erich, anthropologist and archeologist. Dyke took interest in my comparative approach to value study, based on field research—though I did not realize, at that time, how many years it takes. Bob Erich edited and discussed my early work on Arapaho values (published later in *Ethnos*, University of Wyoming Publications, International Journal of American Linguistics). Brooklyn College at this time gathered brilliant and attractive scholars in many departments and created a unique environment for exchanging ideas. I shall mention in my department the warm friendship for many years of Charles Lawrence, Herb Stroup, and the late Rex Hooper, and the exchange of views with Alfred McClung Lee, whose work is discussed in this book, George Simpson, my younger colleagues Sidney Aronson, Oscar Glanz, and Marvin Konigsberg, to mention only a few. Ideas and theories are tested also in the classroom. For many years the interest of my students and their work in this field were illuminating and also helpful (I quote one of the papers, written many years ago). Among them, in this specific project I would like to commend Arnold Wenderoff for his assistance, friendship, and pleasant exchanges of views on his African research.

Unforgettable are my long associations with Italian colleagues at the Universities of Rome, Milan, Pavia and others: the unending and searching conversations with Vittorio Castellano, Franco Ferrarotti, philosopher and jurist, Renato Treves of the University of Milan, author of a *volumetto* entitled *Dogmatism and Critical Spirit*, young Luciano Pellicani, commentator of Ortega y Gasset. Their insights and comments reassured me in my work. Joseph B. Moody, historian, read sections of the manuscript; his criticism and comments—above all his friendship—are always valued.

Library research was carried on mainly in the New York Public Library and library of the Graduate School of the City University. My correspondence on values with Jurgen Friedrichs, University of Hamburg, goes back to 1969. His comments and also bibliographical information were always pertinent and read carefully with appreciation.

During the last two years, when this study was almost completed, I met often with my colleagues from the Graduate School. K. D. Irani and Jacob Stern. Here, in the Commons at lunch, in pleasant and vigorous conversations I still was able to check on some of my findings and hypothesis on ancient and Oriental values and cultures.

My bibliography was revised several times. This type of work is, of course, time consuming. Advice and assistance of my colleagues at the City University of New York Graduate School Library, Claire Bowie, and George Simor have been always very friendly and helpful. For the first time in my work, computers gave fast answers to some problems of editions, translations, and other details.

Special acknowledgment is given to my wife Priva Gross, an art historian, for her collection of architectural sources and her comments and assistance.

May I express my thanks to all those who helped with my inquiry in Italian villages, on the islands of Maine, on the Wind River Reservation of Wyoming, and to my colleagues of various departments, who discussed problems with me; they knew far more than I and were willing to criticize my views. I wish that I could list all the names. May I however mention the late Rev. Dr. Roberts, who settled on the reservation at the same time as Chief Washakie (when I met him in 1946, he was in his late nineties); my Arapaho friends, Ben Friday, Paul

Moose, Jack Shavehead, and Rev. Coach Wilson, and Mr. and Mrs. Tindall of Ethete, Wyoming.

During the last years I had additional duties with the City University Academy for Humanities and Sciences and the Polish Institute of Arts and Sciences. Daily schedules were heavy, indeed, and work on my book had to begin very early each day. Francis Puslowski attended to many of my duties and was generous with his time and helped with tact and a smile. Julia Czestochowska's assistance in those long and tedious corrections and the final copy of the bibliography is appreciated as well. May I thank them all.

Part I
IDEOLOGIES

1

The Directive and Regulatory System

Orientation and Sense of Direction

The search for goals and directions is as old as mankind. While the magical outlook was still powerful, man sought for direction, for a resolution of the painful process of choice, via divination and magical practices. But there was always an area where pragmatic and "rational" choices had to be made, choices that followed or were prompted by previous experience and success. Otherwise man could not cope efficiently with conditions imposed on him by his environment.

In some vital areas, he followed practical and workable ways; in others, he was a victim of haphazard responses, failures and successes, and choices deduced from magic or divination. Again, those ancient practices expressed the need for and a sense of direction, orientation. A sense of orientation is essential to movement, to coping with the environment. Our intelligence, our skills in observation, contributes to our capacity to move and choose. It is a vital quality.

Thus, orientation is an activity of finding ways leading to our goals. The goals are of diverse origin and quality. But to meet the goals and in consequence also to meet or satisfy our needs, ways have to be found that lead in this direction. Sensitivity to the latter, our inborn qualities and skills, contributes to what might be called the sense of direction, the capacity of identifying goals and choosing ways. Thus, orientation suggests an attitude toward the environment at a given time when movement or action is considered and decided.

Direction has to be chosen in many diverse areas of our activity. Geographical orientation has to be distinguished from social-cultural. The latter is concerned with goals and direction within the social system—more, within the various areas of human activity, in the economic as well as in the cultural fields, even in systems of ideas such as arts, education, science.

The sense of geographic orientation is of course essential to human existence.

A hunter must find his way back home from hunting; he must relate the tracks of animals to the environment, must note the relationship and distance of some landmarks, which tell him where he is. The great migratory movements of peoples, which can be traced back for millennia, suggest a developed sense of geographic orientation, shaped already by experience of previous generations.

Geographical orientation is a part of our nature, our personality. Some may be endowed with greater inborn talents and acquired skills in searching out and finding ways and places than others, but still it is a condition of our existence.

Geographical orientation (not goals) is widely observed in the animal world. The "goals" of animals are instinctive. They are responses to biological needs to which the movement is related, but migratory movements call for orientation and direction.

A tern breeds in the Arctic and winters in the Antarctic, eleven thousand miles apart, flies distances of twenty-five thousand miles annually, follows a certain broad path of direction. Instinct? Even if this is instinctive, it points to a sense of orientation, a direction that the bird must be endowed with. The flock follows, imitates, but some must lead, must set the direction.

The experts in this field tell us about components of orientational faculties: the sun, the map, and the compass. But whatever the mechanism is, whatever the elements, geographical landmarks, sun, temperature, there is an inner sense of orientation, choice, a sense as basic as the major, biological senses the birds are endowed with—even if this is only an instinctive response to stimuli.

Hence the frame of reference that results from this very sense of orientation, related to needs and human goals, is neither an a priori concept nor a purely abstract model. It is a consequence of elementary springs of human behavior. It is a consequence of an elementary sequence: need → drive → action → satisfaction. This sequence is considered by Malinowski in his *Scientific Theory of Culture* as a fundamental but also obvious pattern.

By the term *goal* a conscious or unconscious purpose, an end point to which the action is related. The goal of a hunter is to kill the animal. A goal of a magical incantation is a desired change.

A large area of human behavior is goal-oriented. In many situations man follows customs, or general, daily habits. Certainly, a vast area subject to emotions might be also irrational. But in order to survive, especially in our times, man's actions have to be, and were in the past, rational in terms of goals and means, means adequate to achieve goals.

Our orientation is a search for goals and ways; our sense of direction consists of abilities to identify the goals and discover, or choose, efficient ways. We discover the efficient ways by choice; it is a process of distinguishing between right and wrong, efficient and nonefficient, "do" and "don't."

In a geographical orientation the choice has to be exercised by animals too. Moreover, with exception of a few predators, fear is almost a constant companion of animals. Fear is a condition of alertness; it is an instinctive alarm attitude.

During a frosty winter an animal has to make a choice between danger (fear), food (hunger), and shelter against inclement weather (cold). A squirrel in Central Park on a freezing winter day chooses between nuts offered by passersby and exposure to dogs and to weather. In the presence of dogs its distance from its "territorial" tree depends on its evaluation of danger. The distance is a vector product of hunger and fear. The squirrel finds safety on tree branches, escaping from the dogs, running up the tree trunk where it has its shelter. The higher the risk, the greater or more intensive is the fear. Hence, it results in a shorter distance of the animal from the shelter, the tree trunk. The greater the hunger, the stronger the drive for food, prompting a longer distance from the sheltering tree.

The choice is imposed by situations. The exercise of choice becomes part of our nature. Again, our survival calls for both direction and choice. Choice is associated with goals and actions. The exercise of choice is a behavior we observe in our daily life and we experience when we make it. The choice is an ancedent of decision.

The Regulatory and Directive Apparatus

Man acts in many different areas. In his patterns of actions he is guided by what might be called a directive and regulatory apparatus. The former is related to goals, the latter, to norms of conduct. The regulatory subsystem sets the boundaries of our actions. The choice is exercised within the boundaries set by the two parameters: the positive norms or imperatives (do) and negative norms or commandments (don't). The positive norms are associated with expectations of reward.

A band of families or a tribe migrating in search of warmer weather and more abundant food supply is exercising choice and orientation. There is a goal and some sense of direction.

In a simple activity—looking for a spring of water or building a shelter— there is a goal and a norm of conduct. The positive norm in this case is "efficient" or "effective"; the negative, "noneffective." The former suggests a probability of goal achievement; the latter, of failure.

For logical convenience, at this point, we shall call this type of behavior pragmatic as distinct from normative.

To the pragmatic behavior belongs a vast area of human activities by which man attempts to move within or directly affects the environment or by which he deals with and affects directly the material world. His survival calls for effective ways of securing food, water, and shelter. Pragmatic behavior is widely related to our biological needs.

Normative behavior and evaluation are guided by cultural values of right and wrong. A French nobleman who refuses to shake hands with his peer because the latter favors a republic is exercising a value judgment; his behavior is normative.

This division is suggested for logical convenience only, since in real-life situations pragmatic behavior is also affected by values. An Arapaho Indian of the Wind River Reservation abandons a shelter in which a member of his family died. In the Arapaho belief system those who are alive should not remain in a house of death. Relation to his tent or shelter is determined in this case by cultural norms not by pragmatic considerations. However, pragmatic regulatory-directive apparatus is an essential condition of our existence. While we attempt to cope with the environment, acting by means of our effectors vis-à-vis the environment, when our goals are geared to purely material results, the efficacy of our action has to be considered. In reality, however, both areas appear usually at the same time: the pragmatic and the normative.

Both areas, the pragmatic and normative areas are guided by goals and norms, although their nature is different. (We shall return to this theme in our discussion of verification.)

In rational conduct choice is central, the beginning of a conscious process of decision making and selecting goals. Choice, *proairesis*, is a key concept in Aristotle's *Nicomachean Ethics*.[1] The essential meaning of *proairesis* is moral choice, choosing before, ahead. Aristotle devotes an entire section (section 2 of book III) to the concept of choice and its relationship to voluntary and involuntary actions as well as wishes. The ancient Greeks had at least six terms for choice, related to choice of means and ends or objects.[2] This may suggest the relevance of this concept and the precision of its meaning in the ancient Hellenic culture. The choice is present in selection of goals and conduct leading to achievement of the latter. But once goals are chosen, actions conducive to goal achievement have to be selected. Throughout the process of acting, the norms of conduct are applied.

Thus our directive and regulatory apparatus consists of (1) goals or general sense of direction; (2) system of actions toward the latter; and (3) norms of conduct. This apparatus is set in motion once a decision is made.

Actions move toward goals within the boundaries set by positive and negative norms of conduct. Two polar values are needed in the exercise of choice, a positive and negative: do and don't, success and failure, punishment and reward, pain and pleasure, and—above all—good and bad, right and wrong. The actor selects actions (means) and goals (ends) within these two extremes. The limits of choice are set by those norms of conduct. In a rational process, he considers goals that are open and alternative courses of actions leading to goal achievement. (See below chapter 11.)

The choice is exercised in between the polar values. Whether it is a conscious or a spontaneous process of decision making is at this point irrelevant, for the existence of those polar norms can be and is verbally expressed. We may consider the polar values as ideal boundaries. Our adjectives can be expressed in positive, comparative, or superlative—good, better, best—and on the negative side—bad, worse, worst. At first glance we have two scales of evaluation, a negative and a positive. In terms of intensity, each has three different adjective "values" (positive, comparative, and superlative). The choice can be made within those three gradations. In fact, however, our language supplies far more; we may say, (1) good; (2) a bit better; (3) very good; (4) excellent; (5) best under the circumstances; (6) perfect. This gradation could be easily extended (the same on the negative side). Polar values are seldom reached. The choice is exercised within those gradations.

The Italian and Polish usage has a tendency toward superlatives. It expresses a tendency toward polar or close-to-polar evaluations. The actor with a propensity toward superlative expression limits the choice; his judgment has an emotional tendency toward evaluation.

A rational evaluation calls for a careful selection of intensity of gradation in a given case.

The English usage has a tendency toward intermediary norms—positives or comparatives—and not toward superlatives. A balanced, measured judgment and choice call for a careful usage of adjectives that express an intensity of judgment. This cautious, careful use of adjectives in English usage expresses at the same time an accepted or personal style or evaluation.

Joseph Conrad gave us insight into psychology of the English usage in his essay "Well Done". He wrote in 1918 about the language of English mariners:

I don't say marvelously well or miraculously well or wonderfully well or even very well, because these are simply overstatements of undisciplined minds. . . . In the Navy, where human values are thoroughly understood, the highest signal of commendation . . . consists exactly of those two simple words "well done" followed by the name of the ship. Not marvelously done, astonishingly done, wonderfully done—no, only just "Well done so-and-so".[3]

Contrary to the English usage, the Manichean or Zoroastrian tradition has set the two opposites in an extreme way. The world is divided into good and evil. There is only an "either/or." There is no space for compromise. In consequence, in politics there are only friends and foes, angels and satans. There is little, if any, chance for mercy and moderation. The evil must be destroyed, not tolerated, destroyed and eliminated.

Now let us consider the effect of structure of the regulatory norms not only on decision making but also on practical politics.

In English usage and British tradition the amplitude of norms, amplitude between the positive and negative, is wide; hence, many choices are possible. In this wide field between acceptance and rejection there is a chance to find an area of agreement, to select within this area a focal point and to strike a compromise. In an Italian and Polish structure of norms, with the emphasis on extremes (superlatives), the choice is narrower and the achievement of a political compromise more difficult.

In an Iranian Manichean (or akin to Manichean) norm structure, the choice is almost limited to "green" and "red," stop and go, good and bad. There are few intermediate choices. Anybody opposed to a mulla, or ayatollah, is a sinner, perhaps a satan. The Shiite Islam, fused with the ancient Zoroastrian traditions, represents an emotional tendency toward extremes, with few if any choices between the extremes. Those Shiite norms result also in ancient forms of politics, politics of shifts in persecutions, destructive and futile. The persecuted become persecutors; and again after victory the role changes reach extremes. The legitimacy of power and persecution is a negative concept: destruction of evil. And "evil" is the competitor to power.

The norms of conduct do express a regulatory subsystem of our values, a system that sets our actions, our general conduct, on an acceptable path. The positive norm (the imperative "do") suggests the permitted and approved behavior, whereas the negative one ("don't") suggests the morally unacceptable one (commandments). The regulatory system works efficiently when it is accepted by substantial sections of the society, when it is internalized by the latter, and when it is an articulation of culture and of the entire belief system. It is in fact an essential instrument of voluntary, informal social control. (We shall return to shared values in chapter 2.)

A century ago Herbert Spencer wrote: "Few things can happen more disastrous than the decay and death of a regulative system no longer fit, before another and fitter regulative system has grown up to replace it."[4] Breakdown of norms of conduct, of the normative—regulative, to use Spencer's adjective—system (or subsystem), is a symptom and consequence or an antecedent of social disintegration. In a social revolution the old institutions and values break down. They lose their collective acceptance or hold. In consequence, sections of the informal as well as formal (legal) social control break down. The process of anomie, noticed by Durkheim a generation after Spencer, appears in weakening or the breakdown of norms of conduct of the regulatory and/or the directive system—the latter articulated in goals. What is however frequently overlooked are the quantity and quality of the weakening of this normative-regulative system. Spencer wrote about the death of the regulative system. But the weakening or reevaluation (not the total breakdown) of a regulative as well as a directive subsystem may suggest processes of social or cultural changes, transition to a new style of life.

No ethical system can be built without this ideal polarity of norms of conduct within which a choice is made, and choice may be moderate or extreme. The ideal polar values are extreme limits of conduct and choice. Nietzsche, in his *Genealogy of Morals*, rejected the principle of opposition of norms while repudiating and condemning the Judeo-Christian dichotomy of good and evil. He established a new positive and independent standard of "something perfect, magnificently triumphant, something capable of inspiring fear." Thus, in reality, this was nothing else but a new extreme and polar dichotomy, a new opposition of a "superior person" against an inferior one, for the opposites are inherent in the very exercise of choice in a process of thinking and deciding. They do appear even in the rudimentary forms of directive and regulative activities by which early survival was once determined.

Means and Ends

Thus, in any rational action the directive and regulatory subsystems are present in some form. They appear also at times when goals are neither concrete nor rational. Man throughout history attempted to achieve goals born in fantasy and sick emotions by rational means or by means he considered as rational.

Goals and actions, ends and means, appear in all cultures; they constitute a universal pattern of human behavior. In their basic and elementary form they appear in biological needs. Satisfaction of a biological need becomes a goal that results in action toward satisfaction.

It is not an accident that this simple sequence of means and ends, so easily observable in daily life, is at the same time an ancient starting point of a broadly conceived but systematic philosophy. In Western civilization this frame of reference can be traced back two and a half millennia, for it is the basic theoretical premise of Aristotle's *Ethics*, the first known Western theory of rational behavior, of ends and means. Talcott Parsons, who advanced similar frame of reference, began his major work with a quotation from Max Weber: "Every thoughtful consideration of the final elements of rational human action is tied to the two categories 'purpose' and 'means' (*Zweck und Mittel*)." But it is Aristotle who deserves the early credit. Talcott Parsons suggests further that it is impossible to have a meaningful description of an act without specifying the four structural elements: end, means, conditions, and norms.[5] Any action has to be considered in a context of situation, but we shall deal with this later.

The goals set the direction; they reflect our will toward destination and are articulations of our basic biological and economic needs or cultural needs, in a broader sense of our ideology or doctrine. The goals are also consequences of our orientation, search for direction. The limits of behavior are set by those yardsticks we call norms; they regulate our movement or actions. In a simple pragmatic (for example, economic) activity, the positive norms set the standard of efficiency, the negative of failure; in a broader also in a normative sense, they tell what "ought to be done," what is "right." The partisans of utilitarian philosophy may relate the norms of conduct to the polar experiences of pain and pleasure. The positive norms, in their dominant quality, are also called "imperatives." The negative (you shall not) may be called "commandments." The Ten Commandments list the major negative standards.

Our goals in art or ethics differ with such a simple goal as earning our monthly salary. The structure is similar, perhaps even identical, but the content of goals and norms of conduct is different. The former belongs to normative area and the latter to pragmatic, affected by normative. Let us call the former *values*.

To quote Rashdall, "The idea of 'ought' is implicitly contained in the idea of value."

We shall proceed step by step with our discussion and arrive at a definition of values in the next chapters.

Empirical and Normative Approaches

Throughout our entire discussion, a distinction is made between an empirical and a normative approach to values.

Values, to use—at this initial point—Znaniecki's simple definition, are cultural data (for example, concepts of justice, duty), which can be described and studied in a scientific way. A student of values may relate them to social condition, trace their origin. Furthermore, he may analyze their social function, the effects of values on work and production, value-goals as motivation, to mention a few themes of a scientific inquiry.

Scientific method encompasses three major areas: description, classification, analysis of meaningful relationships of facts. Social values can be described, classified, analyzed. Relationships between social values and human behavior, values and actions, in terms of causality or interdependence are open to observation and validation in a qualitative or quantitative way. There are of course limitations: Validation by observation in terms of probability is weaker than experimentation. But in principle the rules of scientific inquiry, scientific in terms of social sciences, apply to the study of social values within its context situation.[6]

A student of values, as a social scientist, studies "what is"; he acts as an observer, not as an actor. He describes the values, but does not evaluate the cultural data as to whether they are right or wrong. During the process of his research, observation, and formation of hypothesis, he attempts to verify his findings, but he does not judge behavior or norms of conducts in terms of right and wrong.

The actor, however, evaluates his own behavior; in a normative approach he judges the others as to whether they are right and wrong. The student-observer describes, classifies the values; he analyzes and relates them to other data and facts. He attempts to confirm his findings, whether they are probable, valid, relatively true. In an empirical approach to values they can be studied and validated by means considered as a scientific method. I can study efficiency of two groups of workers, one with work ethics based on religion and the other with work ethics reduced to profit. The nature of rewards is of course different. I can try to find effects of values on production by choosing similar work conditions, similar product, age groups, and so on and may explore effects of difference of values on efficiency. With all its limitations, it is an empirical study. I'm trying to find out in this case how the different values work and not what is right and wrong.

The normative evaluation of judgment and behavior cannot be scientifically proven or validated. It can be "verified" by comparison with normative standards shared by the actor and his cultural community. This distinction between a normative and empirical approach is seminal.

In an empirical approach we describe, we try to understand *what is* and *how* it works (not necessarily *why*). In a normative approach we evaluate what ought to be; we judge the right and the wrong.

Values: Subsystems and Differing Orders

Values have been defined and redefined for more than a century; the very concept has continued probably since the beginning of philosophy. A historical survey, important and useful as it is, has to be reduced to a lengthy note, since this is not a major theme of this study.[7] Philosophers at the turn of our century, not unlike economists associated the concept with everything that is desired, others with our emotions. Perry considered any interest as a value. Are goals, all goals, values? Is the positive norm ("what ought to be done") identical with goal or purpose?

We may begin with a comparison. My goal today is to repair my automobile. My neighbor's daily goal is to help a needy person, a good deed. Are both goals and norms of conduct of the same quality?

The former is solely pragmatic; the latter, ethical. Efficiency of pragmatic activities is also subject to a regulative subsystem. There is the sense of direction, of course, but the nature of goals is different. Some of our goals and actions are morally indifferent, others are influenced by moral judgment, and still others belong primarily to ethics.[8]

Let us move to another example: Michelangelo working on his Sistine Chapel. Is his goal purely pragmatic or esthetic? Moreover, are the norms of conduct in his esthetic activity identical with those of moral activities? They are different. The philanthropist is guided by his goal to achieve good; a great artist, in an ancient, classic sense, attempts to achieve beauty. Those two idea subsystems are guided by different orders of norms.

Initially, for logical convenience, we have separated exclusively pragmatic activities (for instance, economic), assuming that they exist in such a reduced form, from those guided by norms that are located in idea systems (ethics, esthetics). We shall call the latter tentatively values (for a full definition of values see chapter 5).

However, we have used the phrase "exclusively pragmatic" again solely for logical convenience. For, work is also affected by culture and values. The work of a Renaissance craftsman was affected by values and culture of his time and differed from work, norms of conduct, economic and esthetic goals of a worker in a factory of the early Industrial Revolution.

In terms of method, for the sake of classification we may distinguish activities (a) normatively indifferent (neither guided by nor directed toward value-goals), (b) normatively affected or influenced, or (c) normative, controlled primarily by values.

All these activities and all three subsystems mentioned in our example have different directive and regulative apparatuses. The structure is similar if not identical (the element of choice, polarity of norms, norms of conduct and goals). The very nature of this content, however, is different. The same is true about science, which is also an idea system, different than ethics or esthetics.

Norms and standards applied within one idea subsystem do not work in another one. They are not transferable. Esthetic norms do not work in science. The order of norms is different.

However, the same universe of data, the same facts are subjects of different subsystems and at different times are evaluated—within the latter—by different norms. The same cathedral can be discussed in terms of its cost—by means of economic norms; as object of art—in esthetics terms; as place of worship—in religious terms.

All the subsystems are integrated by the entire culture and by an overall idea system, or world outlook. But still this difference in advanced societies is seminal. In an early stage the various subsystems are not yet differentiated. They are fused within the entire cultural system.

Now we assume that there is a number of idea subsystems and different orders of norms. Let us take arbitrarily three idea subsystems—ethics, esthetics, and science.

Science is an idea system that man has either discovered or created. It is not the only idea system discovered or created by man. Ethics and esthetics are the others, and we could mention a few more. These three subsystems are different areas of human experience. Phenomena or behaviors in all three areas are measured by yardsticks that we have called value judgments or norms of conduct (as shown in Figure 1.1).

Each of our idea subsystems has two extreme polar values—a negative one and a positive one. This dichotomy is a part of every human idea system and of every value judgment. In ethics the positive is right (good), the negative wrong (bad); in esthetics (in the ancient Hellenic sense), the positive is beautiful, the negative ugly; in science the positive is true (valid), the negative false (not valid). Of course, few phenomena, few actions are red and green. There are a number of shadows in our value measurement in between a number of gradations that we express in various ways. Measurement of phenomena within boundaries of those extreme value judgments is, of course, qualitatively expressed in ethics and esthetics.

Behavior and evaluation within each of those idea subsystems are subject to different norms. The norms are different in their nature and quality and are not interchangeable or transferable. They work solely within the context and structure of a subsystem. Michelangelo's sculpture is evaluated as work of art, subject to esthetic and not to scientific evaluation. Aretino had a reputation of a scoundrel (some say, it was well deserved). Literary contributions of this gifted and sarcastic Renaissance writer are judged by literary and not by moral standards. The same work can be evaluated by moral standards, true, but this is no longer literary

Figure 1.1
Idea Systems and Values

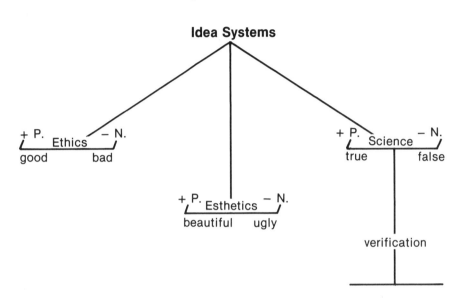

+ P — positive value
− N — negative value

criticism. In such a case, the same data are shifted to another subsystem, subject to a different regulatory and directive evaluation, to a different order of norms.

The goals and norms of conduct of a great civilization belong to an entire system of cultural norms, to the "ethos." Ethics—the moral code—is a part of ethos. Science cannot supply goals of our social institutions. The goals (e.g., justice, equality, knowledge) are normative; they are values of our ethos or ethics. Science may supply the answers about rational ways or means such goals are achieved. Scientific method may be applied to analyze and understand human behavior. But, decision, judgment in ethical matters, does not belong to science. Human life as a supreme value is an ethical norm or standard. Medicine, applying scientific method, is instrumental in preservation of human life. Human life as a supreme value is an ethical, not a scientific, standard.

There is a seminal difference between scientific and nonscientific norms or values. Only scientific findings are subject to scientific validation. By means of validation the verity of our findings is established. Judgment in a scientific process is called a hypothesis or an assumption. It becomes a finding or inference by ways of validation. Validation establishes the tentative "truth" (validity of findings), not a certainty. Once the findings are verified, validity is established; the finding is "true." While we move within the area of science, the finding can be challenged if the validation was deficient or if results were affected by variables not considered by the experimenter.

The hypothesis is tested against hard facts, derived from observation or experimentation. Thus, hard facts, the relationship of facts derived from observation and experimentation, are the basis of scientific validation.

Nonscientific value judgments based on nonscientific norms and standards are not subject to the same process of scientific verification. That an increase of heat results in expansion of iron can be easily verified. Whether Picasso's pictures are beautiful or ugly, or whether they contribute to our esthetic experience, is a value judgment that is not subject to validation, or at least to validation we have called scientific. *A* may argue that Picasso's pictures are ugly and meaningless and *B* that they are beautiful, while *C* may state that neither *A*'s nor *B*'s viewpoint matters since the pictures are neither beautiful nor ugly but contribute to a certain experience. Who is right? *A*? *B*? Or *C*? There is no verification of an objective, scientific nature that establishes the validity of esthetic findings, that settles the matter by way of a process, that is independent of personal sentiments and preferences.

Statistics? The majority vote that Picasso's pictures are just abhorrent does not affect or even invalidate the judgment of the minority. Decision of experts? Wagner's criticism of Mendelssohn's music will not convince those who delight in the latter's work. Neither the former nor the latter may secure any basis for objective validation, a validation of a judgment that once established as a finding or inference serves as a premise of new workable theoretical constructions. All judgments in esthetics are "opinions"; there is no way of establishing an independent, objective test of verity accepted by all those who have adequate knowledge of the field.

Mutatis mutandis—there is no scientific validation in ethics. Efforts were made by Spencer as well as by Kropotkin. In recent years attempts by prominent psychologists to establish such scientific data of ethics did not produce a method of scientific validation of ethical judgments. The findings of Spencer or hypothesis advanced by Kropotkin point to the universality of altruism and mutual aid, and this is a "descriptive" finding derived from speculation (Spencer) and observation (Kropotkin). It is a finding of an observer. It does not provide, however, an actor with a scientific method and instruments of scientific validation of his decision.

Still, the esthetic and ethical evaluation and judgment are of paramount relevance. The absence of a scientific validation does not diminish their significance and function. The utilitarians may argue that the principle of happiness of the greatest number, the principle of pain and pleasure, punishment and reward suggests a scientific premise for ethical norms. Again, the pleasure derived from victory in war does not justify ethically the act. Moreover, should this be a victory of a powerful nation, of a majority over a minor ethnic group, then this act is highly unethical, in spite of the happiness of the largest number.

The noble and great ethical deeds are those indeed that have no utilitarian rewards for the actor. They may be painful rather than pleasurable in terms of personal sentiments or experience.

In nonscientific fields, while scientific validation is absent, or has no application, still there are ways of identification of what might be considered as a "correct or fair judgment," a quasi verification. The scientific hypothesis is tested against relationships of facts. The ethical judgment is tested against accepted or shared standards. The same is true in esthetics. Those standards might be shared by a small group, not by a majority. But within this group standards, sometimes vague, supply the basis for what might be called normative verification. Human behaviors, actions evaluated in terms of ethics, are subject to normative verification. Testing of our acts against a priori established or accepted norms (imperatives or commandments) can be called "normative verification." It is a comparison of an act with a definition, an evaluation of an act in terms of normative definition.

In Judeo-Christian tradition and ethics the Ten Commandments are those explicit standards against which our behavior is tested. In the Roman Catholic church, behavior is tested against dogmas, interpreted by church authorities. In all dubious matters the church sets the standards against which behavior is tested.

Behavior may be tested in ethics against standards or dogma; in esthetics, against intuitive judgment, sentiments, standards established by masters or schools, definitions, or perceptions of proportions.

Perhaps the closest to scientific validation in esthetics were the Greeks with the concept of harmony, reflected in architecture. Proportions in architecture have a mathematical ratio. The very concept of validation has probably evolved from Greek mathematics. The Golden Rectangle which appears in Greek architecture and corresponds to about 1:1.6 ratio, considered as a classic esthetic pattern, could be claimed as such a standard. It corresponds to the proportion of the Fibonacci sequence of numbers and results in this esthetic ratio.[9] Whether or not the mathematical ratio was known to the Greeks, it still appears in Greek art amazingly regularly a permanent ratio. Pythagorean efforts in music and mathematics bear certain similarity: acceptance of or attempt to develop esthetic standards by fusion of scientific findings with esthetic perceptions.

In political ideologies, goal achievements or behavior may be tested against a priori definitions. Thus, achievement of a socialist economy can be tested against an a priori definition of the latter (we shall return below to this theme).

This type of verification follows the medieval scholastic pattern of testing against the opinions, theories of authorities. However, only scientific validation, based on facts, data, and their relationships, supplies in the field of scientific inquiry findings in an objective manner.[10]

We may conclude this section with a general assumption:

1. In advanced cultures, idea systems are differentiated into subsystems governed by particular orders of norms and goals. In traditional societies and cultures a single idea system (e.g., magical) absorbs all or most of the areas of human activities and dominates the various areas. The particular subsystems did not yet evolve as separate areas of activity.

2. Within a closed idea subsystem, standards and norms are particular and different than in others.

3. They are not transferable to other subsystems.

4. Scientific validation has its application solely when data are subject to scientific evaluation, within a scientific subsystem. However, in an empirical approach, values studied within a scientific subsystem as cultural data can be validated. Their relationship to other social data or behavior is subject to an empirical study and construction of a hypothesis. In a normative approach, however, a normative decision—a judgment—cannot be validated scientifically within a normative subsystem.

5. Practical results of normative decisions can be evaluated in a pragmatic and empirical way. Hitler's decision to exterminate Gypsies, based on his ideological premise, can be studied in an empirical (scientific) way, described, related to his personality deviations. His deeds, considered within our ethical system, are considered in terms of moral wrongs. They were evil, bad, cruel. The practical results of his action belong to the pragmatic area (see below) and can be tested. Whether his decision and action were "right" in terms of national socialism has to be tested against the definitions of national socialism. He acts within his ideological system.

The same universe of data, results of social actions, can and usually is shifted to the ethical subsystem and evaluated by ethical norms. Actions, which in terms of pragmatic evaluation are effective, may be at the same time immoral, ethically negative. Political action, though politically effective, may be at the same time morally repulsive.

All three subsystems, however, are a part of and are affected by the entire system (we may call it a super- or mega-system) of ideas, the entire culture. Science, ethics, and esthetics of European medieval culture were affected by the dominant religious outlook and values of the times as well as by nascent social forces and ideas (more about it below chapter 2). At this point, we shall indicate only the nature of this structure.

Resolution of Disagreements

The fact that all three subsystems operate within a larger cultural frame does not change the very quality of subsystems—their norms and value-goals. They are different; with the exception of science, findings are not subject to scientific validation. Second, norms of conduct and values as elements of judgments and goals are not transferable from one subsystem to another. We cannot judge the beauty of a sculpture by means of moral or scientific evaluation. In consequence, disagreements within a given subsystem cannot be resolved by projection of values from the others. Disagreements on esthetic problems cannot be resolved by scientific means, although such efforts were made by the Greeks by fusion of subsystems. At this point we are suggesting as a general assumption this premise, a consequence of the principle of not transferable norms. A political ideological argument on superiority of democracy over aristocracy can be discussed in pragmatic ways in terms of efficiency of a political form. Whether political equality is right or wrong—such a question cannot be resolved by scientific means of a hypothesis evaluated in terms of valid and nonvalid. This is a seminal moral and political issue; it belongs to those two fundamental provinces. Here is a matter of a value judgment, with no scientific validation of who is right and wrong. Disagreements in the political area are not resolved by scientific process: They are resolved by conflict or compromise, by consensus or imposition of rule by force, by ways established by a political culture and skills to deal with problems of power and its distribution.

The same relationship of data however can be evaluated within different closed subsystems:

1. A political act and decision can be scientifically described, related to other facts, to personalities of decision makers, effects, and so on. All such findings are subject to scientific validation.

2. A political decision is also a moral decision; it has its moral effect. Ergo, a political act can be evaluated within the ethical subsystem. Whether the decision is right or wrong—in this area—is tested against ethical standards.

3. A political decision is an ideological decision: Within this subsystem, it is "right" when it is in agreement with the a priori principles.

4. A political decision has practical results; it can be evaluated in a pragmatic way: A political system A leads to a decision B and results in C. But this is testing of results— not the ideological orthodoxy.

We may evaluate the same data within different subsystems, with different orders of norms. Norms, however, are not transferred in such a case from one subsystem to another. In reverse, a universe of data, facts, and decisions is transferred to a different regulative and directive subsystem and evaluated by particular orders of norms. This is done all the time. We test economic results of political systems and moral effects of ideological decisions. The study of the geometric form of crystals is one thing; their chemistry is another. Nonetheless, an inference can probably be made that a chemical composition A results in crystals B.

On a logical level, disagreements within a given subsystem can be resolved solely by ways and norms of that particular subsystem. However, on an empirical, practical level, a normative subsystem may be also (and should be) evaluated by its practical results and not by logical consistency between facts and definitions.

In terms of logic, the evaluation of pragmatic results is already a shift from ideological order to pragmatic. The latter is evaluated in terms of pragmatic results (for example, efficiency) and not by ideological consistency. For example, the socialist organization of a society may be evaluated by its consistency and agreement with the definition or by means of pragmatic validation of results. Then—in pragmatic terms—I ask: Did the socialist organization of society result in (a) higher wages of the working class than those in other countries of mixed or capitalistic economy; (b) better housing; (c) greater abundance of consumer's goods; (d) better health service; (e) peaceful policy toward neighbors; (f) personal freedom and human rights?

Thus we now have moved to a different area (subsystem) that we may call "pragmatic," or policy-testing. We do not test anymore whether the institutions of Albania are truly socialist or not, whether Albania is a "socialist country" in terms of a given socialist theory or not. What we test are the pragmatic, observable results of social institutions and policies. This we shall call a pragmatic test. It is a test of results or consequences of social and economic policies that is usually subject to quantitative evaluation. The pragmatic or policy test is paramount in social-economic planning; in social change it should be distinguished from an ideological test. We may call this subsystem a subsystem of applied policy; we test policies applied in a given case. Of course, policies are rooted in norms, ideological norms. But, the area of practical or applied policies is that segment which crosses the boundaries from ideology to reality. We test practical results of ideological changes, ideological movements, effects of their policies on society in a given social situation.

In an ideological test we "verify" whether decisions conform to ideological norms of conduct and whether goals and changes conform to ideological theory.

To take another example, the administration of Great Britain by its Labour party. Whether Great Britain under the Labour party is a socialist country is one thing. Whether the public policies of the British Labour party resulted in higher wages, shorter working hours, and general improvement of the conditions of the working class is another thing. Such improvement necessitates reform: social security institutions, mixed economy to mention a few. They may fit under the general signifier of socialism. But it should be remembered that the definition of the signifier (the signified) can be changed. (On signifier and signified, see below chapter 4.)

We may as well change the signifier. May I suggest that we use the term *socialist pragmatism* for policies that bring about changes desired by socialist principles: improvement of the condition of the working class, full employment, civil rights, decrease of international tensions, all that irrespective of economic forms.

In terms of socialist pragmatism, a mixed economy rather than state- and centrally controlled collectivization may bring about what is considered to be socialist changes or reforms (in terms of a socialist program). However, this type of economic system may not meet the ideological test; it may not conform to the a priori definition of what socialism is, in terms of Lenin, interpreted by

Albanian ideologists. What indeed matters in life is the relationship between social-economic change, prompted by ideological parties, and practical results.

The social change in many instances is a consequence of political, economic, and social strategies decided by political parties or governing bodies of those parties that have economic and political power.

What is relevant is not whether ideologies of those parties are consistent or not, whether their institutions correspond to definitions. What is relevant are the results; lofty ideologies translated by man into policies may result into social disasters of forced labor, deprivation, and dictatorship. Hence the relevance of a pragmatic or policy test is close to a scientific one, since policies are tested against results, against facts that can be observed. In most cases, quantitative validation is not only feasible, but generally practiced in policy evaluation.

Thus, three major types of thinking, evaluating, and acting are expressed in three different types of verification: scientific, pragmatic, and normative.

Scientific validation is a process of testing a hypothesis against facts by means of observation or experimentation. This validation is an articulation of an idea system we call science or scientific, and it is concerned with description, classification, and understanding "what is." We arrive at this understanding by relating data and constructing inferences.

Pragmatic and policy thinking and acting, by which we affect the environment or relate directly to practical activities connected with our basic and economic needs, form another area. Attainment of targets in this area is tested against results. In a "pragmatic" test we validate effectiveness of individual actions or social policies by the evidence of results. We test the workability of our actions, and goal attainment suggests that operationally the actions were effective.

The pragmatic or policy area is concerned with the factual and practical perception of the situation and effective actions. Here, the major theme is not only "what is" but also "how" to attain practical and policy results.

Testing against results, hence against data, is akin to scientific testing. The policy process is related to science, so scientific methods may have an application.

In the normative area the empirical hypothesis of science, which is subject to testing, is displaced by a normative definition or doctrine. The achievement or nonachievement of a normative goal is tested against an a priori definition or a doctrine or a dogma. We may also call it an ideological test.

The normative definition attempts to answer an implicit question: "What ought to be?" Science determines "what is," whereas practical activity considers "how effective it is."

The study of values belongs to those three major provinces. The philosopher asks the question "what ought to be," what is right and wrong. A sociologist and anthropologist describes, analyzes the structure of values ("what is"), attempts to answer questions of how are they structured, how do they work, and what is their function in a society. His interest extends to the area of origin and change of value systems. A psychologist studies individual values, whereas a sociologist and an anthropologist consider social values, shared values, and their effects.

A social planner is a pragmatist. His task is an effective achievement of policy goals. Collective values and belief systems affect pragmatic actions. It is his task to discover whether a given set of institutions and incentives fosters a given set of policies or whether other options have to be chosen, incentives or institutions adjusted.

The three areas are of course related. It is the method and theory that separate them.

In real life, in politics, no single subsystem is sufficient. In fact, evaluation of an ideological subsystem only in terms of its consistency, only within the norms and tenets of the latter, is tantamount to orthodoxy, dogmatism, and at times even to a harmful exercise. Evaluation of Hitler's politics solely in terms of its relationship to Hitler's norms of conduct and goals may be tantamount to indifference toward, if not silent approval of, his deeds. His policies must be evaluated in terms of pragmatic results and, again, are subject to moral, ethical evaluation. An extreme relativist argues: "He acted according to his norms of conduct and doctrine. How do we know that our ethics is the 'right one'? There are no absolute norms." This type of evaluation, of course, a part of an academic discussion, has to be translated into facts: concentration camps and millions of tortured and murdered victims. Stalin's communist economic system, the communist system according to his definition, has to be considered in terms of its efficiency, practical results, and moral fulfillment. To limit the evaluation again only to its ideological consistency, to agreement or disagreement with Lenin's precepts, is to forget about purges and forced labor camps.

The full evaluation of ideological systems, be they political or religious, calls for "crossing the lines", evaluating the results, the same data within other subsystems: the scientific, the pragmatic and the overall, general ethical code shared by our civilization.

Inference

The directive-regulatory apparatus is seminal in every culture and every society. It is a universal structure in diachronic and synchronic terms.

Social change in a society means affecting its goals and norms of conduct to affect the directive and regulatory structure. Such a change will affect in turn the environment: actions of a social group toward its social, economic, political, as well as natural environment. In reverse, changes in the environment may and usually do affect the goals or the norms of conduct.

Man affects social change by choice of goals and related actions. This relationship of goals and actions in a *rational* social change is organized into empirical-logical, as well as pragmatic, patterns called social planning.

Political change in domestic and international relations is achieved by applying or activating the directive and regulatory structure by identifying goals and mobilizing actions. Patterns of goals and actions in politics are called strategy and tactics.

Notes

1. See Glossary to *Nicomachean Ethics*, translation and notes by Martin Ostwald (Indianapolis and New York: Bobbs-Merrill Co., 1962), p. 313.

2. Six different terms are listed in George Dunbar's *Greek-English Lexicology* (Edinburgh: MacLachlan & Stewart, 1856), p. 51.

3. Joseph Conrad, "Well Done," *Notes on Life and Letters* (London and Toronto: Dent, 1928), p. 179.

4. Herbert Spencer, *The Data of Ethics* (New York: Hurst n.d., Introduction dated June 1879), p. 8.

5. Talcott Parsons, *The Structure of Social Action* (Glencoe, Ill.: Free Press, 1949), pp. xiii, 732.

6. In terms of the German classification of science, the scientific study of values belongs to a general area of *Geistes Wissenschaften*. Today it may be considered as related to or perhaps part of humanistic sociology.

However, Znaniecki suggested a general field of "cultural sciences," and Martindale suggested sociology of culture.

Znaniecki discusses a theory of actions, goals, and values in *Cultural Sciences* (Urbana: University of Illinois Press, 1952), which was one of his last major contributions and which he himself considered as a synthesis of his life work. Znaniecki makes a sharp distinction between a normative and a scientific approach to social values.

Martindale's definition of the sociology of culture embraces three major components: play, art, knowledge. *Sociological Theory of Culture and Problems of Values* (Columbus, Ohio: Merrill, 1974), pp. 49 ff. Huizinga sees in play the essence of civilization. J. Huizinga, *Homo Ludens* (Boston: Beacon Press, 1955).

The study of values crosses the disciplinary lines of separate fields. It is definitely an essential frame of reference of Martindale's sociology of culture.

7. The development of value theories and the debate over the definition of the term *value* call for a separate chapter, if not a volume. The concept is difficult to define and has existed as long as ethics and philosophy. The term, however, with its modern meanings seems to have gained relevance in philosophy during the second part of the nineteenth century, especially in German philosophy. It gained wider currency and interest with the controversial, sometimes contradictory and confused, but at the same time challenging and talented writings of Friedrich Nietzsche; his *Genealogy of Morals* (New York: Tudor Publishing, 1931) is primarily concerned with values and transvaluation.

Noted among scholars and philosophers who advanced the nineteenth-century and turn-of-the-twentieth-century value theories were Franz Brentano, Alexius von Meinong, and Christian von Ehrenfels (called sometimes The Viennese School). Values were related to psychology, to the human emotions, to the faculty of love and hate (Brentano). Meinong in turn argued that values have no absolute worth outside emotions of persons, but they are not simply subjective sentiments, for they are related to a real universe and go beyond personal sentiments. Ehrenfels considered values from a viewpoint of desirability. The value is an object that is desired; worth is assigned to things because we desire them.

Furthermore, George Edward Moore and Sidgwick suggested as the fundamental concept of ethics the central ethical value, and so, it seems to me, did Aristotle, without using this term. Hastings Rashdall in *The Theory of Good and Evil* (1907) advanced a theory of ethics based on two polar values, of good and evil. Rashdall discussed the relationship of good and right. The value of good, he argued, is prior to right in its sequence. I see relevance in his identification of "ought" with the concept of value. "The idea of ought is implicitly contained in the idea of value.... The idea of good and the idea of right are, as it seems to me, correlative terms. It is implied in the idea of the good that it ought be promoted." For an excellent overview see Henry Sidgwick, *Outlines of the History of Ethics*, (Boston: Beacon Press, 1968) with an additional chapter by Alban G. Widgery, First Edition 1886, sixth (enlarged 1931) pp. 306 ff.

Nicolai Hartmann discussed relativity of values in terms of their validity. Relativity of values, he argued, is their historical instability. Still, he continued, in spite of change the existence of value continues. Hartmann attempted to reconcile relativism with the "absoluteness" of values. At certain times values are "valid"; in others, they are not, but their existence continues. See "Das Wertproblem in der Philosophie der Gegenwart" (*Actes du Huitième Congrès Internationale de Philosophie*, 1934). This essay was translated into English and published in Dagobert D. Runes' collection, *Treasury of Philosophy* (New York: Philosophical Library, 1955) pp. 472 ff. (More about Hartmann's major work appears below, in chapter 14.)

In American philosophy values were discussed by John Dewey, *Theory of Valuation* (Chicago: Chicago University Press, 1939); Charles S. Peirce, *Values in a Universe of Chance* ed. by Philip P. Wiener (Garden City, N.Y.: Doubleday, 1958); and Ralph Barton Perry, *Realm of Values* (Westport, Ct.: Greenwood Press, 1968). Perry defined values in terms of interests. We have mentioned here only some of the work in this area, since values were widely discussed and studied and since the American contribution in this field is quoted within the text and listed in the bibliography.

In a broader, historical sense the concept appeared in writings of Wilhelm Dilthey (see H. P. Rickman, ed., *Wilhelm Dilthey: Pattern and Meaning in History* (New York: Harper & Row, 1961, especially the Introduction; Helmut Diwald, *Wilhelm Dilthey* (Göttingen: Musterschmidt, 1963); and, of course, the ten volumes by Wilhelm Dilthey, *Gesammelte Schriften* (Stuttgart: Teubner, 1965–1973).

The concept became implicit and fundamental in Max Weber's work entitled *The Protestant Ethic and the Spirit of Capitalism*, as well as his voluminous *Gesammelte Aufsätze zur Religions Soziologie*.

Max Weber's traditions as well as some of his concepts (for example, *Verstehen*) can be traced to Dilthey. In sociology the interest in this area later found a prominent representative in Max Weber.

Florian Znaniecki in *The Problem of Values in Philosophy* (Warsaw, 1910), written in Polish, gave an early survey of philosophic conceptions of values and credits Hugo Münsterberg with the first systematic work on values in his *Philosophie der Werte* (Leipzig: Barth, 1903). This writer had no access to Znaniecki's general survey, mentioned in his *Cultural Sciences* (p. 173, n. 20). The value frame of reference in Thomas and Znaniecki's major work *The Polish Peasant in Europe and America* was probably initiated by the latter.

In sociology, however, Herbert Spencer should be credited for his pioneering work in this field, *The Data of Ethics*. Although the concept of values is not as explicit as his central premise, nonetheless Spencer discusses the ''regulative'' nature of norms as well as the paramount relevance of the latter for a social system.

In American sociology and social psychology W. I. Thomas and Florian Znaniecki have given relevance to value theory. W. I. Thomas and Florian Znaniecki, *The Polish Peasant in Europe and America* [1915] (New York: Knopf, 1927), introduced value as a central sociological concept, defining it this way: ''By social value we understand any datum having an empirical content accessible to the members of some social groups and a meaning with regard to which it is or may be an object of activity.''

The discussion of values continues with a number of important studies, focusing on the relation of values to the situation or interests, on one hand, and on the interdependence of values and attitudes, on the other.

But the concept of values affected not one, but several theoretical attempts and directions in social sciences. A major school, with its prominent representative, Talcott Parsons, considered values within the action and system, structure and function theories. Talcott Parsons, *The Social System* (Glencoe, Ill.: Free Press, 1951); *The Structure of Social Action*; T. Parsons and E. Shils *Toward A General Theory of Action* (Cambridge, New York, Evanston, 1962). In a personality and culture approach, and in a general theoretical analysis, Pitirim Sorokin, *Society, Culture and Personality* (New York: Harper & Brothers, 1947), and others exercised considerable influence. In cultural sociology and in a macrosociological-philosophical approach, Don A. Martindale, *Sociological Theory and the Problems of Values* (Columbus: Merrill, 1974) critically explored fundamental attempts. Alfred McClung Lee applied the concept in his many studies in sociology and social psychology, in terms of culture and personality, humanistic sociology, and also to problems considered before as social marginality (*Multivalent Man* [New York: Braziller: 1966]). Charles Morris devoted a number of major studies to this special area and wrote about preferential values and choice, varieties of values and semantics. Among his numerous contributions in this field are *Varieties of Human Values* (Chicago: University of Chicago Press, 1956), *Signification and Significance: A Study of Relations of Signs and Values* (Cambridge: M.I.T. Press, 1964); *Signs, Language and Behavior* (New York: Prentice-Hall, 1950).

F. Adler contributed a critical approach in his articles in sociological journals.

Values were also defined for and applied in quantitative research and studies. Again, for the sake of brevity, we shall only mention the work of H. H. Hyman, W. R. Cotton, Jr., Handley Cantril, and E. Borgatta, as discussion of this special area cannot be reduced to a few sentences.

In psychology and social psychology, values were defined and analyzed to limit our sources only to the well-known and basic volume by Gordon Allport, P. E. Vernon, and G. Lindzey, *A Study of Value* (Boston, 1951) (see chapter 15). Philosophical as well as psychological studies were made in search of a scientific basis for universal values (E. Fromm, A. Maslow, and others).

The concept and theories of values have been widely applied in social or cultural anthropology. It is implicit in Ruth Benedict's well-known *Patterns of Culture* (New York: Houghton Mifflin, 1934). Value and value orientations form a major approach of Ralph Linton and Clyde Kluckhohn; we shall mention here Ralph Linton, *The Study of Man* (New York: Appleton-Century, 1936). In a major study by Florence R. Kluckhohn and Fred L. Strodtbeck, *Variations in Value Orientations* [1961] (Westport, Conn.: Greenwood Press, 1976), value orientation is the central concept. Kluckhohn's ''Values and Value of Orientation in the Theory of Action,'' appeared in T. Parsons and E. Shils, eds., *Toward a General Theory of Action* (Cambridge, Mass.: Harvard University Press, 1951). Value orientations are defined as "complex but definitely patterned (rank-ordered) principles, resulting from the transactional interplay of three analytically distinguishable elements of the evaluative process—the cognitive, the affective and the directive elements—which give order and direction to the ever flowing stream of human acts and thoughts as these relate to the solution of common human problems. This definition has been applied to a number of case studies.

The theory of value is not limited to American and European social sciences. In India, Radhakamal Mukerjee applies the value frame of reference in *Social Function of Art* (New York: Philosophical Library, 1958) and *The Dimensions of Values* (London: Allen & Unwin, 1964).

I have listed many studies without any further comment.

This very brief outline of development and definition of the concepts shows not only a variety of approaches but also a variety of definitions. The concept of value is relevant not only for theories. It is a key element of our civilization, whether we find a proper definition of it or not. Nonetheless, there is not a single, all-inclusive definition or variation of a single one, although there is a substantial agreement on the validity of the concept in an operational sense.

This brief note may give only a faint impression of the vast area and complexity. For an excellent, comprehensive, and careful survey of definitions and concepts of values in sociology, see Jurgen Friedrichs, *Werte und Soziales Handeln* (Tübingen: Mohr, 1968). Also a good and specialized presentation and discussion of definitions and methods of identification of values in empirical research, with an extensive bibliography, is William J. Wilson and F. Ivan Nye, "Some Methodological Problems in the Empirical Study of Values," *Washington State University Bulletin* (July 1966).

8. Herbert Spencer in *The Data of Ethics*, pp. 14 ff., makes this distinction and comments, "conduct with which morality is not concerned, passes into conduct which is moral or immoral, in small degrees and in countless ways".

9. Leonardo Fibonacci da Pisa (ca. 1170–1250), medieval mathematician, discovered the Fibonacci sequence. The Fibonacci series derives from adding the two last numbers to obtain the next. For example, regular sequence: 1, 2, 3, 4, 5, 6, 7, 8; Fibonacci sequence: 1, 2, 3, 5, 8, 13, 21, 34. The daisy's opposite spirals ratio of 21:34 and the pine cone's opposites ratio of 5:8 correspond to the Fibonacci series, as do other proportions in nature.

The ratio between any two adjacent Fibonacci numbers is about 1:1.6. This ratio, called the golden ratio, occurs in some geometric figures, but it is frequent in Greek architecture. Fibonacci introduced also Arabic algebra into the Western world and Arabic numbers (about 1202).

Pythagoras (ca. 580–500 BC) in turn discovered the connection between music and numbers and the relationship of various tones in terms of fractions and proportions. Consider J. D. Bernal, *Science in History* (Cambridge: MIT Press, 1971), vol. 1, pp. 303, 332; James C. James, *Mathematics Dictionary* (Princeton: Van Nostrand, 1968), p. 145; David Bergamini, *Mathematics* (New York: Time, 1963), pp. 93 ff. On principles of proportions in architecture see Banister Fletcher, *A History of Architecture* (New York: Scribners, 1961), p. 377.

10. There are of course different concepts and definitions of science and what science is. Furthermore, the boundaries between induction and deduction are by no means tight, especially at an early stage of construction of an hypothesis. A wide area of scientific

activity is deductive in its nature. Nonetheless, inductive scientific validation is and was a process applied by those who practiced science and got results. True, not all areas are subject to such testing. We accept validation, however, as essential. In this sense, I admit, it is a kind of an a priori.

2

Ideologies—The World Outlook and Values

I hope, now, that there is no risk of your misunderstanding when I come to the gist of what I want to say tonight—when I repeat, that every great national architecture has been the result and exponent of a great national religion. You can't have bits here and bits there—you must have it everywhere or nowhere. It is not the monopoly of a clerical company—it is not an exponent of a theological dogma—it is not the hieroglyphic writing of an initiated priesthood; it is the manly language of people inspired by resolute and common purpose, and rendering resolute and common fidelity to the legible laws and undoubted God.

John Ruskin (*The Crown of Wild Olive*, 1864)

... for it is the ideals of a people rather than geography they have outgrown that determine their destiny; and in Kansas, as has been well said, it is the ideas of the Pilgrims, not their descendants, that have had dominion in their young commonwealth. Ideas, sometimes, as well as the star of the empire move westward, and so it happens that Kansas is more Puritan than New England of today. It is akin to New England of the early days....

Carl Becker (Kansas)

World Outlook

The directive-regulatory apparatus is related to and in part located within the world outlook or idea system of a culture. Hence, let us move to the discussion of idea systems or ideologies.

Every society creates a world outlook—a metaphysical or philosophical idea system, a dominant way of perceiving and interpreting phenomena, explaining human existence and the surrounding world and setting the limits of such understanding. When Comte wrote more than a century ago about magical, metaphysical, and scientific periods of human development, there was an element of historical validity in his broad synthesis. He only followed, in this approach, earlier teachings of his one time master, Henri de Saint-Simon.

The history of great civilizations is in fact the history of man's idea systems and their relationship to reality, to the ways man perceived this reality and was motivated to action, affected by values. Values are articulations or components of those dominant, at times powerful, ideologies (which may also be called world outlook).

The general idea system that integrates the society appears as a shared belief system. In early stages of humanity, magic and primitive, strongly ritualistic forms of religion were the two major components of an idea system.

Religion, philosophies of a variety of schools, political ideologies, as well as science are components; at other times, they constitute the totality of our general ideology.

But the idea system has to be considered in its relation to reality, to the society, and to the environment. The dominant values—located in ideologies—set the goals and regulate the conduct. In consequence, they also do affect the social and, to an extent, the physical reality. The belief system affects individual and collective goals and actions.

This context, interrelation between the belief system of the historical period and actual performance, which appears in social reality, is the key to our understanding of a historical era.

History and historical periods appear in this interdependence between idea system and reality. History is understood, as Dilthey indicates, by relating human actions, institutions, expressions of art and science of a historical period to the idea system, the world outlook of those times or *Weltanschauung*, a concept to which he devotes an entire volume.[1] Understanding (*Verstehen*) calls for relating man's action to his (not our) historical period, to the belief system that governs his action and thinking. Man understands some of the nature and behavior of others; he has some, not full, understanding. Hence, relating the others to historical conditions of their period, their society (not ours), he gains a fuller understanding. The concept of understanding, perhaps of an attempt of understanding, forms the basic approach of Dilthey, advanced later by Max Weber.[2]

Every historical period has its particular set of values, its guiding principles; a wide area of his activities is controlled by this normative order. What we study in fact are those external expressions which are consequences of activities of his mind, guided by his world outlook.

The idea system, doctrines, *Weltanschauung* vary, but they can be identified and described in all societies of past and present. The natives of Australia, at times when they met Captain Cook and his companions, had of course their magical and religious beliefs. As we learned from subsequent reports and research, they had their symbols, norms governing their social behavior located in their general world outlook.

The medieval period of Western history is dominated by a religious-theological ideology, and the culture of those times is affected by values, modes of thought of this outlook. Only within the context of this world outlook do the expressions in art, law, even economy gain an understanding. The ideology of those times and its articulations, variety of social structures, institutions—a result of this relationship between the world outlook and reality—form the history of medieval Europe.

A network of Benedictine monasteries, as well as the numerous religious orders, was a consequence of those religious times—that is, times when Catholicism in its medieval expression was a powerful and dominant world outlook. Without this outlook the Benedictine order as well as other Catholic orders would not have been born or extended their constructive work and influence. Moreover, solely the economy did not shape the world view of the Benedictine brothers. To the contrary, the highly advanced economy, the numerous enterprises—mills, workshops, as well as schools and philanthropies of the Benedictine brothers—their organization—that is, the modes of production—were a consequence and an articulation of their religious and theological outlook. The type of economic organization and production was the effect of a religious outlook.

In this relationship, or interdependence between the idea system and its intellectual and material articulations, appears the image of medieval times. The expressions of the religious outlook appear in the norms of canon law, in the institution of the family.

The entire art is dominated by this religious outlook: the fervid building of cathedrals all over Europe, the rules of painting, as well as the subject of iconography. The style of the churches and even the stained glass windows and their esthetic quality are only a part, a component of medieval culture, a consequence of a religious outlook.[3] One of their major functions was to reinforce the belief, validate the faith. Hence, the very architecture of the cathedrals, their psychological impact, the convincing imagery of stained glass windows, which changes the word of religious teaching or sermon into a visual reality, which can be seen. Art is governed by norms, values of esthetics. Esthetics of medieval times was just a component of the religious outlook and imposed the rules of painting and limits of permitted or favored subject matter.[4] Medieval art was an articulation of this powerful faith, of the religiosity of the society of those times.

Indeed, individual life, collective and individual normative goals and norms of conduct become understandable within this context. Saint Celestino, a twelfth-century hermit, imprisoned later in Fumone (in Italy), cannot be understood simply in economic terms of his class position. His life and his afterlife goals were a consequence of a religious outlook, as was his hesitancy when he was offered all honors of papacy.

The belief systems vary of course with various cultures, but they do appear in all human societies that we know. In this sense, they are universal. We are born into them, as we are born into a society. A newborn child begins its socialization process immediately. It is subject to norms of conduct from the beginning. With age and development it acquires the world outlook, which at first is accepted with no criticism nor resistance. The resistance and conflict— if they come at all—come next. The personality is formed and norms acquired within a general idea system, a world outlook.

Intellectual products, says Dilthey, "do not have the consciousness of their origin, therefore, they can become carriers of higher functions".[5]

Change of Ideologies

Every historical period has its set of values that guides the ideological order, the world outlook. Man's purpose changes in history when his world view, the ideological order, changes because the values and modes of thought and their effect on reality are changed. At such point the new directive and regulatory apparatus points toward new and different goals, imposes new norms of conduct.

We do observe those changes not solely in the abstract form of writings or verbal expressions. They appear in articulations, expressions of those ideological and normative systems which affect the reality, the ways of life, behavior, institutions, and man's material products. They appear in symbols, new religious or political insignia, in new ceremonials, musical hymns and songs, in architecture and ways of life. Those changes occur slowly and rarely; at times they mature rapidly in violent revolutions. Changes in values and ideologies mark the new historical eras.

Not all of the culture, not all institutions or values change. This is a complex process, in which some of the norms yield to pressure and others continue. Some institutions survive; others are displaced. But at this point let us limit ourselves to a very general picture, to a general structure of such changes.

Why does such a change occur? Why did such change take place in the past?

Let us state first that causation of ideological and value changes cannot be reduced to a single all-inclusive historical cause.

Interpretation of historical process, of history of ideas, divides students of history and society into several, at times strongly opposed schools.

Major approaches could be roughly divided into three orientations:

1. Monocausal. A single, all-inclusive, major cause of all social transformations is suggested in such an interpretation: a sole and single causal factor acting in all historical cases.

2. Multicausal. Change of ideas and values as well as the general social change is considered as a consequence of more than a single cause; it postulates several causal factors often or mostly acting at the same time.

3. Functional or interdependent orientation. Change of ideas and values is also viewed in terms of reciprocal effects or in terms of interdependent changes of major variables,

major cultural elements. Thus economic and ideological changes are mutually interdependent: Change of any single variable affects the other. Hence the change may
begin at any place: Begin with the initial changes of values and idea systems, and
they will affect the economic system; or it may start with the economic, technological,
political change and affect ideologies and values.

Theories that argue that changes in economic relations, changes in production
affect ideas and values are not only plausible, but in a vast area of cases can be
tested against a historical evidence. However, a monocausal theory, which reduces all changes in ideas and institutions, the entire "superstructure," solely
to the single prime mover—changes of material conditions—is not a sufficient
theory and cannot explain a variety of historical cases. Similarly a class approach
that relates values and ideas to a class position and self-interest of an individual
or group and explains changes in ideological orientations and values as effects
of the former works in some but not in all cases.[6] Those are not false theories,
as they have their merits and evident areas of validity. But they do not encompass
the many complex cases. Those theories postulate that ideologies are a direct
consequence of class position of individuals and groups, but within the same
class, within groups and individuals of similar class position, we may find
followers of several different political parties, ideological or religious orientations. True, values and general orientation of Protestantism were in accord with
norms of conduct of efficient business. But did the class structure cause changes
in religion, or did the changes in religion and value orientation favor and affect
the new economic relations and systems, or were they—as R. H. Tawney in
Religion and Rise of Capitalism may argue—interdependent?

Historical Materialism

A convincing and influential theory of economic interpretation of ideological
changes is the popularly called "Marxist" interpretation.

Marx's and Engels's theories of historical materialism were interpreted and
reinterpreted again for more than a century. A selected bibliography or the past
and current comments and interpretations would easily fill a few chapters or a
volume. We shall limit our discussion here to only a very rudimentary, rough
presentation, as much as it is necessary to further our argument of change.

Historical materialism has been many times presented in a rather difficult,
almost metaphysical way. After all, it is a theory that is largely based on Hegel's
dialectics, and Hegel does not belong to those philosophers who expressed their
views in a clear and understandable manner. I suspect that some of his glory
comes from his difficult and not too clear, oracular ways.

Perhaps, the clearest presentation of historical materialism by Marx and Engels
can be found in *The German Ideology* and in a limpid, intelligible, but orthodox
interpretation of historical relevance in George Plekhanov's essays.

The basic tenets of historical materialism suggest that social economic rela-

Figure 2.1
The Base Affects the Superstructure

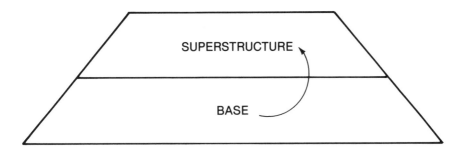

The process of change moves from the base to the superstructure.

tions, class relations in production—that is, modes as well as means of production—decide about the entire historical period and affect all other human relations. In consequence, change in this base affects all the other changes in society, the entire culture, above all, of the ideas, institutions, values, religion.

The modes and means of production form the base, while ideas and values are located in what is called superstructure. The fundamental, initial change—to follow this theory—takes place in the base, and from the base it moves to the superstructure. This can be presented in a simple model (see Figure 2.1). The arrow indicates the movement from the base to the superstructure.

The change in the base— in this approach—is the only necessary and sufficient cause; all other changes are sequent effects. It affects above all the class divisions, class structure, and particular interests. Ideologies form legitimation—we may say today, a rationalization of class interests. Hence values and morals are nothing else but articulation of those interests. They do change with changes in modes of production and with class changes. This change moves from the base to superstructure, from the economic base to the ideological superstructure, not in reverse. This is a rough, very simplified presentation of this theory—rough for sake of clarity.

This division into base and superstructure is indeed a clear and an ingenious methodological device. The Marxist school devoted a major effort primarily to the study of the base and its relation to superstructure.

Engels, however, reinterpreted many times the basic tenets of dialectics and historical materialism in his numerous letters and essays. In the writings of Marx and Engels we may find not one but several, sometimes differing viewpoints on historical materialism. However, they are always within the basic concept of the base and superstructure and a dynamic historical process. This historical process moves by means of a nascent and maturing conflict—the Hegelian thesis and antithesis—which is resolved finally in a synthesis. Well, this provides a convincing, somewhat metaphysical philosophy of history, with an appeal of a new faith, a faith of an era of political creeds that have displaced the monopoly of religious creeds.

Engels's flexible and a broader viewpoint appears, for example, in *Dialectics of Nature*.[7] Here, Engels suggests a theory of reciprocal causation. The base affects the superstructure, but on the other hand the superstructure affects the base. Changes in the base are the cause; changes in the superstructure follow, as an effect. Yet in a next step those changes in the superstructure, in ideologies, become a cause and affect the base.

In his later years Engels, evidently impressed with the social progress of the working classes, with a political and economic advance far beyond his expectations, as well by many debates and discussions, clarified his and Marx's view in a broader and more flexible way, protesting any dogmatism and orthodoxy. In his letters the qualifications of major tenets of historical materialism became clearer and more outspoken. Neither Marx nor Engels, he wrote, denied the relevance of ideas and ideological changes. Nor did they ever consider their theories as an ultimate truth, the last word of the nascent modern social sciences. He objected to the dogmatic interpretation of theories by some Russian scholars (I suspect he had George Plekhanov in mind) who read and interpreted them not unlike holy scriptures or ancient classics.

When an American doctoral candidate asked Engels for comments on his dissertation on a Russian village economy, Engels wrote: "If you have followed the Russian emigration literature of the last decade, you will yourself know how, for instance passages from Marx's writings and correspondence have been interpreted in the most contradictory ways, exactly as if they had been texts from classics or the New Testament, by various sections of Russian emigrants."[8] And Engels himself preferred to abstain from comments of his correspondents' arguments.

Since the turn of the century dialectical materialism has gone through many interpretations and debates. Karl Kautsky wrote his voluminous work on dialectical materialism. With a less orthodox view, so did Henrich Cunov, a prominent economic historian, an ethnologist, and at one time a young associate of Engels (during Engels' declining years). Again, Antonio Labriola, a prominent Italian scholar and theoretician, gave his specific and philosophical interpretation of this doctrine.[9]

However, a dogmatic interpretation of historical materialism continued, and with the establishment of the communist rule in Russia dialectical materialism became far more than a theory. It has been imposed as a state religion, displacing the former orthodoxy of the Eastern church. Now the orthodox way of thinking, acquired before in a religious culture, has been projected into philosophy and politics. The doctrine in its official version became in Stalin's times a required subject in all faculties of Soviet universities.

The interpretation and reinterpretation continues and it is beyond our scope and intentions to present the major trends.

Anyhow, a religious Marxist does not accept any interpretation that does not conform to his creed and suspects in those who have a different view a class enemy, akin to a medieval heretic or a mortal sinner.

Three Major Modes of Change

We may keep this useful theoretical division into the base and superstructure. Our major theme is, however, the superstructure ideas and values. True, the nature of this superstructure has often been differently interpreted; still, the problem is what and how much is located there. It seems to me that Kautsky had argued that some ideas, skills, economic knowledge and the like are also a part of it. But we shall not expand on this, and at this point we shall narrow the concept of superstructure to values, norms, idea systems.

Should we broaden the concept of base to the environment and moreover to political conditions of a given historical time, then we may extend the base to a general concept of a historical situation. We shall use in a parallel manner both concepts and both types of definitions, at least in this chapter.

We shall postulate now that there is not a single way of ideological and normative change, a single causal process responsible for all historical cases, as Plekhanov as well as Bukharin might have argued. Now we shall limit ourselves solely to the major structures, major modes of relationships between the situation, the economic base and ideas. From there we shall move to the "internal" processes of ideological changes.

Three major types of causal relationship between base and superstructure, three major modes of social change, can be suggested.

We begin with the "historical materialistic" mode. The change begins with the changes in means and modes of production; it affects the idea system and values. We have discussed this variant above; to sum up for the sake of clarity: the base or situation is in such case the prime mover of the change.

We may suggest here that in many historical cases such a hypothesis can be supported by data, by proper relationship between facts, pertaining to the changes in production and the changes in ideas and values. However, we may qualify, this change is usually associated with other factors. The great inventions are products of man's mind and ideas.

The second mode, which may find also support in historical data and obser- vation, is the reverse one. The change begins in values and idea systems, affects the economic base, results later in changes in modes of production.

The change in ideologies may affect at first political institutions. A powerful religious or ideological-political movement may result in such a social transformation.

In the third mode all the variables are mutually interdependent; they are tied together in an interaction. One may say they form a *sui generis* system.

The changes in this case are reciprocal. Changes in economics affect ideologies and social movements, and again at the same time changes in ideas affect the economic base. Sometimes they may lag behind for a long time, and adjustment may be slow. Nonetheless, we may face a situation of mutual causation (we call it interaction). It may be difficult indeed to separate causes and effects at times, since the antecedents in stage 1 become sequents in stage 2.

Here the two transformations are interdependent. We may conclude that changes in any of the elements of culture may result in changes of the others. We may begin with religious institutions; they may affect the political as well as the economic. Furthermore, all three may affect the educational system. But let us take exception here. At times the change in one element of culture may not affect the others; some institutions may continue. Real life cannot be reduced to a single theory or a few set patterns. A society may reject economic changes in a variety of ways; it may not assimilate a new technology even at a price of self-destruction. The religious or ideological "superstructure" may be stronger than the changes in the economic "bases." It may as well break, destroy the new economic "base," defeat the groups advancing the change. Recent developments in Iran are only one among many examples. The superstructure may be far stronger than the base.

Now we may return to our initial proposition: There is hardly any social science theory that would work in all cases. Pareto was perhaps the first one who pointed to this quite obvious problem. In some cases the first mode will effectively interpret the nature of social change. In other historical situations the second is at work. And there are changes that lend themselves to the third interpretation. But those three modes are not sufficient.

We may also suggest an additional fourth mode. Whatever Plekhanov's argument against any theory of factors, in other cases—we may postulate—a combination of factors, a number of variables, may affect the ideological change.

Let us add that those three or four modes may suggest only a general direction of change, a general orientation. In a concrete, empirical case of change, factors or variables cannot be easily and sharply separated and questions may arise soon, since some of the factors may qualify into both categories: base and superstructure. Logically convenient, this division, however, is not always clear and is more often blurred.

Unilinear and Multilinear Change

We have omitted in our discussion the political factor for a definite reason: a logical convenience, the sake of reduction of variables. However, distribution of political power is seminal, and social-economic relations may not necessarily correspond to political relations. Political classes may not be the same, and in the past they were frequently different than the economic classes. Control of political power, control of the state and armed forces in an authoritarian system, may decide about choice and direction of an ideological and economic change, may secure a privileged position for a political party and their creed, their ideology. From there, from the position of political control, the ruling group may move into the field of production and of distribution of economic power and foster new modes as well as adoption of new means of production.

Moreover, even when the change in ideologies is affected by a prior change in the base, there is still a problem: In what direction will the change in the ideological superstructure move? What kind of ideologies and values will be advanced and embraced by man and societies? What goals will be assigned to the new productive forces by those in power?

In an orthodox Marxist viewpoint, changes in the economic base follow always a definite, evolutionary pattern and result in identical changes in the superstructure. This is called the unilinear theory of evolution. In such an orthodox historical-materialistic theory, social and economic development moves always in definite stages: from hunting to pastoral life, to farming, to feudal economy, to capitalism; and in its historical necessity it ends with a socialist society.

However, similar changes in economics, (for example, industrialization) in modes of production may be associated with several different types of political systems and ideologies. Neither China, moreover, nor muscovite Russia experienced a historical period of feudalism. Free, independent cities, which were both seats and innovators of European culture, were rather unique and disappeared early in Russia, in fact with the establishment of muscovite rule.

The economic development as well as ideological and institutional development—when it is triggered—is not unilinear but multilinear. The change in different societies may move in several directions, on several different historical tracks, not on a single one. And indeed, both Marx and Engels and later, in his penetrating work and research, Wittfogel indicated clearly this type of multilinear development in their studies of Asian hydraulic or water-dependent societies. Those Asian societies, which had an agriculture based on irrigation, developed different political institutions, political values, and norms of conduct than the European societies, cities, and states. The entire pattern of development of Asian societies was different indeed.[10]

Hence, the historical situation differs, and the pattern of development differs too. Nor is such pattern determined solely by the type of environment, since a similar environment and similar types of production may trigger different historical patterns. The idea system and values, the directive-regulatory apparatus (superstructure), may be also stronger than the economic base and resist the economic change successfully.

But we may move a step farther. The change in economic conditions, change in the economic base (or situation), may result not in a single ideological change, but in several. Within the same class, individuals and groups for various reasons may join different, even opposed, political-ideological camps; they may also choose different goals or follow different norms of conduct.

Furthermore, the same or similar industrial base did work more or less efficiently in association with entirely different superstructures. Here, advanced industrial nations—during the interwar period prior to World War II—may serve as an example. A similar advanced industrial production was associated with political and social systems of fundamental difference.

Postfeudal Japan (we use here the term *feudal* in a very broad sense), with its traditional monarchy and military and conservative systems, extreme nationalism, had an industrial base perhaps less advanced but similar to that of the United States or Great Britain. Both those advanced industrial nations had already a nascent mixed economy. A Social Democratic Sweden had similar industrial plants as Fascist Italy and Nazi Germany. All those different political and ideological superstructures were associated with a similar economic base. During the early periods of recovery, the early Five-Year Plan, the Soviet government, with its dogmatic Stalinist ideology and absolute power of a dictatorship, has transplanted American industrial production in automobiles, tractors, and many other products, and it has established a modern—although autocratic—managerial system in factories and industrial plants.

The relevance, or function, of what was called by the Marxist school superstructure has been not only underestimated by the latter, but it has been largely overlooked. The superstructure is often more powerful than the base; it has strength of its own. The entire idea system, values, and institutions are not simply derivative of the productive forces. They may set the direction of development, since the idea system may determine ways we perceive the changing reality, the choices we make.

Societies may move through differing stages of development. Change in political, social, and economic institutions is not subject to a single, unchanging law of development, determined solely by modes of production. Religion, religious ethos, political institutions, ideological orientation—all affect economic development.

Ideas are not solely derivatives, always dependent on a given stage of production. Ideologies and values form a powerful factor; they have a quality of their own and form a motivating force. This is, of course, not a new discovery—it was reemphasized by Max Weber and others before him. In current political analysis, in our decision making and practical politics, it is so often overlooked.

In history, ideas and values determined many times the choice, the direction, which could be reversed only by other idea systems, not solely by economic forces.[11]

The Sermon and the Dialogue

Certain idea systems have a dynamic quality and a propensity toward continuous change. Here belongs modern science, with its absence of the concept of a terminal and ultimate truth and continuous advance of methods. Error in a scientific pursuit is never fully eliminated; it becomes an element of inquiry. So are doubt and hypothesis. The search for answers never ends.

Western ideologies, with faith in progress, a process of continuous advance toward perfection (while the perfect is never achieved), harbor unusual dynamism.

The concept progress is an open or infinite value-goal, a moving target. Never achieved, it is a goal that is always ahead of mankind, ahead of us. Hence it prompts continuous effort, continuous movement. Since the eighteenth century and the writings of Condorcet, the idea of progress (which originated earlier) has become a dominant Western value. It was reinforced by nineteenth-century philosophy and social sciences, by theories of evolution. Comte, as much as Darwin, suggested an unending evolution toward more advanced forms of life. As different as they were, Spencer and Marx accepted progress and evolution in an axiomatic way. Furthermore, John Dewey, with his theory of continuous reconstruction of society, advanced a related idea of never-ending change, a theory of an imperative of continuous reconstruction of society. True, in the middle of our century the idea of progress has been adversely affected by the advent of totalitarian societies, new forms of slavery, concentration camps, and devastating wars. Yet the vision of an unending advance still survives. We have, however, discovered that what we call progress is not a historical necessity but is achieved by man and his actions. Hence, imperatives of an advanced and good society call for a continuous effort toward a better society, and this in turn demands continuous reconstruction.

But not all idea systems are anchored in dynamic values that propagate man's search and actions toward a better social order or better understanding of the world. Other idea systems and creeds in their specific quality and structure are rigid and petrified with little if any tendency toward change and revision.

Thus, European ideologies and belief systems had and still have this singular quality toward interpretation as well as reform and innovation. This tendency is articulated in well-established ways of communicating and exchanging views and ideas, ways that have indeed very distant origins, since their beginnings can be found at the dawn of great religions and philosophy. Both the Judaic and Hellenic traditions originated this tendency toward creative change, which appeared at first in its prototype and advanced later into well-developed and modern patterns of communication. The two traditions were quite different, representing different ways of communicating and exchanging ideas.

The Judaic tradition is a prophetic one. The prophets carried a single message; this message was a sermon. It was a message of one and ultimate truth. But sermons in the Judaic tradition are interpreted and commented on; they change by way of interpretation.

The different ways and views expressed in comments and interpretations lead in turn to divisions among the believers or followers of the creed, divisions that at the time could not be reconciled. Those who shared the new creed manifested their difference in sects, congregations, and new symbols. Thus, splits changed into heresies and fostered new interpretations and values.

The Hellenic pattern was a different one, it was one of dialogue. This basic way of exchanging ideas was expressed also in philosophical writings, symposia, as well as drama. A dialogue moves by difference, difference in views as well as difference of personalities. Two or more interlocutors may perceive different data, experience reality in a different way, emphasize different aspects, assign different degree of relevance to the same facts, and they still may arrive at a synthesis to an agreement. They may agree at times and disagree othertimes. Thus, the dialogue considers two or more views. Different viewpoints may have an equal relevance, perhaps even an equal validity.

The dialogue fathers and respects doubt, tolerates error. Calm and rational interlocutors may conclude as well that there is no agreement or that there is more than a single truth. Perhaps even two differing arguments may be considered of equal validity. The Israelites believed in one, paramount book, a source of ultimate and all faith. The Jews were a people of one book and one faith; the Greeks, of many books and many philosophies.

It is the dialogue that fathered dialectics, discovery of relevance of opposing views and concepts. Ideas and values grow and change in those dialogues and debates.

In the Occidental civilization the Jews contributed the sermon and also the skills to deal with ideas by methods of interpretation and analysis of a single text. The Greeks, however, gave us the dialogue and appreciation of intellectual courage and imagination in a creative and unfettered construction of new ideas.

But new ideas are expressed in a variety of forms, not solely in those classic ones. Fantasy and imagination are a fruit of human talent, affected of course by historical conditions, but nonetheless a fruit of original and individual thought and inventiveness. A utopia of a new society was born in fantasy by Thomas Moore. Fourier's vision of a perfectly structured community and a perfect social justice was of course affected by the historical period—by the knowledge and interests of that time—but they were also products of a creative mind. A painter, too, is a product of his environment and historical period, but it is his talent and skills, his imagination, that create a new visual image, new style, new forms and colors.

Our initial quotation by John Ruskin suggests a simple observation. The economic base—pure and simple—did not create all the architectural wealth and images of a Gothic, Renaissance, or baroque period. Societies of similar, perhaps identical, social-economic relations created different styles in art and advanced varied and different philosophies. *Si duo faciunt idem, non est idem.* Even if two do the same, it is not the same.

Contradictions

What does it mean that ideas change in comments, interpretation, or dialogue? After all, commentaries and dialogues are no more than vehicles, ways that carry ideas and views. Those are means by which either new ideas are carried or differences in views, inconsistencies, are discovered. Those differences are also expressed in strong opposites, eventually in contradictions. The source of those contradictions may derive either from differences between idea systems and human experience, as well realities that man may witness, or from inconsistencies within the idea system or opposites between different ideas.

First, legal institutions and norms of conduct may indeed conflict with social-economic conditions. This is the case of a changing social-economic base and an old superstructure, when the ideological and institutional superstructure does not fit anymore to the new, emerging social-economic relations.

There is, however, another "external" contradiction: the opposites of ideas that man advances and social realities that he perceives or miseries that he experiences, an ethical contradiction. It is the difference between promise and reality: the promise of the prophets of a political creed and the social-economic realities, the promise of religious preachers and the conditions of life they indulge and defend. It is this difference—the hiatus between ethical, ideological, or religious command and actual, daily practice—that triggers and prompts at times powerful religious and social movements. It is the difference between the ideal and real, the ideal man is taught and commanded and the real he sees or practices; the difference between the teachings of prophets and Christ and the routines of the Inquisition; between the ascetic culture of early Christianity and the political and economic power of the medieval church hierarchy; between egalitarian commands and promise of communism and a society of powerful political classes. Here is one of our historical sources of protest and Protestant movements of all kinds. Those protest movements appear already in sermons of the prophets, who thunder against this dichotomy between religious commandment and the way people lived and behaved in reality, between what was preached and what was practiced. This hiatus is never closed, never resolved, since man advances projects of perfect societies and he, himself, is not perfect.

An ideology of a political party or precepts of a religion are after all directives for human existence, for our daily experience. The function of norms of conduct is to affect both the individual and society and its actions. Here is a nexus between the ideas and the pragmatic order of deeds. Ideas are judged not only by their merits, but also by their practical results. A system called socialist may be tested against its own definitions, its consistency in terms of institutions and law. But its practical effects are tested in a pragmatic way against its results. And here may appear—and usually does—the contrast, more the difference and contradiction between the ideal image of a perfect communist society and a reality.

This difference (and at times agreement) between the normative and pragmatic order is a test of workability of ideas. And the difference, or contradictions, once experienced and perceived, is also in a sense a creative one. It prompts the change, it guides mankind in search for new answers and solutions, and it may also strengthen the fundamental values. When the ideology fails in its practical application, it means that those who have practiced and applied its principles did not reach the value-goals that mankind did expect to be accomplished by a movement guided by such ideas.

Ideas are exchanged and discussed as well as opposed. A creative society is also a marketplace of competing ideas. Ideas by themselves do not compete, of course; individuals and groups who carry the ideas compete between themselves.

Ideas, as already discovered early by philosophers, result often into opposite ideas: Hegel's thesis and antithesis. This does not happen all the time, but it does occur in history. This contradiction may appear between two different orders of ideas—between science and religion—and it may be experienced by groups as well as by a single individual. But it appears also between ideas of the same order. Theories of capitalist economy were followed by opposing plans of a socialist society. The philosophical origins of both were common—the modern, scientific world outlook. Marx's and Engels's work was after all only a sequence of classic economy and Hegelian philosophy. Nationalism of the nineteenth century was followed and opposed by internationalism, which in turn was also a return to the medieval concept of Christian universalism, even if the agnostic partisans of internationalism refuted such roots. Idealistic tendencies in philosophy were countered by materialistic. There is of course a gradation of "in-betweens." Nonetheless, the pair of thesis and antithesis is somewhere there, even if it is less philosophic and Hegelian—less, since internationalism grew not solely as a response to nationalism and the materialistic outlook was not necessarily solely a consequence of opposition to the idealistic world outlook.

In man's quest for consistency of ideas and values an attempt may follow to reconcile or integrate the conflicting orders or to keep them separate, at times to abandon one and follow solely one single and integrated ideology.

However, in a process of answering the dilemma of differing and opposed ideologies, in a search for reconciliation of differences, new ideas emerge; this is at the time a fusion of two or more idea systems. But such a fusion of differing ideologies, or parts of the latter, is tantamount to an emergence of a new one.

Idea systems have "internal" contradictions of their own. Since the early philosophers, attempts were made to create logically consistent systems, which would supply answers to a wide area of problems.

No idea system is perfectly consistent, as there are areas that escape its method and inner logic. It is at this point, when the inconsistency appears in the idea system, when a method cannot provide an answer, when the findings negate the tenets of idea system, or when a search for new methods is begun, that new answers may begin. In science, when what Thomas S. Kuhn called "normal science" does not provide the answer, does not offer a solution or adequate methods, or does not answer the "puzzle" (to use his terminology), a search for new approaches and methods as well as a new revolution in science and ideas may begin. And this is a point when the logical consistency of a theory breaks down, does not work, does not offer answers.

There are no perfectly consistent and perfect idea systems, ideologies, philosophies, or methods that supply answers in all cases, for all experience, and at all times. An imperfect man and humanity cannot create a perfect system. Moreover, a perfectly integrated and consistent idea system would be terminal and final, devoid of innovative qualities in method and approach. Such a rigid philosophy would be tantamount to an ossified creed.

Imperfection and error are creative. Contradictory idea systems, the inner contradiction of ideas, are productive. As a result of those disagreements and negations, new ideas and ideologies emerge. That society as well as ideas change by difference, opposition, and contradiction was discovered early. Dialectics appeared already as a method among ancient Greek philosophers.

There is of course some validity to the theories of dialectics: They are above all theories of conflict. In social sciences they do consider the nature of social conflict, its effects on society, and possible outcomes. In this sense, dialectics is a part of a historical process. However, dialectical theories have been elevated to a dogma of a sole and only historical process, a dogma of a momentous, still mechanical process that moves those unyielding Hegelian determinants: thesis, antithesis, and synthesis. Dialectics in such a creed displaces Providence and creates a social mythology of anonymous and necessary, unavoidable historical forces and disasters.

Contradiction, or dialectics, is not the sole source of new ideas. The human mind is creative, and some idea systems and values foster independent creativity of the human mind, a creativity that prompts also a future advancement of mankind. Nor is there a single pattern, a single road, and an all-inclusive deterministic mechanism for all historical processes and developments.

Let us conclude this chapter with a casual reflection. Scientific discovery or invention begins with an initial concept or hypothesis. But this initial idea, at times based on rudimentary observation, is a creative, intuitive process, which changes into imagination and from there moves to a distinct formulation. Leonardo da Vinci's flying machines as much as the later, successful models of airplanes were a fruit of man's ideas, his imagination. The relevance of the latter was suggested already by da Vinci in his *Notes*. Here at the beginning is the intuitive, a priori process. (Bergson, Einstein, and Popper point to these beginnings.) And here begins the basic change in science and later in technology; from there it moves to experiment and experience. The creative forces of society and man are indeed in the superstructure.

The change in ideas, values, thoughtway, and world outlook mark the stages of history.

Notes

1. Dilthey devotes an entire volume to the "science of world outlook": Wilhelm Dilthey, *Weltanschauungslehre: Abhandlungen für Philosophie der Philosophie* (Göttingen: Teubner, 1960; also vol. 8, *Gesammelte Schriften* [Stuttgart: Teubner, 1962]).

Dilthey lacks the clarity of French thinkers (for example, Comte, of whom he might have been critical) and the straight argument and logical sequence of British and American philosophers (Russell, Peirce, Dewey, or James). The text at times is difficult to follow, and it is equally difficult to find a clear definition. A clear presentation of his ideas may be followed rather from commentary and translations: *Wilhelm Dilthey, Pattern and Meaning in History, Thoughts on History and Society* edited and introduced by H. P. Rickman (New York: Harper, 1961). See also Helmut Diwald, *Wilhelm Dilthey Erkenntnistheorie und Philosophie der Geschiechte* (Göttingen: Musterschmidt, 1963). Although Diwald devoted an entire section to the concept (pp. 204 ff), still the concept is not clearly defined.

In his discussion of method of comprehension of world outlook and various types of *Weltanschauung*, Dilthey emphasized the psychological aspects of the concept. The basic approach explores (1) interdependence, (2) comparison, (3) psychological interpretation.

The basic approach of Dilthey is historical, but the idea systems, beliefs, values have to be explored only in a historical context, in their relation to life and the reality of a given period—in its synchronic meaning—not in their relevance to and context of our times. The idea structure and, above all, the historical period have to be understood. He developed the concept of understanding, *Verstehen*, introduced to sociology later by Max Weber. *Die Weltanschauung* is not solely a product of our thinking, wrote Dilthey; it is a consequence of our relation to life, our life experience, and our psychological structure. The German text here is helpful.: "Die Weltanschauungen sind nicht Erzeugnisse des Denkens. Sie enstehen nicht aus dem blossen Willen des Erkennens. Die Auffassung der Wirklichkeit ist ein wichtiges moment in ihrer Gestaltung aber doch nicht eines. Aus dem Lebensverhalten, der Lebenserfahrung der Struktur unserer psychischen Totalität gehen sie hervor" (Dilthey, *Weltanschauungslehre*, p. 86). The world outlook is formed through the relationship between life and development of the image of the world, the ideal of life (*Lebensideal*), and the world view (*Weltansicht*). See also Diwald, *Wilhelm Dilthey*, p. 205.

2. Theodore Abel in a penetrating article commented that in American sociology *Verstehen* signifies understanding of psychological motives of others, as opposed to a broader historical meaning of German philosophy, although both are complementary. Abel, *"Verstehen* I and *Verstehen* II," *Theory and Decision* February 1975.

3. Max Dworak, Viennese art historian, discussed medieval European art as a consequence or expression of religious outlook and passionate religiosity. In a fruitful way Dworak analyzed the functions of religious art, the way it affected contemporary congregations, reinforcing their faith by visual presentation. See Max Dworak, *Idealism and Naturalism in Gothic Art* [1918], preface by Karl M. Swoboda, translated by R. J. Klawiter (Notre Dame, Ind.: University of Notre Dame Press, 1967). To quote from the preface (p. xxv): "In the introductory chapter, Dworak emphasizes that medieval art is based on the tremendous Christian spirituality of the Middle Ages—a force whose significance for medieval art one can at present only dimly apprehend. He stresses that his intention was not to link occurrences of an economic, social or religious nature with artistic phenomena in a causal connection, nor to derive the spiritual content of work of art from the writing of the great medieval theologians; but rather it was to illustrate that the spiritual content of a medieval work of art and the historic development of its relationship to transcendental ideas and the material facts of life both spring from a common source: the *Weltanschauung of Medieval Christianity*."

4. See, for example, Wladyslaw Tatarkiewicz, *Estetyka Sredniowieczna* [Medieval Esthetics] (Wroclaw: Ossolinski, 1960).

5. Dilthey, *Weltanschauungslehre*, p. 48.

6. On class consciousness see Karl Mannheim, *Ideology and Utopia* (New York: Harcourt, Brace, 1936). Mannheim follows the Marxist tradition. Weber and R. H. Tawney point, however, to close interdependence and independent relevance of ethos and values in the economic development and rise of capitalism. See especially R. H. Tawney, *Religion and Rise of Capitalism* (New York: The New American Library, 1954), especially his chapter "The Puritan Movement," pp. 164 ff., and his interpretation of Weber.

7. Friedrich Engels, *Dialectics of Nature* (Moscow: Foreign Languages Publishing House, 1954), pp. 306–7.

8. F. Engels, letter to Joseph Bloch, London, September 21–22, 1890; also his letter to Dr. I. A. Hourvich, May 27, 1893, reprinted also in Marx and Engels, *Basic Writings on Politics and Philosophy* ed. Lewis S. Feuer (Garden City, N.Y.: Doubleday, 1959), p. 441.

9. See Karl Kautsky, *Materialistische Geschichts auffassung* (Berlin: J. H. W. Dietz, 1927); Heinrich Cunov, *Die Marxsche Geschichts, Gesellschafts und Staatsteorie: Grundzüge der Marxschen Soziologie* (Berlin: Vorwärts, 1920–1921); Antonio Labriola, *Saggi sul Materialismo Storico* (Rome: *Editori Riuniti*, 1964).

10. Karl Marx's article on hydraulic societies appeared in the *New York Tribune* (June 25, 1853; see "The British Rule in India," reprinted in Karl Marx and Friedrich Engels, *Selected Works* (Moscow-Foreign Languages Publishing House, 1958) vol. 1, pp. 345ff. For a comprehensive theory of hydraulic societies see Karl Wittfogel, *Oriental Despotism* (New Haven: Yale University Press, 1963).

11. Alfred Fouillé, in a today-forgotten book, *Le Socialisme et La Sociologie Réformiste* (Paris: Alcan, 1930) (which still had four editions), points to the strength of ideas in socialist movements, particularly the force of a single value—justice—which, he says, "haunts the history of mankind." The basic difference between French socialist ideology and the German in its Marxist expression is, as he puts it, that the French socialists demand justice, while "The Germans say, 'What we demand is not justice, only power' '' (p. 64). Lenin of course followed the latter goal.

3

The Structure of Ideologies

Structure of a Belief System

What was called the world outlook (*Weltanschauung*) or belief system affects and is affected by our practical knowledge of the environment, our knowledge of skills as well as experience, which we have called the pragmatic system. The belief system encompasses the normative-ideological area, whereas the pragmatic deals with the basic needs, production and consumption, territory we dwell in—in a word, the basic conditions of our existence. In order to survive, man must perceive his environment in a way he could be able to cope with. There are of course elements of choice and various degrees of objective perception of the reality. Whatever our debates about objective truth in perception, the fact remains that with total disregard for the realities of our environment, man could not survive. He perceives fire in terms of its dangers and utility.

An animal deals with the environment by means of its sensors or perceptors and effectors. The way an animal perceives the environment affects its relationship to the latter. Again, a condition of its life is perceiving by means of whatever apparatus of perception it is endowed with as well as affecting physically the environment by its apparatus of effectors. By means of the latter, it moves as well as builds shelter or secures food. Man develops skills and tools, extends his perceptors and effectors. The pragmatic imperatives affect in various ways the normative ideological system.

Our perceptions, thoughtways, and actions may be visualized in the form of an arc (see figure 3.1) A section of this arc is pragmatic (*P*); on the other pole, another section is normative (*N*)—affected by our idea system. In the middle, we may identify a marginal section (*M*), affected by both the normative-pragmatic and the pragmatic-normative. The former is the ideological affected by pragmatic considerations; the latter, pragmatic affected by ideological considerations. The size of the middle section varies in various cultures.

Figure 3.1
Perception and Thoughtways

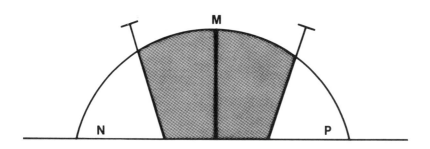

N — normative
P — pragmatic
M — marginal

normative — pragmatic
pragmatic — normative

The ideological-normative system, not unlike other systems of ideas or knowledge, has a logic of its own. Those who who are guided by such a belief system may or may not be cognizant of its inner consistencies and logic, just as an Italian peasant who speaks an excellent Tuscan, Venetian, or Neapolitan vernacular is not necessarily cognizant of the grammar and its rules. Belief systems have both, contradictions and logic.

We shall limit our discussion to an outline of two structures: (1) a general belief system (*Weltanschauung*) and (2) a political ideology. In both systems the values form a directive and regulatory apparatus. But this is not their only function. An outline of the major function of values follows description of those structures.

We may follow the structure of a belief system by steps (see figure 3.2).

Steps 1 and 2 begin with a set of dominant values—the ethos—and norms of conduct (triangle or V_e). Those values are a consequence of the entire normative-ideological system, but they also affect the former (arrows). We may postulate that the ethos, the ethical system that guides and controls the entire system, forms a separate order. (We shall return to this theme in part III.) Next to it the pragmatic outlook has norms of conduct (V_p) and goals of its own; it affects the normative, but this influence is reciprocal.

The set of values governing the entire area of normative behavior forms a

Figure 3.2
Structure of a Belief System

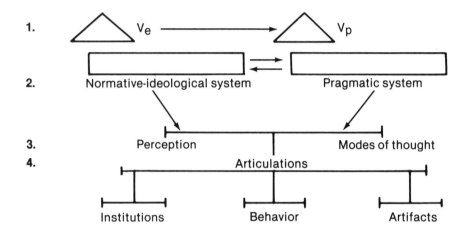

V_e — ethos values
V_p — pragmatic values

hierarchy. It is a set of norms of various intensity or relevance. We shall return to their structure in the next chapter but especially in part III (vertical value structure). It is this set of dominant normative values, the ethos, that exercises the controlling effect, once it is shared by substantial number of individuals. The culture of a group, a nation, or a civilization—a cultural pattern, the institutions shared by a number of nations—can be identified by those shared values. Once they are shared, we call them social. They are social, because a critical number of individuals responds to their appeal or is motivated by those values in their behavior: for example, patriotism or religious piety. By way of an example, we may consider medieval Christianity in times of its relative unity (with some minor sects) as a widely shared belief system. Ethics in this case is a direct expression of the religion. It forms the pivotal component of Christian religion with its concept of sin and its moral and religious sanctions. It is a powerful regulatory and directive structure (marked V_e on our figure).

In step 3, next in this logical structure, the value goals, the norms of conduct, and the entire ideology affect, in a predominantly normative area, our perception and thinking. The nature of the universe was explained by religious concepts.

Selection of facts and their connections into causal links were in a past historical era determined by religious outlook. Of course, next to the normative area was, in medieval times as well, a vast pragmatic field of human activities, where thinking and perception followed practical experience. Nonetheless, religious outlook affected intellectual interest, perception of art, legal institutions.

In step 4 the result of motivation (values), perception, and thinking is externalized in a number of articulations: institutions, behavior, artifacts. Thus the Roman Catholic, medieval world outlook was (and the modern is) guided by a set of value-goals and norms of conduct (ethos) reinforced by the theology (the normative ideology) and especially by the concept and interpretation of dogma. This normative idea system guided the perception of the universe, of the nature of things. The scholastic modes of thought tested data, findings, concepts against the authorities and dogma or against the opinions of recognized theologians, the Bible, the New Testament, and papal promulgations. This belief system was expressed in a set of articulations: institutions, behavior, artifacts (for example, church hierarchy, religious rituals, religious painting).

If we compare this with the rational outlook of eighteenth-century French or Italian Enlightenment, the difference appears on every one of those four levels. Some of the core values—the ethos—were shared, of course, but the difference appears on all other levels.

Social change may affect not values solely, but all the other components.

This structure may of course vary. With further development of human society and modes of thought, particular orders, such as science, ethics, or esthetics, separate from the all-powerful religion and are formed by men and women into particular subsystems governed by their own specific sets of norms. The early development of those particular subsystems may be noticed in ancient Greece. Here, unlike Judaism and Christianity, ethics was formed in a specific subsystem fused primarily with philosophy, this unique Hellenic all-embracing system of knowledge, separate from religion.

Rational and careful planners of social change have to consider values and ideology as a major issue of social planning. The general world outlook—primarily, however, the value structure—may prevent or defeat a technically rational and advanced plan. Affecting only the economic base, by means of new methods and advanced technology, may utterly fail in achieving of planned targets.

Structure of a Political Ideology

A political ideology forms a subsystem of its own. It has a specific directive-regulatory structure, value-goals, and norms of conduct. Some ideologies, whether democratic or socialist or even anarchist, derive from the same general code of ethos, although interpreted in a diverse way (see chapter 16 below entitled "Search of Universal Values"). They are a part of the same community of core or paramount values, in consequence of the same civilization. However, values in forms of goals and norms of conduct are reinterpreted and reformulated by theoreticians and leaders. Through those programmatic reinterpretations, they develop into particular directive and regulatory structures.

A political party, its leaders, and its governing committees articulate a political ideology of their movements in declarations, programs, theoretical publications, and studies. The sources of information are numerous. Thus, an ideology can be described and analyzed. What we are interested in at this point is the structure of an ideology, not its content or verity. A well-developed ideology of a particular movement, with an extensive theory, is a good case for such an attempt. We have selected a socialist Marxist idea system. Advanced by gifted theoreticians for more than a century, it developed a logical structure. At least, a clear structure can be identified ex post facto. A socialist theory gave birth to many movements, to many interpretations. We shall follow, save a few digressions, an orthodox interpretation (one that could be probably identified with writings of N. Bukharin or G. Plekhanov). It is simpler, more limpid.

As structure lends itself to graphic presentation, we have outlined this ideological system (see figure 3.3).

A political idea system has a number of components. The dominant values are at the very root of an ideological system. The entire philosophy is affected by them. Therefore, we have put the values at the very beginning. A writer or a theoretician may disclaim their existence or the fact that they impressed his views. However, the normative, value-oriented goal, the entire normative thrust of the theory, can be easily discerned in an ideology advanced for the good of the underprivileged.

In step 1, on the very top in a graphic presentation are the core values (paramount or dominant values). They are standards and at the same time "generalized goals" or elements of a vision of a future society. This generalized goal appears as distant collective visions of goals of political activities of the socialist parties. (See chapter 7 for a case study of political goal structure in an Italian village community.)

They are presented in form of symbols and appeals. The symbols have the quality of economic, emotional, and ethical appeal. They appear in form of slogans, "iconic symbols" (visual designs), inscriptions, and songs. Here belong such core values as economic equality, social justice, liberty. The concept of equality is, of course, closely related to distributive justice. (We shall return below to core or dominant values in a section on a hierarchy of values.) The core values integrate the entire socialist idea system, appear in all ideological projects, are repeated by speakers at the meetings and by authors in newspapers and periodicals. They form the overall directive and regulatory apparatus. Vague as it may be, it has an emotional and ethical appeal.

The dominant values as symbols (for example, justice, equality, liberty) form the most sensitive element of the ideology, since they are directly related and appeal to economic interests, psychological (emotional) needs and ethical commitments. Here is the mobilizing quality or motivating force that sets the "ideal"

Figure 3.3
Structure of a Political Ideology

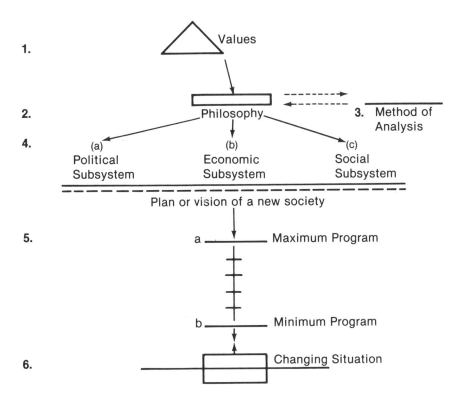

sense of direction of the movement. At the same time, the same symbols rationalize the quest for power, domination, and violence of ruling elites.

Step 1 shows the values, the ethos reduced to the form of a symbol or sets of symbols. They are at the very root of collective appeal and integration of the masses into groups of similar interests and similar normative outlook. Those dominant values affect the general theory of the party: Step 2.

In this general theory two closely interrelated areas have to be distinguished: the main body of the party theory (we shall call it *general philosophy*) and, in our case of a Marxist ideology, a method of analysis, historical materialism and dialectics. The method is a consequence of or derives from the entire socialist theory, from what we have called general philosophy of the party. Nonetheless, once separated, it in turn affects the theory. In consequence, a circular system develops. The current situation is analyzed by theorists and party leaders by means of an a priori method. The findings discovered and validated by means of this method return now to enrich the theory. But the method of analysis, to begin with, was defined by means of this general philosophy (theory). It is only the consequence of the latter.

What is the content of general philosophy? The general theory is based on analysis of social reality in terms of class structure, class struggle, and social contradictions. This structure is traced back historically, pointing to changing forms of exploitation in various historical stages.

The social change is a consequence of the contradictions between the economic base (modes of production) and the superstructure. Furthermore, the theory of a class state emerges as a consequence of the analysis of class society. The general theory leads to a major political inference: the political and historical mission of the working class, the future strategy, and the end goal of a classless society.

Step 3 indicates that while the general philosophy is scattered in hundreds of publications, still a single document of Marx and Engels contains the essentials of method, of historical materialism and dialectics: *The German Ideology*. In a limpid form of "theses" the basic tenets and sense of direction are formulated by Marx, not unlike a church heretic, in those short and convincing *Theses on Feuerbach*. The social reality—that is, the current social processes—is as a rule analyzed by means of this method, dialectics and historical materialism.

The method affects the focus of attention and modes of thought. The study of history is focused no longer on the history of dynasties and on national glory, but on the cruel facts of the history of the working class, its consequence, the class struggle. The war is analyzed as a consequence of economic imperialism rather than a glorious enterprise of a national hero. But it is not the method alone, the directive nature of the core values narrows the field of observation, focuses on facts and issues relevant in terms of directive standards and values. Hence, the core values and method affect the historical perception.

Focusing or narrowing down of our perception and thinking is common in application of scientific method, perhaps in any concentrated cognitive process. But, criticism and flexibility are essential in a scientific approach.

Scientific thinking implies connections of facts, their mutual relationship. Facts alone are useless. A dogmatic method instructs you a priori *what* should be selected and *how* the facts should be related; it identifies a priori the data that should be identified as causal and a universe of data to be considered as effect. Of course, a scientific method is an instruction of how to carry out research, but flexibility and criticism that extends to criticism of the method make up an essential issue.

Thus, a dogmatic Marxist approach guides selection of facts, facts that reaffirm a priori theories, affirmative data. It narrows perception to a point that data and facts, variables, relevant as they may be, are just omitted as irrelevant or non-existent. Data are fed into a rigid theoretical frame of reference. In such a way, a political ideology changes into a faith, akin to religion, a faith based on dogmas and certainties. Add to it elaborate symbolism and political ceremonies, hero worship of geniuses (Lenin, Stalin, Mao), and a political theory changes from science into religion, a political religion.

I shall not deny that every method has limitations, nor do I question the veracity of the theory at this point. The method, that is not flexible but dogmatic, however, is not an adequate scientific tool, since it begins with a dogma and not with a hypothesis. The former cannot be changed; the latter is tentative and flexible, can be changed at any time. In a dogmatic approach a theoretician chooses affirmatives only, facts that support his thesis based on an a priori dogma. In an open, scientific, approach the researcher gathers affirmatives as well as negatives, facts that support and negate his hypothesis; the hypothesis can be changed and has to be revised if the facts indicate the need of revision or even rejection of a hypothesis. The former searches for and believes that he arrives at certainty; the latter moves solely within hypotheses and probabilities.

The method sets the road of modes of thought. More, it decides about the entire theoretical system and its development. In a scientific inquiry the method is its fundamental device, instruction. It is *the* mode of thinking, the essence of a scientific style.

Historical materialism as method guides the perception in terms of focusing attention on conflicts, on contradictions. Thus the doctrine affects modes of thought as well as perception. In consequence, this leads to identification of a distant goal, of a classless society and of a future social system, as the end of political action. The very direction of interest and perception is set by the core values, related to interests and needs.

The theory as well as analysis of the current situation, an analysis arrived at by means of a sophisticated and elaborate method, may serve the interests of the workers, but it may be used also as a rationalization of interests of the party's ruling elites, as well as legitimization of the quest for power.

We have outlined in a very rudimentary way a line of thinking and application of method of an orthodox way. We should add that this was and is an example, an exercise, for interpretations of the theories of Marx and Engels are many, and they differ. So does the application of method.

In step 4 the political theory in turn has to be translated into a plan for action, into concrete goals (in this case goals of a future society, a change, plan of a new or reformed society). What then is subject to such change? The economic, political, and educational systems and institutions and, in consequence, the political distribution of power.

The theory supplies the necessary tools of an outline of an economic system of a classless society, of a collective economy, which meets the imperatives of social equality and justice. The imperatives of political freedom call for democracy. However, in a Leninst approach, dictatorship may be necessary in a transitional period. Here, on this issue of political systems and imperatives of liberty came a split in a Social Democratic camp of Russia in 1903, a split between Mensheviks and Bolsheviks.

The imperatives of equality affect also the educational system and change from elitist to broader school patterns, to mass education.

Now, we have arrived already at a broad plan of a new society, rooted in core values and argued in terms of an advanced theory armed with a convincing instrument: a method of analysis. Here is a plan of a socialist society.

This entire ideological system can be presented as a general plan of the future, hence a vision of a future organization of a society. It is a "social image"—a vision of a future social order. This vision may be pragmatic and suggest a workable plan and indeed the winning party may set up a new organization or introduce reforms. We may call such a plan "a practical plan."

But this plan might be also a visionary image of a perfect society, logical in terms of abstract theory, but hardly workable in terms of present experience and situation (for example, an anarchist plan of a stateless social order is logical, perhaps even attractive, but not necessarily practical). But, someone may argue, it may work. Yes, but at times of appeal it is still a vision of a future and perfect society, of a social system that has all answers. Its mass appeal is in this vision. The French syndicalist theoretician and a brilliant sociologist, Georges Sorel, called visions of future heroic actions and plans social myth, and the term has been quite widely accepted.[1]

Furthermore, we may call utopias visions of the future that are fantasies, unworkable and imaginary, as were the many utopias of the eighteenth century, including one outlined by de Sade.

Some of the visions of the future society are practical; others are more poetic than pragmatic. It is a matter of degrees. But perhaps it is this poetic, visionary plan of a perfect society, of an ultimate, millenarian answer that hides a powerful appeal. In times of crisis and revolutionary tensions and processes the vision gains on strength of appeal. At such time the utopians may win over the practical planners. (See chapters 8 and 9.)

A social myth of the past may be as powerful as a utopia of the future. A distorted history of a perfect and happy past, a vision of a previous, idealized social and political order, may supply a powerful appeal. However, what today is a utopia may be in the future considered as a practical answer.

A nation governed by a republican constitution without a king or dynasty was also a utopia in the early years of the eighteenth century. An eight-hour working day and a free weekend was a social myth.

Karl Mannheim distinguishes utopias from ideology. Ideology is related to the present reality, while utopia transcends this reality in terms of ideas and views of the author of the utopias or the actors who advance the latter. The difference, Mannheim may argue, is the problem of a historical stage to which the standard is applied. Individuals and political parties may differ as to whether utopias are realizeable or not, whether they are practical or not. Furthermore, the ideological orientation of a person affects the view of what a utopia is and whether it is a workable solution.[2]

We have made a distinction between those three forms of future visions: practical plan, social myth, and utopia.[3] Of course, divisions and boundaries are not sharp, not even clear. The concepts are relative, and the workability can be tested only in experience. However, their psychological appeal and sociological function as a distant goal are relevant in our discussion.

Where the attraction of a social myth or a utopia lies, so it seems to me, is in its visionary nature. The vision shows suddenly to a listener or a reader very simple solutions, simple answers—which appear as obvious and workable, as well as practical and just. And sometimes they are. Those answers follow some cherished ideals or simply interests and sentiments. At the same time the answer contained in those visions appeals to emotions, to ideals in a colorful, even poetic way.

We are now at step 5a of our figure. This general plan has to be, however, translated into concrete goals. Direction must be set for action. The ideological system is shared by partisans of the movement, represented by a party. A political theory is not an academic exercise. It has to be translated into actions, actions geared toward a goal. A major goal—an intermediary one—is conquest of power. Hence, the goal must be now presented in a form that would mobilize a broad support of members of the party, voters, or followers. Patterns of actions have to be outlined in order to arrive at those goals. Those patterns of actions are called strategy and tactics (to which chapter 9 is devoted). Now these broad plans are translated into programs, called also platforms or manifestos. The program is an expression of the directive and regulatory functions of the entire ideology. It sets the directions of political actions and normative limits within which this action will move. This program spells out political goals. In a general plan, called program, the interwar socialist movements, as well as the communists, made a distinction between the maximum (5a) and minimum (5b) programs. Let us keep this useful theoretical device.

The general plan results in a maximum program (5a), a major transformation of the present society, the distant goals. In times of revolutionary situations this is a seminal part of a mass appeal, a motivating psychological force. At such times of rapid change the long-range, distant program—"the maximum" program, as it was called at the turn of the century and later—changes into an immediate goal. In times of stability and orderly change, the maximum program cannot be materialized immediately, today or tomorrow after a successful election. Moreover, such a profound or fundamental change may alienate a substantial section of voters, who may vote for change of government, a concrete issue— shorter working hours, social security—but still mistrust a plan for a future, different type of society, untried as yet and risky. Thus practical, concrete goals, derived from the long-range program or at least complementary to the latter, are constructed as a "minimum program" (5b on our figure). Those goals are legitimated by the set of values that dominates the entire logical system.

In an effort to win mass support or due to a compelling situation (or for other, tactical reasons), sections of the minimum program may contradict the maximum one, even the general theory. "Dictatorship of the proletariat"—in fact, dictatorship of the party's central committee or leaders—is an essential premise of communist theory and moreover, a paramount political goal, a consequence of

Leninist (and, at a certain historical period, Marxist) theory of state. The French Communist party advocates democracy and political rights in its electoral programs. A direct call for dictatorship of Soviet type would alienate large sections of the voters; moreover, it would probably repel most of the communist leaders in Italy.

The minimum program is attached to tactics; the maximum, to strategy. Flexible courses of action within the general scope of strategy are called tactics. A general vision of a new society, a complete transformation of the society, at least in our case, corresponds to strategic goals. The minimum program responds, above all, to the dynamic, continuously changing situation. Tactics change with the changes of the minimum program or immediate goals. Tactics and the minimum program are—in a skillful political action—the most flexible and also the most sensitive and changing instruments of party politics (see chapter 9).

Once in power, a totalitarian party (which, while out of power, defends civil rights) may return to strategic objectives (dictatorship). The strategic objectives after all are an articulation of the entire ideological system. The strategy and tactics, let us not forget, are the articulation of the directive-regulatory apparatus of the party. But with time the ideology, the very philosophy of the party, may change. Then of course the change is not only or anymore tactical, but, above all, strategic. It is a beginning of a new stage. This distinction between tactical and strategic changes, between changes of electoral programs and ideology and paramount goals, is of practical political significance. It may be tantamount to a complete displacement of an earlier directive-regulatory structure.

Survival of an ideology calls for two seemingly contradictory qualities: stability and change-flexibility. Stability derives from the "central" regulatory apparatus, the overall strategy, which in turn is attached to general theory (philosophy) of the party. Flexibility is an essential quality of political tactics.

Finally let us consider step 6. Political ideology is meaningful only in its social context. Of course, we may also develop an ideology, abstract or unrelated to political or economic realities. Some of the eighteenth-century utopias were abstract, unrelated to the real situation and distribution of power. However, an active movement guided by its program attempts to affect a concrete social situation. This is especially true in the case of socialist movements.

The social movement represented by the political party affects the situation. On the other hand, a current social process, a social-historical situation, affects the social movement, the party—its tactics and ideology (indicated in figure 3.3 as 6 and two arrows).

The political ideology is not monolithic. Two contradictions affect an ideology: the inner, logical and normative contradiction and the outer contradictions between the ideology and changing situation.

The ideologists and theoreticians discover the inner contradictions between the standards, the core values and specific plans and programs, between the various components of the ideology. The supreme value of liberty comes into contradiction with the plans for a dictatorship of proletariat. Then, the plan for a dictatorship of proletariat (a political system) has to be translated into dictatorship of the party, the vanguard of the proletariat. But even this ideological adjustment is not sufficient. The dictatorship of the proletariat contradicts the reality: It is at best a dictatorship of the ruling committee. Again, after purges, the reality is a dictatorship of a single person. The outer contradiction emerges when values, institutions, and actions are tested against realities, against a political situation and actual performance.

Then the hiatus between the symbolic, ethical relevance of the ideology and actual policies, between the ideal and real, appears clearly. It appeared in a brutal way in a historical contradiction of a Communist promise of a perfect society of social justice and well being, and the reality of Stalin's system of concentration camps and forced labor, purges, and executions. It reappeared in Mao's China and again in Vietnam, or in a genocide of Pol Pot in Cambodia, where a third of a nation was destroyed as a way to construct a perfect society.

This hiatus of inner contradictions gives origin to two processes. One is of legitimation of contradiction. Hence, purges in the Soviet Union or massacres in Cambodia are legitimized as "class struggle," opponents as "enemies of the people," dictatorship as a "transitory stage" toward millennium. The second is the process of emergence of inner political splits, emergence of new parties, splinter groups, and protest movements.

These changes affect, sooner or later, the directive-regulatory order, the goals and norms of conduct. In both cases changes lead to interpretation and statements—revised goals and conduct, values and norms, revised and reinterpreted programs, strategies. Hence the central issue is the directive-regulatory structure.

Logical contradictions emerge with a further advancement of theory. Few if any idea systems are free of incipient, inner, and hidden contradictions and inconsistencies. Once the general theory is advanced further, contradictions may increase. Simple and at a glance convincing theories may become a source of those contradictions. The theory of surplus value reduces the creative process of value and capital accumulation to labor, to the productive processes of the working class. Does an inventor, Edison, Marconi or Westinghouse, produce a surplus value, or a value at all, as compared with an unskilled factory worker? And if he does, is his contribution equal or less or more?

What follows is interpretation. And there are not one, but several.

The same values and basic theories lend themselves to a variety of interpretation and articulations. The content of symbols has not one but a number of meanings (we shall discuss the relevance of signifiers and content below in chapter 4). Perception of the situation varies.

In consequence, identical symbols (identical only in terms of their signs or signifiers) as well as visions of a new society of social justice and economics of equality evolve in a variety of diverse ideologies. The tendencies of a new, socialist society originated communist dogmatic ideologies; pluralistic and flexible democratic and socialist ideologies, and, at the extreme, libertarian anarchist ideologies.

The testing of the ideology against experience uncovers the weakness of rigid and dogmatic theories. The real change, the real social process supplies the data of a pragmatic test against which plans are verified. As long as the ideology is a theme of debates of a closed group, the vision is tested against definitions and theories. It is a normative test that points solely to ideological consistency. Once the plan is put into practice, tested against reality of facts, however, the plan moves into a pragmatic field. Its utility is tested. At this point both the strength and the weakness of the plan appear.

The ideology, an ideology that is meaningful and effective in its major social functions, changes or adjusts under the impact of the altered social-economic conditions. Contrariwise, a party of a rigid ideology may impose its will and control the situation by use of force, violence, and skillful tactics. If the party members do not adjust the ideology to the dynamic social-economic situation or if they do not establish controls by means of force of violence, the party may begin its road to decline. Force may not suffice. The dynamic situation and appeal, the strategies of the opposing groups, may be more powerful and break the control imposed by the party and its armed cohorts.

In a political movement, the ideology is multifunctional. It supplies legitimacy to the movement. It is also, or it may be, simply a rationalization of the new out-elites in their quest for political power, even an authoritarian power. On the other hand, an ideology appeals to the economic needs of the followers, but not to solely economic needs. In a wide appeal it responds to psychological and ethical needs of the voters or supporters, Otherwise, it would fail in its major function—to mobilize individuals and groups. It would fail as a motivating force in a quest of power.

The relevance of religion and ideologies extends beyond an empirical analysis. In those distant and broad ideas and beliefs man finds a deeper sense of life and a meaningful commitment. Visions of a distant, future society, an ideal of justice and brotherhood, whether attainable or not, prompt our humane and noble sentiments and reinforce those values that do not appeal to profit or self interest only. The meaning of religion and sacredness is wider than a church or congregation. No great civilization can survive without such a higher order, which gives a meaning to major values.

The Sermon and the Prophet

In the area that spreads widely from the eastern shores of the Mediterranean and Asia to Western and Eastern Europe, and later in groups diffused all over the world, powerful religious and political movements had similar major components and similar ideological structures. As very different as they were in content and in message, those which continued, which gave evidence of vigor and appeal had four major components: (1) an elaborate idea system with a messianic message, (2) a prophet who carried the idea system and knew how to translate a complex ideology into (3) a powerful sermon, and, sooner or later, (4) a social structure, an organizational apparatus, an autocratic social hierarchy, or an association of free men.

Whether Christianity, Islam, or socialism, the distant goal was messianic; it was a future salvation or ultimate emancipation of man, a world of happiness here or there. Those distant goals, thrown widely ahead, were always anchored in belief systems—religious or secular, political. Before the distant, generalized goal—a vision of the future could be reached—there were necessary, intermediate goals, steps that had to be reached, accomplished. All of them had the same concept of time, a linear one. Goals were set in this "spatialized" image of time, time and space were sensed in a visual way. The concept of time was on a human measure—in decades, centuries, and millennia—but still comprehensible to the human mind (see chapter 14).

The prophet, religious or political, carried the message. Hence he was listened to, whether he commanded a powerful organization or only a crowd of followers who listened, believed, and followed.

The prophet preached a complex ideology or religion, revealed truth or his truth discovered by means of patient scholarship. And this complex idea system was translated either by him or by his disciples into a "vulgate," a simpler form, a sermon—into a language, values, and symbols that could reach wide sections of people, could appeal to their longings or urgent needs of an economic, psychological, or ethical nature. The idea system or religion, often simple at the beginning, grew complex by means of interpretation, and it was again simplified into a vulgate, accessible to many. The sermon may be one of hatred and hostilities or of love, appealing to brotherhood of man, equality, and liberty. The sermon may lead to dictatorship and submission of large sections of a nation or to emancipation and more social justice, a better society. But the strength of the sermon is in its straight and simple message, understandable and powerful.

From the ranks of an unstructured mass of followers sooner or later emerges a congregation of free persons or a hierarchy of religious or political clergy, at a time fused with political militias, armies, and armed orders. Should the latter happen, a humane message of the prophet is now carried by armed men who practice violence as a legitimate way to gain and consolidate power. Ideas, humane at the outset, may suffer now corruption and default.

There were in the past historical movements of a different nature. Their sermon was carried by a rational, calm contemplation and dialogue but also with a powerful appeal.

Notes

1. "Those who participate in great social movements visualize their future actions in the form of images of battles that will assure the triumph of their cause. I suggest calling such images, which were so important in our history, social myths. The general strike and the catastrophic revolution of Karl Marx are such myths," wrote Georges Sorel in *Réflexions sur la Violence*, 10th ed. (Paris: Rivière, 1940), pp. 32ff.

2. See Karl Mannheim, *Ideology and Utopia* (New York: Harcourt, Brace, 1936), pp. 196 ff., also pp. 88 ff., on evaluative and nonevaluative conceptions of ideology.

3. Feliks Gross, ed., *European Ideologies* [1948] (New York: Books for Libraries, 1971), pp. 8 ff.

4

The Appeal and Function of Values

Response to Value Symbols

In the previous pages we have tried to answer the question of how an advanced idea system is constructed. Its very structure reflects the way political ideals have been organized and a general theory has been focused and sharpened into programs and goals. A general philosophy can be contemplated or discussed. However, social change desired by theoreticians and leadership can be achieved once ideas are translated into goals, and further into goal symbols, and become targets of political actions. To move from the level of a theory, a philosophy discussed by few theoreticians, to the level of action and of many, it must be shared by many individuals. Then, if it is shared not necessarily by masses, but by groups (the party) of a critical, effective quantity (which varies since ideas and conditions differ), then they become a motivating social force. Now we may ask the question, What is shared, how, and why?

The extensive philosophy might be entirely unknown to large sections of a group that professes an elaborate ideology, for example, a socialist Marxist one. The appeal is located in value norms, goals, and symbols. Why do they appeal? Because they do correspond to needs, interests, and values structures shared already by the followers. Response to economic programs that in turn represent the interest of the voters is obvious. Here, goals correspond to definite economic needs and interest. Value-goals of national glory or racial superiority may be geared, however, to psychological needs, inferiority complexes, or pent-up hostilities, repressed aggressions. But not all symbols and value-goals are of this nature. Values and symbols of justice, even if they do not appeal to the economic interest of certain groups or individuals, may meet with a supportive response, because they do correspond to a shared ethical order. One may support a program because this is "just"; it is right in terms of his sentiments of justice.

At this point, we may suggest that goals of an idea system may correspond roughly to (a) economic needs; (b) psychological needs; (c) cultural needs; or (d) an ethical order and sentiments.

The values or norms of an ideology might be of course only rationalizations of economic or psychological needs.

Sharing of Symbols

We assumed that the core values of an ideology meet with a response when they are shared.

Now the question should be asked, What does this mean? How are they shared? Values are shared when individuals of different classes or groups agree on their meaning[1] and observe them as guides of conduct as well as standards. This seems to be obvious, and such definitions may appear in a more elaborate form. However, this definition of the term *shared* is not fully valid and calls for qualification.

Values appear in a variety of forms. Symbols identify values, norms, standards. The flag and an image of a tree are pictorial or iconic symbols that correspond to verbal values; patriotism, liberty.

A song, for example, "La Marseillaise," may become a symbol and corresponds to a set of values of the French Revolution. But all those symbols differ from a road sign, which warns that a railroad crossing is half a mile ahead. The first—let us call it as this point a symbol—has an emotional appeal; it contains a value that cannot be defined in a precise, verifiable way. The second contains information. The tracks are there; this can be easily verified. This information is precise, is verifiable, and does not present any difficulty in definition as well as in sharing precisely the same, and not different data: We may call it a signal. An information sign may appear in a variety of forms: a verbal, iconic or even a "musical" signal, such as a military reveille, or, on the other hand, an emergency signal. Hence, symbols should be distinguished from signals.[2]

As we said, symbols appear in a variety of forms. Let us take a verbal form, such as "liberty" or "equality." In linguistic terms this is also a linguistic sign.

A simple linguistic sign consists of two elements: the sound image and the concept. The two elements are intimately united, writes De Saussure, and each recalls the other.

De Saussure uses the term *sign* for the entire entity, introducing at the same time a broader term for content—*signified*—while calling the word images *signifier*. His concept of a signifier and a signified, or sound image and content, is visualized in a simple graph.[3] See figure 4.1.

The concept corresponds to a sound image, and again the sound image corresponds to the concept. The word image is united with the definition. The signified is relevant indeed; the signifier can be arbitrarily chosen. The same definition, content, for example, of the constitution, can be called *A* or *AB* or just by a number. In fact, it is: The same content, the concept of a constitution,

Figure 4.1
Sign

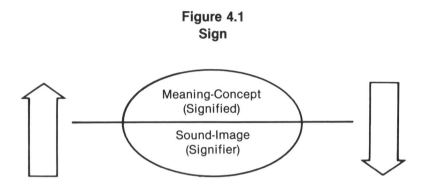

the signified has different signifiers in various languages; the meaning is the same.

Hence, three options are possible:

1. The same content (signified) corresponds without any further change to the same word image (signifier). The signifier and the signified are constant.
2. The signified is constant while the signifier varies.
3. The signifier is constant while the signified varies.

With symbols, value-goals, and standards, a similar thing may happen: The same signifier, the same image or sound, may be used for a different or differing meaning, concept, contents or signified. However, psychologically, a shared signifier—the word or image, the very sound of music, a patriotic song—has an intensive appeal, triggers emotional response, activates sentiments. Iconic and verbal symbols, reduced to signifiers, have their own psychological appeal. Of course, the signifier acquires this quality through a long association with a certain content, as well as a result of individual experience. But once this symbol, in form of an image or sound, has been ''internalized,'' or associated with a belief system, it carries a psychological appeal of its own, as the flag does. Hence, individuals and groups may share the signifier, though not necessarily the signified.

The same signifier, as was said, lends itself to related but still differing definitions (or content). A linguistic sign, ''nationality'' or ''nation,'' may be defined in terms of culture or in terms or race. The word image, ''freedom'' may be defined as freedom of a nation, of a collective, of a group from foreign domination, or of a individual from domestic oppression. What might be shared is only the signifier, a linguistic or iconic representation of the value, while the very content might be interpreted in a variety of ways. "But what people mean when they proclaim that liberty is the palm, and the prize, and the crown?" asked Lord Action in his *Inaugural Lecture*.[4] "It is an idea of which there are two hundred definitions." The British historian Tarn, writing about the Hellenistic civilisation (300 B.C.-30 B.C.), suggests the different meaning of freedom in the Greek and Jewish community. The ideals were different—he argues—even if expressed in the same words." Both desired political freedom, writes Tarn, but to the Greek freedom was an end, expressed in free self-governing community, making its own laws and worshipping what gods it pleased, while to the Jew it was a means, preventing interference with his devotion to a Law divinely given and unalterable by man, and to a God beside Whom there could be no other object of worship. Both praised Wisdom; but, to the Greek, wisdom was a thing which grew with the toil of many brains, while to the Jew it was the fear of the Lord, unchangeable for ever."[5]

The signifier, "La Marseillaise," corresponds not only to a known musical composition, not to the music alone. The song corresponds to an entire set of values. This is the signified of this anthem. The appeal of the French national anthem goes further, deeper than the stirring melody, although the melody per se has a psychological, an emotional effect; it affects moods and sentiments. The music, as we said already, is a sound image or symbol of liberty, equality, brotherhood, fatherland, to mention a few of the major ideals that this song was associated with. The very sound of music recalls the signified that were associated with this signifier—the song and march—through history and experience. The signified, the content of values that "La Marseillaise" stood for changed all the time, but the signifier, the song, was the same: It was an anthem and war song of the nascent and promising revolution, of the terror of the Jacobins, and of imperial France of Napoleon Bonaparte.

A symbol that unites a word image (or music) with information plus a norm, a value, has also an emotional meaning. It corresponds or relates to sentiments, to emotions and psychological needs. Hence, it affects motivation, mobilizes those who share the symbol (signifier) and emotions, even triggers collective behavior.

The strength of an appeal, of a symbol or a value, is perhaps concealed in the fact that the same word symbol, the same linguistic sign, carries a number of related meanings. Most or all of the partisans or followers accept and believe in the same signifier—the same flag, the same sound "liberty." But they do not necessarily share the same meaning, the same signified. The signifier, the word image of "liberty," is visible or audible; the content, the meaning is not. The image conceals a variety of meanings.

The acceptance of the same signifier that corresponds to different meanings (everyone interprets the symbol in his own way) integrates into a single collective, a single group, and activates a number of individuals or groups who interpret the value, freedom in this case, in a different way. But the signifier is identical.

During the first days of the Russian Revolution, slogans and symbols carried various contents. Republic, socialism, democracy, constitution—all those word images, signifiers, represented for various movements and individuals quite different concepts, different contents—the signified. But the symbol has unified individuals and groups who approved a republic, democracy, socialism—the terms that covered a vast variety of concepts that were not necessarily identical or even shared. The symbol, the image, was.

At times the signifiers are identical, while the meaning, the signified, is unrelated, even contradictory. Both Roosevelt and Hitler used the same signifiers, the symbols of freedom, liberation, and nationhood. The meanings, however, were two opposites, polarly opposed concepts.

In the last half of our century this linguistic problem has new dimensions. Symbols of ancient meaning and powerful appeal are appropriated, used, and misused by totalitarian parties and leaders. The word image, the signifier, is filled at times with a content that is but a negation of the ancient meaning. The signifier "liberation" is used by conquerors. The term supplies legitimacy to acts of force and violence and wins majorities at the United Nations General Assembly.

However, qualification calls again for further comment.

The Meaning of Norms and Group Identification

Usually, in daily life and routines, the concept, the signified, does not vary or depart far from the ideal core value or from real norms. Values and norms do not lend themselves to an easy definition. They are interpreted and understood with some difference, but the core, the essence of the norm, is shared; it is shared deeper emotionally than rationally or by means of an emotional, not a purely rational, response. This sharing is reflected in judgment, in decision, in behavior rather than attempts toward definition. Seldom if ever a layman attempts to define a norm or such a value as freedom, progress, justice.

The judgment is, however, exercised and the polar values "do" and "don't," if not fully respected, are followed with some deviation by substantial sections or perhaps majorities. The polar norms of conduct are there, behavior can be observed, and interpretation of norms can be heard. In an Italian village, far more than in a Maine community, the behavior of one's neighbors, friends, and enemies is commented on in terms of approval or disapproval in terms of right and wrong. Views on approved and disapproved behavior, that is, norms of conduct, appear in daily neighborhood gossip, when ladies congregate at the stairs or at the piazza of an Italian village to do some work or business and enjoy their gossip. Men do the same evenings, at numerous bars or taverns. There is a sense of general orientation, direction of conduct, a sense of limits of the morally permissible.

Those sentiments and the general orientation are instrumental in a voluntary social control (informal social control); this directive and regulatory sense results in group cohesion, ability of a collective response to a changing situation.

The same symbol, a signifier, integrates widely scattered opinions and in consequence actual behavior, precisely due to the fact that it appeals to emotions and it is an orientation rather than a rigid formula or concept; it is sensed rather than defined. This is one of its major functions we can observe.

Once we move away from political ideologies to other subsystems, we may find standards, values that are well, even narrowly, defined,—for example, profit.

In my own experience on two American Indian reservations, in Wyoming and New Mexico, I was impressed by this clear presentation of concepts or standards. Even if the concepts did not lend themselves to easy and tight definitions, still their distinct meaning was clearly presented. They were presented in a descriptive and colorful manner rather than an abstract way, although the concepts could be generalized and reduced to abstractions. The defining was done in this case by identification of an in-group that shares a standard or norm and a stress on differences between the in-group and the out-group. The out-group does it in a different way: "We do it that way, differently than you." And usually: "We are better because we follow our standard."

An Apache Indian on the Mescalero Reservation in New Mexico discussed with me the meaning of respect as a norm of conduct. In my previous experience with Arapaho and Shoshone of Wyoming, I have enjoyed long philosophical-religious conversations, related directly to values. The values such as straight-forwardness and veracity were for them real things. I have noticed on the Mescalero Reservation fresh deerskins, stretched and nailed on the back wall of an old house. This was not the hunting season, and I inquired whether there are any rules that regulate hunting on the reservation. The young Apache explained: "Indians do not kill for sport, like those big game hunters who bring trophies from Africa and hang them on their walls. We hunt when we need meat and when we want to eat meat." And from here on the conversation moved to a more abstract, philosophical level and to the fundamental respect for nature, for animals and plants, even if you kill animals. The hunting behavior, as well as the relationship to nature, is governed by a principle of respect. "The major way we live by is respect," he said. "We respect a plant, a tree, the sun, all you take for granted. Our prayer may be short, we thank for what we get: the warmth from the sun, the shadow from the tree. You take it for granted, we do not. If you take for granted, you get used to it; it becomes a daily thing."[6]

In this case, whether this was an individual attitude or a shared tribal standard, whether an ideal or real norm it was distinct; it separated clearly my Apache host from the out-group. In consequence, this concept was instrumental in identification of an in-group; it identified a community of shared values. Here a distinct and rather narrow signifier, narrow in terms of groups, affected group identification and integration with the tribal community. It is the difference between the in- and out-groups that consolidates the in-group. This concept, which we may now call value, is a consequence of a world outlook (*Weltanschauung*) of the Apache. It can be understood only within a context of the culture to which it is related.

Respect for nature points to a general attitude toward nature, to an ethics that differs from one relationship to nature. Neither the Judeo-Christian civilization nor the Hellenic and Hellenistic created systematic ethics toward animals and nature (although we may owe our concept of nature to the Greeks). Our nineteenth-century world view was an image of conflict, struggle between man and nature. It is now that a vigorous ecological trend among the young moves toward a new outlook of a symbiosis of man and his natural environment, toward an outlook of relative harmony rather than conflict. It is a threshold toward a new ethics of nature, an "environmental ethics" of living rather with the nature than fighting and conquering it. An animal ethics is now advanced by the younger generations. Some animals, such as whales and dolphins, have been already adopted as our kin. Some beginnings of animal ethics can be traced also to the ancients. Pythagoras and Empedocles (fifth century B.C.), who rejected the killing of animals, are believed to be founders of this branch of ethics. More than half of a millenium later, Plutarch "places the duty and kindness to animals on the broad ground of affections . . . to which no parallel can, I believe be found in Christian writings," according to Lecky in his *History of European Morals*. In the sixteenth century Montaigne abhorred cruelty toward animals. But those views and attitudes were not widely shared. It is only in this century that a new ethics toward animals and nature is constructed, and this may be as well a major contribution of our era, far more so than destructive weapons.[7]

We spoke about an ideal Apache norm. The real behavior is of course different. Nonetheless, in this case a signifier with a distinct content (signified) exercises its social function of collective identification and coalescence.

Hence, signifiers either may broaden, extend the content, the meaning of values, or may narrow it down to selected groups and more definite meaning. This depends on the relationships of the value of symbols to the entire idea system on one hand and to the social group that the symbol or norm affects on the other. The latter has to be always considered within those two contexts: society and ideology. While the situation or ideas change, the "meaning" of values may change. This means that the signifier continues while the content, the signified, changes, responding to situations.

Social Function of Values

Values mobilize collective actions, integrate groups when they are shared. Sharing means that values are not only individual, but also social. When we ask why symbols affect or mobilize groups, our initial answer is because they appeal to ethical sentiments or to certain needs, economic or other interests that are shared by or present within a collective of individuals, a group.

Values are multifactional, and three social functions are seminal:

1. Integrative. Values integrate idea systems and groups. In one form or another, as core values, symbols, what Durkheim called collective representations, they integrate groups and collectives.

2. Regulatory-directive. Values as standards and norms of conduct set the direction of actions as well as limits of permitted behavior.

3. Motivating. Values correspond to sets of needs and interests. Needs are related to drives and actions. Drives in turn are attached to incentives and rewards.

The core values (super ethos—see part III), the standards and norms, are articulation of the entire idea system and of the respective social system. Neither the value-goals nor the norms of conduct are separate objects that exist independently of man, society, and the idea system they profess. The idea system integrates the society. The values form the central theme of the idea system, suggest the sense of direction as well as set the limits of the system. Change in the core values is tantamount to change in the entire system. A social system, individuals, and groups resist outside attempts to weaken or change the dominant values. Hence, an ancient strategy of permitting symbols, the signifiers, while changing the content, the signified.

After the conquest of Mexico, the native belief system was displaced by Christianity. Ancient dances and rituals, once dedicated to native deities, continued, however, and integrated the Indian Christian community. The Indians performed them now during Catholic holy days; the native deities were displaced by saints.

The signifier, ritual dance, continued. The signified, religion, has been displaced. A conqueror may permit the conquered nation to display the national flag, which symbolizes sovereignty, while real power is displaced and administered directly or indirectly by the new rulers. The old signs carry new norms. A major social change calls for changes of the social goals (shared goals) and norms of conduct; hence the regulatory-directive structure has to be affected one way or another.

When we say that the values integrate and supply the sense of direction to the idea system and society, in a narrower sense this means that by means of standards and norms the system becomes consistent and maintains a certain logical homogeneity. Stability and continuity of a social system, generally of a society, call for a relative predictability of response. The norms of conduct provide this predictability; since I know what is permitted and what is not, I know the parameters. I know how far I can move, where my actions will meet with moral sanctions and, further, with a legal one. In this respect, the system has to be consistent. The stability of a system depends on levels of consistency. The highest consistency is achieved by a coherent and universally binding set of norms, that is, a set of norms that binds in the same measure all members of a society, all citizens in a state, and no individual or class exceptions are made.

In such a case of a universal set of norms of conduct, behavior of all is under the same controls; similar responses can be expected for similar actions.

Institutions and Legitimacy

Where are the values located in institutions? In their very goals and norms of conduct. Education, excellence, search for truth are among the goals of a university; justice, of a court of justice. Those are of course ideal goals and legitimacies. They are articulated in the charter of the institution. Every institution has a charter, accepted by custom, or a written one. The charter states the objectives and the function of the institution. Hence, it exercises at the same time regulatory and directive functions. An institution has an established set of rules of conduct, guided by norms.

Strength of a society, its cohesion, is reflected in its institutions: in their stability, their continuity, and at the same time their flexibility. It is not the document that makes the institution stable and flexible: It is the relationship between the charter and the nature of social order, traditions of the society, skill in the art of government, that makes a good institution. As an example may serve the American constitution, a stable and flexible instrument of unusual quality. It adjusts to changes, which it absorbs by a variety of devices. It works, however, because a critical quantity of citizens follows the norms of conduct and shares the values. It may not work in Argentina. Flexibility is provided by amendments and reinterpretations, even transvaluation of norms.

The courts of justice in Anglo-American systems regulate the meaning of norms of formal social control. By interpretation of laws, above all, by interpretation of the constitutional rights, the content of standards and norms changes. The same signifier, as was already indicated, may have different meaning. The concept of equality and civil rights went through substantial changes in our political and judicial history: from legal slavery, slave ownership protected by law, to emancipation; furthermore, to reinterpretation of equality into equal but separate rights, and eventually to affirmative action that protects—more, gives perference to—minorities.

The signifier did not change; the content did. The meaning was broadened. By means of law and legal sanctions, norms and values are reinterpreted, reinforced. This mechanism of formal control affects of course the informal. In that way the system is changing, but it works as long as the legitimacy, the shared set of values, is strong.

The state is a complex institution. The state controls directly or indirectly many of the other institutions; it is well equipped with sanctions, with a legitimated use of force, whenever the law justifies it.

The legitimacy integrates the state and supplies a binding doctrine of exercise of power. Legitimacy is a doctrine based on a definite set of values, or it is simply a set of values. The legitimacy of the state may be based on wide sharing of common values, on what may be called spontaneous acceptance of the latter, or an imposition by means of exercise of force. The cohesion of the state, its stability, depends either on quality and quantity of a voluntary acceptance of shared values or on effectiveness of imposition by force and coercion. In the first case, sharing of legitimacy by large majorities, with a nonviolent opposition of insignificant minorities, secures stability. In the case of autocracies, to mention ancient Persia and Russia since the sixteenth century, legitimacy was imposed at times effectively by coercion.

Social Control

The regulatory functions of norms of conduct are articulated in social control. Distinction in usually made between formal and informal social control.[8] In a nutshell, informal social control is exercised by a set of norms and rules of conduct shared by the group; it is a general ethos of the group. It is known, accepted, and usually not enforced. However, the limits of behavior are set by what may be called moral sanctions, a variety of forms of criticism and patterns of avoidance: beginning with gossip and ending with anathemas, curses, prophetic condemnation, excommunication, physical exclusion.

The formal social control is armed with legal sanctions. It is exercised by the state, which can impose the norms of conduct, even the goals, by means of laws or orders supported by threat or direct use of force. The state has the legitimacy, and it is the only institution that can "legally" use or delegate the use of force. The word *legally* means supported by enacted laws. In a constitutional state the limits and conditions of use of force are narrowly and distinctly defined and universal (binding all members of the society). The formal social control is administered by laws and legal sanctions.

The mechanism of informal (voluntary) and formal (legal and coercive) social control depends on acceptance or enforcement of norms of conduct and dominant values. The informal social control secures a social order based on consensus, voluntary acceptance of norms (values) and, in consequence, of obligations and responsibilities toward the group or institution. The formal social control is articulated in laws and institutions, and acceptance of norms of conduct is secure by legal sanctions.

Legitimacy of norms and action is, however, a condition of an effective social control.

Legitimacy of a state is primarily a set of values, accepted by or imposed on the subjects or citizens. A wide acceptance of dominant values of the state permits broad informal social control, which secures social cohesion by consensus rather than by command. Where legitimacy is not fully accepted, formal social control is stronger or at times even brutal, and order is maintained by central command, enforced submission to norms, or threat of such enforcement. This type of a political command structure has usually a wide system of negative norms or commandments (you shall not), since the area of prohibited behavior and actions is wide.

Formal and informal social control, legitimacy, and values are not solely theoretical concepts. They do have a relevant, also a historical, meaning. Totalitarian states operate through extensive systems of formal social control, evidence that the legitimacy of the state and of the power is not widely accepted. The order has to be secured by excessive increase of formal control and imposition as well as enforcement of norms.

However, weakening of legitimacy in a social system rooted in consensus may also result in an increase of formal social control and in displacement of customary, informal rules and norms by legal.

Breakdown of Legitimacy

When legitimacy is rejected by large and active majorities, then the maintenance of power, even by means of force, might be difficult and at a point also the coercive apparatus may break down. Individuals and groups in such a case are alienated from the idea system from which the legitimacy derives or from the source of the core values. Where core values are rejected, a process of slow social disintegration sets in, a process Durkheim called *anomie*. However, weakening of or change of the meaning of the core values, values of legitimacy, is indicative of social change, which affect the values.

The breakdown of legitimacy is tantamount to a massive weakening of political core values. The breakdown of legitimacy, when it appears, is visible and observable in times of a revolutionary process. The action of the crowd is at first directed against the symbols of power, be that a two-headed imperial eagle in times of the Russian Revolution or a sentry box in Paris in 1848 or a red flag in Berlin in 1953. De Tocqueville described it in Paris of 1848; a *New York Times* correspondent, in Berlin of 1953. Those symbols represent legitimacy of power; the latter in turn represents values.

Destruction of symbols—when this is an articulation of emotions in time of a revolution—is a preliminary; it might be associated with a future breakdown of operations, of working of the institutions. At such a point—of breakdown— executive orders do not travel through the various links of bureaucratic hierarchy; laws and commands are not obeyed. A new legitimacy is associated with nascent values and institutions; new norms of conduct emerge. Orders of the new power centers are now respected, orders of the old, disregarded. This process of formation of "dual power centers", the formal of the government and the informal one of the revolutionary committee or council, emerged clearly in the Russian Revolution of 1905. The legitimacy of the government was now breaking down; the new legitimacy of the *soviet* was born in that revolution. The orders of the government were disobeyed; the orders of the *soviet* were followed. This was an apparent articulation of change of shared values, change of the directive-regulatory apparatus. Symbols changed too.

Notes

1. Znaniecki stresses the significance "of consensus in judgment about values." This consensus appears when individuals of diverse experience express similar or identical judgment. "Their evaluative judgments concerning certain objects are supposed to express not merely their own intellectual and emotional experiences, but *standards in accordance with which everybody ought to define and evaluate the objects*. Their judgments about the desirability or undesirability of certain ways of acting in situations which include these objects are supposed to express not merely their own volitions that something should be done or not done, but *norms of conduct which everybody ought to consider obligatory for any agents who deal with such situations*." Florian Znaniecki, *Cultural Sciences* (Urbana: University of Illinois Press, 1952), pp. 263-64.

The problem of consensus is, however, more complex, since an acceptance of a signifier is not tantamount to an agreement on content (see below).

2. We have limited the classification of signs to signal and symbols, since those two concepts are relevant for our argument. Morris introduced an elaborate system of semiotic terms. Still another concept useful for further discussion of our theme is that dealing with the response to the sign. The response sequence to a sign has been called an *interpretant* by him. See Charles Morris, *Signs, Language and Behavior* (New York: Prentice-Hall, 1950), p. 17, also "Extension of Terminology," pp. 20 ff.

Peirce developed early an extensive classification of signs and also the concept and term of iconic signs. See his "Logic of Semiotics: The Theory of Signs" in a collection of his studies, Charles Peirce, *Philosophical Writings of Charles Peirce*, ed. Justus Buchler (New York: Dover, 1955), pp. 98ff; also Morris, *Signs*, pp. 287 ff., "Charles Peirce on Signs."

3. Ferdinand de Saussure, *Course in General Linguistics* (New York: Philosophical Library, 1959), pp. 66 ff.

4. "Inaugural Lecture on the Study of History," delivered June 11, 1895 in John E. E. D. Acton, *Essays on Freedom and Power* (Boston: Beacon Press, 1949), p. 14.

5. W. W. Tarn, *Hellenistic Civilisation* (Cleveland and New York: The World Publishing Company, Meridian Books, 1967), p. 226.

6. My notes from the Mescalero Reservation, quoted literally for August 4, 1968. I repeat the content of a single conversation.

7. The ethical relation to animals is quite different in different cultures. Findeisen discusses the forgiveness dance of some Asiatic hunters, a ceremony imploring the killed animal to forgive the deed (*Entschuldigungstanz*). Hans Findeisen, *Das Tier Als Gott, Dämon und Ahne* (Stuttgart: Kosmos, 1956), p. 4. The current development and growth of animal ethics has already produced an extensive literature. We shall mention here only, in an arbitrary manner, some examples: S. and R. Godlovitz, J. Harris (editors), *Animals, Men and Morals* (London, 1971); P. Singer, *Animal Liberation: Toward an End of Man's Inhumanity Toward Animals* (New York, 1977); T. Regan, P. Singer (editors), *Animal Rights and Human Obligations* (New York, 1976); W. Brockhaus and others, *Das Recht der Tiere in der Zivilization* (Munchen, 1975).

A. Linzey in his *Animal Rights and Christian Assessment of Man's Treatment of Animals* (London, 1976) integrates ethics toward animals with Christian ethics. For a bibliography, see: M. Hunt and M. Jeergensmeyer, *Animal Ethics: An Annotated Bibliography* (Berkeley, 1978). The Institute of Philosophy of the Polish Academy of Sciences in Warsaw issued a remarkable volume on ethics toward animals (*Etyka*, Warsaw, 1980, Vol. 18) which is limited largely to Western sources. An informative and useful annotated bibliographical survey by Stefan Sencerz (''Obligations Toward Animal and Rights of Animals'') begins with the Bible and Aristotle and brings the literature through the ages to the present.

8. The theories of social control developed by Alsworth Ross in 1896–1898 were later published in a volume *Social Control* in 1901 (New York: Macmillan, 1924). His theories were slowly abandoned, even forgotten.

A new approach to social control, as well as the revision of the concept, has been advanced by Morris Janowitz, Don Martindale, and Joseph Roucek in Joseph Roucek, ed., *Social Control for 1980* (Westport, Conn.: Greenwood Press, 1980).

An attempt has been made to apply this concept to the contemporary problems of the weakening of informal social control.

5

Definition of Values: Structure of Goals

An Attempt at a Definition

Our general discussion of the nature, structure, and function of norms, values, and goals calls for two next steps: (1) defining of values; (2) narrowing of the theme of our study to the structure of values and goals.

Znaniecki distinguishes standards of behavior from norms of conduct: Standards are evaluations of *objects*; norms of conduct evaluate *activities* in relation to those standards. Writing about prophets, priests, missionaries, propagandists, and others, Znaniecki argues: "Their evaluative judgments concerning certain objects are supposed to express not merely their own intellectual and emotional experiences, but standards in accordance with which everybody ought to define and evaluate these objects. Their judgments about the desirability or undesirability of certain ways of acting in situations which include these objects are supposed to express not merely their own volitions that something should be done or not done, but norms of conduct which everybody ought to consider obligatory for any agent who deals with such situations." Situations are evaluated by actors in terms of those standards and norms. Both are essential in any ideological model, and, Znaniecki continues, they were frequently confused: "Standards refer to objects with which human agents are dealing and norms to activities bearing on these objects."[1]

Thus Znaniecki distinguishes between an ideal court of justice, the standard, and the administering of justice, guided by norms of justice.

Parsons's definition relates to the symbolic nature of values and to choice—search for alternatives, an element of decision making: "An element of a shared symbolic system which serves as a criterion or standard selection of the alternatives of orientation which are intrinsically open in a situation may be called a value.[2]

Perry defines values clearly in terms of "interest." He selects it because it is an old word, and of all the old words "it is the best to substitute for a class of words—'liking,' 'desiring,' 'living' . . . . and distinct from a different group or class of terms: 'sensing, perceiving, thinking.' "[3]

Concepts and phenomena can be defined in several different ways, and still each of those definitions may be valid and correspond either to many meanings of the concept or, in other cases, to the diverse empirical realities. Definitions are guided, as classificatory systems are, by principles of division and selection. It is an abstract, at times an a priori, device that finds its application in an empirical and inductive process. The definition calls for major patterns of relationships of variables: principles and characteristics that can be identified in all cases and embraced by the definition. But some concepts, some phenomena, at least in theory, may have not one but more than one common quality, each subject to different principles of selection. In consequence, the same universe of relationship of data may led itself to more than one all-inclusive definition. Furthermore, definitions may be complementary rather than contradictory. In such a case, the same signifier serves a different content, or the same content is considered from different vantage points, focus, or interest. But the same signifier corresponds nevertheless to one of several relationships of data of the same phenomena. A definition is a reduced image. In this process or reduction, different data may be removed in different definitions. With this reservation we may proceed to a definition that is a consequence of the present approach and discussion and may be considered as complementary to others.

Values are generalized cultural data that are either measures or guides of our behavior or goals. They form a central theme and integrate the entire idea system. However, values are not separate blocs, but are a consequence and an articulation of an idea system or doctrine. They form a shared symbolic subsystem. Social values are shared by various types of groups. In empirical terms they exist not independently, but only within a social context, as an articulation of a shared ideology. Values form the elements of a directive and regulatory order, and every subsystem of ideas has its specific goals and norms of conduct. The values as norms of conduct form the boundaries, within which the choice is exercised. The normative boundaries are seminal for the very existence of a society. The directive and normative order appears in all societies, although the content of norms may vary.

Thus social values exercise three major functions: (1) They integrate society by means of various forms of social control, legitimacy, and symbolism; (2) they supply the sense of direction and pattern of conduct; (3) they are a motivating force and mobilize individual and social action. Values and goals affect the actors and society, and actors by their actions affect other persons as well as the social as well as the natural environment (situation); the latter affects in turn the actors and their values, since man responds to the challenge of the changing situation.

A Short Overview: The Vertical and Horizontal Structure

A distinction should be made between real and ideal norms, similar to the distinction between ideal and real behavior. The ideal values represent the norm that the society sets for an individual or group as imperatives or commandments that ought to be observed. The real norms are those which are actually followed in everyday life, which can be empirically identified in behavioral patterns. Philosophy deals largely with ideal values; sociology, with real norms. This distinction represents the perennial issue between what is and what ought to be.

In the introduction to the second volume of his *Système de politique positive,* Auguste Comte wrote: "The positive study of mankind should be divided into two essential parts: the first, static (*statique*), which concerns the very nature of this large organism; the second, dynamic, which deals with the necessary development (*évolution nécessaire*). . . . In consequence, in an abstract, tentative way, the human order should be studied as if it would be static (immobile)."

What Comte suggested when he wrote his positive philosophy, some time about 1835, was to study human society in two ways: first, the structural order, as if it would be immobile or static, and second, the processes of change, the dynamic aspects. This division into static and dynamic, the study of the structural order on one hand and processes, actions, the dynamics of society, on the other hand, continues as an essential if not elementary methodological division, not unlike study of anatomy and physiology.[4] Anatomy in a sense is equally abstract as social statics. Statics is of course abstract; it gives us an image of the structure, as if one could arrest the working, functioning, of a society.

The study of values and goals of the directive-regulatory order is subject to a similar distinction of static and dynamic.

The dynamic quality of value-goals appears when they activate individuals and mobilize groups. Goals are incentives, associated with rewards. In a dynamic expression, value-goals are causes or antecedents of actions. The latter are effects or sequents of goals.

Values are also structured as hierarchies. In a static approach we may perceive a set of values in terms of a vertical, hierarchical order. Some are intensive and relevant; others, far less. Some are key values that affect all the others; we call them dominant or core values. We may put them on the top of the pyramid, since they affect the other values. The latter are derived and subordinated, derived from and subordinated to the core values.

The dynamic nature of values can be projected in a linear form of a *sequence* of value-goals, and we shall call it a horizontal structure, since it can be presented in a simple linear form of time sequence of immediate, intermediate, and distant goals (see chapter 8). The static approach appears to us as a hierarchy of values or norms, a pyramid of varied qualities and intensities. Visually, this relevance of a scale of value lends itself to a vertical presentation and in consequence, it has been called vertical (see figures 24, 26, chapter 15).

In this sense we may suggest two types of value structures: the vertical and the horizontal. These two types of structure represent simultaneously two levels of analysis. We may say that they represent two vantage points. In other words, we may imagine that the same phenomenon is observed from two different observation points, one on the vertical and the other on the horizontal level. Therefore, the picture that we get from a horizontal view is different from the vertical one, and vice versa, but they represent the same social universe. The horizontal and vertical views are complementary—not contradictory. However, they cannot be applied at the same time.

In addition to the vertical structure of values, and horizontal sequence of goals, we may single out two other types that are seminal in cultural patterns. Goals may reappear in society in definite time intervals, determined either by the rhythm of annual seasons and activities related to the latter or by culture; it is a cyclical goal structure.

Some of the goals are "finite"; they are fixed and well set on the value scale. But there are goals that are continuously moving and can never be achieved. We call such value-goals *open values* or *infinite value-goals*.

Notes

1. Florian Znaniecki, *Cultural Sciences: Their Origin and Development* (Urbana: University of Illinois Press, 1952), pp. 265, 267 ff.

2. Talcott Parsons, *The Social System* (Glencoe, Ill.: Free Press: 1951), p. 12.

For a comparison of definitions of values in recent German sociology, see Jurgen Friedrichs, *Wert und Soziales Handeln* (Tübigen: Mohr, 1968), chap. 2.

3. Ralph Barton Perry, *Realm of Values* [1954] (Westport, Conn.: Greenwood Press, 1968), pp. 6 ff.

4. In American sociology, as early as in 1883, Lester Ward defined the dynamic quality of society or groups in terms of means and ends in *Dynamic Sociology* (Westport, Conn.: Greenwood Press, 1968), chaps 8–14.

Part II
GOALS

6

Types of Goals: Elementary Goal Structure

Predictive and Nonpredictive Behavior

Can we predict individual or collective behavior? In the general lore of scientists the view still prevails that unlike in physics, chemistry, or biology, where processes follow certain universal sequences and are "predictive" (in terms of probabilities), social behavior and processes are not. However, when a man follows a certain direction, his conduct may be anticipated in terms of probabilities; his past behavior and personality, past behavior of groups, even nations—in a word, past experience—supply a certain basis for human foresight; without foresight there is no statesmanship. Results of our actions or behavior may not be predictive, but still behavior may. Of course, our forecast is only a probability, more often than not a very tentative one. Still, foresight in human conduct is exercised in our everyday experience, and it is obvious to a point that we fail to notice it in our daily routine. Thus, I may "predict" or "forecast" that the post office at Forty-third Street in New York City will be open on Monday and closed on Sunday. I can also "predict" that in the Wall Street district mail will be heavy on weekdays, while far less so on Sunday. I know that the firemen in New York will respond—with high probability—within ten to fifteen minutes to a fire alarm.

Thus we may roughly classify human behavior into predictive (in terms of probabilities, of course) and nonpredictive.

The church, city hall, or post office are quite different in their functions, but all of them are institutions, and institutional behavior is predictive, within certain limits. We know that a religious service will take place at Saint Patrick's Cathedral during the Easter holy days, while the post office and city hall in New York will be closed, except for emergency services. There is no certainty, of course. But empirical inquiry moves only within the limits of probability.

Contract law assumes predictive behavior that roughly follows the rules of law. Should one of the partners behave differently, the law is enforced. Romans knew this already well, and legal maxims suggested those anticipations: *do ut des*, I give so that you give me; I expect, anticipate you will give me an equivalent of my merchandise; otherwise we shall go to court and the praetor will act according to the law, forcing you to pay. Legal behavior—within limits of probabilities (provided evidence, and so on)—is predictive. Legal procedures are followed in courts all the time; they set structured and predictive patterns of behavior. The results, however, are not.

Predictive does not equate with *predictable*. *Predictive* suggests only various levels of probability, a probability that an actor or group will move toward a goal, or one of the options, alternative goals, that are open to him. In a narrower sense it suggests that, in a goal-oriented behavior, the actor's choice and selection of a course or courses of action will be determined by his goal. In consequence, knowing the goal, we can infer future actions; contrariwise, goals can be discovered by understanding the function, the nature of actions, in a given situation or case.

Goal-oriented or telic behavior is predictive. A student who intends to become a teacher enrolls in a teachers' college. Provided he is serious about his goal, he will enroll in the required courses, attempt to pass exams, write papers, and study. I cannot predict of course the entire story. I do not know whether he will pass the exams. I may forecast, however, as a probability, that he will take the courses. A student makes a decision, selects a goal, has a sense of direction. The directive nature of goals permits one to anticipate actions initiated toward goal achievement. Actions of the actor may be frustrated, but his actions can be anticipated. Adolf Hitler's goal, stated in his writings, was a conquest of Eastern Europe, especially the Ukraine and Russia. He stated the policy goals and reoriented Germany's industry toward war economy. A high probability suggested that given (a) will and goals and (a_1) armaments as antecedents what follows is (b) hostilities on a variety of levels and finally (b_1) general attack and war. a, a_1 were the antecedents; b, b_1 were the probable results—sequents that could be anticipated. It was a matter of logic and foresight. Foreign policy and statesmanship are above all foresight.

There is, however, an area of behavior that in a practical sense is nonpredictive. John, after a number of drinks, leaves a bar on the Bowery. He may move right or left or walk straight ahead. He does not know where he will move and has no clear intentions. We shall call this type of behavior aleatory or chance behavior (from Latin *alea*: dice, gamble, chance, risk). Aleatory behavior lacks the clear decision making that is essential in goal development or goal perception. Before a decision is arrived at, usually in a predecision stage, a mental effort is made to list the possible courses of actions (options), a kind of an inventory of choices. Selection of a preferred course of action, preferred in terms of the perception of the actor and intent to act in this direction is called decision. John's predecision stage (considering of options) is vague; he may even avoid it mentally since decision making calls for an effort; it may result in sensation of stress, even fatigue. John avoids a predecision stage. Aleatory behavior is a sequent of a vague predecision stage, and, similarly, his decision (since there must be some kind of attention point that signals action) is not a fully conscious one. For the sake of the present argument, we shall postulate that there is no clear or observable decision in this case. Thus, in an arbitrary way, we may identify four types of behavior:

1. goal oriented or telic
2. institutional
3. aleatory
4. other types

Goal-oriented and institutional behaviors are predictive; aleatory is not predictive; and other types constitute a vast category of behavior not embraced by the first three definitions.

The first group is the subject matter of our major theme—goal-oriented or telic behavior. Other categories have been suggested for comparative purposes. It is not our purpose at this point to analyze any further human behavior in terms of prediction or forecast. The distinction has been made for pragmatic and comparative purpose. In an aleatory behavior there is no clearcut, distinct decision, but only a vague orientation. Institutional collective behavior calls for certain routines, rooted in continuous repetition of activities the institution has, however, its purpose—goals and functions. An individual, as a part of an institution, in a subordinated role, may act routinely.

Intelligent executives, the decision makers, are however, cognizant of the goals, of the purpose of the institutions. They direct the entire apparatus to perform the functions vital for the very existence or purpose of the institution as well as the system within which the institution operates.

To act in a routine way means here to follow a well-established pattern, a way of actions—that is, acting and following predetermined steps, usually without questioning rationality or efficiency of steps, with no or little considerations about result. Nonetheless, a well-established path of actions may be at times both rational and efficient (for example, an efficient post office routine).

We shall suggest a hypothesis that even while the goal is irrational, efficient means are rational. Extermination of a religious group might have been a plan of a sick mind, of irrational sentiment, of pent-up hostilities. Rational in this case means logical in their sequence and adequate (in terms of probability), adequate to arrive at and complete the goals (tasks). Rational means were carefully selected, however, to achieve such a goal. There is no more rational and precise process than an industrial one. It has been applied by Hitler's disciples in Auschwitz and many other camps of extermination.

To repeat, the distinction between spontaneous (aleatory), institutional, and telic (goal-oriented) behaviors has a practical implication. The goal suggests a sense of direction, directive behavior. Direction is a major function of the value system. Goal and decision are antecedents; actions are sequents. In terms of probability, of course, once we know the chosen direction—goals or options open to the actor—we may hypothesize the possible courses of actions: the sequents. While observing actions or sequents of an actor, we may discover the "cause" of his actions, his purpose (goal) or objective, which is the logical antecedent.

The frame of reference of goals and actions lends itself as a method, a device in foreign policy forecasting, particularly strategic (telic) forecasting.

Telic Behavior: Directive Nature of Goals

We have called goal-oriented behavior or actions telic. A telic frame of reference lends itself to forecasting; it has predictive qualities. But the study of goals is far wider; it is not limited solely to those predictive probabilities.

A major function of value-goals is a directive one. Goals or ends articulate our sense of direction, and no society, no individual, exists without goal-related activities, for man is telic, goal oriented. The dynamic nature of man and his values appears particularly in patterns of goals, which in turn trigger human action and converge into social processes. Our entire life is built around patterns of interdependent goals. To plan our life means in fact careful consideration of our life purpose, our goals. It is a choice between relevant and less relevant, not solely between pain and pleasure. Our life-style reflects those goals which on one hand are articulations of our needs, responses to outside challenges; on the other, however, they are also expressions of our world view, ideology, for goals do not have a separate, isolated existence. They are responses to our needs and ideas or are pivots of institutions. Their relevance for planning an individual life or for a collective is obvious. The choice of goals may be a matter of survival. The choice of proper sequence of intermediate goals may lead to success or failure, victory or defeat. The relevance of goals has been recognized as both elementary and fundamental in a study of man. It is inherent in the Socratic objective of knowing oneself.

Moreover goal and purpose is a part of our psychology, a condition of our existence. Telic or goal oriented behavior is universal. It appears among children; maturation and goal range extends with the extension of their attention span.

Total prison isolation and complete retirement may result in radical, almost complete reduction or breakdown of meaningful and extended goals. A prisoner may attempt to recreate such targets or goals by means of regular daily exercise, hours of contemplation, prayers, planning goals for the future. Such an attempt may be a condition of mental health and survival.

Reduction of goals in times of retirement may result in unhappiness and isolation. Reconstruction of meaningful goals, to begin with short, daily routine targets, paves the way toward a more active and happy existence. Without goals, we cannot exist. Too many result in stress, reduction to very few, making us passive, inactive and unhappy.

Active life means of course an existence related to a number of meaningful goals. Reconstruction of individual goals is one of the conditions of rehabilitation.

Instrumental and Consummatory Goals

Ancient philosophers made already the distinction between goals that are sufficient and final (ends) and those which are not sufficient, but are only instrumental or means leading to the former. In Aristotle's *Ethics* only final and perfect good is a self-sufficient end; others are means. "We call that which is pursuit as an end in itself more final than an end which is pursuit for something else .... What is always chosen as an end in itself and never as a means to something is called final in an unqualified sense."[1]

The stoics—we learn from Cicero in *De Finibus (On Ends)*—made also a clear distinction between ends *(telos)* that serve, lead to the virtue, and those which already contain the virtue. In terms of definitions both Aristotle and the stoics made a distinction that we call intermediary and distant goals or, also, instrumental and consummatory.

The elementary, fundamental structure of goals does not change. It appears in our daily life, in individual goals, in military strategy, in social planning, and generally in human efforts. Intermediary goals are called tactical, the final are called strategic in military or foreign policy planning. The basic horizontal line is similar. The pattern of tactics, the content, changes. Rudimentary structure continues. We shall call instrumental goals *intermediary*; they are necessary to achieve ends originally projected in our decision. Consummatory goals are those which are either considered as final ends in our project; or are perceived as a successful termination of a process of problem solving; or are tantamount to satisfaction of our intitial needs.

This distinction calls, however, for a qualification. In a dynamic process, goals once considered as consummatory may become instrumental. In a war of limited strategic objectives Napoleon, after a conquest of one province—the original objective—decides to take the entire country. Hence, the initial consummatory goal becomes instrumental. In reverse, in politics of social progress, the end goal of a perfect society is not achieved. However, the means, the process of gradual reforms and other social changes considered by the leaders and followers of the party as instrumental, result only in a gradual reconstruction of a society, a working model, different from the ultimate plan of an ideal society. The latter sets only the sense of direction; it is never achieved. What is achieved are the instrumental goals.

Goals associated with biological needs are directly consummatory in terms of need—goal—satisfaction. True, the satisfaction is temporary, and the need will reappear. Nonetheless, in terms of a present need, goal achievement consumes the need and drive. Thus, a biological need of hunger results in instrumental goals: hunting, fruit gathering, or earning money. Consumption of food is tantamount to a consummatory goal. However, in a sense, it is a semantical problem, too, a problem of definition. In terms of a hunting projection, for a hunter venison is a consummatory goal.

Basic, Pragmatic, and Normative Goals

This distinction of instrumental and consummatory can be applied to all kinds of goals. It is related to the *iter*, the path of our actions; it points to the interdependent nature of goals. The definitions indicate solely whether the goal has been achieved and the total project has arrived at its end or whether the actions have reached a stage goal, an intermediate goal necessary for further steps.

However, goals differ in their quality. Those directly related to our basic needs and drives are called biological, biologically determined, or *basic*. Others are projected in terms of a "product" or a measurable result, for example, construction of a bridge. We shall call such goals *pragmatic*. Still different are goals determined directly by our values and articulations of our world outlook. We shall call them *normative* or cultural goals.

In consequence, in terms of their nature, we may indentify three types of goals:

1. Basic (or biological) goals: related directly to biological drives and needs.

2. Pragmatic goals: directed toward achievement of a "product" or forward concrete, usually measurable, observable results, for example, profit in a concrete financial transaction. We shall call them also "targets," as distinct from generalized, ideological (normative) goals such as socialism or equality.

3. Normative or value-goals: in broader terms, cultural-normative goals, articulation of political or religious ideologies, esthetic systems, or general, moral codes. Here belong such goals as justice, equality, or perfect harmony.

The divisions are not tight; some are overlapping. To some extent all goals are culturally affected. Even satisfaction of biological needs or goals varies with different cultures; for example, food varies in kind of diet, skills necessary to prepare the latter, customary habits, and time of dining (see chapter 3).

Basic and pragmatic goals are consummatory, at least temporarily. In terms of rewards—satisfaction—they differ too from the two latter categories, since satisfaction of those needs or drives is a matter of our biological survival. Hence, they are universal, appear in all societies. Since they are universal and at the same time basic (in terms of survival), they form the premise of unity of mankind. This biological premise of unity appears in forms of imperatives. The ways we satisfy our basic needs differ, but the needs are universal and prompt basic goals and activities related to the latter.

All cultures display some kind of normative-cultural needs and goals. Again, they differ greatly in content and nature. But we shall find those normative goals as articulations of belief systems, such as religion, ethics, or esthetic needs related to culture.

Those normative-cultural needs and their expressions or goals may originate in our unknown, psychological depths. They might be expressions of psychological needs or only rationalizations, sublimations, of biological drives of material desires. What is relevant at this point is the existence of those psychological or normative and culturally determined needs and goals. They are expressed through the means of world outlook, *Weltanschauung*. They may also be anchored in the very roots of our ethical order. It is beyond our scope at this point to search for origins of the latter; at this point, we merely postulate their existence (see chapter 3).

The response to needs differs, since it is culturally affected. In times of a family crisis, an Italian mother may find consolation in a prayer, in a religious service, in the church of her patron saint, while an Arapaho father on the Wind River Reservation of Wyoming would seek it in a sun dance or a peyote meeting, religious prayers of the peyote lodge. The needs are similar, perhaps identical. The ways of goal satisfaction differ. And, to return to our chapter 1, we shall recall that all societies have a normative, regulatory and directive apparatus.

Thus all societies display some patterns of goals, although articulations of those patterns differ. Goals form steps, stages of our life. They structure our daily and seasonal activities. They set periodical accents on our activities.

Elementary Action-Goal Structure

We shall proceed step by step. We shall state the problem and develop the concept as we advance the discussion.

First of all, a question should be asked: What indeed is a goal?

In a simple parlance it is a point of destination that sets the direction of our course of actions. An acquisition of a material object might be a goal and on the other hand a value, a never-attainable ideal. In a goal-oriented action I attempt to reach a point, to control others or nature, to achieve an ideal or an ideal solution. Once the goal is reached, my attempt accomplished, a temporary condition of satisfaction sets in, a sentiment of fulfillment.

Effective actions are necessary to achieve the goals, and they are initiated as a consequence of a decision. In a daily routine of repetitive activities (I go to work, eat lunch, and so on) decision making is, of course, simple, even spontaneous. In a complex situation it is an end point of reflection and choice between options. (More about decisions appears in the following sections.) In the process of choice, goals are first imagined or formulated, and then action follows. They may suggest that goals are not isolated or separate blocs. They are, however, meaningful as components of a relationship: choice-decision, actions, and goals. Decision (choice-decision) is followed by action toward goals.

The choice of actions is, however, reduced by two parameters: the pragmatic and the normative. Actions are chosen that are efficient, means that are considered effective, adequate in achievement of goals. This relationship between means and ends was called logical by Vilfredo Pareto, in those cases when actions, in terms of experience and common sense, were adjusted to goals, that is, when in terms of experience and reason, goals could be reached by actions that were chosen.

The choice of efficient means toward social (collective) goals is exercised within the limits imposed by outside factors, for example, by distribution of political, social, and economic power. Limits set on a choice of efficient means, limits that form the pragmatic parameter (boundaries) of our actions, appear in problem solving. In one case, parameters of choice are tight, and in selecting beween more or less efficient, more or less purposeful actions, the actor has only a limited freedom of choice of options of the less efficient quality. In 1979, American and European agencies planned aid and assistance of the starving Cambodians. Options had to be chosen within the limits of political realities. Two warring governments—one of them unusually cruel and genocidal, the other supported by a conquering and aggressive government—set the limits of choice. Each of them, it was anticipated, might divert aid from the needy in order to feed the armies and not the hungry populations. The agencies must choose between the two; none can guarantee maximum of efficiency in delivering food and medicine to the starving and the needy.

In other cases the pragmatic parameter is wide. The planners have to choose the most efficient options, the optimal, what is considered best in a given situation. The parks of New York City are neglected, and rehabilitation is urgently needed. But young people need also vacation and rest. Money is provided for summer activities of high school students. The planners decide to split the time of the young people between paid part-time work in parks on one hand and games and other leisure activities on the other hand and to allocate resources to both accordingly. They consider such a use as optimal in terms of the interests of the youth and community. They could have used all for leisure.

In addition to the pragmatic parameter the choice is limited by normative considerations. The normative boundary imposes moral limits, or limits derived from ethos and world outlook, also law, on choice of options.

India has one-fourth of all the cattle of the world; it is estimated that it has more than half as many cattle as humans. Religion and custom, however, prohibit slaughtering of animals. The choice of relief policies in a famine-stricken India is limited by its normative parameter: respect for animal life. Thus, people would rather die than kill the free-roaming cattle. Incidentally, India developed ethics toward animals; the Western culture, beyond some rudimentary rules, did not.

In a relief action, for example, for India, the planners and decision makers consider or should consider the pragmatic as well as normative imperatives. The goal is to supply food to people affected by the famine. Relief organizations work within the "pragmatic parameter": What follows is a fast, efficient action to purchase food, ship it to areas of famine, distribute it. This is, of course, essential. However, the choice of food and ways of distribution should respect the religious and ethical sentiments. Thus the choice of pragmatic options is in this case limited by normative considerations or limits (parameters).

The goals of our action are directive; the pragmatic and normative parameters are of regulatory nature (see chapter 1). Now we may add to our model the two parameters (see figure 6.1).

The two subsystems, the normative and the pragmatic, operate within parameters set by two polar values, the positive and negative (see chapter 1). The positive pragmatic polar value corresponds to "efficient"; the negative one, to "nonefficient." The normative positive value is "right"; the negative is "wrong." The "fence," the parameter, consists of two boundaries, the positive and the negative. Parameters are ideal limits. The positive, polar value is seldom if ever fully achieved. An attempt is made to come close to, to approach, the polar positive value. In reality, we move between "more" and "less," more or less efficient, more or less right. The "top" of this measure is an ideal of perfection, in our culture a limit that is seldom fully attained.

In advanced societies, there is a distinct third parameter, the legal one. Goals and actions should conform to legal imperative. A legal parameter is also normative. For the sake of simplicity, we shall reduce our model to two parameters.

Goal systems and norms of conduct form general boundaries within which our daily life moves; they set in fact limits on our activities. Our existence, however, is not reduced to a single goal pattern and its parameters. We follow several, not a single one, and move within several boundaries. Society changes when new goal systems (also new parameters) emerge.

Are the normative limits or boundaries always respected? Do they in fact always, in all cases, restrain our will and activities?

The normative parameter limits of course our choice of actions, choice of what we call options. Even military action is usually limited by normative and legal consideration, expressed in declaratory acts and international conventions concerning civilian population, war prisoners, or open cities. The differences in strategic schools or doctrines are expressed also in normative considerations or limits of warfare. That all antagonists are the same in war, equally ruthless and brutal, is not true, although all wars are "dirty," violent, and brutal. True, the normative parameter may be totally lifted. This is in fact the nature of total war.

The force of limitless evil may be countered, contained, either by equally or more brutal actions or by higher intelligence and more sophisticated strategy. A civilized government cannot choose the former. Skillful use of potential forces (deterrent) but, above all, intelligent method of resolution or reduction of tension, attempts at construction of peace, are strategies that follow the ethical imperatives, and optimize the pragmatic within the latter.

Figure 6.1
Goal and Parameters

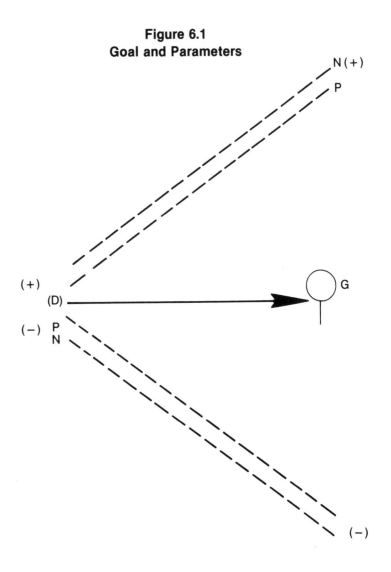

Decision (D)
Action ——→
Goal ◯ G
Normative parameter N
Pragmatic parameter P

Parameters — — — — —

Positive (+)
Negative (−)

Decision→action→goal moves within the positive (+) and the negative (−) normative and pragmatic parameters (N and P). Parameter is a boundary line that may vary. We may use both terms, boundary and parameter, interchangably.

Options and Alternative Goals

The elementary process of decision making can be reduced to three essential steps, to a simple, practical pattern:

1. Analyze the situation and decide on a goal.
2. Project the goal or goals ahead, into the future.
3. Plot efficient actions in order to achieve goals.

Such conscious sequence is at the same time rational and logical. Not all human behavior is rational, subject to a careful and disciplined self-evaluation. Nor are we always guided by pragmatic considerations. However, a large area of our behavior is pragmatic. And this is also the case in less advanced societies, whose logic is affected by magical beliefs. Also in those cases a substantial area of decision and actions is pragmatic, empirical in terms of observation, even experimentation. Man would not survive otherwise.

At a point of decision making, a rational and thoughtful actor considers ''What else can I do?'' with the same means at his hands. He may ask the question ''What is most important at this moment?'' In other words he asks what are the priorities, or what are the goals he may choose, or generally what kind of alternatives or options are open. After careful consideration, or at times spontaneously, under an impulse or ''a guess,'' he selects what he considers as preferential.[2] Preferential goals here mean goals ''more desirable'' than others; preferential actions may mean more efficient, safer, in accord with my moral consideration, to mention a few.

John Dewey wrote somewhere that man thinks when he must. But daily life asks for decision and choices in trivial and well as in relevant matters. Even at lunch in a cafeteria, we choose a sandwich from a number of different kinds; we select a lighter or darker coffee. In relevant matters, choice as a mental process is tiresome, may result in stress.

A decade or two ago the first floor of Macy's in New York City had an extensive section where ladies' hats were sold. This was a laboratory where human behavior could be easily observed, studied from a remote corner. One could see rows of ladies, sitting at tables equipped with mirrors. Each of them had a few hats at hand, nervously trying one after another. Seldom were they relaxed. They made their choices—trying to find a preferential option, a better-looking or more practical one. The number of options was extensive, and therefore choice was difficult. A final decision in such—at the first glance—a simple matter took considerable time. After twenty or thirty minutes of my observation, some were still there. It was evident that the process of choice in most cases was not easy and was tiresome. The problem, for us, may seem irrelevant; still the choice was exercised. The ladies were thinking, they were evaluating the esthetic merits of the headgear. They compared the hats, selected two or three, and eventually decided on a single one (or more), the preferentials.

We choose, decide on preferential goals all the time. The ladies of Macy's store were not unusual even in their specific interest. Here, in choosing hats, options are many; dangers are not present.

In a disaster situation choice must be done, too, but options are few, at times reduced to two choices: between survival and destruction. The time span for decision making is usually short, and absence of a decision may be tantamount to a greater personal and group calamity.

Those are, however, extreme cases. Listing alternatives can be a spontaneous mental effort, simply a commonsense approach to a problem. However, it may be also a careful, methodological approach of a political strategy and economic planning (more about this in following sections).

Adolf Hitler's strategic goal, we may assume, was conquest of Eastern Europe, the Ukraine, and Russia. He stated his goals in his writings. He could have attempted his plan attacking first either Austria or Czechoslovakia or Poland. The problem was the sequence of intermediary goals, which was conditional on the final, strategic one. He had at least three alternatives or options and selected an attack against Czechoslovakia as the preferred one.

In social planning the choice of effective policies is of course crucial. The legislators and executives intend to introduce a national social security. This goal can be reached in a number of ways: (a) Private insurance companies are given this task with public subsidies. (b) A public health system is introduced (as in most of the continental states). (c)An autonomous health insurance system under tripartite control of unions, business, and government is established.

In both cases the modes of thinking, the thoughtways, are analogous in terms of methods (one of policies of destruction; the other of policies of benevolence), while goals and intentions are diametrically different, opposed. In the former case the normative boundary is removed; in the latter, reinforced. If we reduce in both cases the decision making and choice of courses of action to one stage R (research), a single model (figure 6.2) is suggested.

1. The decision makers consider the problem and situation (R or research).

2. They set the goals (G).

3. They list alternative courses of actions or options toward the goal (A_1–A_n).

4. They select the prefered course of action (option) (A_p).

This is the way a rational policy decision is made, although pertinent criticism of this method deserves a more extensive discussion (more about this below in the section on strategy in chapter 8).

The actor may also evaluate goals, not policies, and perceive a number of alternative goals or options from which he selects one as a preferred one. A student, after his graduation from a high school, considers a number of profes-

Figure 6.2
Decision Making: Selection of Preferred Actions (Options)

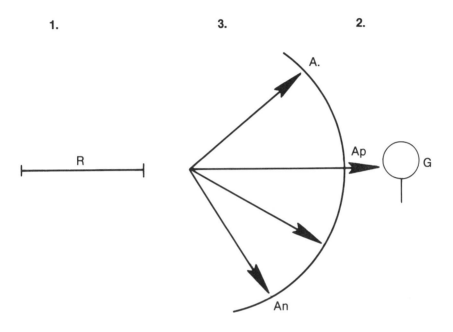

R.   Research
A 1   Actions-Options (Alternatives)
A p   Preferred Action (Option)
G   Goal.

sions and related studies: teaching, engineering, dentistry are his options, and he selects of course one, considered at a given moment as a preferred one. But he may be also forced to substitute his goals: Tuition for dentistry is too high; he is unable to pay his way through college in dentistry; he substitutes his preferred goal and decides to become a teacher. The same is true in political strategy; even strategic goals are substituted. Needless to say, goal substitution is already related to options and alternatives. What we choose, especially in a rational political strategy, is the possible.

In addition, in a practical, daily situation, new goals may emerge, while we are attempting to achieve those previously selected. The purpose of actions may be of course changed during activities.[3]

In policy decision, construction of goals and constancy to purpose may depend on past experience, routine, or an established pattern recognized as binding as well as efficient. Josephus Flavius, a Roman and Jewish historian, who wrote his books in excellent Greek, gives us an insight into Roman military and political decision making. Information was carefully gathered by the Romans about the situation and then, after careful evaluation of means and ends, a firm decision was made. The goals were stated. Once goals were established, they were pursued in a brutal way, if this was the most efficient way, with no deviations from the established purpose.

In battle, nothing is done unadvisably or left to chance. Consideration invariably precedes action, conforms to the decision reached consequently. Romans rarely err . . . .
They consider, moreover, that well concerted plan, even if it ends in failure, is preferable to a happy stroke of fortune, because accidental success is a temptation to improvidence, whereas deliberation, through occasionally followed by misfortunes, teaches the useful lesson how to avoid recurrence.[4]

Man responds in the past and present to similar circumstances and situations, affected by his idea system, choosing available alternatives. Either he chooses by custom, habit of mind, or he applies his reason and invents new answers, and the technological and scientific advance offers new, more effective alternatives, unknown before.

Human organization grew more complex; technology, more advanced. Hence the response is also more efficient, flexible in its way. The content of our response changes, but the elementary structure of perception → choice → decision → action → goal has the same rudimentary order. True, it is refined now, sophisticated, disciplined—but the linear sequence and its basic architecture continue.

Notes

1. Aristotle, *Nicomachean Ethics*, book 1, translation and notes by Martin Oswald (Indianapolis and New York: Bobbs-Merrill, 1962), p. 14.

2. See Charles Morris, *Signs, Language and Behavior* (New York: Prentice-Hall, 1950) pp. 79 ff., on apprising and on the terms *preferable* and *preferred*.

3. Florian Znaniecki discussed more extensively the change of purpose during actions or process in *Cultural Sciences* (Urbana: University of Illinois Press, 1952), pp. 224 ff.

4. Josephus Flavius, translated by Thackerey, Henry St. John *The Jewish War* (Cambridge: Harvard University Press, 1976), vol. 2, p. 607.

7

Formation of Goals: Needs and Stimuli

Biological Needs and Goals

And now I shall start with a question: When and how are goals formed? To begin with, they are formed in response to needs and outside stimuli and in all cultures in response to basic needs. But this is not of course the only way goals are formed.

Bronislaw Malinowski built his theory of culture around the concept of basic needs and satisfaction. Wrote Malinowski: "By need, then, I understand the system of conditions in the human organism, in the cultural setting and in the relation of both to the natural environment, which are sufficient and necessary for survival of group and organism." Learned behavior, institutions, argued Malinowski, must be organized in such a way as to satisfy the basic needs. In consequence, needs form the boundaries of culture and choice. In a different culture, however, needs are satisfied in a different way. Needs are universal; the ways they are satisfied differ. The basic needs have a corresponding system of cultural responses. Malinowski in a synoptic device, drafted a chart of basic needs and cultural response.[1]

BASIC NEEDS	CULTURAL RESPONSES
1. Metabolism	1. Commissariat
2. Reproduction	2. Kinship
3. Bodily Comforts	3. Shelter
4. Safety	4. Protection
5. Movement	5. Activities
6. Growth	6. Training
7. Health	7. Hygiene

To follow his system, needs must be satisfied. They appear in the form of impulses: action ("act") and satisfaction follow. Malinowski calls it "permanent vital sequence incorporated in all cultures.'' Again, this sequence can be presented in a simple graph with corresponding biological impulses, acts, and satisfactions:[2]

Impulse	$\rightarrow$	Act	$\rightarrow$	Satisfaction
hunger		ingestion of food		satiation
thirst		absorption of liquid		quenching

We shall stop here, since further listing of biological needs, important as it is, for the present discussion is immaterial. Malinowski's argument that his comparison of two entries, biological needs and cultural responses, is neither a hypothesis and, moreover, not a fictitious nor even constructive theoretical argument makes good sense: "We merely summed up the sets of empirical data; we placed them in juxtaposition; and we drew a few inferences, strictly inductive and empirical again."[3]

This pattern of vital sequence is later repeated in our discussion of biologically determined and pragmatic goals.

Malinowski advances further a theory of derived needs (derived from the basic ones) and lists imperatives necessary for the very existence of human society.[4]

To repeat, no single theory (argued Pareto) covers and explains all human actions and processes. The same is true with biological determinism. It does, however, explain a vast area of human activities and goal formation, and indeed, it is convincing in its logic and rigorous reasoning.

Biological determinism stresses the universality of needs and, in consequence, the unity of mankind. It does not, however, explain the fact of profound differences in values and culturally determined goals. Why and how can we explain those obvious variations? The difference in natural environment has been suggested as the major cause since times of Thucydides. But again, it does not encompass all cases. Cultural difference, differences in values and institutions, appear in the same environment.

Furthermore, the normative area of human activities is also related to needs, normative, ethical needs that may not necessarily fit the definition of derived need. Arguments of biological determinism and utilitarianism are logical in their broad reduction of ethical acts to their utilitarian or biological function and nature—in a very broad sense. But this interpretation, logical as it is, reflects an interpretation of philosophers and their thinking that overlooks the relevant motives and deeds of the actors. To quote Cicero (in his criticism of the Epicureans), ''nature has also endowed us with higher ends than pleasure.'' Or to quote Joseph Conrad, ''All great virtues are based on self denial.'' Those are not necessarily prescriptive maxims. Self-sacrifice and dedication to goals and values remote from self-interest and direct utility are frequent, if not as common and universal as the utilitarian acts.

We shall postulate here the existence of specific, ethical needs, needs anchored in an ethical order. This ethical order has a directive-regulatory quality. Some of the ideologies and religions habor ethical or related specific normative needs, although a vast area of normative arguments of an ideology or political philosophy is indeed or could be considered as rationalization of interests and emotions.

The ultimate origins of normative or ethical needs (urges) is, however, beyond the scope of our subject matter. We start at a point where the latter appear. The problem of the ultimate roots of our ethics and ethical goals may lead us into this unending debate, which was originated, if not only continued by the Greek Epicureans and stoics, continued by utilitarians and idealists; it is a dialogue that does not end in a simple synthesis, if it ends at all.

Need Goal as a Cause of Actions

Nonetheless, the sequence of needs—imperatives—and responses suggests a logical frame of reference for formation of goals and actions. A need goal becomes a cause; action follows as an effect. It sets the need as an antecedent; the drive action, as a sequent. This is also a classic monocausal sequence, composed of three elements: cause; logical nexus between cause and effect; effect. Knowledge of a single cause or effect suggests the probability that the other will happen. If I know the cause (antecedent, need), I can anticipate, in terms of probability, action toward effect (sequent, response). Knowledge of the response (sequent, effect) suggests the source of actions, the need (antecedent, cause).

The connection between both, the nexus, is a logical inference, a consequence of our thought process, which connects the two data. We shall not elaborate any further at this point the complex problems of causality.

Our individual and social actions are anchored in goals. We are conscious of some of the goals. Such goals are usually identifiable, sometimes even visible. The biological needs are reflected in goals that are easily identifiable. For instance, hunger will produce action toward satisfaction. Goals are related to those actions and can be identified through this relationship. Similarly, groups and institutions have goals that are easily identifiable. A trade union has economic and sometimes also political goals that can be easily identified. Modern psychology teaches us that there are psychological needs that might be repressed, blocked, or subconscious. Those psychological needs appear as rationalized or sublimated goals that trigger our responses. Pent-up, repressed hostilities, frustrations, may respond to political appeals of aggression, once a definite target of aggression is offered by a political leader, or once emotions are articulated and translated into goals. Ideology in such a case is a rationalization of emotions, sentiments (Pareto, Freud, Dollard).

We speak about rational action when the individual, conscious of his goals he selected, chooses actions logically related to those (identifiable) goals. In terms of his perception and probability, those goals may be achieved by chosen means. Aristotle's definition of rational has not lost its color: ''The rational element has two parts: one is rational in that it obeys the rule of reason, the other in that it possesses and conceives rational rules.'' A man whose goals are controlled by reason and who, in his action, follows the rules of reason acts in a rational way toward national goals.

An outside observer, who notices what may be called erratic, bizarre, or in certain cases deviant behavior, may consider them as unrelated to definite needs or goals. He may call them, therefore, irrational. They are or may be expressions of hidden, repressed, or nonconscious psychological needs, also not normal, and result in goals that neither he nor the observer identifies. ''Killing with no motive,'' we read in the papers. A drive for power and domination in a youth who could not channel otherwise his urges for control and power might have resulted in mugging and killing of a passerby. To hold a man or a woman at a gunpoint might have given him the fulfillment of a subconscious search for domination. Here was a person totally under his control and mercy—he is the lord of life and death. Here the emotional need harbors the goal.

To sum up, then, goals are expressions of needs or of their combination. Not all needs are directly or indirectly utilitarian, economic, or biological. Psychological, emotional, or normative needs result in strong motivation and goal orientation. The needs produce drives or urges, expressed in individual or group behavior, in the form of actions. In consequence, the following sequence can be suggested: There first appears a need, which results in a drive or action toward a goal, which is now identified or chosen. The goal suggests to the actor the probability (hope) of satisfaction. The actor reaches the goal. What follows is satisfaction. Hence goal need may be considered as a cause; action, as an effect.

Goal achievement results in longer or shorter satisfaction. Such a consummation of need interrupts temporarily or weakens the drives and actions. A goal results into action if there is a will behind it, a constancy to purpose strong enough to carry the necessary effort. This nature of the purpose was stressed by William James in his *Psychology*. Here comes, however, a strong qualification. Not all goals originate with outside stimuli or easily identifiable needs. Even greed—and mankind experiences greed everyday—is not tantamount to a need. Many of the wealthy accumulate money, spend their energy in making money, although they do not need such an amount of wealth to meet their needs.

Moreover, goals can be constructed; they may be produced by ideas that originate in our imagination, as a consequence of our esthetic, ethical sentiments, curiosity, and wish to create, or to understand. Of course, we may translate these kinds of wishes into needs. A wish to fly, which appeared in mankind early, was not a result of a direct or utilitarian need.

Society needs a broad image, an ideal anchored in core values, for without such a broad ideology or religion a historical civilization cannot survive or advance. Such an image results into distant goals, ideal goals to be sure, but still, they supply the very sense of direction. Without such a guideline a complex society becomes stagnant and passive. But in this section we shall continue solely with needs.

The Sequence of Goal Formation

We shall start with the simple, almost obvious example: individual, biological needs, goals, and satisfaction. It is this sequence, identified by Malinowski, that has a universal quality. Moreover, in a more elaborate, sophisticated form, it appears in all patterns of a horizontal goal structure. The elementary goal structure is indeed biological in its pattern, as suggested in Malinowski's models.

John comes back from work and experiences hunger. His hunger is an awareness of an urge to eat and of a need to satisfy his urge, which appears in a form of a tendency, a spontaneous direction. It results in a predecision stage of imagination. The tendency toward satisfaction of our biological drive appears in a concrete, cultural setting. A hungry Japanese student may imagine a bowl of rice; an American student, bread and cheese in the form of a sandwich. John imagines a delicatessen and a cheese sandwich. Thus, the goal is developed mentally, intellectually, he imagines the picture of his meal. The choice and decision follow. Thus action and goals are closely related to imagination. John's behavior was clearly telic or goal oriented.

Step 1. Biological subconscious urge is transformed into a conscious hunger and need of satisfaction.

Step 2. Tendency toward satisfaction develops, leads to

Step 3. The image of the goal. The process of development of images of goals shall be called imagination.

Step 4. The imagination results in a choice process:
        a)   evaluation of options (imagination of alternative goals)
        b)   selection of preferred goals
        c)   decision to act

Step 5. That leads to action toward the goal and goal achievement.

Step 6. Goal achievement is followed by

Step 7. Satisfaction. What may follow is imagination of new goals.

Imagination and Goals

Imagination (Step 3) is an important stage in terms of decision making, but more in terms of a general tendency to action. It is a stage of reinforcement of a drive, urge, or tendency; it prompts action. It is indeed a seminal stage in advertising and propaganda, since it is a predecision stage when the actor "lists" the choices in his mind. At this point he is hesitant, sensitive to outside persuasion and image. Our choice can be channeled, diverted by outside manipulators toward directions, choices that they control or that serve their objectives. The moments or time of choice is a stage, a moment of hesitation, inner weakness; it is a time of search, when a person looks for direction and also for an escape from the psychological stress of making a choice. A psychological outside push may prompt a decision.

Imagination is of course an individual process (in terms of individual decision making). However, manipulation of imagination and choice making of many persons transforms the individual choice into collective; it affects opinion, choice, sense of direction, of a "target group," the group a manipulator attempts to win. This may result into similar decision and action of many individuals, hence of a group.

The manipulators and propagandists attack or affect our "imagination," by which we mean here man's ability or propensity to produce mental images of his goals, wishes, or desires. The advertisers, playing on our imagination, harp on craving for a cigarette that an unhappy smoker is trying to arrest. They may also play on our status desire, by associating the habit of smoking a cigar with the good life of ambassadors or other important personalities. Thus the culturally determined desire for social mobility is reinforced and associated with smoking habits. Those advertised images become or affect our own mental images, awakening or reinforcing wishes and drives. This in consequence leads toward formation of goals. Thus the stage of image formation or imagination changes into an end point of imagination of goals at which action is released. Needs are also created, urges reinforced, excited by musical, visual, or hortatory commercials, which appeal to our imagination. The objective of the advertiser is to prompt actions—decisions toward the advertisers' goal, which then becomes also the actor's choice.

In this narrow sense, we may define imagination as the development of mental images of possible goals, as proximate causes of action. The urge, the need, and imagination in this case are closely interrelated.

Thus the urge appears as a latent tendency that affects our imagination. Images of goal satisfaction appear in our mind after recollections of past experience or earlier perceptions.

Back in 1949, on the Wind River Reservation in Wyoming, I arrived early, about 5 A.M., at the Plains Indian camp, where the sun dance, a religious ceremony, was performed by the Arapahoes and Shoshones. During the sun dance the dancers are subject to severe rigors. They fast and abstain even from drinking water, sometimes for three days. It was the second or third day of this ceremony when the missionary, Rev. Coach Wilson, and myself stopped at the big grass house where the sun dance took place. After a while the ceremony came to short halt. We shook hands with our friends, who so proudly took part in the ritual of penitence and self-discipline. One of my Indian friends, after greetings, said softly, close to my ear, "I feel like having bacon and eggs and a big can of beer." Thus the hunger affected his imagination with an image of bacon and eggs and beer. The images of our goals, in such a case, appear in our mind in a kind of daydreaming. It does not seem to me that we are always conscious of it. The images reinforce the urge; they remind us about the drive, which still awaits satisfaction; an individual, however, may delay satisfaction by exercise of self-control, called discipline. In absence of restraint, action follows toward goal satisfaction. The need or desire reflects both: the absence of satisfaction and the presence of drives. In this case the image was a consequence of past experience and was indicative of present culture. My friend did not desire venison, antelope, or buffalo meat although he was hunting antelope.

The goals, as so many psychologists teach us, may not directly reflect the very nature of our drives and needs; the goals may sublimate the drives or they may result in displacement or substitution.

Hence, satisfaction of biological needs appears in a cultural context. The needs or drives are universal, but the cultural context of satisfaction varies. So it seems does the imagination of goal satisfaction vary. In different cultures the images of needs are different.

Malinowski in his analysis of vital sequence points to the cultural phase through which a drive must pass before it reaches the goal of satisfaction. We eat at established hours. Our dinner is usually at the table with our family. We may enjoy radio and news. It is a cultural situation. The preparation of the meal calls for skills; tools have to be used. Our dinner is also a result of cooperation, division of labor. The hunger is satisfied in a cultural situation and context that is different in an Italian or Chinese village. The hunger drive is present in both cases. Food, the goal, is too. But the way hunger is satisfied is different.

To reach the goal, the drive passes through the cultural phase, which consists of a meaningful relationship of persons and their cooperation, skills, tools, and a cultural situation.[5]

The Path of Normative Goals

Goals, however, are not solely results of biological needs or even biologically derived need. The biological sequences is primarily oriented and directed by basic needs, a result of biological drive. Cultural, normative, or ethical needs result in value-oriented action.

In the evening I have a desire to listen to music. This desire moves my imagination: Should I play baroque music, romantic or modern? My preferred choice is baroque. I make the choice or decision and set the record in my record player. After an hour of listening, my wish to listen desists.

We may replace now urge or need by desire or wish, and the path of biological need–goal formation can be applied to the formation of cultural goals (see the model we devised in "The Sequence of Goal Formation").

Step 1. Desire or need.

Step 2. Tendency, urge to listen to music continues.

Step 3. Imagination of various composers and styles.

Step 4. Preferred choice of baroque.

Step 5. Action: putting the record on the turntable, playing it.

Step 6. One hour of playing or consummating the goal.

Step 7. Satisfying my wish.

Thus, the wish or desire and the latent imagination of the goal, which set the direction of my activities or normative goals, are a consequence of our general value system, world outlook, and personality. They are value-goals.

Incidentally, imagination is the "locus" of human creativity. In a broad sensory and emotional sense musical composition is a result of an "internal" act, of aural imagination. It his later years Bethoven hardly could hear, but he composed in his imagination. Musical composition is man's creation. Goals are also constructed here.

Leonardo da Vinci described imagination as a "rudder of thought". He distinguished "pre-imagining"—the imagining of things to come, and "post-imagining"—imagining of things of the past.[6]

It is rather interesting that attempts to achieve culturally determined value or normative goals follow a similar if not identical sequence to those which are basic. Achievement of such goals as education, the need of some kind of esthetic experience and satisfaction, activities that give us moral satisfaction move through a sequence that begins with a need or stimulates a desire. We may put "begins" in quotation marks, since these sentiments that generate needs or desires may be at times hidden in still deeper, nonconscious levels or our psyche.

The Path of Pragmatic Goals

The analytical sequence of six or more steps has a wider application. We began with simple cases of hunger and want of music, but a general decision-making process in business and politics follows a similar pattern since there is only one general path, *iter*. It begins with perception of the situation. First, the situation is perceived and evaluated, before a decision is made. Perception of the situation at the first stage may be pragmatic, but the choice of means, the decision, is limited by normative consideration. Even perception—as it was already indicated—is affected by our values, by one's moral code (chapter 2). An English diplomat may perceive American diplomats kidnapped in Iran in 1979 as victims of a political highjack and an outrage, violation of international law. Ayatollah Khomeini perceives the same fact, hostage taking, as a religiously legitimate and moral act. The same facts are perceived, but their evaluation at the very moment of perception is different. Our perception is affected by our idea system (world outlook) and ethos.

Not all goals are a consequence of our present needs. In addition to the standard need goal mechanism, needs and goals emerge or are created as a consequence of an outside stimulus. Furthermore, goals may also develop as a consequence of a creative or constructive intellectual initiative, a result of our imagination and thinking. Initial beginning of such goal formation may originate far deeper in our psyche in unknown or not yet discovered needs. They may originate with creative needs expressed in urges to write or to compose.

But let us begin with the stimulus. Man, within his cultural set of values, responds to the stimulus, and this response begins with his identifying a need to react and setting of goals that would answer the challenge. Thus the stimulus again is translated into a need.

Stimulus is usually produced by change of situations: situation A changes into situation A_1. After a torrential rain, flooding follows in Morristown, New Jersey. The situation changes; the community must respond to a new situation. It is a matter of survival. The mayor and his staff must make a decision. This change of situation forces the decision makers to action, provided that their idea system, their world outlook, prompts and activates such an attitude. In a different culture a similar situation may prompt different decisions, actions, and goals. A Buddist monk may simply move, with no attempt to fight or control the elements. Provided a cultural attitude, a set of values, the perception of change shall activate the will of the mayor to act. He identifies the need. The need to act is created by our active attitude toward the environment.

Again, the actor may imagine the choices of actions and goals. In a rational, logical process he evaluates the options. From several options he chooses one that he regards as most effective. The choice is then translated into a decision and action toward the goal.

Again the process of goal formation and action moves through all the steps of the analytical, horizontal sequence, in addition to the initial one—change of situation and perception. We may again list the steps of goal formation and decision making, this time, for example, for a social-political decision maker who has to respond to a critical change.

We shall call the initial steps 01 and 02, thus keeping the original numbering intact, for the sake of comparison and application of the same model.

Step 01. Situation A changes into situation A_1.

Step 02. Change of situation is perceived and results in

Step 1. Need or will to act.

Step 2. The tendency, the intention to act, continues and leads to

Step 3. Imagination of options. In the case of decision making, listing of options open to actor.

Step 4. Decision. There is a difference between the hesitant, insecure period of goal formation, when urgency or pressure is absent and decision making in an urgently critical case. At this point, the actor has to decide one way or another; otherwise he invites destruction or passive acceptance of events. The decision is the "end gate" that produces action, provided, of course, that the actor has this essential ingredient, *the will to act.*

Step 5. Courses of action or policies are carried out.

Step 6. Goal achievement.

Step 7. Consummation of and satisfaction with decision making.

Brevis iter per exempla: a short way leads by example. We shall use an imaginary one.

01. Unemployment jumps from 5 percent to 15 percent.

02. Office of Labor Statistics as well as the Executive branch of government perceives this change in terms of a need for action.

1. The need for action is stated by the government, an action toward full employment. This attitude and evaluation of perception is a consequence of values and idea systems of the decision makers who control the government at this very moment.

    The opposing group may consider any public intervention in economic field as unnecessary, or more, incompatible with the function and concept of state, and in consequence inadmissible. Actors with such world outlook may not act at all since they believe that the working of the economic system will solve this problem. In a fundamentalist, religious country, the decision makers may take a passive view; in times of famine, let the people die. It is the will of heaven. Thus, perception and decision are in this case affected by values, modes of thinking, idea-systems, as indicated in Chapter 2.

2. Tendency and will continue toward actions, to meet the goal of full employment. This will can be observed (heard or seen) in the debates, in mass media, in the Congress.

3. Imagination of a response to changed situation sets in. Various plans are discussed, criticized, and evaluated.

4. A policy of public works and subsidies to private business is decided, and a decision is made.

5. Policies toward the goal of full employment are carried out (organization of public work, subsidies for private business).

6. Let us imagine, in an optimistic mood, that unemployment dropped to 4 percent.

7. The goal has been achieved and the initial need consumated.

8. The project has been terminated.

In an empirical study of goals and action a distinction has to be made between what is in our path (*iter*)—empirical, observable (even experimental in terms of simulation)—and what is not. The process of goal formation and decision making, as long as it is individual, is not observable. The process of thinking, while everyone experiences it, is not subject to observation. We have the knowledge of those processes by means of individual introspection and conversation. While he drafts a plan, uses perhaps a piece and paper, man thinks, assigning priorities, suggesting solutions. We may understand his notes, but his thought processes, unless verbalized, are neither, visible nor audible. Collective decision making, however, is observable. It appears in forms of committee meetings, sessions of parliaments and courts. At these meetings the changes in situation are described, and responses in terms of possible courses of actions are discussed. There is one general pattern or path of goal formation. The path, the sequence of steps in a structure of normative, or culturally determined goals and actions, is similar—more, identical—with the one related to basic, biological needs or goals. The path begins in both cases with needs, goals are projected ahead, and what follows is a process of imagination, decision making, action toward goal, goal achievement. Satisfaction follows goal achievement. This is the end point of the sequence of the path. This seems to be a universal pattern of goal formation and action. The steps are followed on all stages of culture. They are different in content, perhaps, richer and precise in imagination in more advanced cultures, and the control of reason might be more effective. *But the steps, the path, is the same or, better, similar.* Furthermore, the same pattern appears in complex goal-oriented actions: in military strategy, social-economic strategy, or political strategy (more in chapters 9–11)

What Does Rational Mean?

Our discussion was narrowed down to a single category of rational, goal-oriented actions. We did not attempt even to extend our scope to nonrational or deviant behavior.

The question may be asked, What is rational? It is not our scope at this point to explore psychological, emotional, or ethical origins of those actions. In defining rational actions, the relationship between goals and action is seminal. However, rational action is not easy to define. To avoid extensive digressions, which in this difficult case cannot be conclusive, we have borrowed Pareto's definition of logical action as a working definition. Thus action "which uses means appropriate to ends and which links the former with the latter" is logical.

"To avoid verbosities, which could only prove annoying," continues Pareto, "we had better give names to this type of conduct. Suppose we apply the term of logical action to actions that logically enjoin means to ends not only from the point of view of the subject performing these, but from the standpoint of other persons who have more extensive knowledge—in other words to actions that are logical both subjectively and objectively in the sense just explained. Other actions we shall call nonlogical (by no means the same as illogical)."[7]

Actions are logical when they are "adequate"; this means that the choice of action has been guided by empirical consideration of goal achievement.

Irani fuses the normative ends with pragmatic ends in defining rationality: "Rationality in action implies the adoption of appropriate means to acceptable ends and to balance them when they are in conflict. This implies the ability to recognize and evaluate relevant evidence."[8]

The choice of a goal or an option may be even a result of astrological fantasies. But once a decision is made, its implementation may be logical in terms of the workability of means even though the goal itself might have originated in a haphazard manner.

Rationalism is of course also a broader concept. It meant and it means control of human actions by reason. Hence, rational action is logical in choice of means.

But rational means also a disciplined control of emotions, a search for truth by a systematical intellectual effort. The supreme rule of reason, at least for philosophers of the Enlightenment, involves also an ethical judgment that imposes moral limits on human action. We shall use the term *rational* in its narrower sense, that of a logical-rational choice of means. However, the logical conduct per se is not necessarily moral. Logical conduct might be (in terms of our ethos) moral, amoral, or immoral.

To conclude, once an awareness in the form of a desire, wish, or need appears, whether consciously or not, man begins to search or outline in his mind targets or perhaps only vague goals of his future action. It is at this stage of the imaginative process that the goals or thoughts of action are formed. A popular saying, "I shall figure this out," expresses this process of imaginative thinking and relating facts and figuring the consequences or effects.

Goals are related to action, and in a rational process probabilities of success, of goal achievement, are considered. From this stage of imaginary goals we move to decision making. In the rational, educated political or economic decision-making process of a government, the stage we called imagination takes form of a careful study and listing of options; this process of imagination of goals and policies is usually carried out by a group of advisers, experts, and decision makers and extended to a further exchange of views and evaluation of probabilities of effects. The goal becomes real once actions that may secure goal achievement are marshaled. There is of course a difference between actions and goal achievement, and the desired goal may never be achieved or may produce different, unexpected results. In case of action frustration, action might be repeated or substituted.

Notes

1. Bronislaw Malinowski, *A Scientific Theory of Culture* (Chapel Hill: University of North Carolina Press, 1944), pp. 75 ff. 90, 91 ff.

2. Ibid., pp. 77 ff.

3. Ibid., pp. 108 ff.

4. Ibid., pp. 125 ff.

5. Ibid., p. 171, "The Theory of Needs," and p. 137, "The Instrumentally Implemented Vital Sequence."

6. Edward McCurdy, *The Mind of Leonardo da Vinci* (New York: Dodd, Mead & Co., 1940), p. 182.

7. Vilfredo Pareto, *The Mind and Society*, edited by Alfred Livingston and translated by Andrew Bongiorno and Arthur Livingston with the cooperation of John Harvey Rogers. (New York: Harcourt & Brace, 1935), vol. 1, p. 77.

8. K. D. Irani, "Rationality in Thought and Action" (manuscript, 1981).

8

Horizontal Sequence of Goals: Goals and Incentives

Horizontal Goal Structure

At this point we shall separate the last links of our sequence of goal formation, the sequence that begins with need or stimulus (see Table 7.1) and shall concentrate attention exclusively on decision → action → goals. We shall return to or reduce the complex analytical model to the initial elementary one (see figure 6.1). This separation is also relevant in terms of immediate (proximate) causality, which precipitates action. The goals associated with the will that the goal generates becomes an antecedent (a cause, in our daily terminology); actions, in turn, become a sequent or an effect. Information about the antecedent permits a hypothesis, an educated guess about the sequent and vice versa. Information about an antecedent (decision) suggests the nature of a future sequent (course of action) to be taken; again, observation of actions (sequents) suggests what may be called ''an educated or informed guess'' about the cause (decision). Relevant goals are organized in patterns called projects or plans. Goals are plotted in terms of time and space and can be visualized as temporary stations on a linear, horizontal action path. We shall call such a sequence a horizontal value or goal structure (see figure 8.1). The time space is indicative of relevance or of pragmatic considerations.

Horizontal Goal Structure

A project can be visualized as a linear, horizontal path divided into stages, or segments. Stages are courses of actions directed toward stage goals. The time distance of stage goals is determined by their nature, relevance, function, risks, and conditions of success. Goals, which can be achieved at a set time, might be not available anymore later: for example, a deadline for a grant application, opportunities in business, an opportune political situation in foreign policy plan-

Figure 8.1
Horizontal Goal Structure

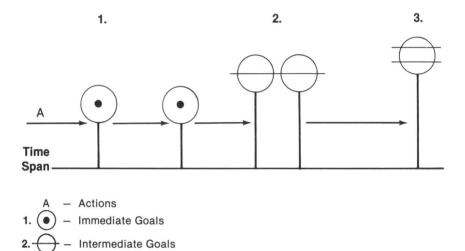

A   — Actions
1. (•) — Immediate Goals
2. ⊖ — Intermediate Goals
3. ⊖ — Distant Goals

ning. In consequence, on a horizontal line and in terms of time distance we shall divide goals into immediate, intermediate, and distant.

In terms of function, goals plotted on a horizontal line may be instrumental or consummatory. Goals are instrumental when achievement of those goals is a condition of the next step, of the next stage, and eventually of achievement of the end goal and completion of the project. The final or consummatory goal depends on completing the intermediary stages and achievement of instrumental goals which are tantamount to means.

A consummatory goal is the end goal of a project; it is the desired and projected end. An end goal of a project may be only a stage of a wider plan (see chapter 6).

However, goals may be plotted on a horizontal line in terms of time and priorities, and they may be unrelated to a distant objective. Hence, goals are independent and at the same time consummatory, when achievement of immediate and intermediate goals is not necessarily related to the achievement of a distant objective. Contrariwise, goals are interdependent and instrumental at the same time when attainment of immediate or intermediate goals is a condition of successful achievement of distant goals. An entrance examination is an immediate and instrumental stage for a student to reach instrumental intermediate goals— to complete required courses—in order to reach the consummatory goal of his stage of life: his college education.

This horizontal approach and perception of man's activities is a dynamic one. An observer perceives an actor moving from one goal to the next, from immediate to intermediate to distant. They are the milestones of his actions.

We have divided goals in a horizontal sequence into:

1. immediate, intermediate, distant
2. instrumental and consummatory
3. independent and interdependent

However, those divisions do not indicate the nature or the content of goals.

Targets and Generalized Ideological Goals

In terms of the content of goals we shall distinguish the pragmatic or concrete targets from generalized, ideological goals. This division appears in historical, social movements, especially in political ideological movements. Pragmatic, concrete promises of reward, concrete targets, are usually put as immediate or intermediate goals. We shall call them targets, in distinction from the broad, visionary promise of a perfect state or society, a vision of social salvation, the eighteenth century utopias of a perfectly organized society or more practical and equally visionary nineteenth-century plans. Those generalized goals appear in political ideologies as distant goals.

The generalized goals are at times akin to the religious visions of a new millennium which were carried by movements called chiliastic, (from the Greek *Khiliastos*). Sometimes broad, general goals prompted mankind into new eras, guided movements of emancipation of serfs, and slaves, guided general improvements of work conditions toward more social justice as well as peace. They were productive, chiliastic visions.

The generalized value-goals are primarily ideological in the sense that they are related to ideas of ''what ought to be'' and standards of right and wrong. A generalized value-goal, such as progress, socialism, or democracy, is symbolic and therefore normative. It represents a vision, a proposed social system, rather than a concrete objective. In consequence, its achievement or lack of achievement cannot be verified empirically or inductively. The evaluation of achievement is usually made by comparing it with an ideal type of social system. The empirical hypothesis, which is subject to testing against data derived from observation or experiment, is displaced here by a normative definition of a social system or theory (see chapter 6). (This difference in validation between normative, generalized goals and targets has been already discussed chapter 1.)

Concrete *targets* (or pragmatic goals) are practical and empirical, individual or social objectives (for instance, the establishment of an eight-hour working day.) Their attainment can be validated by what we may call a pragmatic test, the evidence of result. We test the workability of a policy and consider that if the individuals attain their goal, operationally the actions were effective.

The eight-hour working day is a target of a socialist ideology, while land reform is a target of an agrarian democracy. Socialism and agrarian democracy are generalized value-goals. Concrete targets are frequently derived from broad ideology and are also normatively and culturally determined. We may take a very concrete target—the construction of a road—that may be set forth as a social target. Determination to build the road may come from consideration of economic and environmental conditions, the peoples' values, and the political program, or military plans.

Distinction between those two types of goals appears in verification: Achievement or nonachievement of generalized goals is tested against a priori definitions of an ideology. Targets are tested against concrete data of achievement or non-achievement of such pragmatic goals: here achievement or nonachievement of an eight-hour day.

The normative goals, however, are articulated also in targets: construction of churches, chapels, cathedrals, houses of parliament, monuments to political leaders.

Hence, in a very broad sense, intermediate goals of political programs are instrumental. They are means and articulations of those distant normative goals. In this sense, targets and normative generalized goals are at times mutually interdependent.

The normative goals (or the generalized goals of political ideology) supply the sense of direction and invigorate the will of individuals, mobilize collective action, which we call mass movement.

Mass Appeal of Targets and Generalized Goals

Elaborate political idea systems and their programs have an arsenal of symbolic goals and targets. Their appeal depends on the nature of the situation on one hand and on the group to which the appeal is directed on the other. In times of relative stability of the system, concrete targets are usually effective in affecting political behavior, for example, voting. The targets were and are usually located in the so-called minimum program of the historical ideological parties, for example, socialist parties of Europe or in platforms of American parties (see figure 3.3). Here are the goals that the party promises to deliver within the next parliamentary or congressional periods. Why do the targets work? They do appeal directly to individual interest and at the same time to value symbols (for example, social justice). They are in fact priorities associated with an appealing reward system, for example, minimum wages, affirmative action, eight-hour working day, lower taxes. The social targets appeal to the voters, while there is a high degree of public faith in the stability and workability of the social political system, its ability to change or to deliver the targeted objectives. The minimum program's emphasis is near or immediate rewards; hence its attractive quality and dynamism of immediate goals. American unions in times of strikes are typical here. The goal is simple: "more." The targets are usually well defined in terms of salaries, working time, or fringe benefits, while generalized goals—broad, symbolic ends of a new, different society—are absent. The first questions an American leader may ask about are, How do you get there? Where do you begin? And what shall I get out of it? Thus immediate goals with substantial rewards attached are the motivating incentive of resolute strike action.

While the targets—immediate goals—appeal in times of relative stability of the social and political system, appeal of the symbolic ends (the generalized goals) increases when there is instability of the system, when it breaks down, especially in times of revolutions. At such time the faith in the working of the existing political system is declining. Self-indentification with the political system and loyalty grow weaker, and in consequence, legitimacy of power is affected too. New values and idea systems (or revived ancient ones) gain, since substantial sections believe that collective and individual targets as well as symbolic ends cannot be met anymore by the present political system, and only an entirely new political, social, and economic system has the capacity to deliver material, civic, as well as moral rewards. At such a time distant symbolic ends advanced by theoreticians, ideologists, and activists begin to affect sections of society. The existing system does not provide security anymore, or at least the perception of personal and group insecurity prompts individuals and groups to support and struggle for a new system, which would provide security. Achievement of one or more immediate goals would not do anymore. Moreover, perhaps the latter cannot be achieved within the existing system. Hence symbolic ends, representing a vision of a new, ideal society, increase in their effective mass appeal. It is in those times of revolution and social upheaval that the symbolic representations of the future appear as a practical alternative or as a necessary, perhaps the only feasible, answer.

An appeal of social return to utopias of the past, to a previous stage, an ancient and glorified religious, economic, and idealized political system, one that secures rewards to certain classes or sections of societies, had similar effects in times of destabilization as did utopias of the future. In those cases change, progressive reform, is perceived as a threat to individual and group security, and indeed it may in fact be a real threat.

At the end of the nineteenth century as Moslem religious revolt in Sudan was led by Mahdi against the British. The British rule and abolition of slavery, associated with this colonial government were indeed a threat to economic security and privileges of the substantial slave-trading class in Sudan, to the Moslem clergy, and to those natives who profited from the slave economy—and they were many. Mahdi's appeal to religious revival, even fanaticism, was well loaded with political, economic, and, in terms of the actors, religious and moral rewards.

The trading classes—in case of a victory—would retain their economic primacy and slave commerce; the Moslem clergy would keep its full control; and the native rulers would maintain their political power. Religious incentives should not be underestimated. Again, the latter have to be considered in terms of idea systems, modes of thought of the actors in terms of their thinking habits and doctrines, not ours.

Mutatis mutandis—the situation in Iran in December 1979 is instructive. The revolutionary process, no doubt, was well advanced. Leaders (or part of them) succeeded in their appeal to return to their past utopia, to a belief system that, they hoped, would give them security, to values that remained powerful in spite of outward acceptance of material comforts and some of the ways of industrial societies. Women took on their traditional and unattractive garb, symbolic of subservience and inferior status, and some did it with enthusiasm, to an amazement of those who believed that quest for emancipation is a natural propensity of man.

In times of political and economic stability utopias of the past or future are interesting curios, exhibits of man's imagination: Some belong to an intellectual museum. But utopias transform society in times of revolutions and from a social myth change into reality. Society moves at such times toward the chiliastic goals of a perfect society. Events and complex social tendencies may move in many directions. One road may pave new ways toward a better society—on the road of progress, invented by philosophers and prompted by social movements. But utopias may move also on another road, at times as distant from the imaginative dreams of philosophers and prophets as the dungeons of the Inquisition were once from the Essenic ideals of a Christian community.

And now let us consider the pragmatic goals, targets, and generalized or symbolic goals in terms of their static and dynamic quality.

In an analysis of their static, "anatomical" structure we shall ask above all a question: Where are targets and symbolic goals located in a political ideology? In a dynamic approach the question is, How are they plotted on a horizontal line, in a horizontal goal structure?

This brings us back to our analysis of a political idea systems (Figure 3.3). Here the generalized, symbolic appeal resides in core values (at the very top) as well as in the general philosophy of the movement. In a more concrete form symbolic goals form the vision of the maximum program. Targets are located at the very bottom; they form in turn the core, the powerful appeal of the minimum program.

Now, we shall turn to the horizontal structure, to Figure 8.1. Targets appear in this model as immediate and intermediate goals; the generalized goals are the distant ones.

Preferred Goals: Priorities

This horizontal structure of goals—spacing of immediate, intermediate, and distant objectives in time—is not only an academic and purely theoretical assumption. It is also a rational and logical way of projecting individual and collective goals. At times this type of projecting is spontaneous; in political or economic planning, however, projecting of goals in terms of sequence of goals has to be carefully considered, effects anticipated, providing of course that the planners are rational and plot their action in terms of logical-empirical sequences.

A detailed case of goal structure in an Italian village may serve as an example of a horizontal goal structure related to actual needs; it furthers discussion on priorities and incentives.

The tenant farmers and the farmers, as much as the laborers in this village, we shall call it Bonagente, belonged to the major Italian parties. Most of them were Social Democrats, Communists, or Christian Democrats. In spite of diversity of politics, they seemed to be clearly distinguishing between three types of goals: (1) immediate, (2) intermediate, (3) distant. The distant goals represented the broad social vision or affiliations, broad social symbols such as social justice, equality, freedom. The immediate political and social-economic goals were pragmatic targets: roads, water, and electricity. Whether we discussed the problems of the community with the Communists, or the Christian Democrats, or the Social Democrats, the answer concerning the immediate goals was almost always the same; in spite of strong party differences, they agreed that these were the most urgent problems of the community. Some gave preference to water; others, to roads. These were what may be called preferential goals. As an intermediate value-goal, land was usually mentioned: improvement of land or distribution. The views of the members of the three major parties differed on the intermediate and distant goals. Some were for land reform without indemnity, whereas others believed that the present owners should be paid for their land. The distant goals were vague, expressing social myths or visions that they could not elaborate in a more definite way. They were, however, presented in a form of recognized and established symbols.[1]

In this case the general goal structure was independent: achievement of the intermediate (land distribution) or distant goals (a socialist state or social justice, although the latter was vague) was not determined by the immediate (roads, water, electricity). As mentioned, the immediate goals were preferential. The actors and the group suffered because of deficient water supply, bad roads, absence of inexpensive electric energy (above all, absence of adequate light, refrigeration and the like). All those needs were perceived, moreover experienced and later discussed at political meetings. All were logical and attainable within the existing political, economic, and social system.

We may postulate a situation when an actor desires several goals. However, in terms of his potentialities, he is unable to achieve all of them. Furthermore, achievement of one of them (or a few) at this very time may preclude success in attainment of the others. In such a situation the actor selects a goal or goals he considers (a) being the most relevant, (b) being the most advantageous, (c) having the highest probability of success, or (d) having the least risk. The goals selected are preferred (or preferential) goals. Some choice is exercised in selection of means. Means chosen that way are called "preferred courses of action." Preferential value goals are *definite* when the choice of a goal precludes achievement of nonselected goals; they may be only *delayed* when the selection of priority does not preclude their achievement. In our case selection of preferential goals was considered solely as delayed.

The choice of immediate goals signifies in this case, as well as in others, that the urgency of needs or relevance of those goals and values prompts the actor to assign to those goals priority in relation to intermediate and distant goals. Priorities are goals that must be met in the shortest, immediate time span. In a linear goal structure they precede all the other goals, plotted in terms of time distances. In terms of advantage they are not necessarily the most profitable. However, they are preferential in terms of urgency or relevance.

Proper assignment of priorities is a test of efficiency and wisdom. The choice between "important" and "unimportant" may be considered as test of intelligence. It distinguishes a statesman from a minor politician. Yes, but what is relevant and what is not are also relative.

Emperor Bokassa of the impoverished "Central African Empire" spent a substantial part of this empire's budget to purchase in France for himself an ornate throne, crown, uniforms for his guards, and other paraphernalia. All those artifacts had a high priority in terms of his coronation, a direct articulation of his drive for power. What was relevant in terms of his interest and values was irrelevant for the welfare of his poverty-stricken subjects. Thus, priorities and preferred goals are directly or indirectly connected with sets of values, ideology, and personality of the decision makers.

Goal—Incentives

The horizontal goal structure appears in our daily life. It is applied spontaneously, as a matter of repeated routine or after careful planning in elaborate projects, so as to trigger or intensify our activity in economic production or in political struggle. Goals set the direction of our actions and are incentives at the same time. They affect and reinforce our will to act.

First, we shall begin with a short discussion of the types and content of incentives, and then in the next section we shall return to the ways that goals or incentives are plotted in a project, in terms of time and type. Selecting and plotting of those goals have a definite purpose: To increase productivity, to intensify our actions. Hence goal incentives are plotted in terms of immediate or intermediate and distant goals, independent or interdependent. Incentives in turn vary in their nature: They appear in a variety of content and in diverse association. Hence incentives are pragmatic-utilitarian or normative, positive or negative, single or fused. Man applies a variety of goal incentives and administers their combination in his attempts to achieve his economic, political, or ideological goals.

Goals, as we have said before, correspond to needs. They are formed as a reaction to outside stimuli; furthermore they may be as well a fruit of our creative mind. But we may realize the need, visualize the goals, and do nothing. Goals may continue to exist only in our imagination unless there is a will to act, a will to change. It is the incentive, primarily the expectation of reward or gratification, but also the sentiment of fulfillment of duty, that triggers or reinforces the will. Incentives vary in their intensity. In an economic enterprise profit is the incentive and can be measured precisely in terms of dollars and cents. The higher the profit—or the lower the risk—the stronger the incentive is. In a political struggle future exercise of political power may be the incentive. Political power means control of instruments of power, symbolic or material instruments essential in decision making and in enforcing decisions. Political power is often instrumental, not consummatory. The conquest of political power is instrumental in social reform. Even such obvious reform as establishment of social security cannot be achieved without political power.

In our daily life incentives are reward systems inherent in our goals; or to put it in reverse, we may assume that goals that do result in dynamic action are associated with strong rewards and expectations of satisfaction of our needs. Urgency of needs on one hand and quality and quantity of reward on the other reinforce the will to act, mobilize our will to coordinate efforts toward the goal. We may call this type of incentive a positive one. On the other hand, fear of punishment may also increase the incentive. A worker who is threatened with the loss of his job as a consequence of low productivity may increase his effort. We shall call such an incentive a negative one.

But intense need or biological urge affects the incentive in the same way. A low wage in a hunger-stricken area may supply a stronger incentive than a higher wage in a community in which high wages and easy access to food and commodities prevail. Man may manipulate punishment or reward (positive and negative incentives), and manipulation of both is associated with the intensity of incentives. At the other end of this, what Malinowski called the vital sequence, the need may be reinforced or manipulated, the drive channeled toward action. The need may be reinforced by advertising or by increasing direct pressure by means of force and deprivation. Hunger and fear are negative incentives.

The reward (or incentive or goal) system is closely related to the entire situation within which it operates. It is related to the needs, values, and goals of the actors, to the social context within which his needs appear, to the ways the needs are satisfied. Because of this close relationship with other variables, especially with culture, it is difficult to set simple and universal rules that control the intensity of incentives. A string of glass beads in times of Stanley and Livingstone could prompt strong incentives in the Congo and reinforce the will to serve as porters, but the same string of beads would not move a dockworker to lift a piece of merchandise in London at this time. Nonetheless, some general approximations, based on our daily and commonsense experience, are well known to all of us.

It seems that those incentives directly or indirectly related to our basic needs, to biological needs, are strong and universal. However, we cannot reduce the entire mechanism of incentives or wishes to basic needs. Nonetheless, the basic needs and urgency of their satisfaction are elementary. The stronger the needs, the more intense the incentive becomes. Incentives of higher economic gain, or higher gain by a lesser effort, are indirectly—and at times directly—related to this elementary mechanism of need satisfaction. Even when higher incomes and high standards of living cut loose this immediate relationship, which may be observed in a primitive economy, still the ancient, elementary sequence seems to continue in the modern society of high technology and comfort. We may not feel the immediate danger of hunger; an increase in income may mean an increase in luxury. Nonetheless, some kind of ancient, primitive insecurity is there. We shall call this entire category of incentives pragmatic or utilitarian. Higher salary is in this category, which deals primarily with material rewards. However, shorter working hours or preference in education also belong to the same category.

It is obvious, of course, that in our economic activities the appeal to individual and material rewards is seminal. We work in order to eat and live in the way that makes us more comfortable or happy. An economic system, a factory, cannot expect high productivity on low positive rewards. Shoes cannot be produced on enthusiasm and appeals to party loyalty by workers who are hungry and do not share the political religion of their leaders. However, canals can be built on positive incentives—on good wages and plenty of food, as the Panama Canal was built by American enterprise—or on negative: forced labor and punishment—Peter the Great built his capital city and Stalin his collossal waterways (see chapters 10–11). Material rewards and the general category of utilitarian and pragmatic incentives are both individual, since they do appeal to individual interests and needs, and they are social when shared by a group action in a similar or the same situation and result into group expression.

Of course, material rewards are not the only source of our incentives, not the sole way toward gratification. Normative and cultural goals have provided a powerful motivation throughout history. Normative imperatives—ethical, esthetic, ideological principles or standards—do and did affect our decisions and the intensity of our actions.

In our daily parlance we usually make a distinction between"moral" and "material" incentives. But what we call moral encompasses a far larger area than the moral and ethical norms. Normative imperatives—ethical, esthetic, ideological—provided a powerful motivation in our history. Economic incentives and goals are often associated with the former. However, neither Mozart nor Chopin (nor so many others) was guided by utilitarian incentives or solely by what we call material goals. This world would be an ugly, evil, and dull place indeed if material gain and political power alone had shaped our destiny and culture.

Many sculptures and paintings of the medieval cathedral are located in distant or hidden corners of those immense architectural structures. I realized this rather suddenly climbing the Tower of Pisa. I noticed a number of details of the adjacent cathedral, details difficult, perhaps even impossible, to notice from the green square, from the ground level. Only part of them were visible from the tower; others were hidden from human eye unless one climbed the walls and the roof. Think about the artists who did this work, located somewhere in the cornices of the Cathedral of Florence. Who will see or notice the art of those details or decorations?

What kind of incentives mobilized the will and energies of those artists? Was it only money or purely utilitarian ends? Of course those artists were not indifferent to money and distinctions, for they had to earn a living, for some a comfortable one. The strong motives, however, were supplied by esthetic, normative rewards. It was the will, striving toward excellence and perfection, loyalty to an ethos that this hidden art expresses. Millennia of art testify to the presence and existence of rewards stronger than or as strong as material rewards or utilitarian satisfaction. Principles and values—artistic, esthetic, and moral—were the guides of mankind in moments of its greatness.

The rewards of work well done, high-quality products, their utilitarian but also artistic aspects, were widely shared by medieval artisans and are still present in crafts all over the world.

Scientific instruments of the Renaissance as well as of the baroque period are at times masterpieces of art, not of utility only. The beauty of antique instruments, not solely their utility, strikes a visitor at the Museum of Science in Florence. They, too, fuse two standards: utility, the pragmatic one; and esthetic, the cultural or normative.

At this point we shall make a distinction between single and fused incentives. Single incentives are associated with a single, at times powerful, type of goal or reward; for example, economic, such as profit or salary. Fused incentives are associated with several different types of rewards. Fused incentives are probably the optimal and most efficient in the modern postindustrial society.

What I perceive here as an association, a fusion of incentives, appears probably to an actor as a single goal that—only in a close evaluation or analysis—consists of several diverse goal rewards. Goal systems are associated with a variety of material and normative rewards, with ethical or esthetic gratification.

We shall assume a wide category of cultural and normative goals related to needs that are not—directly or indirectly—material, pragmatic utilitarian goals. There are motives hidden in our values or norms where reason meets with emotion; this border line is not subject to empirical observation and testing.

The imperative of duty (in its ideal form) is tantamount to a commitment not necessarily associated with rewards. Still, duty is a paramount incentive, a motivation toward a normative goal. Existence of a reward does not negate or diminish the relevance of reward-intensive goals, as well as strong appeal and motivation whenever rewards are tantamount to a visible and obvious advantage.

To conclude, expectations associated with goals that reinforce the will to act are called incentives. Those expectations are either rewards or punishments. Incentives are positive when associated with rewards, negative when the expectation of punishment, expressed in fear, prompts the action. The positive incentives are associated with a will of achievement; the negative, with fear and avoidance.

Fulfillment of duty—serving an ideal or normative system, achieving a normative goal—is also an incentive. In man's economic activity the normative, positive incentives are not sufficient. However, fused with economic rewards, they have formed in the past incentive-intensive goals.

Thus reward-intensive goals can be either of a single type or of a fused, associated with diverse types of incentives.

Horizontal Goal Sequence as a Pattern of Gradual Rewards

The actor moves from one goal to the next, and this sequence supplies dynamism to projects. Goals prompt our action.

The horizontal goal sequence lends itself to a variety of incentive patterns. Either those patterns are a consequence of the very nature of the project, or the pattern is intentionally plotted to prompt the action, to increase productivity by manipulation of the incentives. We shall postulate that the horizontal sequence of goal rewards suggests a number of combinations of diverse intensity. By such combinations efficiency can increase or decline.

Goals as incentives can be plotted in a variety of ways: at this point four patterns are outlined (later we shall list eight).

First, the initial or intermediate goals call for sacrifice; the end, consummatory goal is associated with major reward. It is the distant or final payoff associated with the consummatory goal that supplies incentive to action throughout the entire project. In such a case, priorities are instrumental and necessary steps of a project. All goals are interdependent. The achievement of immediate or intermediate goals opens the road toward a reward system. Organization of a union is a high priority for workers on a plant. Once this priority is met, a strike may follow. A successful strike leads to negotiation and, in consequence, a salary increase. Thus, the workers of the plant moved through four steps: (1) immediate goals, organization, is associated with sacrifice (firings and the like) and no reward; (2) intermediate goal, strike, is associated with no reward and sacrifice in pay; (3) intermediate goal, negotiation, is neutral and carries no reward; (4) distant, consummatory goal, salary increase, is associated with reward. Rewards are associated with the last stage or contract. In consequence of a strike or negotiation, the priorities—in this case, paying union dues or striking—called for sacrifice as a condition of higher rewards.

Do those initial goals have no reward? Definitely no material reward. However, some kind of normative incentive is present. The union supplies a general ideology, a set of values of solidarity action. It is a utilitarian value, true; its utility is obvious, tangible. Nonetheless, it is there. This type of incentive pattern calls for ideological support. The entire combination has fused incentives: initial, noneconomic; consummatory, economic.

In the second pattern all the goals of a project as a horizontal sequence are associated with material rewards of various intensity. The end goal, however, suggests the largest share, the most attractive rewards. Goals may be independent or interdependent.

In the third pattern immediate and intermediate goals are associated with basic rewards (satisfaction of biological needs); the end goal is punitive. This pattern fuses negative and positive incentives.

In the Siberian Tayga, in those forests of the Soviet Northeast, a shrewd although harsh goal-incentive structure was instituted, probably in the early days of Stalin's rule. The system was in force in 1940–1943, when the forced labor camps were filled with Polish citizens, rounded up and deported en masse, under military and police guards, after the Soviet armies, allied at that time with Hitler's Germany, occupied the eastern provinces of the republic. The same incentive pattern was applied also to Soviet forced laborers.

The forced laborers were paid in food and small amounts of money. Initial allotments were very low, not sufficient to satisfy their daily needs. The workers were hungry. But after a short time of a few weeks, production quotas were set and associated with food and monetary reward. Those who delivered higher quotas received more food. Again, in a few weeks rewards were higher; quotas increased. But by now the higher rewards called for physical strength and intense effort. Many could not make it. The process of selection began. And so it went for six months: At every stage quotas were increased. Still less could make the quota, and more were left on lower allotments. After six months the project came to an end. All—the most efficient workers and the slow ones—had to start from the beginning, from the lowest level, and the pay was the same for all. After a few weeks quotas were set again, then increased gradually. It was a cyclical pattern. A new cycle began every six months.

The initial quotas were tantamount to a starvation diet. A slave worker faced the choice between the pain of fatigue and overwork on one hand or hunger on the other hand. He could be relatively well fed and dead tired or less tired and dead hungry.

The normative parameter was in this case displaced; the pragmatic (efficiency), maximized. The project was plotted in terms of intermediary goals on a path, carefully distributed over a time span of six months. None of those goals was instrumental for the workers. All of them, immediate or intermediate, were consummatory in their nature, and the final goal after the six-month stage was punishment, not reward: All rewards for work were cancelled. Hence, with every stage, rewards were increased. But all those stages led to the end goal of punishment.

For the planners the project had a different meaning in terms of rewards. The purpose of the entire project was solely to increase efficiency and production. For the planners there was not a six-month consummatory goal—only a series of intermediary goals of various intensity, all of them instrumental in terms of the annual quota of the camp. The annual quota of the project was the consummatory target. The mechanism of this horizontal goal-reward sequence was simple.

Three needs were competing in this slave work gang: hunger, physical fatigue, and craving for sleep. Satisfaction of the former could be made only at the expense of the two latter. At first, hunger was strong. During the first stages craving for food was more intensive than the two others. With intensive and extended work, hunger was satisfied by those who made the quota, but fatigue and the craving for rest and sleep was growing stronger and advanced to a preferential position. At the last stages work was slowing down. Many were tired, but not yet intensely hungry. Fatigue became more intense. The decision to slow down and rest was chosen at the expense of hunger. For the planner now the project was not fully efficient anymore. Less wood was cut, as fatigue set in. In order to increase efficiency, the need had to be increased, manipulated. Intensification of hunger was a sure device. Hence hunger was manipulated. It was at this point that the gradual, higher quotas were terminated abruptly. Now all workers were reduced again to a single status—of a lowest food ration. Now the hunger in turn grew stronger than the craving for sleep and rest. The high priority of survival in this subarctic climate prompted the choices and priorities: Bread and soup moved again ahead of rest and sleep as a top priority with an urgency. To delay the satisfaction of hunger was painful. So the system worked again for those who survived; rations were increased with the delivered quotas. A full cycle lasted six months, which was probably the maximum, rather than the optimum, of its workability. An efficient system is not necessarily moral. Contrary to economic theories, the slave system had its application in an industrial age, and it had its rules of efficiency.

The weakness of Stalin's reward system was in its hiatus between ideal and real. The ideal—and the propaganda slogan—was normative. Workers were supposed to produce because—in theory—they owned the industry (as much as I own the Brooklyn Navy Yard). Others were to produce in the interest of a communist state. But in an enterprise that produces goods and is guided by economic standards of efficiency, rewards must be geared to those economic imperatives. Goals consist of fused rewards: Civic, exclusively normative incentives do not work in a factory or in a coal mine. It is a matter of experience—an obvious thing—that good work calls also for a share of economic rewards. The breakdown of positive incentives resulted into another extreme: forced labor, the lifting of normative imperatives. Goals and rewards are not separate blocs either. They are part of the entire fabric of the system within which they were formed or imposed. (We shall return to this subject in chapters 10 and 11 on planning.)

This type of goal sequence was practiced in ancient Rome: Gladiators were well fed and pampered before the circus performance. But the end goal for most of them was a cruel and unnecessary death. One could call this pattern the gladiator's sequence.

The fourth pattern is one plotted on a horizontal line, with rewards increasing with every subsequent goal, but with a reward and no punishment at the end.

Actually eight or more goal incentive patterns can be plotted:

1. sequence of equal rewards, assigned to all goals (intermediate and distant): (for example, a monthly salary)
2. sequence of increasing rewards with every following step of goal achievement (higher rewards with increasing productivity)
3. sequence of equal intermediate rewards and high consummatory payoff
4. sequence of equal intermediate rewards and low consummatory payoff (for example, a handyman on a monthly salary with a low retirement benefit)
5. sequence of increasing intermediate rewards and high consummatory payoff (for example, a corporation president, with an increasing monthly salary and a high bonus for completion of a project)
6. sequence of increasing intermediate rewards and low consummatory payoff (the teacher's sequence: increasing salary and half-salary retirement)
7. sequence of increasing intermediate rewards and consummatory punishment (the gladiator's sequence)
8. sequence of no intermediate rewards and a high consummatory payoff.

We shall limit the combination of patterns of those eight. However, far more could be plotted, especially by fusing incentives.

Time Span as Related to Self-Discipline

In all those quite diverse cases discussed above, *the structure* of goals was similar, if not identical. It was a horizontal model; that is, a number of interdependent or independent goals were projected in time: Some of them were instrumental, while others were consummatory. The time span between need decision and expected goal achievement or satisfaction is relevant, at times crucial, in all those cases. It is seminal in individual projects as much as in social planning. Decision in a situation may depend on those rough estimates: How long will it take?

We may suggest a hypothesis: The shorter the expected time span between the commencement of action (decision) and the projected goal achievement, the stronger the incentive to act. The intensity of incentives is increased by reducing the time span toward goal achievement (expected reward and satisfaction). Delaying of goals or rewards weakens the incentive to act.

The time span affects to a lesser degree an actor whose goals are associated with normative rewards, with values, especially with single normative orientations. In this case the idea system supplies the permanence, the structure. Religious goals in history supplied an architecture of goals of unusual strength and distance (see chapter 14). Secular idea systems at times are related to religion; here belong utopian, visionary political ideologies. The leadership of movements motivated by such vision in our times was willing to sacrifice a generation for the sake of the next one. This generation must endure misery and slavery for the sake of freedom and happiness of the next. Such a goal structure and idea system supply also legitimacy for political power and license in its exercise. The few of the central committee get an immediate reward—political power and economic privilege—at the very onset of this voyage to the distant uptopia.

But goals compete, and an actor has to choose between competitive goals. The urge of basic needs or attraction of material and monetary rewards is powerful. In consequence one must exercise will, the will to postpone or sacrifice immediate rewards in order to attain more distant (at times), normative goals. We call discipline or self-discipline such an exercise of will in control of drives, urges, and incentives. Self-discipline is a learned behavior of self-control. The child is born with capacities to learn to exercise the latter, but it is not born with it. It is a result of experience and learning, which begin quite early and not solely by a punishment and reward system, but by experience and also by imitation. In time of adolescence a variety of initiation rites in traditional societies, requiring endurance or even pain, are (in terms of one of their functions) exercises and tests of self-discipline.

Self-discipline affects the goal sequence and priorities. Self-control permits extension of goals and also construction of such a goal sequence in which the distant goals dominate the entire path. It reverses or modifies the general rule that the shorter the time span between action and reward, decision and expectation of goal achievement, the stronger and more intensive are the incentives, the stronger the will to act. Due to self-discipline, immediate, "visible" goals can be delayed or surrendered for the sake of achievement of distant goals. Distant goals are in such a case the preferred ones.

Great, complex civilizations were built by extension of goals. In hunting and gathering cultures, goals are short and close to immediate needs.

Notes

1. For an extensive discussion of goal structure in an Italian village see: Feliks Gross, *IL PAESE*, Values and Social Change in an Italian Village, with a Preface by Vittorio Castellano (New York: New York University Press and University of Rome, 1973), pp. 59-120.

9

Strategies

Strategy and Tactics

We shall define the term *strategy* as an art and method of achieving individual and collective goals. Strategic goals are achieved by a combination of actions. Thus goal and actions form the two major components of strategies. Actions are also called means, and goals are called ends, for we use the term *strategy* in its broad and contemporary meaning and use. Originally it was a term connected solely with military action. Today, however, we speak about strategy in politics, in games, or even in achievement of personal goals. The meaning of this term has changed considerably; it has been broadened.

Hence, strategy is a pragmatic relationship between ends and means. Means are "efficient" when their choice results in achievement of ends. They are more or less efficient depending on the proper quantitative and qualitative choice of actions, quantity or quality of effort, and the resources necessary to the successful achievement of goals.

Strategy is a pragmatic design. Strategy deals with identification of efficient means in achieving goals. Hence strategy is concerned with economy of human effort in achieving desired ends. Its purpose is to achieve the best results or desired goals with the least effort, resources, and losses.

Seldom if ever are strategic goals achieved by a single thrust. Thus the road or design toward achievement of the strategic goal is plotted in terms of inter-mediary stages that are oriented toward immediate and intermediate target goals (objectives). Stage objectives are interdependent goals: Successful achievement of one stage objective is a condition of achieving the next one. A strategic design plots actions stage by stage. Immediate and intermediate target goals are related to the end goal. They divide, however, the entire strategy into stages. The stage objectives are arrived at in turn by a combination of actions, movements within the stage. Those actions are attached to flexible goals. This combination of

Figure 9.1
Strategy and Tactics

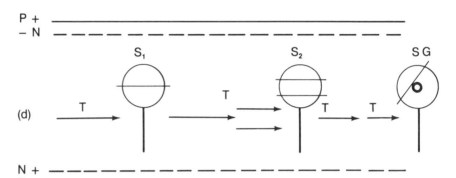

Strategy and tactics develops within pragmatic (P) and normative (N) boundaries (parameters). Strategy moves from (d) decision toward stage goals S_1, S_2. Every new stage is determined by previous stage goals (S_1, S_2) which are mutually interdependent. Every stage approaches the project toward the strategic goal SG; strategic goal sets the direction and purpose. Movements within the stage are tactics T T. Strategy and tactics develops within the pragmatic (efficiency) and the normative (ethics, law, customs) boundaries or parameters. Lowering or lifting the normative (movement toward − N) may increase the efficiency (pragmatic P +) and reverse.

coordinated actions with flexible goals is called *tactics*. Tactics is concerned with the current and continuously changing situation. Hence, tactics is flexible in terms of goals and actions.

Strategy is concerned with the overall direction and end goals. It is tantamount to general policies. Tactics, in turn, refers to the specific and detailed, to the intermediary actions and movement that are meaningful only in context of the strategies (see Figure 9.1). Thus the purpose of tactics is discovered and understood by identification of strategic goals, for tactical actions and goals are only components of an overall strategic design.

Strategic design is a general project or pattern that outlines the major direction of action, sequence of targets, and sets the central purpose: achievement of a strategic goal. It is a plan that charts the course of actions initiated by a decision maker.

The general structure of strategies follows the horizontal sequence. Strategies are plotted within the imperatives of the two parameters: the pragmatic and the normative. The normative parameter of strategies consists of "rules of the game," customs, usages and moral norms, values shared by partners and communities or considered as universal (*N* in Figure 9.1). Rules of the game are accepted norms of procedure, "the ways things are done," observed or to be observed in relationships, contests, or even conflicts within which strategic actions advance. Customs and usages may determine those procedures, not unlike what happens in a legal action.

But legal norms are not identical with moral. A moral norm encompasses a broader area of activities. In this section our discussion of imperatives (parameters) will be limited to normative (morals and legal) and pragmatic (governing higher or lower efficiency).

Moral and normative (in the broad sense) imperatives have an impact on the choice of effective actions, for they limit the number of options by eliminating those which are outside the "normative fence" and hence do not conform to moral commitments, to rules and customs.

Dialectics of the two imperatives affects the choice of means. Moral and pragmatic imperatives are at times contradictory or conflicting. In this conflict is the drama of choice and decision making. Total lifting of moral restraints was advised for two millennia by some major political and military writers or strategists as a way of maximizing efficiency of means.

Tactics are flexible, adjusted to changing situations. The strategic end goal and the general thrust of a given strategy are constant. What varies and should be considered as flexible are tactics and stages, their distribution in time and space, even their quality. Their sole purpose is to serve the strategic end.

Strategic goals in political projects of governments change seldom; their change is tantamount to the change of a general direction—more, of basic policy, even ideology (doctrine). Tactics change frequently since the situation within which a political actor operates is never static and changes all the time. Therefore identification of a strategy and differentiation of strategy from tactical goals are seminal for an understanding of an entire strategic design and a forecast of future actions. This is especially relevant in foreign policy analysis.

We shall use the term *strategy* for a logical and planned organization of goals and actions. The action is logical and empirical when means are adequate or have a probability of adequacy for achieving ends (see chapter 7). The goals might be conceived by a sick mind; they might even be irrational, conceived in a fit of hostility. However, the pattern of actions toward their achievement might be at the same time precise and logical, adequate for achieving the ends.

Thus strategy may be visualized as an organized, divided pathway, divided into stages and tactical events. Such a pathway is a structure, a mental image, or a projection of future actions. Strategies—military, political, or economic—affect the existing situation and result in maintenance or change of situation, relationships, and the entire system. They form a dynamic component of planned social change.

We have outlined a structure of goal-oriented actions, patterns that we called strategies. However, our discussion on strategy and rational actions toward goals calls for a caveat.

All strategies, and here belongs the military strategy or the foreign policy strategy too, are concerned with *plans*, intellectual attempts in designing ways that certain goals may be achieved. But they may never be achieved. Planning, projecting, and achieving are entirely different propositions. Nor do we postulate that such plans, or the selected path, are necessarily rigorously followed by the actor. Circumstances and accidents, changing situations, and man's own folly, emotions, or irrational reactions may change or abandon the routes of action; furthermore, goals may be not achievable or achieved by different ways.

In terms of our present discussion strategy is no more than a plan, a pattern of goals and actions, ways an actor intends to choose in order to reach his goals.

What an actor intends to do and what he does indeed may be two different things. Still, planning ahead, projecting in a rational way is the path to efficient approaching toward or achieving of goals.

Strategy of Armed Conflict Actions

War strategy is probably the most ancient, practical, and efficient theory of goals and actions; it is a conduct of a military enterprise with a central end goal: to break the will of the adversary, to destroy his army.

The aim of strategy in its early and also advanced, but ruthlessly pragmatic, concept is clear and definite. To quote Karl von Clausewitz, "War is thus an act of force to compel our adversary to do our will." The goal is victory, and Clausewitz's victory is unconditional, if not merciless; it follows primarily the pragmatic lines; the normative parameter, a system of ethical restraints or humane considerations is removed. Efficiency remains the guiding principle; efficiency here means defeat in the shortest time and a total one: "Victory consists not merely in the conquest on the battlefield, but in the destruction of physical and moral forces and this is usually attained only in the pursuit after the battle is won," continues Clausewitz.[1]

The desire of peace produced visions, utopias of a perfect world, which seldom, however, are workable. Peace did not generate an equally strong will, equal to that of war. The promise of a road to peace was through war, proclaimed too many times as the last one. Until perhaps the recent, post–World War II times, peace did not produce attempts for a workable theory and practice of strategy.

The strategy of peace does not culminate in a victory, triumphal, visible in its celebration. It does not, or should not, bring spoils and immediate rewards to victors. Perhaps because of it, theory and praxis of peace making did not generate powerful desires in political leaders of antiquity or of later historical periods.

However, Clausewitz's definition expresses views of one school. Liddell-Hart, a leading British military theoretician, defines the strategic objectives with considerations for a lasting peace settlement. He recommended magnanimity in victory rather than a defeat of total destruction. It is a strategy of restraints, of normative limits even in an enterprise as brutal as war.[2]

It is not our purpose to discuss in this section controversial issues of military theory. What is relevant for our subject matter is the very concept of this term, the very content of this word, its elementary, generally accepted meaning. In its original ancient Greek form *strategia* means military skills. Such is its meaning in Xenophon and Thucydides' writings. Military skills mean of course conduct of actions toward victory. Its general meaning points to careful selection of intermediate goals and effective actions directed toward the end goal—victory. It is the theory of goals and actions that interests us here, for a strategic plan in its structure corresponds to our horizontal goal structure. This is the basic model, generally applied in goal-oriented activities, strategy being a major one. Strategy is plotted in time and space. Immediate and intermediate goals must be reached before the end objective, victory with its rewards, is achieved. Strategic goals are targets, as they were defined below (see chapter 8). Defeat and victory are pragmatic, concrete objectives.

Furthermore, the courses of military action move within the two boundaries or parameters: the normative and the pragmatic. Reduction of the former increases a number of options and, in consequence, the probability of efficiency of the latter. Strategic goals and tactical aims form the directive system, while rules of warfare, customs, moral imperatives are normative considerations, and their relation to efficiency guides the regulatory apparatus. The relevance of the moral (normative) boundaries is also associated with the rewards attached to the strategic goal: The rewards, the spoils victors expect to get out of this violence enterprise.

The normative ethical parameter, a moral value structure of right and wrong is a fence which bars, elimates options conflicting with its imperatives or commands. It is a limiting factor, restricting the choice of offensive and effective means. A strong normative parameter of course, affects, the pragmatic one. Thus, the use of force and violence is restricted not only by moral imperatives and commands, but also by accepted and shared rules of the game, by international usage, as well as international conventions and law. At least in theory, civilized and humane government fighting defensive wars have fewer options than totalitarian ones (e.g., Hitler's Germany) and are limited in their choice of efficient means. Cruelty was at times (not always) efficient in breaking the will of nations.

There was a difference in the moral parameter between the Allied armies and the Nazi war machines during World War II, especially in their treatment of the civilian population. Of course, "war is hell," as a military leader once said. But, there are differences in patterns of warfare, in spite of the fact that it is plausible, to suggest that all wars are equally brutal and ruthless. The eighteenth century European wars of limited strategic objectives observed, for a short time, rules of military behavior, even customs of gallantry. There were limits set to total license and brutality.

The French Revolution originated the "people's war" when an entire nation and all its able bodied men were armed. This was an initial step toward the twentieth-century total wars when the difference between the military and civilian population disappears. Both groups are exposed to the same threat of total destruction. Weapons are aimed against the civilian and military population. Totalitarian warfare has lowered, at times has reduced entirely the normative parameter. Wars differ in history not only in the use of weapons, but also—paradoxically as this may seem—in brutality, in moral, normative considerations.

This relationship between efficiency and a moral code of armed conflict is crucial. Even though naked force is a tool of an armed conflict, the imperatives of force and efficiency have limits and contradictions of their own. War is not only a conflict of leaders and rulers because armies and people organized for war may, at a point, exercise their own will. The army command or army units or underground partisans may favor a cessation of hostilities and may even surrender to an adversary whose war objectives are limited and "reasonable," and whose moral code and military behavior can be trusted. This kind of adversary may even encourage commanders to seize the opportunity and make the decision and agree to surrender or compromise.

The interdependence of pragmatic and morals or ethical codes, (normative), at times dialectical in a conflict, is not an abstraction. It has its practical relevance in a general conduct of public policies.

Both theoretical and practical was man's paramount interest in what was called the art of war by Machiavelli in his treatise, *L'Arte della guerra*, published in 1521. War was a major collective activity and profession since the times of tribal society and the emergence of the state. Defense against human predators and against conquest, organized massive robberies, legitimized later by history and historians, absorbed probably as much or more energy, effort, and time than daily labors to produce food, clothing, and shelter. The ruins of castles in Europe, the walled cities, even the villages in Umbria and other Italian provinces, the Acropolis of Athens and those of lesser-known places like Alatri in Italy, the Great Wall of China, and the Maginot line—here are only a few monuments of human toil, massive effort in search of security. Man had to defend himself against his most dangerous enemy: man.

Whether a war of defense or one of conquest and spoliation, the military strategic aim is similar, to use Clausewitz's words again, "to compel our adversary to do our will." It is strategy that suggests the end goal of military action, of use of power.

Military and Political Strategy

However, military goals are not identical with political objectives. The military strategy is an instrument or means toward political goals. At least in theory, military strategy is subordinated to political strategy; it is a part of an overall or grand strategy that encompasses the entire system of actions and goals on several levels: military, political, diplomatic, economic. Thus the political goal of a defensive war is different than one of conquest.

Strategic Forecasting

The nature of goal sequence in strategy and tactics lends itself to forecasting. The goal is the proximate cause, an antecedent, while actions are effects or sequents. Information about or knowledge of the antecedent (goal) suggests of course the probability of sequents (effects) or, in our case, actions. Information about Hitler's political goals suggests his probable course of actions: military, political, and diplomatic actions. Those actions are anticipated in terms of options. We do not forecast that since the political goals of an actor are A, ergo B will follow. He shall take a course of action B. In forecasting, the mode of thinking is tentative. What we do anticipate is that (a) given the existing political situation, (b) knowing from past experiences the strategy and tactics of a political actor, and (c) assuming strategic, as well stage or tactical, goals of the decision maker, then (d) all courses of actions open to the actor are listed. We do not identify one possible course of actions. We do not state, Since A's goal is $A+$, he will follow a policy A_1. What we anticipate is an "arc" of probable actions. At this point we do not postulate that the actor A will definitely select action B. We postulate that given (a), (b), and (c), he may choose courses A_1, A_2, A_3, or P. Here are the options he will probably choose. Now from all options we select those which offer the actor the highest payoff under present or future anticipated conditions. Here is the probable course or courses of actions.

This mode works of course in reverse too. Knowing the actions (sequent), we can identify the probable antecedent (goal). Let us assume that in times of Mao, the Chinese began to build roads toward India that pointed to their strategic rather than their economic relevance. In foreign policy forecasting we ask a simple question: Why are things done? What is the goal? The answer: A probable goal might be the invasion of India.

The distinction between the tactical stage and final strategic goals is seminal in forecasting the actions and understanding their meaning.

Few strategies are available and practiced in a given historical period. Discovery (or invention) of a new strategy and tactics marks a drastic political, even historical, change for which mankind usually pays its price of sacrifice and suffering. A strategy has typical sequences of goals and actions. In its early application the strategic innovators have the advantage of surprise, of the unexpected. The adversary whose thinking is geared to past experience expects a sequence of goals and means associated with known and different strategic design. However, once a strategy is applied and repeated, an intelligent observer or adversary learns the sequence of goals and stages. In consequence, once the innovator moves, his opponent may guess from the antecedent the sequence that may follow. He already knows from past experience how his opponent moves. Since there are few strategies available and practiced in a given historical period—furthermore, since changes in types of strategies seldom occur—their structure lends itself to a forecast. Strategic forecasting has a general application. It can be applied, as well to grand strategy, political strategy, and above all to foreign policy forecasting.

Political Strategy

The art of gaining control of the state or some of its institutions is called political strategy. The goal is political power of the state. In a democracy political strategy suggests accepted and legal courses of actions in winning elections. In a violent transfer of power the strategic goal is the capture of instruments of power by use of force and coercion and consolidation of power. The grand strategy of politics, however, is concerned with the uses and administration of power, once control of the state has been won.

Field strategy of politics answers the question, How can one get power? Control of political power is here an instrumental goal for the grand strategy and a consummatory one of the field strategy.

Grand strategy of politics answers the question, Power for what? The goals of grand strategy articulate also the legitimacy of power. In a democracy the uses of power and the goals are set within the constitutional imperatives.

The choice of violent or nonviolent means affects the ends. In a civil war the contest for control of power is waged by two or more organized armies, representing two or more opposing political camps in a nation divided. In revolutions and civil wars the strategic goal is similar to the one in war: Break the will of the adversary, overthrow him, deprive him of his control of the state.

A democratic society operates by means of what might be called a civic regulatory system, civic norms of conduct. Laws, rules of the game, customs, ethical considerations (the normative and legal parameters) impose strong imperatives, brakes on political behavior, and regulate, as well as limit, the choice of efficient means toward political victory. Even personal relations between the contesting candidates are restrained and controlled by rules and laws. The defeated congratulates the victor and leaves the field unharmed. This difference between violent and nonviolent strategy, however, is closely associated with the nature and strategy of political struggle. In a violent confrontation the goal is to force the adversary into submission, to weaken or destroy his political effectiveness, frequently to destroy him physically, as well to kill if possible.

Achievement of control over the state apparatus is not a sufficient goal; it is often only an instrumental goal. The grand strategy of politics is formulated in electoral platforms, in a program, and in a wider sense in ideology and doctrines. The latter answers the question, Power for what? The future use of power calls for a program, a plan. Exercise of power now becomes means. The doctrine, a declared ideological goal, tells only part of the story, for ideology is also a legitimacy of political payoffs for the leader and the party, rewards associated with victory.

Political power in itself is a major reward for men of politics. Power in itself, power over the state or institutions, control of other persons, is a highly desired and valued commodity. It is a value in itself. Power is also instrumental in achieving personal goals. However, political status, glory, and money are not the only rewards, for political power is also instrumental in those attempts to achieve broader and visionary goals, or in an issue-oriented movement it is necessary in problem solving, as well as in assisting one's fellow man. It would be a mistake to underestimate the strength of ideas and values as motivating drives of individuals and groups. Fulfillment of idealistic goals is a meaningful reward.

Different goals call for different personalities and talents. To win or conquer on one hand and to exercise power with skill and moderation, with minimum of coercion, on the other are two different goals and different things. They call for different qualities and reflect different personalities. Seldom are both qualities fused in a single individual. Those who know how to conquer power might be ignorant of the art of government.

Notes

1. Karl von Clausewitz, *On War* (NewYork: Random House, 1943), pp. xxi, 3. Clausewits finished his manuscript in 1827.

2. B. H. Liddell-Hart, *Strategy* (New York: Praeger, 1960).

10

Social Planning and Ethics

Social Planning: A Strategy Definition

We shall proceed with the definition of planning gradually, step by step, from general to more specific. The resulting differences in major types of planning are not a consequence of an abstract exercise. The types are related to major patterns that were practiced by planners and decision makers of our century.

The major dilemma is the problem of ends and means: considerations of efficiency versus ethical-moral, normative considerations (normative boundaries) in choice of means. In its very essence it is a problem of social control by use of force and coercion, on one hand, and freedom, or various degrees of free associations, on the other.

Strategy and tactics constitute the art of achieving goals effectively. Planning, social economic planning, is nothing else but a specific type of strategy. It is governed by the same principles as strategy is. It faces similar problems. The structure of goals is similar, since it is the same major pattern of achieving objectives. Planning is a rational and economic way of achieving goals: by means of least effort, with a minimal or optimal allocation of resources in optimal time necessary for efficient achievement of goals. It is above all a choice of adequate means in order to achieve desired ends.

Planning is an art akin (but not equivalent) to science. The function of the scientific method is an intellectual economy and concentration of intellectual effort with the purpose of achieving valid and verifiable results. Thus maximizing efficiency in goal achievement with a minimum of allocation of resources and effort is a component of planning. Principles of economy of effort and expenditure are not sufficient, however seminal they may be. The concept, or at least a major category of social planning, is identified with public interest, with the welfare of underprivileged, with assistance to the needy, with protection of the exploited. It is considered a beneficial activity. In such context and within this narrowed-down definition, normative imperatives are major determinants of goals and conduct.

Scientific inquiry, science does not seek beneficient, normative ends. The end of scientific inquiry is scientific validity of its findings (truth). The uses of sciences—this is a different thing. Science is instrumental, can be used for good objectives or bad. In this sense planning can also be defined solely in instrumental terms.

To begin with a concrete project: for example, a rehabilitation project in the South Bronx of New York City. The planning project moves within the limits imposed by normative and legal imperatives of public interest or social welfare, norms of conduct far more restrictive and forceful than in political strategies.

The normative parameter has two dimensions: the customary moral and legal. A construction company cannot impose on its workers a twelve-hour working day because it violates the laws of the land. The city government must employ minorities (Blacks, Hispanics, Orientals) even if this is not enforced by law, since norms of affirmative action or accepted norms of fair employment are guidelines of city policies. Even if moral norms are "stretched" or disregarded, policies cannot move beyond legal limits, since laws have sanctions and can be enforced by the authorities.

Military strategy, at least in theory, is also restricted by international conventions. The latter cannot be enforced, however; they are often observed due to reciprocity. Nonetheless, enforcement of international conventions is hardly possible. Political strategy in a democratic and legal state, for example, New York State, is of course limited to such options that are considered fair or at least tolerable and legal in a political competition and conflict (unlike a revolutionary strategy).

The goal of military strategy is subordination of the adversary. In both military and political strategy the result may involve change in the relationship of the two adversaries; the objective of one of the parties is to change the relationship of sub- and superordination and change the distribution of power. The goal of social planning is different. To begin with, its goals is not a subordination. In most cases there is no adversary. The objective is a material and social product.

The goals of social planning, however, cannot be easily reduced to a single general end and a single concept of beneficent planning. The term *social planning* has been widely used. Hitler and Goering practiced a kind of social planning, and so did and does the British Labour government. The ends and means were quite different, although both were industrial, technologically advanced societies. *Si duo faciunt idem, non est idem.* This issue moves our discussion to the second step.

The Origins of Terms

The term *social planning* is a historical product. It is an articulation, on one hand, of ideologies or doctrines and, on the other, of an attempt of man to respond to social problems created by the Industrial Revolution and later by modern, rapid industrialization. Traditionally, social planning was considered a problem-solving device, beneficial to those for whom it was designed.

Planning is of course an ancient art. The ancient Greeks and Romans had their planners. They founded cities, built highways, fountains, and aqueducts. The idea of social planning, however, as a professional activity of urbanists, economists, sociologists, and administrators was advanced during the interwar period. It became a profession requiring technical skills to outline and draft the plan, as well as administrative skills to execute the plans.

Planning, as we understand this term today, is a consequence of the nineteenth- and twentieth-century doctrines. The term gained popularity and relevance in the 1930s for two major reasons. In the West the Great Depression called for a rational response; social planning was the answer to mass unemployment. This was the major challenge and the central problem. In the East, in Russia, after a devastating war and revolution the need for reconstruction of the Soviet economy called for an organized action. Stalin's Five-Year Plan, with all its brutal methods, attracted general attention. In Europe, America, and the Soviet Union social planning became—though not overnight—a kind of social engineering, a strategy of social change and problem solving.[1]

As was said before, goals of social planning and the entire strategy are an expression of ideologies and hence of the normative nature, the value orientation. The growth of the theories of social planning is primarily associated with two major, moreover powerful, ideologies: the socialist one and much later that of the welfare state, a derivative of the former.

The socialist theory in its pristine, perfectionist period called for a plan of an entirely new and perfect society. Indeed, there were many of such plans. The theory implied a plan of a new society, techniques of construction of a new social system. The eighteenth- and early-nineteenth-century socialist theoreticians were not only analysts of the existing society, but also planners of a new one. Soon, however, they were split into two major camps. The more extreme groups advocated—in search of a perfect society—total and revolutionary changes. The more moderate wing, later called reformist, advanced a melioristic vision of a better society and a gradual change wherever possible by means of a democratic state. The reformists fathered the idea of a democratic welfare state, although they did not coin this term. The term came into use much later, in the middle of our century.

The change toward the welfare state did not come easily. It was a hard uphill struggle, at times by revolutionary means, at times by orderly, a parliamentary actions. The change in public attitudes was slow. Long working hours and low wages had an official legitimacy in precepts of economic science. Economics did not protect the most essential component of wealth: labor. With the flow of time, step by step, the immediate social goals of the working class—the eight-hour working day, health and unemployment insurance, public housing, labor legislation—were won; moreover, they were also generally accepted.

Thus the idea of the welfare state advanced gradually, long before the term was invented. The beginnings can be traced decades before the Revolution of 1848. Louis Blanc, one of the leaders active in that revolution, was an early theoretician of this doctrine. In consequence of its history the meaning, the semantics, of social planning was identified with beneficial activity and problem solving, with a general method to foster rational organization of economy and society.

To repeat, the concept was associated with a normative, value-oriented goal of a better or perfect society organized in a rational way. But what kind of a society is it or should it be? There was not and there is not a single answer. The idea system, the values and doctrines, as well as experience of the planners varied.

The Two Meanings: Total and Beneficent Social Planning

Social planning was not always humanitarian and beneficial.

There are two meanings of this concept and method: One is a historical concept. The other is an empirical and practical method or concept employed for a variety of objectives, a general technique, a strategy. With this distinction we move toward the third step of our discussion.

As was said, social planning is an intellectual attempt to design a strategy to achieve social goals. Planning, in this very sense, is instrumental. It is a tool that may serve a variety of objectives, good or bad ones. It can be used by those who build and those who destroy. Extermination of Jews and Gypsies by Hitler and his associates called for a systematic and practical plan. Their goals were morbid, inhuman. But achieving those goals required rational, logical, efficient means. The goals might be antiethical, irrational. But achieving irrational goals calls for means that are rational, logical, empirical, adequate to achieve such ends. Contrariwise, a historical concept of beneficent social planning suggests systematic and rational intellectual activity, oriented toward equally rational and beneficial goals. Here belongs planning of social reforms of broad projects beneficial to man, attempts toward a well-working and rationally organized economic system: to build cities, to plan for populaton and food, proper distribution of energies, natural resources—in sum a logical-empirical action for the good of man.

For want of a better term, we shall use *beneficent social planning* to mean a strategy directed toward achievement of social goals considered as beneficial for and by those for whom they are planned and in a broader sense for the good of society. Our initial definition followed this tradition, and my personal sympathy (or bias) counsels to keep the term *social planning* for this meaning of the term.

However, this is only a narrower sense of the term *planning*. Planning or projecting of goals is an intellectual activity, a preparatory stage toward actions that are and were practiced by man since he built the cities or organized armies.

In an objective, empirical descriptive sense the intent of social planning is to affect the existing situations, social systems, or selected social groups by such policies that result in social change designed by the planners, whether it is beneficial or not. At this point we may call it a general and pragmatic definition of social planning. Of course, one could argue that destruction of Jews and Gypsies was beneficial to the partisans of Adolf Hitler and his associates. This is, of course, a moral insanity. The term is relative only if our ethics is indeed entirely relative or if we accept a radical relativistic viewpoint. This division into beneficent and pragmatic definitions is useful, even seminal, in terms of distinction of options, selection of means toward ends. In terms of beneficent planning the options of the planners are strongly narrowed down by moral, ethical imperatives, by the moral ethical boundaries. In terms of a pragmatic definition of social planning, in a definition that sheds ethical and broader, normative imperatives, not unlike Clausewitz's strategy, all means are good as long as they end with success. The moral ethical boundaries, the normative parameters are not adequately considered.

Therefore we shall call this type of planning absolute or total planning if it is guided, regulated totally by considerations and norms of efficiency and results and (in contrast with beneficent planning) the normative parameter is removed, totally lifted. This may lead toward, and in fact it was, an expression of totalitarian methods and totalitarian state. In the latter case, we may also call it totalitarian. At this point we touch on a crucial issue of means and ends: Can man achieve beneficent ends by ruthless, even cruel means? Or should he? Here we are again at the dilemmas of the previous chapter. This is the basic dilemma of the contradiction between beneficent and totalitarian planning. But, as we shall see, the problem is even more complex.

Means and Ends

Means are courses of action. Ends are strategic goals, often distant objectives.

With the modern issues of means and ends, we are back at the issue of contradictions, even conflict, between the two major sets of values and norms of conduct: ethics and efficiency. Similar contradictions appeared already in a general discussion of strategy. It is a crucial issue of modern large-scale planning, modernization, and rapid industrialization.

To recall our definitions: Total planning lifts the normative imperatives; it is guided and regulated solely by one set of values: efficiency, workability, results. In beneficent planning, limits are imposed by normative, regulatory imperatives of our ethics, customs, laws protecting the weaker against exploitation.

The question is, of course, Do the ends justify the means? The question—Do ends justify means?—harbors a historical conflict within our civilization, a conflict that spans and stains our past history, a history of religious wars, of mass terror of the revolution. The same issue reappears in modern time. The ideological content is different, but the nature of the problem is much alike. It is again a problem of conflict between efficiency in goal achievement and ethics. After all, in a sense the Inquisition was efficient in Spain in its goal of consolidating the power of a single church hierarchy and a single interpretation of Christianity. Moslems, Jews, and Protestants were eliminated one way or another, not unlike political opponents in our times.

In social and political planning of our century this dilemma is as valid and as tragic as in the past.

The discussion of this issue is not an empirical and inductive exercise, for it is not a scientific issue, but a relevant and moral problem. The premise of a normative assumption of a shared, postulated universal even absolute set of values is a preliminary frame within which the relationship of means and ends has to be considered.

Providing this assumption, four relationships are feasible and were practiced in the past:

1. Beneficent planning for beneficent goals. Good ends achieved by good means. We may as well use broader terms—positive and negative—and suggest positive ends achieved by positive means. In this case, beneficent and humane goals are achieved by similar policies.

2. Total planning for beneficent goals. Good (positive) ends achieved by bad (negative) means. Beneficent goals can be achieved by ruthless, ethically negative means: for example, a housing project built by forced labor, a railroad constructed by a system of labor camps. In practice, negative means are tantamount to excessive use of coercion and forced labor. (We shall return to the first two alternatives.)

3. Total planning for negative goals. Bad (negative) ends achieved by negative means. Adolf Hitler's goal—armament for a war of conquest achieved by slave labor— provides an example. Ethically harmful ends, destructive in terms of humanity, are achieved or attempted by similar means.

4. Beneficent planning for negative goals. Bad ends achieved by beneficial means. In terms of logic this fourth combination is feasible.

Positive Means and Positive Ends: Beneficent Planning for Beneficent Ends

Each of those four combinations has a specific impact on the relationship of what is morally or ethically acceptable and pragmatically efficient.

The goal of social planning is conceived as a positive, beneficial result: a material product or a beneficial change in social relations achieved by means that are similar (beneficent). But efficiency is a paramount component of social planning and of a rational plan. Still, in their attempts to maximize efficiency of effort, the planners are limited in their choice of options by normative imperatives fenced in by the normative boundaries. The production of the plan has to be beneficent. It is expected that the plan will have positive effects for those for whom it is planned, but also for those who work, who are employed in production. For example, an irrigation system is planned in order to improve economic conditions in a depressed area and to prepare the land for effective cooperative farming. The product—as the planners perceive it—is beneficial for the residents of the area. But, on top of it, it should also be beneficent to those who dig the ditches and canals.

In consequence the principle of economy of effort and allocation of resources, in this case, is subject to revision and adjustments. What the planners seek in this case is the optimum and not the highest, the maximum, payoff. Their options are fenced in by three boundaries: the pragmatic, the normative, and the legal. (For the sake of simplicity we shall include the legal parameters in the general category of normative.) The pragmatic principle of efficiency must be adjusted to the normative-moral and normative-legal.

Within the legal and customary norms, or imperatives of ethics, the planner has freedom in choosing such options that maximize efficiency. On one hand a change to more attractive incentives or rewards may increase human efficiency; on the other hand a shift from a labor- to a capital-intensive project, modernization of tools and equipment, maximizes productivity.

This interplay of the two norms of conduct, the pragmatic and the normative, within which the choice is exercised, regulates the conduct of planning.

In the past, in the Western industrial nations, improvement of technology, working conditions as well as salaries and working hours, were those elementary devices that contributed to higher efficiency. What might be called "the industrial environment"—the nature of the workshop, its location, its access to work— may have had an effect on work efficiency.

The issue of means and ends has, however, current implications. It gained in relevance with the industrialization of the Soviet Union, with the famous Five-Year Plans, and with problems of modernization of traditional societies. Modernization carried out by principles of the first option (good ends, good means) calls for different policies, perhaps even technology, than the second option, which involves coercive measures.

Modernization of the former type involves careful evaluation of existing culture and values; furthermore, planning calls for adjustment of technology to the existing culture, attempts of preservation of at least some of the institutions. It calls for respect for differences in culture and religion.

Selecting the first beneficent option in traditional societies may slow down the process of modernization; coercion, at least on the surface, may seem to be a shortcut, although this is not necessarily true. Noncoercive cultural change is slow. It gradually affects social stratification, values, and institutions. Noncoercive, evolutionary change is also a consequence of a philosophy that calls for preservation of cultural heritage, at least in some vital areas. A rapid, forced change may on the other hand result in complete disintegration of native cultures.

Good Ends and Evil Means: Total Planning for Beneficent Ends

The second case is one of total planning for beneficial ends.

In practice the second option postulates that ends justify means. Moral and humane considerations in the choice of options are disregarded for the sake of a successful achievement of what the planner and decision maker considers as paramount and beneficial ends. The ethical parameter in human conduct is lifted. All means are good to achieve a perfect society. Hence it is also the issue of total planning in service of a noble and just goal. The present generation becomes just a manure for the new, perfect society and happy, joyous generations. Hence the pragmatic postulate decides about choice of options (means).

But there is another aspect of this goal of a perfect society. The vision of the future ideal society is at the same time the principle of legitimacy of power. Ruthless means applied toward an end of a future perfection are in fact ruthless means toward consolidation of power of the ruling party. The idealization of an end is in such a case a rationalization of a pragmatic and ruthless goal of an oppressive and total power.

In our times in large areas of our globe this choice of options, of means toward a better society, became seminal. It is a historical issue. It reflects also a fundamental dialogue and controversy, a consequence of the search for a just and workable social system. It is the controversy and conflict between meliorism and perfectionism, a contrast of two approaches toward an ideal type of society based on egalitarian values of social justice. In modern times the vision of such a society can be traced back to the eighteenth-century plans of utopian socialists. Those images and end goals of a perfect society resulted in two major trends: perfectionist (total) and meliorist (reformist).

The vision of a perfect, in contrast to a better, society is conceived as a static and terminal vision (goal) of a society, an ideal conceived by theoreticians. It corresponds to the extremes of ethical norms and of ideological constructs. The practical merits of such social images are hardly even considered. The logical and ideological imperatives displace any practical considerations. The plan is perfect; it is an ideal. Its protagonists consider any compromise or change as dangerous deviations tantamount to treason. Here are the chiliastic, general goals that Georges Sorel called "social myth" (in his *Reflections on Violence*), a term that came later into general use (see chapter 3).

In a perfectionist outlook a total change and the beginning of the millennium are just around the corner, only days after a successful revolution. The perfectionist is in search of and struggles for a single goal of a perfect society now. What this "now" means in reality is a different problem. The melioristic outlook is less inspiring, but it is a practical image of a better society and gradual change; it is a "practical plan" (see chapter 3). The two different approaches toward a new society are, of course, a consequence of different historical conditions, but also of different personalities and values. The difference between perfectionism and meliorism led in consequence to two different approaches in planning, the total and beneficent.

A meliorist outlook is a continuous change and effort toward a better, not a perfect, society. The immediate and intermediate goals have to be reached all the time. They pave the road toward a better society. The ideal type of society is far away. The ultimate goal of a perfect society cannot be achieved. It does not exist, since the image of the ideal type of society is changing too. Thus the meliorist moves slowly, advances a better society. He is a political protestant, whose faith is free from dogmatism and fanaticism.

A perfectionist discovered the ultimate truth, cherishes absolute faith, accepts only a single image of a perfect society, an ideal he perceives and agrees upon with no compromise. He rejects all deviations from his ultimate goal and works and struggles solely for this final end goal (consummatory goal) of a perfect society—a social myth or even a more distant utopia. For Lenin those who disagree are either enemies of the people, of the class, or traitors. The perfectionist has strong faith and dogma. But his ideal type of society is also tantamount to total power, total power for him—the incorruptible idealist. Since he strives for perfect justice, for the perfect ultimate goal, all means are justified. The meliorist strives for optimum, a compromise goal at a given stage, while the perfectionist calls for the shortest road, the maximum and total planning.

Where is the major ideological difference? The basic difference is in the dominant or core value, in the dialectics of the collective and individual.

The consummatory values, the hierarchy of core values in both cases, are different indeed. For the meliorist the person, the existing and future individual, is a major core value, the end goal. For a perfectionist it is the state, the collective, society. For a meliorist the state is a means; a person, an end. For a perfectionist the state, society, is an end; the person is only a means toward this end and can—more, should—be sacrificed in the interest of the collective. The historical contrast of the collective and the individual appears in this issue and the choice between the perfectionist and the meliorist vision of a new society. Here is a dilemma of reconciliation of the two principles, a problem of complementarity of the collective and personalist principle rather than one of conflict.

In total planning, normative considerations are removed and the pragmatic effectiveness, efficiency in goal achievement, is considered as the only measure, the only regulatory device in the choice of options. We shall see later, however, that the latter are also limited this time by a binding doctrine, by a political dogma. Absolute total methods in politics guided by a sole consideration of consolidation of power were of course practiced in Europe and Asia, had its theorist in both continents.

Negative ends, bad in terms of our set of values, are efficiently achieved by equally negative means. But now the question has to be asked whether a goal that is beneficent can be achieved at all by negative, ruthless means, whether the choice of such means does not defeat the very ends. Should we change the description of goals and instead of "good" goals suggest "desirable"? Then, of course, the case is different and, at the same time, relative, and the question is: for whom?

Goals of Adolf Hitler and his associates were "desirable" for them. In terms of our ethics they were negative, harmful. Hitler's planners used slave labor. The cost was minimal in their perceptions. Human life of Slavs and Jews was cheap. They could not sell slaves; the only thing they could do was to work them to utter exhaustion and death. The dead ones were replaced easily. Plans executed in that way—in terms of Nazi planners—were economic, efficient, since slave labor was cheap. But in this case bad goals, morally negative ends, were achieved by negative means.

The communist theory advocates the primacy of ends: the perfect, socialist society based on equality, social justice, and freedom. The Communist vision is a perfectionist one; it is a vision of a perfect society. All means are legitimate to achieve effectively the perfect end. The ends supply legitimacy to means. In this case positive ends of social justice and human perfection have to be achieved by negative means of dictatorship, coercion, terror. For the sake of historical clarity we shall limit the time span to Stalin's rule. Historical evidence on forced labor, terror, and purges is abundant and easily accessible.

The Soviet case is quite different from Hitler's. The core values of the communist philosophy, in terms of the ideal, are at the opposite poles. The distant, generalized goal of socialism and communism is a society free of exploitation of man by man, a classless society of equals, a final stage of emancipation and self-realization of man.

In Hitler's planning the regulatory and directive subsystems were in agreement. His end goal was a society of a ruling race, *das Herrenvolk*, over all others. Force, ruthless, unfettered force, and its use for the sake of the racial state constituted a declared and practiced policy, part of the ideology. Exploitation of "inferior" races by the ruling one was a promise and commitment. Means and ends were in agreement. Holocaust, subjugation of Slavic peoples—all this was in the books. Only the naive did not trust his promise.

The communist ideal set of values is, however, in fundamental conflict with practice. Unlike the first case, means and ends are contradictory—more, in conflict. The politics of daily life is distant from the ideal, the promised perfect state. And the ideal is never reached. To the contrary, it becomes more and more distant. In 1917 the promised land was around the corner. A dictatorship of the proletariat was proclaimed as a transitory stage to a perfect society, freed even from the coercive bond of the state. After more than half a century dictatorship continues.

Planning of a socialist economy, considered an end goal of a perfect social justice, was arrived at by means of coercive measures, including forced labor. Fear was the major political tool in constructing the future perfect and ideal society, not yet achieved. In consequence, formidable undertakings, such as the White Sea Canal, Stalin's accomplishment, were carried out but with human losses equal to those of war. This canal (1932), covering a distance of 227 kilometers between the White Sea and the Onega Lake, the Moscow-Volga Canal (1936), and the Volga-Don Canal (1952) were built by enslaved labor at a cost of many thousand lives; those are only examples of a long list of forty-six truly gigantic projects.[2] Indeed, until the death of Stalin a gigantic planning of a new economy and society was carried out in the way pyramids were built. Peter the Great carried out his equally gigantic project of a capital city of Petersburg by such means. Historical credit must be given to Khrushchev for his courage and will to reveal the facts at the Twentieth Party Congress of the Communist Party. The plan was gigantic and was carried out by coercive means considered probably as the only feasible and efficient way.

Forced labor, however, was not Stalin's invention. It was a part of the system— of the theory of means and ends, the ends that justify the means. Forced labor was proposed by Trotsky as early as June 26, 1918, and general principles of compulsory labor were introduced by a decree of the Central Executive Committee on October 31, 1918. Trotsky, for the first time, proposed collective (family) responsibility in the same memorandum to the *Sovnarkom.*

The 1918 decrees were directed against the middle classes, against those who could be labeled as the bourgeoisie. In 1919, however, Lenin as chairman of the Council of Workers and Peasants Defense signed a decree forbidding coal miners to leave their work. On April 15, 1919, forced labor camps were established by a decree of the Central Committee.[3] From that time on, mobilization of labor by coercive and military means was continuous. The method has also produced a substantial number of decrees, ordinances, and memoranda. The mobilization was carried out by arrest or simply by surrounding squares and streets and impressing citizens into ranks.

In times of revolution the fabric of society had been disintegrating—one may argue—and coercion was an emergency measure. However, no attempts were made to try on an equal scale humane means. What is essential is that planning toward what was considered as beneficial ends was carried out by means adverse to final goals.

Two questions have to be asked: How does the choice of means affect the ends? And, second, are those coercive means always more efficient than other options based on rewards?

The end, the distant vision of a perfect state, is a moving, infinite goal, never fully achieved. A better society, a betterment, a melioristic ideal is an achievable goal. But even here, this is not a terminal goal, a final rest for all of society. Society calls for continuous reconstruction, continuous change and adjustment. John Dewey, in his *Philosophy of Reconstruction*, points clearly to this dynamic nature of social betterment. The life of a creative society is a dynamic process. In consequence, there is no final ideal or end that society will reach at one time, a perfect social terminal. The process consists of our actions, our means. We move from one stage to another. Upon reaching one stage goal, we move again to the next one. The lifeline of a society and persons is a road marked by stages and intermediary goals. The road in itself becomes an end, since the end is subject to continuous change.

In those gigantic projects of Stalin and Peter the Great the time span toward achievement of major stages extended over an entire lifetime of a generation. The generation of a take-off stage may never live to see the end of a project, of a stage. The means that were chosen, ruthless and coercive for individuals employed in such a project, mean daily personal and family suffering and humiliation. Of course new elites, new ruling classes, emerge in such a process; although privileged, even they, experience teaches, are never indeed free from fear. It is soon discovered that the perfect state is a distant ideal. The beginning of the millennium is not around the corner. The long-range plan calls for sacrifice of one generation as a price of happiness of the next one. In our times Pol Pot and his organization in Cambodia made such a plan. His intention was to start at a "zero point." Towns were abandoned; hospitals, universities, and schools were closed. Mass migration of the population was carried out. Masses of population were moved from one province to another. Thousands of Cambodians were beaten to death or shot for the sake of a perfect society they are supposed to enjoy. Although Hitler's and Pol Pot's political creeds were opposed or at least different, next to Hitler's millennium Pol Pot's construction of a future, perfect society was probably the cruelest experiment of our century.

Evil means applied toward beneficent ends, at least in planning, were self-destructive. Plans were extended for generations. Hence, for the generations of the Russian Revolution their own life span was one of those means sacrificed for Stalin's plan carried out by coercion and forced labor. Those generations did not witness any withering away of the state, or enjoyment of all the abundance and well-being promised in an ideal socialist society, of perfect freedom and justice. For those generations, for our generations, the chosen means corrupted and defeated the ends.

Long-range coercive planning is only a segment of public policy, a policy closely associated with political power. A major objective is not solely planning but also consolidation and enjoyment of total, or at least extensive, power.

Hence coercive, long-range planning calls for and creates new institutions and organizations. The major one is, of course, an enforcement apparatus, an extensive political police system. Different from police systems in democratic countries, one of its major functions is mobilization and supervision of forced labor. Institutions have a tendency toward self-perpetuation. Members of the security apparatus enjoy in such systems special privileges. They have higher salaries, better access to food supplies, housing, and other resources. The tendency toward self-perpetuation is reinforced by their privileged social status. Thus the enforcement apparatus, which controls means of violence—weapons—has a key, strategic position in those types of societies. It grows in significance with time and extends its control. An organization planned as a transitional and temporary one becomes well entrenched and permanent; it becomes not only an instrument, but an advocate of a coercive system. Once an institutional apparatus is formed and consolidated, it may continue even for centuries. Self-perpetuation of such institutions, of a coercive apparatus becomes tantamount to perpetuation of privileges for the ruling political classes.

Let us return at this point to the incentives, to their division into positive and negative.

There are times when the incentive system breaks down. Still, water and food, shelter, as well as other necessities must be provided for the entire community and society. In times of revolutions and disintegration of society voluntary incentives, rooted in rewards, may break, almost completely collapse, especially in some strategic areas. Moreover, major institutions disintegrate in such times of rapid social change. What then? How can one reorganize the broken fabric into a working society? Some French historians argue that this indeed happened in later stages of the French Revolution. Jacobin centralism, coercion, and terror constituted the only option left—it might be argued—to reintegrate the society into a workable and functioning state.

We have already indicated below that the positive incentive system may fail. The building of a society from such total collapse, disintegration, or catastrophe when voluntary, positive incentives do not work anymore, when there are no strong rewards available, leaves little choice. At such a moment, coercion—what was called negative incentives—may remain as the only alternative. Let us assume such a condition; let us even assume that it was at such a point that the leaders of the French and Russian revolutions resorted to extreme forms of coercion, to mass manipulation of fear.

There are times when voluntary social control breaks down, when coordination of efforts based on values, customs, or rewards has to be substituted by a coercive, command structure. There are times that the fabric of society disintegrates. However, it is an art of government and a matter of wisdom to set limits in quantity, quality, and time span of coercive, formal social control in work as well as in social, economic, or political reconstruction and to devise ways of transition to a system based on positive incentives and reduced coercion.

The coercive measures, as it was said before, are not isolated. They are only instruments of an entire system. They are also means toward consolidation of total power. And unlimited power is a commodity highly desired by men of total politics. Hence, such a transition is difficult. However, there are ways of transition to more humane and less coercive means. Such a change was accomplished in the past and may be in the future by violent or nonviolent changes in power structure, by displacement of ruling elites and ascent to power of new groups. But there are also options of gradual change of the entire system and a movement toward a melioristic change even within a coercive system.

Monistic and Pluralistic Planning

The term *social planning* is used widely; it encompasses a variety of methods and theories. We repeat the initial distinction of total in contrast to beneficent planning. Total planning is unrestricted by moral consideration in its choice of means toward achievement of goals. Historical experience teaches, however, that total or absolute planning has been at the same time dogmatic, limited in choice of options by imperatives of the doctrine. In terms of past history, absolute planning while disregarding humane consideration was at the same time fettered by doctrines. Thus Soviet planning under Stalin or Chinese planning under Mao were absolute and at the same time dogmatic.

The term *monistic* describes a planning doctrine that imposes limits on choice of options and experimentation due to a binding, political ideology. The options and their workability are tested against the precepts of a single ruling doctrine rather than hard facts.

In contrast, the kinship of pluralistic planning with the scientific, inductive sequence has an impact on the entire concept and definition of planning. By pluralistic planning here we mean planning unfettered by ideological dogma or a single political or economic doctrine. Pluralistic planning suggests that individuals and groups are engaged in economic activities, attempting to achieve a variety of different goals, by use of a variety of types of economic means. It implies, furthermore, not one but a variety of economic doctrines, freely discussed and applied: freedom of choice in selection of means toward ends, as well as freedom of choice of ends. In consequence the planner is free to select means toward established ends, guided solely by consideration of efficiency of means and their compatibility with public interest and established norms of conduct. He chooses policies and experiments. Similarly to science, his experiment may succeed or fail. The planner as well as the administrators, those who execute the plan, accept the risks of failure, the principle of fallibility, or error. Error is an element of the scientific process, since there is no certainty; should a policy or an action not succeed, a pluralist either tries another option (alternative) he anticipated in his plan or postulates that the goal is not achievable and, in consequence, he substitutes the goal.

A plan may also fail because the means do not work; the plan is not "operational"; things must be done differently due to circumstances that interfered or could not be anticipated; new, unknown variables appeared and were not accounted for.

Last but not least, a rational planner cannot exclude a terminal and negative option: (a) Under existing historical conditions, (b) under the present level of our knowledge and science, (c) given the allocation of cost and resources, (d) the problem cannot be solved at all or within the time span indicated by decision makers. This is not an encouraging suggestion, but in terms of simple logic, such an option is one of the contingencies, one of the probabilities. It may serve as encouragement to think and work hard to find the ways and a workable, productive option.

An empirical planner accepts a failure as well as an error as one of the possible outcomes of the experimentation in and adventure of planning. If it does not work, we try something else. If one tool does not work, another may. This is a practical way of thinking, a commonsense notion of daily life.

In monistic planning things are quite different. Planners are limited in their choice of alternatives by an ideological, theoretical dogma. A doctrine and a rigid sociological or political dogma are imposed by the ruling elite and control their actions and planning. The doctrine is an official creed, not unlike a political religion. It is considered as perfect. Here are ideas and precepts that must work, since they were conceived or advocated by a genius, be he Marx, Stalin, Mao, or Pol Pot. In such an approach, plans cannot fail. There is no place for chance, probability, or error, since the doctrine is perfect and based on certainty and dogma. And since planning in those cases is closely associated with political power, plans can be enforced by political means, even by use of mass violence. (We shall return to this theme in chapter 11 in our discussion of options.)

Monistic planning assumed in the past a single center of planning and economic initiative. Here is its major weakness. Individuals and society have a variety and a multitude of economic needs. New needs appear continuously, as a result of dynamic social changes or individual activities. This multitude and variety of needs cannot be met by a single initiative and administered by a single decision center. No central committee can understand and meet all the needs and goals of a complex, large industrial society. This can be answered solely by many points or centers of independent initiative. Those diverse initiatives of imaginative men and women have to be coordinated one way or another. But their dynamic response should be rewarded rather than punished.

A multitude of needs appears in a multitude of individual and group goals. Again, the latter have to be coordinated or integrated; however, frustration of so many obvious and legitimate goals and needs affects adversely both individuals and society.

In contrast to absolute and monistic planning, the choice of options in pluralistic planning is unrestricted by theories and doctrines. In a pluralistic approach the choice of options follows the ways of experimentation. Goals can be reached by a variety of means. Options are listed and results anticipated or tested. Options that are most efficient within the constraints of the welfare of those who work and for whom it is done are the preferred ones. Options are tested against facts (achievement or failure of goals) not against a doctrine. (Options are the major theme of our next chapter.)

Absolute planning has thus far practiced coercive methods and large-scale employment of forced labor. Absolute versus beneficent planning involves also the issue of free labor versus a coercive one, free versus state-controlled unions.

The term *planning* encompasses a variety of modes of thinking and methods of problem solving. The difference between a pluralistic and monistic one is seminal; it has practical consequences.

World Outlook and Common Sense

Planning in terms of alternative choices is, as was said, a matter of logic, but also a part of a broader *Weltanschauung*. It is a consequence of a world outlook that accepts doubt, the right of an individual to choose, to choose his religion, his political affiliation, and, within limits of the system and of his talents, his avocation.

There is no society without political power and some kind of coercive social control. Nor do all societies fit into a single political, social, and economic system. Diversity of culture calls for diversity of social political systems. Our issue here is one of social planning only, social planning free from excessive coercion. No scholastic, verbal ploy shall succeed in an argument that coercion is always present in all manual or industrial work, that threat of hunger is nothing else but a form of coercion. Coercion, coercive social planning of our times, has its known and clear expressions: concentration and forced labor camps, mass deportations, wholesale expulsion, mass terror, purges.

The contrast between absolute and monistic planning on one hand and beneficent and pluralistic on the other is a contrast between totalitarian and non-totalitarian systems. This difference appears in the choice of means toward goals.

But the exercise of choice is also a matter of simple logic—more, of human nature. The exercise of choice is pertinent not only to human behavior. It can be observed among animals and experimented with. Even under a totalitarian rule this craving for exercise of free choice cannot be destroyed. The ruling party totally blocks certain areas of human activities. Real barriers are established by means of an enforcement apparatus and terror. Still, even under those most adverse conditions individuals will continue to exercise their choice and will in areas where barriers were not yet established or where controls by the government are not yet effective. Persons of initiative and independent views will attempt to move slowly into areas where they do not meet a major resistance or where their action is not yet fully noticed or, due to conditions, is silently tolerated.

In the end, those who are daring will attempt—hesitantly at first—to cope with, and later to move, the barriers.

To conclude, in planning that seeks beneficent ends, means and ends should be in agreement. The norms of conduct, what was called above the regulatory subsystem of behavior, should not conflict with the end purpose, with the very direction, with goals. A better society is not built by application of cruelty and naked force. The agreement of norms in choice of means and ends is seminal. Planning conceived solely in pragmatic terms of efficiency and results misses the central purpose of man and humanity.

Notes

1. A flood of publications on social planning, interestingly enough, began after the Great Depression. At this time "economic planning" appeared in numerous titles; 1932 seems to be the beginning. Here are a few of those volumes; among the earliest, most of them were socialist theoreticians: Harry W. Laidler, ed., *Socialist Planning and a Socialist Program* (New York: Falcon Press, 1932); G. D. H. Cole, *Economic Planning* (New York: Knopf, 1935); Henri de Man, *Planned Socialism* (London: Gollancz, 1935); International Federation of Trade Unions, *Economic Planning and Labor Plans* (London: I.F.T.U., 1935); Sir William Beveridge, *Planning Under Socialism* (New York: Longmans, 1936); Mary Flederus and Mary Van Kleeck, eds., *On Economic Planning* (New York: Covici, Friede, 1935); A. N. Holcombe, *Government in a Planned Democracy* (New York: Norton, 1935); League for Social Reconstruction, *Social Planning for Canada* (Toronto: T. Nelson & Co., 1935). For a more extensive bibliography see: Harry D. Laidler, *History of Socialism* (New York: Thomas Y. Crowell, 1968), pp. 921 ff.

2. See Aleksandr I. Solzhenitsyn, *The Gulag Archipelago Two* (New York: Harper & Row, 1975), pp. 81 ff., 591 ff. At the construction of the Belomor Canal (a forced labor project) during just one winter, 1931–1932, it is estimated that more than 100,000 persons perished (p. 98).

3. James Bunyan, The *Origin of Forced Labor in the Soviet State 1917–1921: Documents and Materials* (Baltimore: Johns Hopkins University Press, 1967), pp. 55 ff., 70, 71 ff.

11

The Logic of Planning

The Questions Asked

Every one of us does some individual, personal planning all the time. What does such planning involve? In terms of our common sense we ask at first the right kind of questions: what shall be done and why? Here are typical steps of choice, decision, and action: (1) the present situation is discussed and problems are evaluated in terms of priorities; (2) goals are identified; (3) means to reach the goal are considered; (4) a decision is made; (5) actions toward goal achievement are carried out. This path of thinking and doing is not necessarily conscious, but there is a logical pattern that we will follow.

In social planning the sequence is alike, but questions have to be asked and answered all the time.

Thus, a planning project can be reduced to answers to four major questions:

1. *What is the situation now?* What is the *problem?*
2. *What should be done* and for whom, in order to respond to the problem? What are the priorities and our goals in this case?
3. *How can we do it?* What are the means, or
4. Preferred courses of action?
5. *How much will it cost?*

The last is a question of allocation of resources, identification of sources of financial as well as of other forms of assistance.

In consequence of a general analysis the planner identifies the problem and assigns top priorities for problem solving. The key issue has to be located.

The next question (goals) concerns the product of planning. The goal of planning is a product that consists of a subject and an object. The subject of planning is a section of population or a group for whom the project is planned. The object corresponds to the material product or laws necessary to meet the needs of the subjects.

In an overcrowded section of the city a housing project may suggest an answer. But any housing project, any building, any object as such is not a sufficient answer. The question has to be asked, For whom? Who should profit (*cui bono*)? A housing project may be a boon for real estate business. Luxury apartment housing—those half-million-dollar co-ops of the rich—instead of supplying homes may displace the underprivileged population. The subject is seminal. The object—the product—is an articulation of those needs that the project meets; it is a result that creates new conditions for the people.

Thus the goals of planning are expressed in its material and social results; they form the product and are the result of planning.

The Five Components of a Planning Project

The plan, the written and operational project, follows closely the four questions. The logic of problem solving, the rational and abstract way, is simple. Where the difficulties appear, of course, is in its application, when it is tested against the social, economic, political, and geographical conditions that the complex environment, the goals, are projected into.

Thus a logical outline of a plan is this:

1. (What is?) The situation and the problems to which the plan has to respond are identified. It is a survey or descriptive and analytical presentation of the situation.

2. (What has to be done?) Goals are identified and formulated. The goals are expressed in terms of social and material products, economic and social results.

3. (How can we do it?) Options, courses of actions open to the planners (means), are listed.

4. (What is best?) Preferred options (optimizing goals and policies) are noted.

5. (How much will it cost?) Allocation of resources, a budget, is determined. Financial resources are identified.

Planning Models

We shall use this outline of planning for developing equally simple models.

The logic of planning is also a rational way of looking into the future and answering a challenge, avoiding negative effects.

Our first planning model (figure 11.1) presents an initial forecast. We postulate that *rebus sic stantibus* (provided present conditions), situation A will move into situation A_1. We postulate also that situation A_1 is considered a negative one or not desirable. It is an adverse, a detrimental, even a disastrous situation; for example, increase of drought and population growth in territory A will result in overpopulation and hunger within time span A_1. The change from A to A_1 is an unintended, uncontrolled process. The major, identified variables move toward an anticipated but adverse situation.

The danger of a detrimental outcome (situation A_1) we postulate further, can be avoided, however, provided there occurs outside interference, which will affect a different direction of this process. This outside interference is a set of courses of actions, a new variable, a result of rational planning initiated in order to avoid the negative situation and by means of new action to reach the goal of planning, the positive situation B. In consequence, by means of our planning the process is redirected.

In this case situation A may change in two directions: into an adverse or negative one or into a desirable, "salutary," or positive one. The former is not intended; it is a process. The latter is intended; it is a set of actions, a new variable initiated by planners. The goals of planning in this case are pragmatic, verifiable targets: increase of food production, irrigation, population control.

Our actions are not unlike an experiment. A new, outside variable is introduced

Figure 11.1
Situation and Planning

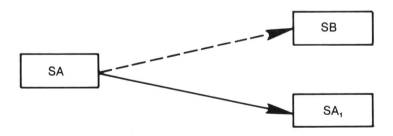

Situation SA will move – under present conditions – to SA₁.
The planner suggests courses of action toward a desired and salutary situation SB.

into a situation, and effects (or sequences) of this new factor are tested against results of our plan. Of course the difference between what we may call pragmatic on one hand and scientific experimentation on the other hand is seminal. A basic postulate of scientific experimentation is that it can be repeated in identical conditions and it will result in identical effects. The planner does not control the field of his experimentation as a physicist does. Moreover, social economic conditions might be repetitive but never identical in their new reappearance (for example, strikes).

In addition, this mode of responding and planning is in fact also a reflection of a doctrine, of a theoretical assumption, even when free from dogmatic determinism. We do *believe*—in our approach—that a given historical situation can be answered in many ways: that man, within limits, may control and direct his destiny, for a situation (save singular cases) does not determine solely one single and necessary course of events. In an approach unfettered by radical determinism, social processes can be affected and altered by man. The situation lends itself not to one but to several responses.

Planning is a humanistic activity. It harbors a strong belief, a faith that man can change the situation by his will and action. It is also a rationalistic act, based on belief that reason and proper use of intelligence and knowledge give us power and choice to improve the human condition. Hence planning is an outcome of a world outlook, a belief system. It calls for a definite set of values, norms of conduct.

Now the question is asked, *How* can we avoid a negative outcome? How can we solve the problem and improve the conditions? The logic of planning lends itself to presentation in the form of an operational graphic model, which suggests the sequence of three steps adequate to achieving the goals. It answers the question How.

For logical convenience we begin by reducing the outline of a plan from five steps (survey, identification of goals, listing of options, choice of preferred option, allocation of resources and cost) to three (survey, identification of goals, identification of courses of action or listing of options).

Step 1. The planner proceeds with research (survey) of the present situation *what is* (*SA*); he explores and identifies the problem (*P*).

Step 2. In response to the problem and to the current social process, he suggests an answer (*what to do*) articulated as strategic goals (*G*). Goals are thrown ahead into the future situation (*SB*).

Step 3. Now the question is asked, How can we achieve the goal? (How can we do it?) The planner postulates that a goal can be achieved in many ways (A_1, A_2, A_3, A_4). In a pluralistic approach he is not limited by a single doctrine, for a situation can be answered in a number of ways, and a goal thrown into the future can be reached by a variety of actions.

In consequence, the planner suggests alternative courses of action, called options (A_1, A_2, A_3, A_4) to achieve strategic goal G. This results in change of the situation into *SB*. See figure 11.2.

Thus, the model has been reduced to those three steps. Next comes (4) choice of preferred courses of action; (5) allocation of resources; and (6) decision. Decision ends the stage of planning. From the decision the path moves to implementation; the plan is translated into virtual action toward goals.

Validation

The three steps are subject to three different valuations: scientific, normative, and pragmatic. Thus not all of the steps can be validated by scientific means (see also Chapter 1).

In step 1, survey of the situation, the study of the situation is carried out solely within a scientific frame of reference: true and false, valid or not valid. The method can be challenged, of course. Sampling may be considered as not adequate or analysis of data as biased. But findings must be verified, validated by

Figure 11.2
Planning

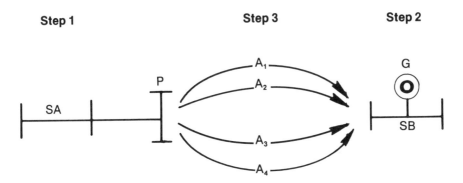

Step 1	**Step 3**	**Step 2**

1. SA — present situation
2. G   — Strategic goal
        in a new situation SB
3. A_1, A_2, A_3, A_4 — alternative policies

scientific means. The hypothesis is tested against the results. The criticism of methods or results is limited to scientific procedures; adequate verification decides whether results are valid or not.

In step 2, the goals are either generalized, normative symbols or pragmatic targets (see above, chapter 6). In the first case they are subject to an ideological test; in the second, to a pragmatic. For example, the planning of a socialist state. Whether a socialist state has been achieved or not is tested against ideology and the definition what a socialist state is. This is not a scientific test. In fact, it is a normative evaluation.

Targets are tested against results in a pragmatic way. If my target is a housing project, its erection is the test. The result of my actions is at the same time a pragmatic test. It testifies to the effectiveness of my actions. The proof of the pudding is in the pudding. However, the very choice of targets might be determined by normative—ideological—considerations (see, chapter 2).

Overpopulation can be answered by deportation or free emigration, voluntary population transfer, increase of employment opportunities, and so on. Public housing for the underprivileged might be advanced by party A and opposed by party B, because their basic ideological doctrines are different. The plan for a housing project is the consequence of my welfare state ideology. An administration with a different ideology may choose another goal—labor camps, perhaps. Hence goals can be practical or not, right or wrong. They are not necessarily valid or invalid.

In step 3, listing of options, the choice of my actions follows pragmatic considerations. I choose means that are efficient, that give results. Actions are tested against results, and this type of validation was called pragmatic. We are testing workability of options: whether they work and give the expected results or fail, are not workable.

In beneficent planning this stage is more complex, however. The choice between effective and noneffective values is still limited by normative imperatives (of right and wrong).

The planner lists the options first, and in the next step he chooses the most adequate, the preferred options. The choice of the latter is a rational compromise of selecting the most efficient one within the imposed or postulated normative limits (adequate or inadequate).

An inductive, empirical process begins with a hypothesis, which in a next step is tested by experimentation or observation. Results of the latter suggest a generalization or an inference that is based on verification or on failure of experimentation or observation.

Validation of policies follows a similar but not an identical sequence. The planner begins with a relationship of data, a kind of hypothesis: Preferred courses of action (A) put into operation will result in an anticipated product (B), he argues. The policy (A) in this type of a pragmatic hypothesis has to be considered as an antecedent: the result—goal achievement (B)—as a sequence. It is a cause-effect relationship, a relationship of two sets of data that are tied by a meaningful connection (called by Pareto a logical nexus, by Pearson a meaningful connection). *A* is a cause of *B*; *B* is a product (an effect) of *A*. Introduction of policies, of an artificial or outside variable, is similar to experimentation. The operation is akin to experimentation, and calls for continuous observation. Why then do we call this test pragmatic instead of scientific? First of all, the planners cannot repeat identical conditions. Conditions may be similar but are never identical and completely under control of the planner. A scientific verification means that the same experiment, performed under the same conditions with the use of the same instruments (open to other experimenters), will yield the same results. Second, the decision and the goal are guided by both normative and pragmatic considerations. The goal is not scientific. A planner is not after scientific validity, after truth (in terms of scientific probability) alone—the only scope of a purely scientific approach. What he attempts to get is practical and workable results. Still, in its nature, in its structure, the pragmatic test is similar to scientific validation.

To summarize, within the first step (survey) the planner moves between two polar values: true or false, valid or invalid. In the second step (goals) the polar values change to right or wrong or, in the case of targets, practical and impractical. In the third stage (actions) the polar values change again: the positive norm of conduct is now workable, effective; the negative, not workable, not efficient. In beneficent (humanitarian) planning the positive polar value of actions is adequate; the negative one, nonadequate (adequate is both efficient and morally and legally acceptable).

What follows is that disagreements on those three levels are subject to three different types of resolutions.

Disagreements on findings of survey can be resolved in an objective, scientific way: scientific validation. The verification alone is the measure.

A disagreement on generalized, ideological goals cannot be resolved by scientific means. The disagreement is answered in this case by political means. The preference of goals (for example, conservative or liberal) if we can use this term, is decided either by a compromise or simply by new distribution of political power. If, however, the parties involved seek efficient targets—the best housing with minimal cost, the most efficient and least expensive maintenance—then, of course, the nature of the disagreement shifts from an ideological to a pragmatic level, subject to a pragmatic resolution.

In the third step, a search of proper options is considered in pragmatic terms of results and workability. A disagreement on choice of preferred courses of actions can be resolved only ex post facto, by testing results against the former. Results tell whether party *A* or *B* was "right" in terms of efficient means.

This difference—the very nature of those disagreements—has a practical meaning and significance. In practical life a scientific validation is pretended in areas that belong to a nonscientific idea system, and disagreements cannot be resolved by methods that simply do not work in this area. Here belong ideology and religion. Important as they are, they work in different ways (see chapter 1).

An ideological disagreement cannot be resolved by a scientific test. Such a test will not tell whether it is right or wrong; the test will not work outside the scientific system. Moreover, in most cases ideological disagreements cannot be resolved by a pragmatic test.

Assuming that the Nazi and fascist systems worked, Lincoln Steffens was impressed by fascist efficiency. Let us further assume—for the sake of argument—that Hitler's Nazi state worked, that it had high industrial capacity, advanced methods and equipment in production, and efficient bureaucracy. This does not make it right and acceptable in terms of my ethics and views. It remains always a system based on prejudice and brutal, cruel exploitation of subject ethnic groups. Pragmatic efficiency in this case is not even a premise, a bridge for a compromise between two opposing political parties. The necessary condition here is also an elementary set of shared values. And this is absent.

Alternative Actions or Options

Actions or policies should be (1) rational, adequate to achieve the goals; (2) efficient, in terms of economy of effort and cost (they are selected because there is a probability that goals will be achieved with lesser efforts and lesser allocation of resources than other options, or at the same or higher cost but with higher quality); (3) in agreement with our normative imperatives. And in consideration of the latter condition adjustment has to be made within the first and second conditions to reach an optimum balance between all three.

In practice, we may postulate, there are a number of ways to reach the same goals. Once the goal has been established, the planner considers the many diverse alternative courses of actions or options that are open and conducive to goal achievement. We have already called such an approach to problem solving a pluralistic one, contrasted with a monistic approach. Now for the sake of logical convenience we shall define here an orthodox or dogmatic monistic school. In our age there have been and are partisans of monistic philosophies and approaches who in daily life act in a pragmatic way; they disregard at least some of the doctrine. There are others who adhere closely and dogmatically to the doctrine. For the sake of logical convenience we shall consider here a dogmatic monistic school that narrows down the choice due to imperatives and methods imposed by a political and dogmatic doctrine.

The monistic school postulates that given the existing situation, which must be analyzed solely within the parameters of this only doctrine, there is but one solution and a single course of action open toward the goal (for example, collectivization of agriculture during a food shortage). There are no alternative courses of actions, no options. Moreover, only one response is feasible to answer the challenge. A monistic approach offers no, or very limited, flexibility; it does not suggest experimentation with various alternative courses of actions. True, there are at times situations that offer a choice limited to two polar answers. A typical one is a disaster situation that suggests only two options—destruction or survival—and only one avenue is open to reach the latter. But not all disaster situations are of this nature.

When facts disagree with the theory, a pluralist and pragmatist says, It's bad for the theory. The theory must be dropped or changed; it does not work; another solution must be suggested. To the contrary, a monist says, Should the facts disagree, negate the theory; it's bad for the facts; the theory will not change. Should the Marxist theory fail in problem solving in farming, it is bad for the farmers, for the peasants, not for the theory. The theory has the support of internal security forces, armed militias, and the party. The farmers do not.

We may recall that the pluralistic approach is not fettered by a single doctrine or by an imperative of a single a priori selected problem-solving approach. For successful planning, flexibility is essential as well as freedom of choice, and this includes freedom to commit an error, even to fail.

In a pluralistic approach planning is considered as an experiment. Like any experiment, the plan may succeed or fail. If it fails, another option has to be chosen to reach the goal, or goals have to be substituted.

In a monistic approach the doctrine is based not on a hypothesis but on a dogma. A dogma is an article of faith that cannot be changed. A dogma is an a priori acceptance of a method or concept, philosophy considered as a certainty, philosophy that cannot be challenged. Even in case of failure of the plan, since the doctrine is a dogma, it cannot fail for those who believe in its certainty. And if the plan fails? Then it is not because the doctrine, the theory, does not work, an orthodox partisan will argue, but because some wicked people, evidently enemies of the people, have been chosen, by a grave error of course, as managers of the plan. Hence it must be sabotage perpetrated by those wreckers. The show trials validate the hypothesis of treason and sabotage. The doctrine or the theory is, of course, perfect. It must work.

Then comes a new interpretation of the perfect doctrine. True, reinterpretation of the doctrine is feasible, but only in terms of the early or late writings of the prophet—the major theoretician of the movement—or in terms of theories and interpretations of his pious disciples, those recognized and approved by the party.

However, a pluralist looks at the failure of a plan, above all, as a failure of an experiment due to an error, an error of the planners and decision makers in choice of means as well as perhaps in selection of goals. A monist validates his theory against an a priori definition, a pluralist, against the data, the facts. The only test of his validation is the product. If the options or courses of action that were chosen result in a product that was planned, then the policies worked. They were effective.

The product might be very adequate, fair, poor, or a total failure. The strength, the quality of policies, is evaluated accordingly. This is an experimental and pragmatic approach. We try whether our policy works and look what the results are. If the policy works and gives some result, it is valid or adequate. If it does not, it is invalid or inadequate, that is all. Error or failure is not only possible but is, moreover, a legitimate component of any experiment. Flexibility, freedom of choice of options, of answers to the problem, is a condition of an empirical and pragmatic approach, contrasted with a doctrinal and monistic approach. The latter is akin to the scholastic approach and method, which paved the way to inductive and empirical verification, as Alfred North Whitehead suggests, but it is also very different indeed. In a scholastic approach findings are tested against authorities, against the views and precepts of prophets, their disciples, or recognized masters. In an inductive and empirical approach the findings are tested against facts.

A democracy that recognizes a plurality of goals accepts the same plurality of methods and means within the broad limits of legal imperatives. A single, dominant, a priori doctrine imposed on the planners limits the choice of policies and forces solutions that may not work.

The question, however, may be asked, How do we find the right optimal measure? Our basic assumption suggests that the same problem can be solved in many different ways. In other words, the same goal can be achieved not by one single set of actions, but by more than one. Thus the planners consider not one but a number of options. After listing the feasible options, the preferred one is selected.

The preferred option is one that, in terms of a rational forecast, is (a) adequate (the chosen means are sufficient in terms of logic to achieve the goal); (b) the most efficient (highest payoff); (c) within the normative imperatives; and (d) within a reasonable expenditure of resources. The preferred options are tantamount to optimal.

Planning: Science and Common Sense

The sequence of planning, outlined above is of course not the only and a necessary sequence. On the other hand it is not a figment of our imagination nor exclusively an a priori logical and deductive construct. The sequence of planning that follows closely the general sequence of goals (horizontal goal structure) is also a result of a *sui generis* observation of ways that planning has been done in the past, as well as a kind of theoretical and rational effort in answering a question: How is rational planning done? It is an attempt to understand the rational and logical modes of thinking of those who attempted to achieve distant and complex goals. To repeat Thomas Huxley's dictum, what has been attempted is just organized common sense. "Science is, I believe, nothing but trained and organized common sense...." wrote Thomas Huxley. "A detective policeman discovers a burglar from the marks made by his shoes, by a mental process identical with that by which Cuvier restored the extinct animals of Montmartre from fragments of their bones." Planning has been carried on since man projected his cities, roads, cathedrals, and schools. There were goals that had to be implemented. Again, to quote Huxley, "The man of business will find himself out to be a philosopher with as much surprise as M. Jourdain exhibited when he discovered that he has been all his life talking prose."

Any rational plan has at least the five components, the five questions of what is (situation), what should be done (goals), how it should be done (means), other options, and at what it will cost (allocation of resources). Plans are written and carefully documented. Whether a plan is a short position paper, once called a problem paper, or an elaborate, extensive, even voluminous document, its outline will contain the answers to those questions.

Alternative Goals

Instead of alternative actions, a planner may consider alternative goals as a way of formulating his projects. Thus he attempts to meet the needs or answer the challenge of a situation by identification of a number of goals. In such an approach, after a survey of the situation he proceeds with identification of alternative goal options. One may argue that alternative goals are, in fact, nothing else but policy options. To an extent this might be true. In an overpopulated city a planner may consider several answers: (a) financial incentives and job offers to those willing to emigrate; (b) new housing projects within the city; (c) closely connected satellite cities with low-rent, public housing; (d) mass deportation in a totalitarian state.

All those options may be considered as immediate or intermediate goals guided by a strategic objective: in our case, to lower the density of population. An alternative goal calls again for choice of options and preferred alternatives.

However, this division between alternative goals and policies, options, is by no means sharp and precise. Policies and goals merge; they are not separate blocs. Closely interrelated, they represent at times the same set of data perceived from different vantage points. Logical convenience, as well as method, calls for separation of interrelated data by means of theoretical concepts. But daily life, behavior, and practice are complex and interrelated. At times they do not lend themselves to such separation by distinct and rigorous concepts.

Military and political strategies or foreign policy planning, unlike social planning, face counterstrategies and opposed courses of action. A political actor or planner who faces a strong counteraction and competes with his adversary for an identical goal must consider risks or cost too high. In consequence he may substitute his original goal for another.

However, substitute goals call also for careful choice and planning. A prudent planner who faces interdiction of his original, preferred goal has an anticipated response and substitute. Thus he may fall back on another policy objective without a major disadvantage. While facing an adverse situation, he has a ready plan where and how to retreat, to reorient his actions.

12

Distant Goals

Goal Range and Culture

Cultures and civilizations differ in the nature of their goals or major objectives inspired by religion, political beliefs, or various needs. They differ also in terms of goal ranges, the time span of goals, time and individual as well as collective attention span needed to achieve the objectives, hence they differ in duration of projects and plans. This difference in goals and their time span is an indicator of a historical period or of a civilization, for in those projects and goal-oriented activities not only are expressed needs, but so are ideas, beliefs, will, and organization of effort.

The strength of needs and ideas can be observed in the quantity and quality of human effort, in man's will to construct, to build churches, parliament houses, university campuses, aqueducts, or ancient temples.

Let us begin with simple, even obvious, examples of two sets of different pragmatic goals—directly related to urgency of basic needs: hunting and agriculture. From there we shall continue with complex (ideological and religious) goals.

Hunting requires shorter goal ranges than farming. In hunting societies goals are geared to immediate needs and objectives. Spacing between immediate, intermediate, and consummatory goals is not as far extended in time as in farming. In hunting the time distances could be measured in days, sections of days, or hours, while in farming measurements are made in months, weeks, and days. Farming calls for far more intermediary steps (instrumental goals) than hunting.

Rewards in hunting are almost immediate, once goals are reached. Goal spacing is, of course, short: (1) Decision (usually a group goes hunting); (2) readying cars, rifles; (3) meeting hunting company; (4) action (hunting); (5) if successful, goal (reward or achievement) becomes visible; (6) return home. All this is a matter of hours; the entire project of an Arapaho hunting party in Wyoming's Wind River Reservation might have taken a day or two. In one case, I remember, when it was combined with lumbering in the hills, a few days were planned, but the participants did not specify the number of days at the outset.

Now I shall mention major stages in farming. Each one could be considered as a separate project, subdivided into intermediary goals. Each stage of a farming project is as definite and complete as the entire project of hunting. However, the goal of a stage, unlike hunting, is instrumental and intermediate; it is not associated with rewards the actor works for. A hunter brings venison for his meal. The farmer, after ploughing, is finished, has no rewards whatsoever. He prepares for new labor, a new project of sowing.

The goal structure in farming is far more complex; it calls for an extended structure of intermediary, instrumental targets before the consummatory goal is achieved. Thus we may list at least six major stages of a farming project, each stage in terms of allocation of time, cost, and effort equivalent or more to the entire hunting project: (1) preparing soil, fertilizing; (2) ploughing; (3) sowing; (4) harvesting; (5) storing; (6) marketing.

The change from hunting to agriculture is tantamount to a shift from an almost immediate, tight sequence—need → goal → action → goal achievement → reward → satisfaction—to a horizontal goal sequence extended in time and highly complex, structured by a chain of instrumental, intermediate goals.

Such a change of goal structure is tantamount to a change of personal habits and tribal way of life.

The Arapahoes of the Wind River Reservation took to agriculture very slowly and in a passive way. Even with the short growing time in this part of Wyoming the shift to agriculture is not easy. On one hand goals are extended; on the other the content of effort is different. An Arapaho hunter does not engage in systematic daily work and chores. This type of work is done by women. Because of the nature of work, a shift from hunting to ranching is perhaps more attractive, and the Arapahoes moved rather slowly in this direction. This is of course not a universal omnipresent rule. The pattern of evolution, of change, is not unilinear, but is multilinear, and people live and lived on this earth who did not move in a historical evolutionary way. Many of them disappeared and did not change their way of life. However, the nature and the distribution of work in time and differing structures of goals favor certain types of transitions and make others more difficult.

The change of production, of means and modes, affects of course our goal structure. The economic change is in fact a change of goals. However, the initial change may take place on both or either of the sides of a culture: the material economic or the normative ideological.

Normative changes, changes in values and beliefs, may occur within the same, existing economic system and later affect the economic. The ideological change is an antecedent in such cases; the economic, the sequent. We may postulate that either the economic or the ideological change or both are antecedents of changes of goals. (A monistic approach limits the hypothesis of change to a single major variable (see chapter 2).

Goals have been extended in history with changes of beliefs, religion, ideology, philosophy, and systems of theoretical and applied knowledge. With the development of religion, philosophy, and science we may observe the development of the more distant goals and elaborate goal structures. The distant goals require self-discipline, restraint, patience, and planning. The satisfaction of immediate goals is postponed for the sake of more distant goals. Our science and arts have developed due to this type of restraint—self-discipline—and continuous extension of goals, goals that require extensive, long effort. The ascetic medieval life in the monasteries permitted extension of goal ranges—substitution of a distant goal for an immediate one. To transcribe books, entire volumes, an unusual attention span was necessary, an attention span supported by faith, the strong religiosity of those times. An unusual self-discipline, talent and also dedication were present. Beautiful and careful lettering as well as illuminations of those manuscripts testify to time span of work and preferential goals, not necessarily chosen for simple, utilitarian reasons.

Expansion of Christian faith took centuries. This was not solely a spontaneous process. There were also plans, projects of evangelization, forced or voluntary. Christian leaders, churchmen, and rulers probably anticipated their goals in terms of centuries and millennia.

A measure, or at least one of the measures of civilizations, is the nature of goals and particularly the goal structure and the time span of distant goals or targets (for definition of targets see chapter 8).

We may suggest here a following hypothesis: First, in the early stages of human society goals are short and cyclical; that is, goals do not extend over days and weeks, perhaps months. Cyclical goals, goals that return in regular time intervals of seasons, appear already in those early stages of mankind (see chapter 14).

Second, with the development of our society, on the advanced levels of culture in urban societies, projects appear with an extended goal range. This goal range extends to years and generations.

Finally, the long-range projects are not solely a mechanical consequence of economic changes. They are at times primarily articulation of religion or world outlook, idea systems of the ruling groups. The longer-than-a-generation goals in past history were associated with religious beliefs or visionary ideologies. However, in the latter part of our century there are projected pragmatic goals that span two or more generations.

In the history of the Mediterranean, European, and American civilizations the time span of goals varies; it reflects the major characteristics of culture:

1. In the early hunting and early farming periods goals were short, seldom exceeding an annual time span.

2. During the great periods of the Egyptian civilization the time span of major construction projects (temples, pyramids) extended to periods longer than two generations, occasionally as long as almost two centuries.

3. In the Hellenic civilization the time span of goals of major religious construction projects declined to decades, usually below the Egyptian level. In exceptional cases (for example, Olympieion in Athens) it extended even to ten generations—over three hundred years.

4. In Roman times in their construction of temples and pragmatic projects (bridges, theaters) the time span was still further reduced below the Hellenic one.

5. In medieval Europe the time span of goals of major religious architectural projects extended strikingly to centuries. The upper limits, even if exceptional, are five hundred to six hundred years.

6. With the Enlightenment, rationalism, and the Industrial Revolution (in the eighteenth century) long-range goals were associated with secular projects and ideas. They grew much shorter—usually did not exceed a decade, and seldom were planned longer than a generation. The time span of major construction projects grew shorter than in Hellenic and in medieval times.

7. During the nineteenth and early twentieth centuries individual goals of a life span were generally accepted in Western Europe and particularly in the United States.

8. During the second half of the twentieth century, in the scientific-technological period, some of the major secular goals are extended over two generations. This extension of goals is a consequence of development of a new outlook and is related to space and environment.

Time Range (Distance)

We shall call a time span estimated or necessary to achieve a goal, a time range, or distance. It is a time span between the decision, the end gate of the decision, and the goal or reward. We may assume such exact points often as theoretical or abstract, since in our daily decisions it is usually difficult to pinpoint in a precise manner the final point of decision and goal achievement.

The goal range is a matter of horizontal or cyclical approach (see chapter 14). Distance on the scale represents the time element. The time allocation plays a significant role in goal structure. The time element is tantamount to an effort, attention span, sacrifice of other rewards; it is in consequence the cost of the payoff. It also calls for allocation of resources. The distant value-goals require a far longer attention span, and the attention span is a matter of culture, personality, and also training.

The point of decision may be difficult to ascertain, for at times it is not fully conscious. The nature of the goal is indicative of the type of decision. The engineers who build the aqueduct of Rome, the *aedilus* in charge of the project, allocated the approximate time and cost in a less or more precise manner. He could not begin his work just off hand, without plans. We know about many of those edifices and how long it took to erect them.

The major construction projects are expressions of culture—however, of culture and the general idea system that governed behavior and decision of the ruling classes. It was the ruling classes who made the decision and controlled the instruments of power.

The distances of goals represent a variety of structures of goals: at certain historical periods amazingly distant and powerful, spanning centuries; in others limited to years and at most decades.

A series of data has been selected to illustrate our hypothesis and to draw a few inferences. However, before we move further, it should be stressed here that this historical outline of goal structure is again no more than a hypothesis that calls for initial and a posteriori qualifications.

We have selected for comparison architectural projects (goals) that are religious or ideological and represent direct articulations of the dominant idea system: for example, churches, cathedrals for medieval times, or projects that are pragmatic, but also culturally determined, such as bridges. The selected examples are representative illustrations of time and culture. They are social goals (since their execution calls for a group effort and social or political power). Furthermore, we have selected only the long-term and most distant projects. The everyday life projects of a working family were of course patterns of daily and annual sequences with some planning ahead. We have selected for comparison only those cases that suggest distant, and probably most distant, goals in architecture or represent either some of the largest or the most representative cases. Examples selected are also articulations of the dominant idea and belief system, above all religion. Dominant may mean in this case most widely professed or preferred by the ruling classes, that is, groups in control of the instruments of power necessary to erect those structures.

Below, the selected data on time of construction of major projects in four millennia are indicative of goal ranges and goal structures in architectural projects. How do we know that the builders of a cathedral had those goals? They built the cathedrals; here was the goal. The cathedral is a sequent, an effect; the decision to build was the proximate cause, expressed in a project or a plan. Furthermore, the time range expresses a historical attention span—in many cases an attention span of several generations. It is a ''social'' attention span—an attention span of many tied by the same idea system. In this sense they are cumulative goals of several generations.

Dates of duration of some major projects either are not known or could not be located.[1] In consequence, they were not included. The sample is not a random one, nor is it an irregular sample. The examples have been carefully selected in terms of their relevance. They are representative examples, indicators of culture and its period. But the emphasis in selection is put on duration. Examples of longer duration have been selected, since the purpose is to identify the most extensive projects that are articulations of normative or pragmatic goals. The purpose is to find the distant ranges of goals, not the immediate. In the latter sense the sample and in consequence data and means are skewed in favor of goals of a distant time range.

Difference in Dates

The dates of duration of construction, particularly dates of commencement and termination, differ at times substantially in various sources. For example, Banister Fletcher gives 1089–1131 (42 years) as dates of building the Abbey of Cluny; Gimbel instead gives 1088–1109 (see note 8). Both Fletcher and Gimbel are historians and scholars of great merit. How shall we choose? We have chosen Fletcher in this case, since his work is primarily concerned with detailed study of history of architectural samples. We could not consult original documents in all those numerous cases. Moreover, in many examples such documents do not exist; what does is a historian's record or mention. Perhaps in some cases there is a discrepancy between a symbolic act (consecration of the ground, installation of the altar) and actual commencement. But those are minor differences.

In numerous cases a cathedral was at first constructed, and later rebuilt, or sections of the church were built later. How shall we establish the duration of a project?

We may take here several examples.

There are some indications that in Roman times there was a church where the Cathedral of Chartres is now. There are also some records that in 743 and again in 858 the cathedral was burned, there was a fire in 1020, and a crypt was completed in 1024. The church (its architectural plan of today) was rebuilt in 1194–1260. The spire was built in 1507. However, some work went on. Fletcher gives 1194–1260 as the time of erection of the cathedral. We have chosen 1020–1507, since work began again after the fire of 1020. Of course it is in a way arbitrary. A longer period could be chosen too. Let me add that a historian of the Chartres Cathedral (Robert Branner) tells us that "substantial remains of older monuments are to be found."[2]

Now the perception of an art historian may differ with ours. We are concerned with a historical attention span, with a goal—to build a church, a cathedral, to rebuild a burnt one, a project that stretches over generations, that once neglected (as in the case of Cologne) is resumed again after years or even generations and continues. The spiritual need or the religious emotion or imagination of a project and the action toward achievement are always similar or the same. It is the duration of a will and need of generations, anchored to an ideological, religious need—what we may call a historical will—and a renewed goal, that is relevant in terms of the time distance of goals. That was the reason we have chosen the date of 1020, indicating that by that time the need and goal were already established.

There are many such cases. Take Westminster. The church in its location was built in 616, became a Benedictine monastery in 960, and was rebuilt in 1055–

1065. For the same reason as in the case of Chartres, we took 960–1065, although some historians may take 1055–1065.

Again, consider Saint Mark's in Venice. Fletcher gives dates of construction as 1042–1085; Gimbel gives 1095–1500. The initial Basilica of Saint Mark was founded in 868. In 1042–1085 the plan was completely transformed and the cathedral completed. The facade was again reconstructed—as we see it now—in the fifteenth century. We have chosen 1042 as the beginning and 1500 as the termination. And so it goes: Lincoln Cathedral was erected during 20 years (1072–1092) and rebuilt completely during 128 years (1192–1320). But, the spiritual need and goal, the historical attention span (not a basic need of hunger or shelter), was there all the time.

The choice was tiresome and not easy. We were guided in those cases by a somewhat arbitrary sense of approximation. It has all the shortcomings of my own errors and deficiencies.

The differences between sources as well the way durations were chosen do not affect, however, the basic findings and inferences. Nonetheless, we had better repeat, our findings at this stage are no more than a hypothesis and an approximation. See table 12.1

General Inference on History of Goal Range

The time span of projects suggests the range of goals; for statistical convenience we may suggest units of annual duration or of decades and generations. The major construction projects associated with ideological–religious goals—belief or religion—were able to generate the longest-enduring (what might be called) social attention span. By the social attention span we shall mean the continuation of a collective effort to achieve a goal, whether such a goal is attempted by means of command of autocratic, oppressive ruling classes, by slave labor of Egypt and Rome or by free labor of medieval craftsmen.

Some of the Egyptian religious projects spanned nearly two centuries and many generations. The time range of those projects was longer than the Greek and Roman. The time range declined when major cultural and political centers move to Greece and Rome.

In Greece the structures were not as colossal as the Egyptian, but still the major projects extended to two, even three, generations—70 years—and a century in their social attention span; this suggests extended, even if interrupted, efforts. It took 180 years to build in Egypt the Temple of Horus in Edfu, 99 years for the Doric Temple of Zeus in a Greek colony. However, major Egyptian temples were built in several decades and two or three and more generations: Luxor, 92 years; Sebek, 159; Hathor, 178; Isis, 37; the Pyramid of Gizeh, 23. Most of the Greek temples were completed in decades, but also in generations: Olympieion in Athens, 306 years (this is indeed a case of long duration); the Great Temple of Apollo, Selinus, 70; but Theseion, 5; Parthenon, 15; Nemesis,

Table 12.1
Range of Major Projects, 2700 BC – 1970 AD

	Dates	Time span in years
Egypt, 2700 BC – 68 AD[3] *Tombs and Temples:*		
The Great Pyramid in Gizeh, built somewhere about 2700 BC, took probably more than twenty years. The Greek historian Herodotus mentions twenty years; he estimates that 100,000 workers were employed. Egyptologists estimated twenty, thirty, and even more than fifty years duration of the construction of pyramids. We shall accept a probable thirty years. The Tombs in Beni Hassan (39 tombs), which belonged to a provincial great family, were built during 2130–1785 BC; hence a time span of 345 years. However, this seems to be a "crescive" project, which grew with each new generation and was not derived from an initial plan.	2700 BC	30
Temple of Luxor	1408–1300 BC	92
Temple of Horus, Edfu	237–57 BC	180
Temple of Isis, Island of Philae	378–341 BC	37
Temple of Hathor	110 BC–68 AD	178
Temple of Sebek	145 BC–14 AD	159
Temples: Greece, 550 BC–132 AD[4]		
The Theseion, Athens	449–444 BC	5
Temple of Apollo, Bassae	450–425 BC	25
Parthenon, Athens	447–432 BC	15
Temple of Nemesis, Rhamnos	436–432 BC	4
Temple C, Selinus	550–530 BC	20
The Great Temple of Apollo, Selinus	520–450 BC	70
Temple of Zeus, Agrigentum	510–409 BC	99
Temple of Segesta, Sicily	424–416 BC	8
Temple of Apollo Epicurius, Bassae	450–425 BC	25
The Olympieion, Athens (the stand on the side of the Doric temple was commenced in 515 BC)	174 BC–132 AD	306
Temples: Rome, 14 BC–313 AD[5]		
Temple of Mars, Rome	14–2 BC	12
Temple of Concord, Rome	7 BC–10 AD	17

Table 12.1 *(cont.)*
Range of Major Projects, 2700 BC – 1970 AD

	Dates	Time span in years
Temple of Venus, Rome	123–135 AD	12
Trajan's Basilica, Rome	98–112 AD	14
Constantine's Basilica, Rome	310–313 AD	3
Cathedrals and Churches: Eastern Europe, 532–1078[6]		
Hagia Sophia	532–537	5
Kiev—Desyatinnaya Church	989–996	7
Pechora Church	1073–1078	5
Saint Sophia Cathedral, Novgorod	1045–1052	7
Cathedrals and Churches: Western Europe and Mexico, 449–1880[7]		
Baptistery Ravenna	449–452	3
San Vitale, Ravenna	526–547	21
Saint Mark's, Venice	1042–1500	458
Le Puy Cathedral	1050–1150	100
Cathedral in Pisa	1063–1092	29
Baptistery of Pisa	1153–1278	125
Cathedral of Milan	1386–1813	427
Saint Peter's, Rome	1506–1626	120
Lincoln Cathedral	1072–1092	20
rebuilt	1192–1320	128
Cathedral of Santiago at Compostella	1075–1128	53
Winchester (continuous work on this cathedral)	1079–1528	449
Cathedral in Salisbury	1220–1258	38
West facade	1258–1265	7
Chapter house	1263–1284	21
Wells	1180–c. 1425	245
Westminster Abbey	960	
rebuilt	1055–1065	10
Notre Dame, Paris	1163–c. 1250	87
Amiens Cathedral	1220–1288	68
Rouen	1230–1365	135
Beauvais Cathedral	1247–1568	321
Strasbourg Cathedral	1230–1365	135
Chartres Cathedral	1020–1507	487
Rheims Cathedral	1211–1427	216
Cathedral of Cologne (begun in fourth century, present foundation stone; finished according to original design)	1248–1880	632
Cathedral of Mexico City	1563–1667	104

Table 12.1 *cont.*
Range of Major Projects, 2700 BC – 1970 AD

	Dates	Time span in years
Monasteries: 1131–1522[8]		
Belem, near Lisbon	1499–1522	23
Betalha, Portugal	1387–1415	28
Cistercian Church, Alcobaca, Portugal	1158–1223	65
Abbey of Cluny	1089–1131	42
Major Architectural Examples: United States, 1789–1970[9]		
Saint Patrick's Cathedral, New York City	1858–1879	21
State Capitol, Virginia	1789–1798	9
United States Capitol	1792–1867	75
New York City Hall	1803–1812	9
Empire State Building, New York City	1929–1931	2
Rockefeller Center, New York City	1931–1939	8
World Trade Center, New York City	1961–1970	9
Bridges: 109 BC–1964 AD[10]		
Pons Mulvius, Rome	109 BC	1
Pons Fabricius, Rome	62–21 BC	41
Bridge of Augustus, Rimini	14–20 AD	6
Roman Bridge, Alcantara, Spain	105–116	11
Trajan's Roman (Timber) bridge on Danube	104–105	1
London Bridge	1176–1209	33
Bridge of Saint Esprit (on Rhone River)	1265–1297	32
Ponte di Castel Vecchio, Verona	1335	1
Santa Trinita Bridge, Florence	1567–1569	2
Southwark Bridge (Iron Arches), London	1814–1819	5
Britannia Railroad Bridge, Wales	1845–1850	5
Tower Bridge, London	1886–1894	8
Brooklyn Bridge, New York City	1869–1883	14
George Washington Bridge, New York City(Decision made, 1892; construction commenced, 1927)	1927–1931	4
Oakland Bridge, San Francisco (Decision made, 1929; construction commenced, 1933)	1933–1936	3
Golden Gate Bridge, San Francisco (Decision made, 1929; construction commenced, 1933)	1933–1937	4
Verrazano-Narrows Bridge, New York City	1960–1964	4
Theaters: 23 BC–1969 AD[11]		
Theater of Marcellus, Rome	23–13 BC	10
Colosseum, Rome	70–82 AD	12

Table 12.1 *cont.*
Range of Major Projects, 2700 BC – 1970 AD

	Dates	Time span in years
Odeion, Athens	161 AD	1
La Scala, Milan	1776–1778	2
Great Theater (Opera), Warsaw	1825–1832	7
The Opera House, Paris	1861–1874	13
The Opera House, Cologne	1870–1872	2
Lincoln Center, New York City	1959–1969	10
Selected Structures Considered at Times as Record Achievements, 1887–1970[12]		
Eiffel Tower, Paris	1887–1889	2
Rockefeller Center, New York City	1931–1939	8
Empire State Building, New York City	1930–1931	2
World Trade Center, New York City	1961–1970	9

4; Temple of Segesta, 8; to mention some. Rome seems to be far more secular; the span of major constructions is contained within a decade or a few years more. Compared with Greek temples, the time of construction was shorter: Temple of Venus in Rome, 12; Trojan's Basilica, 14; Temple of Concord, 17; and Constantine's Basilica, 3. None extends over one generation.

The increase in time span came with the religiosity of the medieval times. During the most intense period, which extends from eleventh till beginning of the sixteenth century, this religiosity was articulated in religious architectural projects that extended in their social attention span for several generations, even centuries. The Cathedral of Cologne is one of the most impressive: 632 years of construction span. The project was interrupted, of course at times forgotten, but resumed again and continued. The attention to this project spread over generations. Many of the medieval projects extended for centuries: Saint Mark's, 458 years; Milan, 427; Wells, 245; Chartres, 487; Beauvais, 321; Rheims, 216. However, some were shorter: Rouen, 135; Mexico City, 104; Notre Dame, 87.

In a historical comparison of the time span of goals of the ancient, medieval and modern worlds, the medieval civilization strikes us with the constancy to purpose, tenacity of effort. The powerful architecture of distant goals has its parallel image in those cathedrals. Distant goals of construction also had their intermediate stations, which at the same time connected the old and the oncoming generations of architects, administrators, and churchmen. Those architectural projects extended over several generations, were integrated by a single, religious world outlook and by wide acceptance and permanence of the dominant values.

The religious theme prevailed in art and philosophy as well as literature. Pitrim Sorokin considered the medieval culture as representative of a unified *ideational* or idealistic system as contrasted with the earlier and modern sensate culture. The *ideational* culture is based "on superrational and supersensory reality of God, although differently perceived" in various cultures. "Its major premise was that the true reality is partly supersensory and partly sensory that it embraces the supersensory, plus the rational aspect and finally the sensory aspect, is blended into unity, that of the infinite manifold God''. The sensate culture is the modern, this-wordly sensory, empirical, and secular. ''It is based upon and integrated around this new principle-value: The true reality and value is sensory.'' To state that the age was dominated by religion and religiosity is both more accurate and simpler. But at this point we shall not argue Sorokin's theory any further.

Analyzing the nature of medieval art, Sorokin indicates (not unlike Dilthey or Dworak a generation or two before) that the major topics of art are religious. He supports his argument with statistical data. He indicates the fact, which is of course well known to students of history of art, that sculpture and paintings were overwhelmingly religious: 10th–11th centuries, 94.7 percent; 12th–13th centuries 97.0 percent.[13]

Sorokin compiled statistical data on religious and secular art by century:

	Religious	**Secular**
Before 10th	81.9	18.1
10th–11th	94.7	5.3
12th–13th	97.0	3.0
14th–15th	85.0	15.0
16th–17th	64.7	35.3
17th–18th	50.2	49.8
18th–19th	24.1	75.9
19th–20th	10.0	90.0
20th–	3.9	96.1

The dominance of religiosity is the same as that expressed in architecture—in churches and cathedrals. Sorokin's data suggests the most intensive, religious period in medieval art to have been between the eleventh and thirteenth centuries, when the religious theme in art increased to 97 percent. This is also the era of commencement of the extensive—perhaps the most extensive (in terms of centuries, not decades)—time span of cathedral projects, for example, Wells, Saint Mark's, Winchester, Rouen, Beauvais, Rheims, Chartres (see above). Cathedrals and churches are solely articulations of dominant culture, of the idea system that at the time governs society. Already by the sixteenth century European culture had become increasingly secular. This is reflected clearly in Sorokin's data on art topics: By the sixteenth century the religious subject had declined to 64 percent; by the seventeenth, to 50.2 percent. With the advance of the Enlightenment, rationalism, and the Industrial Revolution, religious topics in art declined rapidly to 24.1 percent in the eighteenth century, and in the scientific age, the twentieth century, they are reduced to 3.9 percent. In the twelfth to thirteenth centuries secular topics amounted to 3 percent. In the twentieth century the reverse was true.

With rationalism, the Enlightenment, and the Industrial Revolution, major projects moved again into decades and periods shorter than a decade. The person, society in a single life span, became a measure of an industrial and architectural project. With the weakening of faith the goal became shorter. Man wished to enjoy in his lifetime the fruits of his effort. The architecture shifted to secular projects: theaters, bridges, highways, houses of parliament, and office buildings became symbols and articulations of the new rationalistic and pragmatic civilizations. The emphasis was on efficiency—to achieve the goal with the least effort. The change in technology had some effect, especially technical advance in transportation. The technology of building changed little—for centuries—from the early Babylonian and Greek pattern. Iron, glass, and concrete entered the historical scene in the middle of the nineteenth century (although the Romans applied concrete as mortar). Still a major religious project, Saint Patrick's Cathedral took twenty-one years (1858–1879).

Probably the longest time range in the United States is represented by the Capitol in Washington—seventy-five years. The State Capitol of Virginia and New York City Hall took also a decade or more (Virginia, 9 years; New York, 9). The Capitol in Washington as well as that in Virginia are also articulations of a new political belief system—democracy, republic, in turn a consequence of the Enlightenment and rationalism.

Qualification of Data

Overall (save important exceptions), the time range of construction projects spanned generations in Egypt and several decades in Greece, then declined in Rome to more than a decade, increased to several centuries in medieval times, and declined again to decades or more in times of the Industrial Revolution and rationalism.

The sample was a priori qualified. I do not intend to hide or even defend the weakness, perhaps an inherent weakness, of this rough quantitative approach. It is no more than an attempt, a hypothesis. Nonetheless, in spite of shortcomings, this approach permits one to see historical changes in collective goals or intentions of major projects within a time span of four millennia. Moreover, the time range of those goals is an indicator of culture, of a historical period. It is an indicator of a series of immediate and intermediate instrumental goals, which preceded successful termination of those projects.

Nonetheless, we shall continue with the criticism. The series are short, in consequence, and this affects the statistical means as well as the nature of standard deviations. But statistical abstractions of series of data telescope the varieties of numbers into a single data, a single product of quantitative orientation. Those single statistical products facilitate—more, permit—further discussion and analysis, open new vistas.

The data were selected in an arbitrary way. In consequence, a selection of different data (of construction of other buildings) would give us different numbers, different means. But I shall argue here, similar to ours. Those numbers are only approximations and no more than tentative data. What we suggest here is a hypothesis. In a time span of 4,000 years, the means of goal range and the historical attention span of major religious buildings and constructions indicates substantial variations (table 12.2) - (despite some deficiencies in data). Medieval Europe suggests a civilization of a most extended time span of religious architecture, with the means of over 180 years; next comes Egypt, with more than 112 years; followed by Greece with more than 57 years. Short, life-size goal distance with a means of more than 11 years characterizes the secular and pragmatic Roman civilization. The structure of goals of medieval Europe is powerful indeed. (See also figure 12.1.)

Table 12.2
Means (in Years) of Goal Range and Historical Attention Span of Major Religious Architectural Construction Projects, c. 20th century BC – 19th century AD

	20th c. BC – 1st c. AD Egypt Pyramids, Temples	5th c. BC – 2d c. AD Greece Temples	15th c. BC – 4th c. AD Rome Temples	6th c. BC – 11th c. AD Eastern Europe Cathedrals	50th c. BC – 19th c. AD Western Europe Cathedrals
Years	112.6	57.7	11.6	6	180.6

Table 12.3
Means (in Years) of Goal Range of Major Secular Architectural Construction Projects in Europe and U.S.A., from 2d century BC – 20th century AD

	Bridges	Theaters	Major Examples in U.S.A. (of longest duration)
Years	10.29	7.12	20.00

The data, reduced to means, suggest substantial historical differences of time ranges of constructions. But are those different project durations solely a consequence of the belief system? This question seems to arise instantly after perusal of the variety of time spans.

It has been several times reiterated that goals are not separate, independent units. They are only expressions of basic, pragmatic needs or belief systems. This general qualification is, however, not sufficient.

Major projects selected in our sample are indicators of culture, belief systems, yes. But their completion depends on political and economic conditions, that is, stability or instability of the system, which makes such a project feasible. Long-term projects require also political economic systems of long duration. Such systems have either flexibility or adjustment and reconstruction (British or Amer-

Figure 12.1
Top Time Ranges of Major Religious Architectural Construction
Projects of longest duration (based on table 12.1)
(Atypical unique and extreme deviation excluded.)

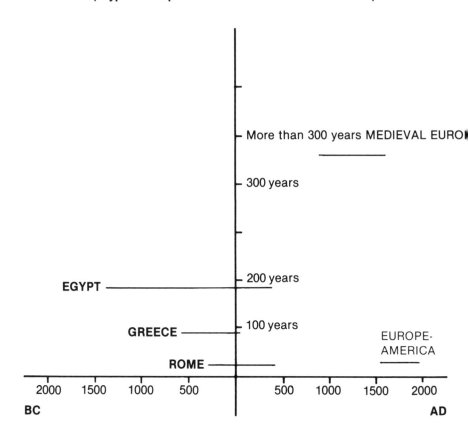

ican political systems) or rigid stability of absolute political control (Oriental despotic rule).

But within any of those systems, completion of a project is determined by four variables, which are present in all cases and which, therefore, we shall call *essential*. In addition, factors may and do affect the projects that either are unique in a given case or do occur at one time and not in another. We shall call them incidental. Those four major variables are:

1. the organized will to attain the goal as well as urgency of the need
2. the belief system, general ideology, values that affect the goals

Figure 12.1a
Time Range of Major Projects, 2000 BC — 2000 AD

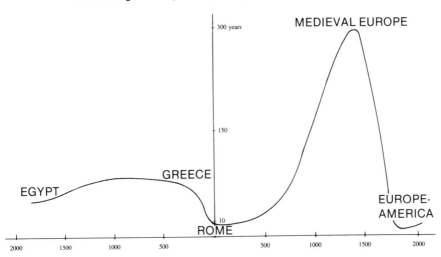

Changing time range of major architectural projects & constructions

Egypt – Europe 2000 B.C. – 2000 A.D. Europe and America.

3. technology, including skills and availability of materials; the means of production
4. organization and skills in organizing, mobilizing the effort; financing and decision
   making

"Advocatus Diaboli" Criticism of Data

Let us now argue against validity of our major hypothesis and see whether the confrontation of negative and positive data will still support the initial hypothesis:

1. The duration, the time range, of goals is culturally determined; it is not solely an outcome (direct or indirect) of needs that are basic or of obvious biological, practical utility.
2. Goals of long or the longest time range were, in the past, articulations of beliefs, particularly of religion.

Roman temples were built in a shorter time span than the Greek ones. In addition, the Romans advanced this magnificent, pragmatic piece of architecture: the bridge. The ancient Greeks left little evidence of their bridge building.

The Romans, so it seems, were superior in organization to the Greeks. This excellence of Roman skills in organization of the government as well as of the army or of engineering is stressed by outside observers, historians of unusual power of observation, for example, Polybius, who was of Greek origin (2d century BC) or Josephus Flavius, a Hellenistic, Roman-Greek-Jewish historian. The Roman sense of order and organization, the logic of an organized life, of stability of social relations, is expressed in the institutions of Roman law, a system that survived and keeps its vitality even today.

They had a well-organized engineering corps with an institutional head—the *aedilus*. The work was supervised by engineers and crews of skilled craftsmen organized into semimilitary guilds. They were sent all over the empire.

Financing of bridges and public works was also well administered and stable. Those of a military nature were financed by the treasury; others, by townships. Ways of mobilization of manpower were set: Military bridges were usually built by the legionnaries; nonmilitary, by forced labor.

The classic textbook on architecture, Vitruvius' *Ten Books on Architecture*, testifies to the interest and skills of the era. This unique manual, written during the first century AD, has chapters on aqueducts. The Romans had indeed superior organization, technical skills, methods of cost allocations, mobilization of labor, as well as advanced technology.

The Roman applied two major innovations: They discovered or learned the use of cement, and they applied the arch in architecture, an arch that they probably borrowed from the Etruscans. The Greeks did not know cement, nor were they fully familiar with the construction of the arch. It is the arch that spins the strong, lasting bridges, whether in Rome, Italy, or Spain; we might mention the long and beautiful Pons Fabricius of Rome (62–21 BC) with its perfect system of round horseshoe arches or in the bridge Alcantara, Spain (105–116 AD). Furthermore, out of three materials—wood, stone, and bricks—stone was used by the Greeks in their major projects, whereas stone and bricks were used by the Roman builders. In the Acropolis of Athens the stone dominates. On the Forum Romanum of Rome stone shares its presence with extensive use of bricks. And to move to the port of ancient Rome, Ostia Antica, what exquisite brick work one can observe. This unusual application of various sizes and forms of bricks one hardly can find, even in medieval Gothic, which applied the bricks in such a profusion, at times combining it with stone. It is of course easier to transport bricks, and the building can be finished faster. Wood was probably used in private dwellings, but the vestiges of its use disappear rapidly.

Granted the difference in all three variables, which favored a shorter duration in the construction of great Roman temples, in our sample the duration varies from three to fourteen years. Moreover, Christian temples—the churches built between the twelfth and sixteenth centuries—were architectural projects of extensive time range, of several decades or even centuries. Italian architects of the fourteenth or sixteenth century had more advanced building skills or technology than the Romans. Construction of tall towers is indicative of this. It can be further argued that the fact that the Romans had great skills could have resulted in more magnificent temples, if they had wished to build them. Pons Fabricius took forty-one years to build. This indicates that Romans had the will as well as the capacity to advance long-range projects. But they invested their energy and taste for this type of work in major secular projects.

Temples and theaters are major architectural articulations of ancient Greece. Roads, aqueducts, bridges, *thermae* (baths), forts, and forums are articulations of Rome. The Greek is symbolic of a culture guided by philosophical, religious, and esthetic values; the Roman is pragmatic and secular. The state, later the *imperium*, generates the ideology of political power, the source of economic well-being of the ruling classes. Ideology and values appear in all those examples in major projects and in the range of distant goals.

Those who built bridges, roads, and theaters expected to see and use those projects in their lifetime. Hence they built their projects within decades. There are exceptions of course.[14]

Financing and decision making patterns—in addition to needs and will, ideology, organization, and technology—may extend or shorten the completion of a project. Both variables may be considered as an extension of the general category of economic and social organization. Here, indeed, differences are substantial too. Hence, in some cases, construction of medieval cathedrals was interrupted simply because there was no money. Intervals due to such interruptions could be quite lengthy. In addition, war and social unrest, not unfrequent occurrences in those times, could further extend the duration of such projects.

Let us move now from those distant times to current history, to our times. Until World War II it took four or five years to build a highway in the United States. Now the building of a highway lasts longer. The reasons are in the nature of cost allocation and financing. Money comes from different sources, especially from the federal government, which imposes conditions and restrictions, especially environmental restrictions.

Decision making and planning may extend the project in time. However, careful planning also secures efficient conduct and completion of the project.

Thus construction of a playground (one to one and one-half acres) in New York City takes a time span of about two and one-half years: eighteen months to design and nine months of construction. Larger parks, those over two acres, take three years: two years to design and one year of construction.[15]

If we begin with intent, the stage of predecision, imagination of a project, then some of the modern, efficient construction projects extend over two, even three, generations.

The first vision of a structure that would connect Brooklyn and Staten Island, New York, and would span the two islands over the Narrows appeared as early as 1888. At this time, however, a tunnel deep under the water was planned. In 1923, shafts for this tunnel were constructed, but work was abandoned. In 1930 Mayor La Guardia took the initiative, suggesting this time a bridge over the Narrows. Eventually the City Planning Commission decided on a master plan of highways and major projects, including the Brooklyn–Staten Island Bridge in 1941. Construction was commenced on January 13, 1960, and completed and opened to the traffic on November 21, 1964.[16] Hence the entire project, from intent till completion, took almost seven decades. However, actual construction took four years.

Finally, let us consider the "incidentals," this general variable of the unexpected occurrences or incidents that reflect the vicissitudes of human history.

Here belong war or plague, which struck Byzantium in times of Justinian (sixth century), so realistically described by the historian Procopius in his *History of the Persian and Gothic Wars*. At such time the craftsmen abandoned their task.

Findings: Time Range of Religious Construction Projects

We have assumed that the duration of the projects is a product of four major components, which we may visualize as vectors. We have put a larger number of variables into those four major categories: (1) will; (2) ideology and values; (3) technology; (4) organization. Moreover, projects have to be considered within a context of the political system within which they originate. Stability or flexibility of those systems is a condition of completion of projects stretched over decades and generations. And now our findings.

Granted that duration of those projects is affected by incidental occurrences, still the strength of the values and ideology, as well as of the will, dominates the patterns of distant goals. This pattern appears in a general overview of major architectural projects during four millennia of organized building activities.

I shall grant all the deficiencies of our exercise that were indicated before. I shall add an additional one: accuracy of data. Some of the historical data may not be necessarily accurate, but I assume that the critical quota of examples suggests correct approximations. Again, in spite of all those shortcomings, a pattern emerges in a broad outline. Of course there are exceptions and variants. They do appear in standard deviations.

Cathedrals, churches, monasteries—all those articulations of Christian religiosity of medieval times indicate an unusually long, sustained collective and historical will and attention span. The projects are at times interrupted, but still continued. How then can we explain the short time span within which cathedrals and churches were erected in Eastern Europe during the sixth to eleventh centuries? The Hagia Sophia in Constantinople was completed in a short time span of five years (532–537). This phenomenon would call for detailed discussions. All those churches, however, were built in the frontier lands of the Christian world. External pressure and aggression called for rapid consolidation of political and religious power.

In spite of all those other factors, determinants affecting the duration, the long range of architectural projects associated with religiosity, appear clearly. The decline of such duration is also noticeable, for example, in Greek and Roman projects, the latter being shorter.

The religious projects are of longer duration. However, secular, pragmatic construction throughout the ages are of strikingly similar time spans.

The Range of Pragmatic Projects

Let us turn now to time span of secular projects: theaters and bridges.

Within a range of more than two millennia the time span of theater construction is strikingly constant.

The construction of a theater, back from 23 BC until the present, takes from a year to about a decade, at most a decade and a half.

The Colosseum of Rome (70–82), the Opera House of Paris (1861–1874), and Lincoln Center in New York (1959–1969) were projects of similar time range, in spite of change in technology. Lincoln Center is of course far larger than the Paris Opera. All of the theaters of Lincoln Center seat over 13,600, less than the Colosseum of Rome used to. The Colosseum seated 45,000 persons; some even estimated 50,000.

The Colosseum—is this building a theater? Its function was not "theatrical" in the Hellenic sense. Historians of architecture list the Colosseum in a special category of amphitheaters. It is indeed a special architectural structure. It is not a "stadium." It compares perhaps with Madison Square Garden. However, because of its architectural qualities and its entertainment function, although brutal and cruel, we have included the Colosseum in theatrical construction. The time span tells us: This is the social attention span of those projects that belong to the largest in theater building. This is the time and cost that man was willing to allocate to his entertainment: ten to fifteen years.

The time range of bridge building is similar. Whether in Roman times or today in the United States, man is willing to give a decade or more to a bridge. The maximum span of bridges changes, of course. The advanced modern technology permits man to extend their length. It could be argued that change in technology shortens the time of building bridges. This is not the issue. There were always rivers, heavily populated on both shores, all over the world. The will, technology, and values to build a bridge were not there. Even technology alone does not suffice. Planners estimated the length of the bridges not only in terms of available technology but also in terms of need and time. The Roman governor of a province, the *aedilus*, in charge of engineering, considered the project in terms of Roman perception of need and duration of his office. It was not very different later. Hence the project is imagined, measured not solely in terms of space but also in terms of the time span needed for completion of the bridge. Still one has to consider and admire the six Roman arches of the Alcantara bridge, carrying a roadway of 50 meters (170 feet); it has served travelers for about two thousand years.

I have selected examples of projects of long duration as evidence of distant goals and social-historical memory. However, distant goals as well as those of the limited short time range of the modern industrial and postindustrial age not only testify to advanced technology, will, and energy but are also indicative of values and modern economic ideology.

The difference between quality and quantity is a major difference between the medieval way of production and the industrial economy. The medieval craftsman was guided by standards of quality, even beauty, rather than by principles of precise calculation of time as well as efficiency per time unit. To quote Werner Sombart, the medieval craftsman was wanting *Kalkulatorischer Sinn*, a computing orientation; he was deficient of what might be called "calculatory sense."[17] Modern industrial production is associated with a broad and precise application of quantification. Efficiency is a major value, a goal, and a norm of conduct in economic activity. Efficiency in a rational method of production is of course measured in terms of the quantity of a product in a time unit, provided that a standardized, often high quality is maintained in a product unit.

Years back, at the capitol in Denver, Colorado, an informative chart for visitors indicated all the measurements of the construction, all in numbers. One could find in it every "how many" and "how much." One would hardly expect a chart, reduced almost entirely to numbers, providing information about the Louvre or Westminster Abbey. The former was a clear articulation of the industrial age. The numbers you can see in Westminster Museum are old bills, bills for restoration of a chapel as well as for the hat of Lord Nelson. They strike you rather in terms of how much you could buy for a pound at those times and how little today.

In addition, next to efficiency, functional, and often esthetic values, a new value appears in modern production and architecture, a value that brings an element of modern sport into man's productive effort. This value is the "record," the very idea of being the fastest, of producing most in the shortest time span, of reaching the goals, the frontiers of the impossible. The "record time" in itself becomes a goal, an articulation of a philosophy of work and competition. The record, speed (not patience and humility), or the faith in myself becomes a value.

The values of Greek athletes, and of most Roman racing sportsmen and onlookers of the gory gladiatorial games, were "Herculean." The sportsmen of those times did not count records. First, they did not have stopwatches. The victory was the goddess; and the sheer strength of muscles—Hercules—was the god. Strength, physical prowess, victory—those were goals and virtues to be admired. Emperor Commodus, who fancied cruel, gladiatorial sports, used the title of the Roman Hercules, which still can be seen on coins of his time. The modern athletic and related racing sports have two major value-goals: victory and record. The first is no different than the ancient one. The record, measured in precise units of time and space, is a modern one. The concept of the record— unknown before—is of course also an articulation of efficiency.

The planners, builders, architects now take pride in time record. Eiffel builds a steel tower, the "tallest tower" of his time, in two years and three months. It does not serve any purpose at this time; it does not claim beauty. It is a monument to a record: the tallest structure constructed with only steel.

Here we cite some of the official Empire State Building information with its emphasis on record, on facts and figures, dating back to February 1956.

"The Empire State Building was built at the intersection of probably one of the world's busiest corners, where 40,000 vehicles and 200,000 pedestrians pass by every day. Since there was no room on the streets for the storage of materials, delivery schedules (much like railroad timetables) were timed so that steel was in place in the framework eighty hours after it left the steel mills in Pittsburgh. The metal skeleton required twenty-three weeks to complete, and the masonry was completed in eight months; both (I understand) are engineering feats without parallel.

During the peak periods of building, more than 1,900 were on the direct payroll of the builder and 1,500 were employed on the site by subcontractors. There were 1,500 different industries, ranging from marble quarries in France, Italy, Belgium, and Germany, were involved."

We learn further, among a flood of data, that the administration maintains and repairs 20,000 doors and locks a year, cuts 15,000 keys a year; cleans 6,500 windows twice a month; cleans 210 rest rooms nightly; and removes seven tons of paper every night. There are 1,106 wash basins, and 386 urinals; 200,000 gallons of water are used daily.

Now on beacon lights: Each separate light uses a 2,500-watt, short-arc mercury bulb and generates 450 million candlepower, roughly the equivalent of 15,000 automobile headlights. Together, the four beacons throw out 2 billion candle-power, the equivalent of almost 60,000 automobile headlights. This is the brightest continuously burning manmade source of light in the world.[18]

In all those data there is an element of record, of speed and victory. Production is a serious business, yes, but it becomes also a sport, a game. The quantification of life itself is also an articulation of our perception of society and world, of our world outlook. Not only the view from the Empire State Building but also the data about this once tallest building in the world, constructed in only twenty months, are impressive.

Both types of data, of the major architectural projects' longest and shortest time spans, are articulations of will, values, beliefs, or ideology in addition to skills, technology, and organization.

The former testify to the social-historical attention span; the latter, to the relevance of pragmatic norms of efficiency, not necessarily of urgent needs. There was no urgent need to build an Empire State Building in record time. At least the lore tells us about the function of fantasy and imagination at the origins of those unusual projects that begin with a vision in the human mind.

The new industrial ideology has its effects on time span of goals. A record short time becomes a goal in itself. It is the speed that is a major standard in sport; speed again becomes a major value in this sport-oriented industrial philosophy. Hence the tendency is to reduce the time span of goals. Still, in spite of this philosophy, the time span of some pragmatic project remains strikingly constant.

Historical Memory and Attention Span

One question may be still asked: Were those long-range goals, stretching over generations, conceived and firmly established at the commencement of the project? The answer is tentative; it is a hypothesis rather than a definite finding. Each case would call for separate research, and it is doubtful whether adequate sources could be located to ascertain considerations of goals and time ranges of projected medieval cathedrals. In some cases, one might guess, architects realized the magnitude of the projects. Some were envisaged in shorter time spans; however, incidental factors, such as war and pestilence, interrupted the plan. In others, money was the issue; projects of some churches were delayed for financial or economic reasons. The goals, I imagine, might have changed while projects were under way. Additional sections, enlargements, chapels were suggested once the buildings were under way or even finished. Imagination or fantasy is prompted by reality. Rulers, churchmen, architects who saw the building visualized embellishments, improvements, corrections, or additions. Similar circumstances might have occurred with old bridges, especially those of a long span.

Whatever the original intent, those major monuments of architecture express a continuation of perception of need and will—more, a social and historical memory, a memory transmitted and maintained from one generation to the next, not solely by single individuals but by groups. Those groups, structured in organizations and institutions, keep and transmit this memory by means of conversation, public utterances, lore, and above all carefully preserved records. This historical memory expresses in turn the attention span of a society that allocates resources and efforts to an original goal, which in turn may generate new ones. Again needs, imagination, will, and new skills may prompt individuals and groups to revise and extend the projects and in consequence the initial goals. It is the initial need and goal as well as constancy to purpose that prompt the project and keep it alive through decades and generations. Maintenance of a project is related to its actual use—not to its erection—from its commencement to its completion.

Those needs are an articulation of a world outlook we call historicism (Meinecke calls it "historism" in a somewhat different sense).[19] This historical interest, attention to the past, the historical sense varies in intensity and articulations. In some cultures, for example, in India, it seems to have been absent, or at least far less intense, than in ancient Greece or Rome. In the early historical periods it appears in religion, in lore, legends, and ballads, later in chronicles and laudatory records of the rulers, and eventually in careful recording, critical evaluation, and criticism.

However, history has also a definite, "useful" social function. First of all, it integrates society; it integrates generations in time, while social organization integrates society in space. Furthermore, it integrates and transmits experience, skills, and knowledge of past generations. It supplies legitimacy for control of land, space, property, even wealth. Its major social function, however, is continuation of culture, of values and goals. Historicism is a determinant of a dynamic, active civilization. The Jewish religion harbors history. Greeks and Romans advanced what might be called empirical and analytical history, a secular one. All three professed idea systems and values generated a historical outlook.

The Cathedral of Cologne took 600 years to build. Its construction was frequently interrupted. The Cathedral of Milan took over 400 years; the Baptistery of Pisa, 125; Saint Peter's of Rome, 120. What this means is that the historical memory of generations and the memory of many individuals, the social and historical memory, continued. The goal was an articulation of this memory.

Change of Distant Goals in a Postindustrial Society

The vision of future goals and planning began to change in the United States and Western Europe a decade or two after World War II.

The faith in progress broke down among the intellectuals. The vision of unlimited progress in wealth and the well-being of mankind has been displaced by a pessimistic vision of a planet afflicted with radioactive waste, with overpopulation, with its water resources polluted, raw materials exhausted, energies depleted. With a population growing faster than the food supply the days of catastrophe could be even forecast by skilled demographers. But an ideology of a rational and scientific man who has the knowledge and skills to cope with difficult challenges continued. So did the will and energy to act. The new outlook affected the goals, prompted long-range, distant objectives.

Science is an idea system next to its scientific values and goals; the scientific outlook affected our ethics. It reinforced the sense of duty and moral obligations, it fostered the concept of public interests: "We know what the problem is. We shall find a way to cope with it."

From the perception of unlimited wealth and abundance of resources we moved to the perception of limits and our limitations. Instead of planning how to use the resources with almost unlimited cost allocation, groups and individuals began to plan how to preserve resources, limit the use, preserve, conserve the environment. The new, in fact conservative, outlook of conservation rather than expansion called for long-range planning and goals plotted in terms of decades, centuries. The vision began to expand again. This time, it was not religion but science that prompted the long-range visions.

Social and economic short-range and also long-range forecasting was of course in use for many years in demography, economics, even education. Now, however, a new discipline has been suggested—futurology—directed as much toward the future as history is toward the past. Whatever the merit and criticism, it is an expression of a new outlook toward time distance and distant goals. Though often a pessimistic outlook, it is also a challenge and call for action.

Our habits of thinking have been directly or indirectly affected by this changing situation perceived in a rational way, by means and methods of a rigorous idea system: science.

We begin to count time in decades and millenia (year 2000) in addition to our ancient Roman outlook of years and centuries. In scientifically oriented groups exponential time concepts, doubling time is now frequently used. Finding and hypothesis are now frequently used. Finding and hypothesis are now formulated that way. "There is an upper limit to the fresh water run-off from the land areas of the earth each year, and there is also an exponentially increasing demand for that water. . . . World population since 1650 has been growing exponentially at an increasing rate. . . . Estimates for 1970 were lower than forecasted. . . . The economic growth of individual nations indicates that differences in exponential growth rates are widening the economic gap between rich and poor countries."[20]

Scenarios of the future and forecasts for the future are mostly pessimistic. Production increases, but population increases faster. The gap between rich and poor nations increases. The major problems and goals ahead are measured now in decades, generations, even millenia.

Ideology, Technology, and Goals

It seems that the more complex and active a civilization is, the more careful its choices become. This complexity appears usually in sequences of goals, in large numbers of intermediate goals and a growing, immediate daily commitment.

The elementary goal structure of need or stimulus, drive, action, and goal is continuous in all those patterns. The number and nature of intermediate goals change, as do the distances. In a historical development the goal distances extend or decline, while idea systems or beliefs as well as needs and stimuli vary.

Technology, as well as science, supplies tools—not goals of a better society or a philosophy of life. The major guiding goals of mankind are found in ideas and values. They are hidden at times in those various endeavors we have called humanities.

Technology and science do not necessarily make a better man and a kind humanity, but they offer us tools and knowledge with which mankind can be made better. Recall Petrarch's dictum: "*Plusculum scio melior non fio*" ("more knowledge does not make me a better human being"). We may say, however, does not *necessarily* make me a better human being.

Thus far the powerful time span of distant goals originated with normative goals, with religions and secular ideologies of visionary quality akin to religion.

The time span of a series of goals forms a temporal parameter of our existence. This temporal border line of goals breaks the infinite nature of time and creates spiritual, psychological dimensions we are able to perceive—more, to live with.

Within those temporal borders of goals we find our home within the infinite. This is our temporal environment. History shapes our perspective, outlook, and perception of the time environment. Within those two environments of space and time man acts and plots his goals, which have a similar underlying structure, although they vary in quality or nature in their very purpose.

Notes

1. For example, the theater in Epidaurus, designed by Polycleitus and built about 350 BC is a good example of an extensive construction project. The theater is an expression of Hellenic culture, a culture of drama and dialogue. However, I could not find data on duration of the construction of this extensive project, which has seats for about sixteen thousand. The same problems are present in the theater of Dionysius, built about 500 BC, which seats eighteen thousand spectators.

2. Robert Branner, Ed., *Chartres Cathedral* (New York: Norton, 1969) pp. 71 ff.

3. According to *Encyclopedia Britannica* the pyramid in Gizeh was built during the fourth dynasty some time about 2600 BC. Quoting Herodotus on the time span of construction, Kingsland estimated on this basis that it took twenty years to place 315 blocks each day; this could be done, I suppose, only with an enormous work army. See *Encyclopedia Britannica* (1979), vol. 14, p. 964; William Kingsland, *The Great Pyramid in Fact and Theory* (London; Rides, 1932), quoted in Peter Tompkins, *Secret of the Great Pyramids*, (New York: Harper & Row, 1971), p. 234, also p. 219.

Sir Banister Fletcher, *A History of Architecture on the Comparative Method*, 17th ed., revised by R. A. Cordingley (New York: Charles Scribner's Sons, 1961), pp. 27, 35, 43, 44, 49.

4. Fletcher, *A History of Architecture*, PP. 112-139. I assume that the dates suggest the time span of construction. Fletcher used c. for *circa*,—for example, "c. 590 BC The Heraion, Olympia"—when dates are approximate.

5. Ibid., pp. 187–201. Temples were selected with adequate dating. The Pantheon of Rome should be listed, of course. However, the time span and dates of erection are obscure. Despite the inscription dating 27 BC, the stamps on the bricks indicate the first quarter of the second century: D. S. Robertson, *A Handbook of Greek and Roman Architecture* (Cambridge: Cambridge University Press, 1943), pp. 246 ff.

6. Fletcher, *A History of Architecture*, pp. 271–80 and *Encyclopedia Britannica*.

7. Fletcher, *A History of Architecture*, pp. 258 ff., 421 ff., 534 ff.; Fred H. Allen, *The Great Cathedrals of the World* (Boston: Haskell & Post Co., 1886); *Encyclopedia Britannica*; R. Forneaux Jordan, *A Concise History of Western Architecture*, 2 vols. (New York: Harcourt, Brace, 1970), vol. 1, p. 136; various monographs, for example, Branner, *Chartres Cathedral*. Other sources were consulted too. However, I found Jean Gimbel's *The Cathedral Builders* (New York: Grove Press, 1961), not only fascinating and original in his approach, but also highly informative in his chronological landmarks section (pp. 185 ff.).

8. Fletcher, *A History of Architecture*, pp. 343 ff.; Gimbel, *Cathedral Builders*, pp. 185 ff.

9. Fletcher, *A History of Architecutre*, pp. 1147 ff.; also information from Saint Patrick's Information Center (letter of July 1, 1957), John Cardinal Farley, *A History of St. Patrick's Cathedral*; (New York: Society for Propagation of the Faith) and other sources, especially correspondence, answers to letters, or direct inquiry.

10. *Encyclopedia Britannica*; p. 174-182. Fletcher, *A History of Architecture*, pp. 239 (I quote data on Pons Fabricius, Rome, on Fletcher's authority), 608, Charles S. Whitney, *Bridges: A Study of Their Art, Science and Evolution* (New York: W. E. Rudge, 1929); pamphlets, information in response to letters of inquiry from the Port of New York Authority (for example, the Hudson River Bridge, 1930), the Research Department of the San Francisco Chamber of Commerce (for example, world's two largest bridges, San Francisco Bay area), and the Golden Gate Bridge twentieth Anniversary. This writer began to collect sources on the range of goals and time span in 1957.

11. Fletcher, *A History of Architecture*, pp. 209, 1086; *Encyclopedia Britannica*, *Wielka Encyklopedia Powszechna* (Warsaw: P. W. N., 1967).

12. Pevsner, Nikolaus, John Fleming and Hugh Honour, *A Dictionary of Architecture* (Woodstock, N.Y., Overlook Press 1966, 1976); American Institute of Architects, *Guide to New York City* (New York: Macmillan, 1969). Other sources include the Public Relations Department of the Port Authority, letters and printed materials from the Empire State Building Corporation.

13. Pitirim Sorokin, *Society, Culture and Personality* (New York: Harper & Brothers, 1947), pp. 598 ff.; Sorokin, *The Crisis of Our Age* (New York: E. P. Dutton, 1942), pp. 20 ff., 44 ff.

14. Here may belong the Pont de la Guillotiere in Lyons, France, commenced in 1190. It was continued in spite of the frequent destruction by high floods. See: Whitney, *Bridges*, p. 85.

15. From personal inquiries to the Department of Transportation and Department of Parks and Recreation, New York City, 1979–1980.

16. "A Bridge Grows in Brooklyn," *New York World Telegram*, special section (November 20, 1964), p. 2, quoted by David J. Goldstein in "Sociological Conditions and Time Span of Urban Construction" (Brooklyn College, 1967).

17. Werner Sombart, *Die Vorkapitalistische Wirtschaft* (Munich and Leipzig: Duncker and Humblot, 1928).

18. From printed and mimeographed information dated 1956, courtesy of the Empire State Building management. This author received immediate answers to his inquiries to management of those major constructions of our century—Rockefeller Center, San Francisco Chamber of Commerce, and World Trade Center of New York—and others in 1957 and in additional inquiries in 1979. The promptness and efficiency in answering casual inquiries were striking, in 1957 as well as in 1970. Let's hope we can keep it that way.

19. See Friedrich Meinecke, *Historism: The Rise of a New Historical Outlook* (New York: Herder & Herder, 1972).

20. *The Limits to the Growth*, a report for the Club of Rome's project on the Predicament of Mankind, by Donella H. Meadows, Jorgen Randers, William Behrens III (New York: Universe Books, 1972), pp. 33, 40, 53.

13

Social Rhythm and Cyclical Goals: Time and Goals

Three Types

At the dawn of mankind nature structured the annual recurrence of human goals. The change of seasons set narrow limits of natural and changing conditions within which man's basic needs of food and shelter had to be met. The annual rhythm of those changes dictated a regular, recurring response to the needs. And needs resulted into goals and actions. Goals are at the very nature of things.

Thus the goal sequence we have called horizontal is not the only dynamic structure. Three major types of goals could be distinguished in terms of their dynamic quality: (1) horizontal (in their simple and complex structure), (2) infinite, and (3) cyclical.

Infinite goals are only a variation of horizontal. Their nature presupposes a series of antecedent and attainable goals attached to a set of ends that are fixed neither in time nor in space. They are the moving targets we follow. The infinite goals are ideals of perfection, utopias, what Georges Sorel called "social myths"— distant, attractive visions. Man does not and cannot achieve an ideal of a perfect state, since by definition what is perfect is always ahead of man, who is not perfect. But utopias of a perfect, ideal state, of a perfect society, of a City of God, appeal to our emotions, generate visions of a perfect future, as well as will an action, and keep us moving in pursuit of an image that is always ahead of us (more about below).

The cyclical goals, unlike the infinite, are concrete targets, which reappear regularly, or almost regularly, after a certain time span with actions they are associated with. They are integrated into our economy, culture, idea systems. Typical are those associated with the daily and seasonal routine and rhythm of time. The seasonal changes in the environment call for similar annual responses to the challenge. Ploughing and harvesting have to be done at definite times, and both activities result in simple goals, such as ploughing a definite acreage or harvesting in time before a rainstorm. Hence some major cyclical goals are in fact a consequence of imperatives of nature and survival. True, they are affected by culture, by what Malinowski called "a cultural phase"; nonetheless the origin of a seasonal goal structure can be traced to the latter. There are, however, cyclical goals that are not always and necessarily a result of those natural—one is prompted to say biological—imperatives. We shall call them cultural or normative cyclical goals. They are often (but not always) associated with the former.

Religious rituals and festivities, as well as customs, are frequently associated with agrarian, hunting, or pastoral seasonal changes, even goals. Thus the seasonal cyclical change results into recurrent rituals. They express a rhythm of individual and collective life. All those activities generate goals that are multifunctional. Next to economic function, customs and religious ceremonials reinforce group solidarity and continuity.

The strength of those seasonal effects on man declines with his technological and scientific advance. A New Yorker is differently affected by those changes than an Eskimo of the far North. Better protected against the adversities of seasons, the former is not forced to change his way of life to such an extent as the Eskimo does. His work pattern continues with little, if any, change. But the cycle remains and continues. So does the rhythm of life. The Easter Parade on New York's Fifth Avenue and winter sales at Macy's mark the seasonal rhythm. To buy a new spring outfit becomes now an activity and a goal. Parades honoring Columbus, Saint Patrick, and Pulaski, those secular, manmade rituals that have no connection with imperatives of nature, occur at the same time each year. They result in annual goals expressed in numbers of participants, excellence of music bands, impressive displays of costumes. The goals and rituals are now adjusted to fit the cultural change.

In agriculture the seasonal changes continue with their powerful imperatives. Now the targets of productions are paramount; religious celebrations associated with agrarian activities have almost disappeared in modern, Protestant societies. The rational approach to production, the primacy of efficiency, displaces customs, rituals, and their creative, esthetic ceremonials.

The annual rhythm and its consequences, the cyclical changes in the way of life, have a universal quality. All mankind is affected by seasonal changes, by movement of the earth, and must respond to the latter. Degrees of this effect vary, however, and cultural response varies in various societies.

This rhythm results in various cyclical goals. The abstract concept of targets, goals, ends may appear late in language and usage. But goals are built into our activities; they supply direction to the latter. They do exist objectively, even if man does not realize that what he is attempting to do is to achieve a goal. Goals do not have their own independent existence, but our existence is anchored to goals. Goals are closely related to concept of time.

The time concept of early societies seems to be primarily cyclical and tightly integrated with changes in the environment, such as flowering time of certain trees and plants; longer periods may be associated with human aging. Such is the concept of time of the Maenge people (of Papua), which bears similarities with other early societies' concept. Periods shorter than a year are noticed by the shift of sunrise on the horizon. Periods longer than a year are perceived by the succession of age sets into which the population of any village is divided. The flow of time—not its sections, demarcations, or time units—is typical in such a time concept.[1]

At this early stage, seasonal-economic and seasonal-ritual rhythms of life can be noticed, next of course to the daily, cyclical changes. Permanent social organization, beyond an extended family or a local group, is hardly noticeable as yet, or perhaps is in very early stages, but at the same time complex periodic rituals are already a rather suprisingly vital institution.

The seasonal nomadic cycle is also common among the advanced pastoral peoples of Asia and is akin to the ways and economic traditions of the once powerful nations of the steppes.

Social rhythms and cyclical goals continue with a change, a transition from hunting to a pastoral and agricultural stage. As before, at this stage seasons affect human life, although man responds in different ways to the climatic changes. In the process that we call "modernization," in the process of fusion of the traditional way with the industrial and technological innovations, the traditional rhythm (or its rituals) often survive. It is usually integrated with the new recurrent ceremonies or activities brought by the innovative changes. The new cultural pattern may carry also new rituals, ceremonies, and seasonal goals, rhythmical divides of communal life. A total disruption of this traditional annual rhythm associated with cyclical goals, a result of external, economic, and cultural pressures, affects the entire institutional structure and culture. It may also contribute to social disorganization.

Activities, which in a general theory may appear as solely economic, or determined only by economic needs, are, in a concrete, empirical case, prompted by economic and noneconomic determinants.

It is simple to say that an Arapaho Indian of the Wind River Reservation is a nomad, but what does this mean? Why is he moving? When? An Arapaho moves not of economic necessity only. There are several celebrations both of religious character and of plain entertainment. These are periodical and cause the Arapaho to move with his family. There are a large number of such celebrations, and they definitely conflict with the requirements of good farming in Wyoming and with the economic progress of the Arapahoes.

Let us start with July. July 4 is regarded by an Arapaho as a big Indian holiday. He closes his house, takes his family in his car and moves to the city of Lander (20 to 25 miles distance) for the big celebration of the American national holiday. Before he goes to Lander, however, he irrigates his land and cuts the first hay. Upon his return, he irrigates again, and then goes to the Sun Dances (usually a distance of 5 to 15 miles). Again he closes his house, takes his wife and children, and moves to the vicinity of the large grasshouse where the Indians dance. There he spends three days celebrating the Sun Dance. This is usually toward the end of July. After the Sun Dance he cuts the second hay crop.

Beginning in August at campfire and in tents, the Indians talk a lot about horse races at the coming rodeo at Thermopolis. There the Indian participates in all the usual events such as riding half-wild horses. In August, an Arapaho takes his family in the car and moves for three or more days to Thermopolis. At Thermopolis, an Arapaho enjoys great festivities connected with cattle and horses, races and all kinds of games in which he actively participates. Afterwards, he talks for weeks about the great games. Upon his return from Thermopolis to the permanent base, an Arapaho might go up to the mountains as a rider for the Arapaho Cattle Association for a week or so. In such a case, he takes his family with him either by packhorse, team, or car, makes a camp at the pasture, and after a week he returns again to his permanent base.

After hunting and lumbering in Fall, the Arapaho returns shortly before Christmas to his permanent house. He finds his family often in the log-house, yet many still prefer to spend even the winter in tents. Again, an Arapaho will not spend too much time in his home. Christmas is near, and for the Christmas holidays the whole tribe congregates around the big wooden dance house close to the Mission Church. Tents are pitched and a whole village mushrooms suddenly for a few days. The Arapaho celebrates Christmas holidays in a tribal way. Although the Arapahoes have long accepted Christianity, the Christian faith operates within the Arapaho cultural system. Christmas is celebrated through traditional Indian rites and dances and by the Arapaho tribal group as a whole. But the religious content of these rites is, in its own way, Christian.

After Christmas, an Arapho moves back to his permanent base and prepares for trapping. April 15, all trapping ends. An Arapaho returns home and works in his fields, mends fences, takes care of cattle, and stays home all through June until July. The periodical movements, the rhythm of Indian life is in this case determined by needs and objectives of a very different nature. But all of them are well integrated into a single annual, cyclical sequence of goals and activities, a coherent life style.

This periodic, cyclical rhythm, articulated in recurrent goal structures, has organized the flow of time of individuals and communities since the dawn of mankind. The rhythm creates what may be called a "vital routine," a vital and repetitive sequence of activities anchored in needs and goals. Our existence is attached to it. It is a vital clock of a society, the time stations are like the hourly signs of a clock. But the movement is determined by a complex working mechanism.

The break came with the Industrial Revolution and with the factory system. The annual cycle of seasons, the change from winter to spring and summer, has always a vital effect on man and society. Still, there is a difference between a small preindustrial settlement and an industrial complex of tenement houses, slums, and red brick factory buildings. Moreover, with the shift of employment to industrial work the seasonal rhythm and pattern are not as vigorous and decisive as in an agrarian community or in workshops of craftsmen.

Now the seasonal change, the annual rhythm in factory and office, is displaced by economic cycles, by the smooth and rational but monotonous run of the factory. Men, women, and children are integrated with the machines. It is the machine, the factory equipment, and the fluctuation of the market that affect the economic time schedule. Rituals are mostly gone—with exception of traditional trades, religious holidays are reduced. But still in a variety of ways religious and secular holidays give us a wholesome interruption of the monotony and in the Christian community a sense of joy rather than repentance.

The harvest is anchored to nature, to soil and climate; industrial product, to the machine, which runs the same in all seasons, well sheltered at one time in red brick buildings.

Annual Rhythm and Cyclical Goals in the Western Medieval Economy

In the early stages of mankind, in preliterate simpler cultures, work and leisure or production and religious rites were not separated as yet. Efficiency and rational production were not the sole guiding principle of native economy. Work was less regular, less systematic, and also less disciplined than in what are called advanced societies, agricultural or industrial. The economic goal, such as profit as an abstract, independent, and separate concept, seemed to be absent. At a later stage slave labor was already fully separated from leisure and from its deeper cultural context. But here efficiency or output was the only goal of work, inefficient as it may have been. Rational, regular, systematic work, with its emphasis on efficiency, measured achievement of production targets, developed slowly and made its definite entrance in times of the Industrial Revolution and the capitalistic stage.

Development of advanced culture postulates continuity and a certain level of stability that in a modern, dynamic civilization calls for continuous change and adjustment. Thus creative change and stability are only two aspects of the same process. Continuity of political power was a condition of development of great civilizations. This was as true in authoritarian, despotic Oriental civilizations as in modern democratic ones.

Social stability and continuity are anchored in institutionalized, long-range, and periodical goals. They do become permanent divides of time and organize our life. Since goals call for release of action, they energize our will, reinforce intentions and mobilize our potentialities, sustain efforts toward achievement.

Medieval Europe had an efficient and sturdy goal structure: powerful, long-range goals and vigorous cyclical goals, both fused with intensive religious beliefs shared by the community. Throughout medieval times those two strong goal structures guided daily and annual life: the long-range goals anchored in religion and the cyclical—associated directly or indirectly with nature and production—integrated with religious rituals. The cyclical goals are powerful, but so are the long-range goals of cathedral builders or builders of universities.

In basic agricultural production the goals are imposed by seasons. Here man's activities are guided by those seasonal tasks, and his goal structure is integrated with his work and environment.

Thus in agricultural production the rhythm of seasons and necessary, sequent stages of production create a permanent system of "natural" recurrent goals. On the other hand, idea systems—for example, religions of fixed holidays associated with economic activities—create similar divides distributed in time, in an annual cycle. Those divides become goals to look forward to, celebrate, and enjoy. Easter and Christmas are major divides, but also days to celebrate, days of sorrow and merriment. In Roman Catholicism, as in other Christian denominations, the beginning and the end of agricultural activities coincide with major holidays or even with certain saint's days. A popular proverb tells you what should bloom on a saint's day and on what other saint's day snow should appear. Those rhythmical and seasonal divides, associated with religious rituals and celebrations, formed in medieval times a natural sequence of goals.

The association of work and religion, work and art, work and leisure, continued in medieval Europe. Economic, cultural, and religious recurrent activities—goals of seasonal rhythm—were visualized, fixed, represented in plastic arts as well as in calendars, and reinforced that way.

The fountain of Peruggia, *Fontana Maggiore*, between the Cathedral of San Lorenzo and the Palazzo dei Priori, was built about 1275. Its lower reliefs consist of a panel representing activities of various seasons, gathering fruit in summer, harvesting, making wine in fall. The rhythm of the year was displayed all the time to burghers, as well to peasants flocking around on a market day. Each of these seasonal activities is an image of goals, cyclical, recurrent, built into the very nature of our life.

In addition to the necessary chronology, medieval calendars were inventories of goals fixed into an annual timetable. Thus the calendar of the Fecamp psalter, illuminated about 1180, illustrates various seasonal activities, tantamount to goals. The postholiday leisure of January is presented by a picture of a noble or a priest in the process of overeating and drinking. The cold February promises to a gentleman a comfortable warming at a fireplace—no specific goals or activities. March is the time of viticulture, illustrated by peasants pruning plants, binding the wine, digging, transplanting; June is illustrated by laborers raking grass, mowing grass, gathering hay, building haystacks; a man weeding fields symbolizes July; in August men work hard, cut corn, fruit. On the September pages we see men harvesting and then treading grapes in a large barrel; on another page a peasant carries grapes and tastes a glass of wine. October is pictured by a peasant sowing, a woman spinning, a horse pulling a harrow; the November page illustrates a peasant harvesting acorns; December before Christmas is an anticipation of feast—a picture of slaughtering of pigs and curing of meat.

The Fecamp calendar is not unique. Seasonal activities and festivities appear in a series of miniatures, probably of the Bologna school, 1307–1318, owned by the Morgan Library.[2]

What we see in those illustrations are expectations, "imaginations" of the future, images of future activities. Those imaginations are future goals, some of which should or even must be met because they are necessary, the alternative being starvation; others are pleasant and desirable. A medieval peasant, as much as his lord, moved in time from goal to goal. These goals were clearly defined by imperatives of occupation and by the very nature of agriculture attached to the rhythmical movements of seasons and months. Similarly, his religious life, reflected on the pages of those calendars, was tied to recurrent, seasonal saint's days and holidays. Seasons began and came to an end with saint's days or holidays; so did new tasks. Religious celebrations, days of holy communions or festive worship, were not only time divides, but expectations or goals distributed in time. This was a system of well-established and regular repetitive tasks that formed the parameters of man's life and actions. His actions moved within this time and goal system. The goals were social and individual. They were collective, since they were shared by the entire community, their achievement depending on participation of others. Achievement of those seasonal production goals in farming depended on cooperation and mutual aid of neighbors or of more distant community members. But survival of the family was also tied to those goals. Such a closed goal system secured at least a certain peace of mind, freedom from anxieties in a dangerous and insecure medieval world of invasions, cruel persecutions, and, above all, strong beliefs in unknown and secretive evil forces, devils, haunting spirits, and sorcery. Inside these goal-time parameters there was a kind of spiritual refuge one can still rediscover today in a remote Italian village community bound by faith and tied to seasons by their way of life and by farming.

Medieval Crafts and Seasonal Rhythm

The nineteenth-century industrial worker did not enjoy this measure of communion with nature, this forceful, annual, rhythmical goal system that organized the life of individuals and of the community, gave regularity to man's life, marked by different tasks.

Their periodical attainment secured a rhythm of achievement and renewal. Of course life was hard; deprivation and misery were frequent visitors. But a festive holiday, a saint's day, a name day was again a day of renewal and spiritual uplift.

With the long working day of twelve or fourteen hours required of the nineteenth-century factory system, an industrial worker saw only the mornings and evenings on his way to work. Industrial slum cities had few trees and meadows.

The medieval urban society—especially its productive classes, the crafts—was attached to the annual seasonal rhythm of time, to its powerful divides of holidays, and to the annual return of the saint's days. The patron saint played an important role in daily life. His name was frequently invoked; hopes and prayers were tied to his attention and heavenly concern. The name days were family holidays linked with worship of the saints. The daily chores and work were long, but, contrary to what one may expect, the number of workdays per annum were often limited and the number of holidays quite substantial. We have some fragmentary sources and data on workdays. Work in the Bavarian mines during the later sixteenth century, may serve as an example.

Out of 203 days 123 were holidays.

Out of 161 days 99 were holidays.

Out of 287 days 193 were holidays.

Out of 366 days 260 were holidays.

Out of 366 days 263 were holidays.[3]

Work was not yet fully separated from the general belief system and leisure; it was not "rationalized" or geared to a single objective—efficiency.

Moreover, medieval towns were relatively small; fifty thousand dwellers was already a large one. They were close to gardens, fields, meadows, and woods and were not separated from nature and the life of the fields, woods, and rivers.

Some holidays were probably only local or even half holidays. Some saint's days, however, could extend for two, even three days. Today in the villages of the Julian region of northern Italy most of the communities celebrate local holidays of the patron saint. Those holidays, known as *sagras* extend in some villages to three days. Again, on certain saint's days, fairs that mark beginnings or ends of farming or gardening or initiate a scholastic year are divides to which both recurrent initial and end goals are tied.

In medieval urban life the saint's days and guild holidays, fairs, feasts, and celebrations supplied the annual rhythm to the crafts, as the seasonal changes did in agriculture. Annual work was not a single, long, uninterrupted span of time, monotonous, tedious, and oppressive. An artisan, whether a master, journeyman, or apprentice, followed customary time segments, which had their festive beginning and ending. He looked forward to those days, his time goals, as a student or college instructor looks forward to the ending and beginning of a term.

We have it still, a happy although greatly diminished inheritance, rather secular, with some religious survivals and color: Christmas and New Year's, Easter, Memorial Day, Labor Day, Columbus Day, Armistice Day, Thanksgiving–and a new cycle begins again.

The Clock and the Abstract Time: Daily Cycle and Goals

There are two major cyclical patterns that affect mankind and are universal in its nature: seasonal and daily changes. Day and night are recurrent and call for recurrent activities and daily goals. This cycle results in a daily routine, a sequence of activities adjusted to the daily rhythm of a community. Hence division of the two natural sequences of day and night into twenty-four hours, into a horary system, was a major change in perception of time and in organizing goals and activities. Day and night became a horary concept, divided into two major segments and subdivided into precise time units.

A new period in the history of labor began with the application to daily routine of this careful and precise division of time into hours. A rational unit of time had been created, an abstract time unit that did not exist in nature as a single element. Now the quanity of produced goods could be related to an abstract time unit, which in turn could be measured as a test of higher or lower productivity. The hour, divided into minutes and seconds on the face of a clock, had been detached from holidays and seasons. Abstract, rational numbers displaced the images of life, of work, of feasts, and of experiences of seasons.

Man's systematic division of time belongs of course to ancient history. It appeared already in ancient Oriental societies; was and is a crucial element in the development of great civilizations.

The division of a year into twelve months of thirty days goes back to the Sumerians, about 3500 BC. Each day was divided into twelve sections (*ges*), equal to about two of our hours, and each two-hour period was divided into thirty parts (*danna*), equal to about four of our minutes. Babylonian astronomy introduced the division into twenty-four hours. Egypt had the same. The time in medieval monasteries (monastic time) was divided into twelve daylight hours (starting with sunrise) and twelve hours for darkness. Hence the length of hours varied with seasons.[4] The concept of minutes and seconds appeared by the second century, in Ptolemy's astronomy.

Transformation of the hourly segments into precise equidistant, rational, and abstract units did not appear as an unexpected and unusual innovation, an augury of a revolution in the perception of time. The clockwise routine of life moved slowly through religious institutions and recurrent prayers. The prayers were also of rhythmical nature, divided into a cyclical movement of day and night and recurrent daily routine. The prayers in medieval times were time goals, marking beginnings and ends of daily chores and life. The time concept is a value, and the hour, the hourly division, slowly became a symbol—not only a signal, an information.

After the disintegration of the Roman Empire and the devastating barbarian invasions the Benedictine Order was the major civilizing force in Europe. Its monasteries were models of rational, economic enterprise, with proper use of water systems and the beginnings of organization of production. Saint Benedict introduced a seventh prayer time to the devotions of the day. The bells of the monastery rang seven times in twenty-four hours following a papal bull.[5] The canonical hours, as they were known, were marked by the sounds of bells, dividing the day and organizing life and work.

As early as the thirteenth century, medieval engineers were fascinated by the idea of a chronometer that would move by means of gravity. In the meantime, however, sundials and the flow of water were used for time measurement, a principle known for a long time. By the twelfth century the market for water clocks, at least in some parts of Europe, was substantial. By 1183 a guild of clockmakers existed in Cologne, and by 1220 the clockmakers occupied an entire street.[6] There are the thirteenth-century records of mechanical clocks, and by the fourteenth century bell towers were built and the clocks—even if they did not yet have dials and hands—struck the hours.[7] We can still admire the oldest surviving and working mechanical time device, dating back to 1386, the clock of the Salisbury Cathedral.

The mechanical and astronomical clock was greatly advanced by a prominent physician and astronomer, Giovanni de Dondi. The work took sixteen years and was completed by 1364.[8] But by 1335 a chronicler recorded the clock of the church of Saint Gothard in Milan, the first clock that struck equal hours. "Public clocks also rang equal hours in Genoa in 1353, in Florence in 1354, in Bologna in 1356, in Ferrara in 1362."[9]

The time signals, later associated with sounds of bells and still later with music, brought the community closer together, broke the dull silence of long hours; it was an embellishment of life. At the same time the hourly signals organized life, created a new, hourly rhythm of work and life and, moreover, definite points of beginning and terminating activities, quantitative and precise parameters for goals set in time. A time unit became also an economic value. The nature of economic goals were changing.

All this, of course, came later, with manufacturing and particularly with the Industrial Revolution. By the second half of the nineteenth century inexpensive, standardized watches were being mass produced in Switzerland and the United States. The time unit became an abstract concept, detached from changes in nature and seasons. Time was differently experienced. At first man experienced the time cycle by all his powers of observation: He sensed changes of temperature, he saw changes in the position of the sun, and he observed the changing colors of trees and plants, birds coming in spring and leaving in fall. The changes of time were perceived above all visually and were not abstract. Those changes were a part of nature, of his closest environment.

There were of course sundials since ancient time. They were, with few exceptions, not as visible as the clocks of the cathedrals. In ancient Alexandria there was an obelisk—*gnomon*—located on a public square. The shadow of the obelisk told the hours to those who knew how to read the time, as did Eratosthenes, who measured the world's circumference. But in the sun a sundial the time was not yet abstract. The days divided and the hours were still parts of the natural movement of the sun (when man believed that the earth was static). Time was on its way toward being an abstraction—but at this point it was still a perception of nature.

In the medieval city, however, the hourly ring, the hourly rhythm of time, was perceived by hearing. In some towns, for example, Cracow in Poland, a trumpeter announced both midday and midnight, playing a traditional tune. Hence the hourly, abstract time divides were primarily aural, identified with a sharp signal or with music or chimes. By the fifteenth and sixteenth centuries in most European cities the hourly division was both audible and visual. Time appeared now on the face of the clock of the church tower; it was prominently visible.

By the end of the nineteenth century it was also an abstract number on a dial, a hand, an indicator no different from those that measure the pressure of steam or the intensity of electricity. The image of time was changing. It was again primarily visual now. In daily pragmatic activities time had been translated into space, spatial units that appeared on the dial of an inexpensive pocket watch. Every working man got used to it. Human life and activities are structured within two cycles—the seasonal and the daily rhythm of day and night. Both were affected by industrialization and the factory system.

With the advance of the Industrial Revolution this coherent and vigorous goal and time cycle, rooted in seasons, in nature, was weakened in factory towns. But the precise time units and horary division suggest a new and efficient way of staging and attaining goals. Now recurrent, daily, cyclical goals of urban and industrial life were short. Get up early to go to work, return home, collect a weekly pay. They were monotonous, dull; the working man became a part of a complex, manmade mechanism.

Rationalization of Time Units and Goals

The twenty-four-hour division of the day has, of course, very ancient roots. But here we are concerned with the rationalization of time, with time as an abstract unit. When the spirit of rationalism succeeded in the construction of new, rational constitutions in America and France, its partisans and enthusiasts attempted to extend the rule of reason to all fields of life, including time, to conquer its nature.

The French Revolution introduced a decimal time division, a follow-up of the metric system. The decimalized hours were introduced in the fall of 1793. This was a challenge to all owners of clocks and watches and to watch makers. How was one to change all the faces and mechanisms, to adjust them to the decimal divisions? A new ten-hour "deciday" imposed over the "old" twenty-four hours was suggested—a complete unit indeed. But by 1795 the law was tabled. It is still there.[10] The act of the Convention is, however, indicative of a general tendency toward the rationalization of time, toward abstraction of the concept and separation from the bonds it had from its origin.

A parallel introduction of the new calendar in 1793 reduced further the holidays. The new decimal system reduced leisure of the working people. The month was divided now into three decades and the tenth day was a rest day. That way, the time cycle was separated from the religious traditions. This reform was abolished in turn by Napoleon Bonaparte in 1806.[11]

Thus the tendency toward an abstract concept of time, a quantitative unit of time associated with a doctrine, with an independent theory rather than nature or religion, with the current needs of a new society and the new philosophy, has been expressed in those reforms of the French Revolution. The concept of time, as a value, is an articulation of an ideology or belief system. The French attempts to change the time unit were a consequence of a new idea system of the ruling political classes.

The Industrial Revolution and Decline of Cyclical Rhythm: Linear-Horizontal Time and Goals

With the Industrial Revolution the annual cyclical rhythm of production anchored in seasonal goals and recurrent religious landmarks of the calendar was to a large extent, in industrial work, complemented by a linear time, by a continuous, infinite run of the machines to which men, women, and children were attached like parts of a mechanism, displaced as yet by new technical devices.

During the triumphant Industrial Revolution, in 1835, when two rational goals devoid of humane consideration, profit and efficiency, were the dominant economic goals, Andrew Ure, economist, enthusiast, and what could be called theoretician of the new industrial system, defined the factory as the integration of men and mechanical devices into a single economic machine, propelled by a central power. Human beings were considered just as an essential part of it as was any mechanical device: ''The term *Factory system*, in technology, designates the combined operation of many orders of work-people, adult and young, in tending with assiduous skill a series of production machines continuously impelled by central power. ... This ... involves the idea of a vast automation, composed of various mechanisms and intellectual organs, acting in uninterrupted concert for the production of a common object, all of them being subordinated to a self-regulated moving force.''[12]

Individual and collective production goals were no longer fused with regular, seasonal, climatic changes, with spring, fall, or summer. No phase of factory production was associated with rituals, festivities, and merriment. The goal for the worker becomes his pay. In those early exploitative stages, goal achievement depends on the quantity of production within a time unit. The rational society and a Protestant one abolished the saint's days and numerous holidays. It was more work-less leisure. The half-pagan cyclical rituals, which embellished work and production, were gone by now. The goals in production were measured by time and money. The change in the nature of goals was substantial and affected life. Profit and efficiency became now the values, the norm of an hour as an industrial symbol.

It took years before working time was shortened, labor was humanized, and salaries could meet the needs of a decent, if not prosperous, standard of living and eventually could permit a new, far more humane and dignified life style. All those changes appeared in the structure and nature of goals. The dominant time and goal pattern in industrial work changed from cyclical into linear, horizontal.

Time and Goals

The existential imperatives dictate, of course, a certain pattern of goals. The seasonal cyclical and linear goal sequence in a long, historical perspective was a consequence of the nature of production at a historical stage. The effects of existential conditions and needs are only one component—through admittedly a major component—of goal formation. Goals are not plotted in an ideological vacuum. Furthermore, even pragmatic, existential goals are affected by what Parsons called nonempirical or normative ideas. Parsons closely followed Weber when he stated: "The question is not whether non-empirical existential ideas are always to be found in social systems, but whether important features of these social systems can be shown to be functions of variations in the content of these ideas.[13]

The same applies to actions and goals, since both are affected by idea systems.

A question may be asked: How shall we attack, in our particular case, the problem of goal formation?

It seem that crucial in this approach is the concept, moreover, the perception of time. Goals are stations in a duration of time. Goal sequences form what might be called fixations of sections of duration. The horizontal or cyclical goal structure is nothing else but a succession of goals, structured in duration of time. Hence succession of goals is in fact experience of time perceived by our senses. By means of setting goals on a continuum of time, sections of this continuum become separate blocks. Once intervals are carefully established and measured, time becomes "spatialized." It is visualized in terms of space, for example, on a sundial or the face of a watch. This again is subject to visual perception. It can be experienced by our senses.

Goals are those divisions of time. They may of course appear as segments of a cycle and/or a section on a continuum.

However, the idea system, the belief system, affects the concept and perception of time. In Western philosophical systems time was discussed or defined in terms of flow, motion or change, duration, succession. It was considered as an absolute concept; as relative to an observer; as objective or subjective. Furthermore, time was defined as an a priori, nonempirical concept or as a phenomenon experienced by man. Among philosophers as early as Heraclitus (500 BC) or Aristotle, time was conceived as flow, dialectical change, or motion.[14]

The concept of time is a fundamental component in the development of science and Western civilization. Needham, comparing the Western civilization and China, calls it "the greatest question": Could there have been a connection between differences (if any) in the conceptions of time and history characteristic of China and the West and the fact that the modern science and technology arose only in the latter civilization?[15]

The concept of history is, of course, a consequence of our philosophy or ideology of time.

Needham makes a distinction between Judeo-Hellenic and Judeo-Christian-Iranian concept of time. The former, argues Needham, is fundamentally a cyclical concept of time; the latter, a linear one. The Chinese culture, with its strong historical sense, according to Needham, is akin to the Judeo-Christian-Iranian.[16]

It seems to me, however, that in Hellenic philosophy and history both concepts were perceived and discussed. Heraclitus' concept is of the flow of time; Aristotle's concept of time as motion is linear; the theory of revolution of political systems in turn is cyclical, as is Hesiod in poetic terms. Greek historians— Herodotus or Thucydides—have clear, linear concepts of time, although their philosophies do not suggest an idea of progress, which appears in Europe about two thousand years later.

The idea and the value of time differ in various cultures, and those differences between Indian, Chinese, and Western ideas of time have been suggested before by students of great civilizations.

The Judeo-Christian concept of time is easily comprehensible in terms of duration, succession, and time interval. It is concrete in terms of days and years. In a sense it is pragmatic. First of all the divine time is no different than the human perception. The world, according to Genesis, was created in days, in a human measure.

In Indian lore "a thousand *mahayugas* (four thousand million years of human reckoning) constituted a single Brahma day, a single *kalpa*; dawning with rec-reation and evolution, ending with dissolution and re-absorption of the world spheres with all their creatures into the absolute."[17] Here the divine and human concepts of time are different; in terms of human life and generation the former is enormous, almost incomprehensible, and above all it has no comprehensible clear time stations or human goals. The Judeo-Christian concept of time is historical and at the same time futuristic. Major Jewish holy days are integrated with the historical lore; they have religious and at the same time historical meaning. Christianity introduced daily saint's days, integrated with the annual calendar they form, to suggest again the clear divisions of the flow of time, a clear succession.

"Past, present, and future belong to transitory beings," writes Zimmer on the Indian idea of time. "Time is a becoming and vanishing, the background and elements of the transient, the very frame and content of the floating processes of the psyche and its changing perishable objects of experience. Past, present and future contradict and exclude each other.''[18] Here is a hopeless, destructive flow of time.

The messianistic message in the Judeo-Christian lore sets a distant future goal; it is teleological. This messianistic ideal and idea of salvation have been projected later into political ideologies. Political messianism appears as a not-so-distant vision of a perfect society or utopia or as a rather immediate goal of a better society. Hence past, present, and future are comprehensible in terms of the human mind; it has definite stations in the present and future. Here time is integrated with goals and becomes that way a comprehensible, concrete datum. It is historical time and futuristic time. It is a history of human actions and goals, achieved or failed. It is this time concept that lends itself to plotting, ''placing'' goals or targets that appear as milestones in time.

The concept of measured, quanitative time, time conceived in operational and pragmatic segments, is seminal in historical thinking as well as in planning, constructing, producing. In Indian culture the interest in history or historical thinking is secondary, irrelevant in comparison with ancient Greece, with Rome, and in a different way with China. The culture is rather contemplative, concentrated on the infinite and universal, not on the concrete and different.

Indian books of history, writes Nakamura, are few, and there is or was little interest in historical, rigorous discipline. History is integrated with legends and poetry; the emphasis is on art rather than hard data.[19]

Time Instruments and Goals

Since the goal structure is so closely associated with the time concept, let us still hear Needham's arguments. A strong historical sense, although different from the Western one, appears in Chinese culture. Already by the first century AD China had its Bureau of Historiography. History was written in terms of dynasties. Here, suggests Needham, ''we may be putting a finger on one of the keys.'' The key question: Why did China not lend itself for development of Galilean concepts? Time in Chinese culture, according to Needham, was concrete to a point that it could not be ''uniformized into abstract, geometrical coordinates, a continuous dimension amenable to mathematical handling.[20]

The Chinese had after all a practical time concept that was, if not identical, close to the Western, a time concept concrete, divisible in terms of time span. They had the engineering skills. Crucial for the invention of a mechanical clock was the invention of escapement, which the Chinese perfected prior to the Europeans. The mechanical clock was devised in China in the twelfth century, two or three centuries before it was constructed in Europe.[21]

Mechanical devices may be used for different functions and objectives. The same or similar inventions or discoveries might be attached to goals that are not only different but contradictory. Moreover, the world outlook, the overall idea system, results in concepts that affect the society's and individual's vital aspects of life. The abstract concept of linear time, divided into abstract hours considered as separate blocks, as measures of our activities, furthermore as time divisions to which goals are attached, has become a part of Western culture and had an impact on the structure of goals of the Western world and from there on mankind.

As the astronomical clock tower was built in China by the end of the eleventh century, perhaps two centuries earlier than in Europe. The major social function, however, was different. The clock was guarded by the imperial authority and official astronomers, since only the emperor had the right to promulgate the calendar and this act was an exercise as well as a reinforcement of the legitimacy of power. "Acceptance of the calendar was tantamount to the recognition of imperial authority," Needham writes. The control of calendar, time divides— were instruments of state authority and bureaucracy. Control of the calendar and of annual ceremonies was one of the instruments of power. It was a part of power over and control of the world outlook. Needham continues: "Owing to this close association between the calendar and state power, any imperial bureaucracy was likely to view with alarm the activities of independent investigators of the stars, or writers about them, since they might be secretly engaged upon calendrical calculations which would be of use to rebels planning to set up a new dynasty".

The social function of astronomical time and the clock in China were different than those in the West. In consequence, the invention of the clock in China had different effects than in Europe.

The Chinese imperial monopoly of astronomical clocks and prohibition of independent time calculations had a negative effect on investigation and engineering of clocks and watches. It had an impact on the economic development of China. "That they adopted our way of measuring time so late has, at least in the majority of Eastern countries, handicapped their economic and industrial development," comments Jean Gimbel.

The fact that the Catholic church adopted—even spearheaded—the new attitude toward time, permitted and built bell towers, had also its effect, Gimbel argues, on the earlier medieval industrial revolution. The Eastern European Orthodox church did not allow installation of mechanical clocks in its towers until the twentieth century.[22]

Time instruments, clocks, and personal watches, essential in daily quantification of time, were a basic invention, an essential component of both the industrial and the scientific revolutions. It affected the nature of plotting human goals, above all economic goals of efficiency, which we can set in precise terms and relate to achievement. Efficiency as a major economic goal is but a relationship between quantity (and quality) of product and number of time units necessary for its production.

The Abstract Pattern of Time and Goals

In terms of his existence and daily, pragmatic activities man experiences time in three ways: cyclical, rhythmical, and linear.

All three ways are cultural articulations of the very nature of the universe, especially the cyclical and rhythmical ones. The former is associated primarily with the daily-nightly twenty-four-hour cycle and change. It is above all the cycle that exists in nature, and it is experienced by man. A single experience corresponds to a cycle; repetitions correspond to a rhythm. Hence cyclical and rhythmical experience of time is related; moreover, it is at times the same experience.

However, short intervals and cadence—what we typically call rhythm—appear also in nature and experienced by man as cadence, sound. The sound of waves in rhythmical. With the advance of agriculture the sound of digging by man at work appears as a cadence. It is rhythmical. Karl Bücher, in his classic, today forgotten work *"Work and Rhythm"* *(Arbeit und Rhythmus)* suggested the affinity between work and rhythm, work and music. He illustrated, if not validated, his imaginative hypothesis with a vast number of examples of so-called primitive music, music and rhythm of early primitive forms of agriculture.[23]

While the experiences of cyclical time is rather visual, we can see that the change, the rhythmical time, is primarily aural; we hear the regular beats of change.

However, when I say cyclical, rhythmical, or linear time, I state already an abstraction. Since in nature I do not experience a geometrical cycle or a Euclidean line. True, I hear the beat, the cadence of rhythm, but the very statement that this is a rhythm is a finding, a consequence of relating data; and a generalized term for a variety of phenomena that appear or are heard in equal intervals is an abstraction.

What happens here is this: Time is spatialized, presented within a space, or it is presented, in the case of rhythm, in abstract cadence; that is, experience is projected into sound. The sonification of time appears in our clocks, the rhythm the tick tock of the pendulum. Visualization of time appears in dials or, as in electronic presentation of time, in numbers. The even rhythm has been expressed visually in electronic watches and clocks, showing fragments of seconds. The three types of time, associated with the experience of natural phenomena, are then abstracted and spatialized in three forms: (1) dial-cycle, (2) wave of equal intervals (rhythm), and (3) line (see figure 13.1).

Now the spatial, visual abstraction of time, not the sonification, was relevant in the development of science and goals.

These abstract cyclical, linear, and rhythmical concepts of time are cultural articulations of our universe. Since they are associated with our daily experience, further abstraction was made with the precise, horary division. The cyclical and linear geometrical forms lend themselves better to equidistant horary imagination and division as well as to broader application in practical life and science than the rhythmical one.

The linear, visual concept of abstracted time, divided into precise equidistant units that can be separated and used in our estimates as individual, independent blocks (the kilowatt hour, and so on), had a seminal impact on our outlook, on

Figure 13.1
Spatialization of Time

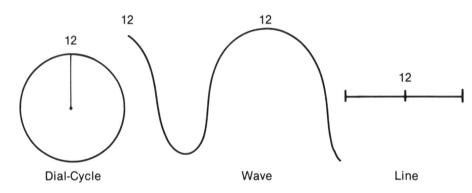

Dial-Cycle   Wave   Line

plotting our actions, and in consequence on the entire structure of goals, especially in production.

It is the cycle of day and night that exists in nature and is experienced by man. Equidistant hours as units, as separate blocks, do not exist in nature; they were created by man.

The twenty-four-hour horary division marks a daily rhythm, recurrent activities, and a repetitive daily, vital routine. The linear concept lends itself to long-range planning; it is a unit of measurement in rational economic production. The linear, horary subdivision into minutes, seconds, and further fragmentation of the horary units was both a consequence and at the same time an essential device in the development of science. The advance of precise quantification of time coincides with the advance of horizontal, linear goals in production and of complementary cyclical goals which encompass time blocks of days and seasons.

Horary Division and Social Goals

With legitimacy as a major function and with the rigid control of time measurement and related instruments the horary system did not achieve in China — in the eighteenth and nineteenth centuries—the pragmatic relevance that it did in the Occidental culture. The struggle for the eight-hour workday, for a reform that is fundamental in our modern civilization, could advance only in societies where the rational and abstract time concept had been fully accepted and assimilated into the general culture. Once everyone, or the majority of working people, had a watch in their pockets, calculation of effort in terms of precise units became a matter of daily routine. The factory system was run on horary signals and units. True, the emphasis was on efficiency and profit. The product was measured in time, and the goals of factory owners were now formulated in terms of production in time units. But the demands of workers, social reforms, were also expressed in precise terms of shorter working hours. The eight-hour workday became a major goal, a target of the nineteenth-century labor movement. In its programmatic slogan, "Eight hours to work, eight hours to sleep, eight hours to play, eight shillings a day," it carried a simple message in terms of a future cyclical division of the day.

In terms of our classification of goals the eight-hour workday was a clear and pragmatic target, unique in the history of mankind, since it was a humane target of universal appeal. This time not a social myth, not a generalized goal of a perfect society carried a powerful and at times worldwide movement of organized labor, but a clear, "quantitative" target had this unusual appeal.

The shortening of the workday was a major social target and value of the nineteenth century. It came to fruition with the end of World War I, which in fact marked the end of the nineteenth century.

The next target was the reformation of the workweek, another segment in organization of our time. In 1930 the forty-hour workweek, called at this time *La Semaine Anglaise*—the English week—was still a distant target, achieved by the British. The English term *weekend* was slowly assimilated into other European languages. A shorter workweek had been achieved in almost all the democratic, industrial nations by the middle of the twentieth century. The thirty-five- or thirty-seven-hour workweek has been adopted in some industries.

In the latter part of our century new targets have emerged, directed toward the reformation of the annual cycle. Summer vacations have now been extended. The nineteenth-century target was the limitation of the workday; in the first half of the twentieth century the shortening of the workweek became the immediate target; during the latter part of the century a new target of working time is an extension of the annual vacation time, shortening of the annual work.

An increase of our productive capacities through the potentialities of science, technology, and industry create conditions of this reformation of time, of adjustment to the annual cycle. The industrial nations can now return to reintegration of man with nature and seasonal cyclical rhythm and goals.

We can afford a creative change. Traditional holidays, associated with the seasonal, annual changes, could be again combined with longer vacations. Every season could be initiated or terminated by biweekly or weekly vacations. This seasonal cyclical rhythm in the United States, for example, is already anchored in Christmas, Easter, Memorial Day, and Labor Day. The seasonal vacations could be staggered within a period of a few weeks within which various branches of industry could distribute vacation time:

1. Christmas—New Year: winter biweekly holiday
2. Easter—spring: weekly holiday

3. Memorial Day—August: staged biweekly holiday

4. Labor Day: weekly holiday

The leading industrial nations could well adopt such a time schedule as a method of reducing unemployment. We produce more than we can consume so that we may easily afford more leisure and more freedom of choice.

Six-week vacations, spread within an annual cycle coinciding with seasons, may contribute more to our happiness and mental health than millions of dollars spent on problems that overwork and stress create.

The new cycle, daily and seasonal, moves between work and leisure. With expanding leisure more of our personal goals may shift into the time span free from factory and office work.

An increase in our leisure coincides with a new ecological and social movement, whose major concern is to preserve nature and to protect the earth and all forms of life against the harmful effects of industry and the ruthlessness of man.

Thus the extended leisure and our understanding of ecology, our willingness to fight for preservation of our natural environment, may mark industrial man's more active return to the seasonal cyclical rhythms and to recurrent goals, goals dependent on free time, independent from factory goals.

In the early stages of human society, life is dominated by rather short, cyclical time and goal sequences. The long-range, linear, horizontal goal structure of extensive projects and plans stretching over years and generations does not appear at this stage. Those noncyclical projects in building temples, aqueducts, and bridges appear of course with the advanced civilizations, and by their very nature they are linear. With the advancement of urban civilization those horizontal, linear time and goal perceptions become paramount. Now the time span of goals is extended. The goal structure becomes more complex. The cyclical daily, weekly, and annual goal structure continues, of course, both in towns and agriculture. The two patterns are fused and vigorous. The structure of long-range construction goals is powerful.

In the third stage the linear perception of time and goals moves toward abstraction and precise quantification. The process of precise quantification of time, abstraction, and visual presentation is parallel with industrialization. The rationalization of equidistant horary time is in turn applied to measurement of efficiency and setting of economic industrial targets. The cyclical type continues, of course, but the linear abstract time comes to dominate the factory and industrial systems.

With the shortening of working time and general improvement of working-class conditions the cyclical goal and time structure seems to win a new relevance. It may lead to the renewal of the strong accents of seasonal divisions of an annual cycle, this time in a highly advanced postindustrial society.

Hypothesis of Infinite and Finite Value-goals

A question may be asked now: What were the value goals that contributed to the rapid technological and social change in Europe and America.[24]

This continuous change is of course a result of a number of interacting and inter-related variables. Nonetheless, value-goals form the directive and "regulative" apparatus of a culture. They reflect the ethos and determine the general thrust, moreover the nature, the quality of the process.

In our culture, value-goals such as success, perfection, knowledge and social progress, are without an end, a terminal point, without a "roof" or a "ceiling." They may be called infinite or open values. There is no final, terminal goal for an automobile or an airplane, no limit to the achievement of speed, comfort, price. Every year cars are turned out. Their market attractiveness depends on the advance in relation to the previous year, and we always expect more—more comfort, more safety, more speed. The inventors of supersonic planes are searching for more speed.

No airplane is the ultimate, terminal model. The producer makes changes again and again, attempts to turn out a "better" product, or a less expensive one. The change, continuous change in a way of thinking and doing. It is a value which shapes our market economy.

Wisdom was defined by Socrates as the understanding of one's own deficiency in knowledge. Knowledge is not finite, absolute, terminal.

Perfection has no terminals. One never reaches the end point of perfection. Things always can be done better, or more.

The concept of science and knowledge, is unlimited. In other words, we do not conceive knowledge and science as a system limited by definite boundaries, as an object or an entity, a wholeness which in definite time will be entirely conquered by the human mind, a totality which in a definite time period will be achieved. We discover certain elements, units which form a part of this totality; but the totality, the concept of knowledge and science is unlimited.

The concept of validity in scientific discovery is often an approximation. This was stated early by Pierre Simon Laplace in *Philosophical Essay on Probability*, a lecture delivered in 1795, "Nearly all our knowledge is problematical. . . . Probability is relative in part to . . . ignorance, in part to our knowledge."[25] He argues, that human mind is not perfect, that it can never embrace all knowledge, all the vast data, hence, the significance of probabilities.

The concept of hypothesis, is by definition a flexible approximation. The French mathematician, H. Poincaré, wrote a century later in his *Science and Hypothesis*: "To the superficial observer, scientific truth is unassailable, the logic of science is infallible." Poincaré indicates that science and scientific findings are hypothesis; they imply continuous change, the possibility of continuous improvement.[26] In short, the quality of science is infinite, unending. Similarly, today, this concept tentative validity, of the endless search for truth, is reemphasized in current discussions. There is no end to science, as there is no end to a library where books are continuously collected, where new books relentlessly open new vistas or destroy old concepts.

Social progress too, has been conceived as an infinite value. Condorcet wrote in 1795 in *Esquisse d'un Tableau Historique du Progrès de L'Esprit Humain*: "we shall find from past experience, from observation of the progress which the sciences, which civilization have made up to the present time, and from analysis of the course of advancements of the human mind and the development of its faculties, the strongest motives for believing that nature has assigned no limits to our hopes"—no limits, no end—no ceiling.[27] Again, Herbert Spencer wrote about a century later in *Social Statistics*. "Progress . . . is not an accident, but a necessity. . . ." Though Spencer believed that perfection can be reached, still the very concept of progress is for him a result of a universal law and must continue.[28] Again, a continuous, limitless change.

Since those optimistic times, much has changed. The idea of progress was modified by some, abandoned by others. Its meaning is broad. It is still a powerful vision for most of us, a moving target of a perfected society. The rapid advance of technology, improved standard of living of the working class testify to its validity in certain areas and in our time.

But not all of our values in our culture are of this nature. Only certain concepts and symbols have this dynamic quality. Nor are they necessarily equally shared, or even accepted.

Moreover, traditional societies are governed by sets of value-goals, that we may call finite. The latter have a definite end point, a terminal. The actor knows the limits; he knows how far he should go. Culture and custom set the boundaries of his activities. Such norms do not enhance social change and may affect the economy of traditional societies.

Bronislaw Malinowski lists three categories of economic motives of the natives of the Triobrand Islands: "Hunger, Love, Vanity." However, definite limits are set on economic activities.[29] A motive of unlimited success is absent, although there are competitive contests in harvested wealth. A Trobriander cannot advance beyond certain culturally accepted limits. His success is limited by customs, social attitudes, and beliefs in magic. If he is too successful, his magic might be too strong, dangerous to society. "A man may be attacked because his gardens are too good; he can then be accused of emulating his betters, of not giving a fair proportion of the crops to the chief, and to his relatives by marriage, and thus acting disloyally." A Trobriander, after satisfying his needs, works for "urigubu," gifts given on a maternal line.[30] Competition in gardening does exist, of course, but gift-giving, reciprocity, and mutuality are seminal in this culture— not profit. Those traditional normative imperatives are an economic driving force, quite different than profit or unlimited success. Social limits are imposed by the culture of the society, by the urigubu institution, and by the structure of society. "It is important to remember", writes Malinowski, "that the glory of gardening . . . is always subordinate to the rules which make accumulation of food a privilege of rank. . . . No commoner must become too rich or work for anyone else but those really in power. Ill health, or even death by sorcery, rather than renown, would then reward his labours.'' Dangers of magic form the sanctions which make the limits of accumulation effective.

The Arapaho Indians of the Wind River Reservation of Wyoming were, in their own way, cognizant of value difference. An old Arapaho once made a pertinent remark. We were sitting in the ''green circle'' where they usually met at noontime when a plane flew over our heads. ''You white men,'' he said, ''cannot sleep. When you sleep you think about a faster plane. You write a book, you are not satisfied, you write another one, you make money, you cannot sleep, you want to make more money. We Arapahoes are different. When we make some money, or kill antelope, we eat, enjoy, make a feast, go and talk to friends, we do not look for more.''

Needs renew continuously our activities and generate goals, as for instance hunger does. But, in the case of open, infinite goals—it is the goal that generates action; moreover it is the goal that starts the process and generates the urge and the need. The sequence is reversed.

Notes

1. Michel Panoff ''The Notion of Time among the Maenge People of New Britain,'' *Ethnology* (April 1969). Panoff compared the time concept of the Papua with ecological and structural concepts of time of the Nuer in Africa, discussed by E. Evan-Pritchard in ''Nuer Time Reckoning,'' *Africa* (1939). See also John Mbiti, ''African Concept of Time,'' *Makarere Sociological Journal* (February 1965). Mbiti discussed concepts of time of some societies in Kenya, especially the limited use of the future tense. (The references were found in *Sociological Abstracts*.) Felix Gross, ''Nomandism of the Arapaho Indians of Wyoming: Conflict between Economics and Idea Systems,'' *Ethnos* (1949):1-2.

2. For details see Olga Koseloff Gordon, ''Two Unusual Calendar Cycles of the Fourteenth Century,'' *Art Bulletin* (September 1963), and *The Calendar Cycle of the Fecamp Psalter* (Marburg: Verlag des Kunstgeschichtlichen Seminars der Universitat Marburg, 1967).

3. H. Peetz, *Volkswirtschaftliche Studien*, quoted by Werner Sombart, *Die Vorkapitalistische Wirtschaft* (Munich and Leipzig: Duncker and Humblot, 1928), vol. 1, p. 37.

4. H. Alan Lloyd, ''Time Keepers,'' in J. T. Fraser, ed., *The Voices of Time* (New York: Brazilier, 1966), p. 388 ff., 399 ff.

The Egyptian hours of one-twelfth of the day and one-twelfth of the night did exist since about 2000 BC. On ancient measuring of time, see a very informative piece: Otto Neugebauer, ''Some Fundamental Concepts in Ancient Astronomy,'' in *Studies in the History of Science* (Philadelphia: University of Pennsylvania Press: 1941), pp. 13 ff.

5. Lewis Mumford, *Technics and Civilization* (New York: Harcourt, Brace, 1963), p. 13.

6. Lynn White, Jr., *Medieval Technology and Social Change* (New York: Oxford University Press, 1966), pp. 119 and ff.; also E. Volckmann, *Alte Gewerbe und Gewerbegassen* (Wurzburg, 1921), p. 129, quoted in White, *Medieval Technology*.

7.   Mumford, *Technics and Civilization* p. 14. also Gimbel, *The Medieval Machine,* pp. 153-155.

8.   White, *Medieval Technology,* p. 126. For the history of clocks see a fascinating chapter in Jean Gimbel, *The Medieval Machine* (New York: Holt, Rinehart & Winston, 1976), pp. 147 ff. But above all see: David S. Landes *Revolution in Time*: Clocks and the making of modern world. (Cambridge: Harvard University Press, 1984). This manuscript was however completed when this volume appeared.

9.   Gimbel, *Medieval Machine,* p. 168.

10.   Arthur Klein, *Measurements* (New York: Simon and Schuster, 1974), pp. 99 ff., 120 ff.

11.   Ibid., pp. 116 ff.

12.   Andrew Ure, *The Philosophy of Manufacturers* [1835], 3d ed. (London: 1861), p. 13.

13.   Talcott Parsons, "The Role of Ideas in Social Action," in *Essays in Sociological Theory* (Glencoe, Ill.: Free Press, 1964), p. 26.

14.   For a survey of those concepts see Cornelius Benjamin, "Ideas of Time in the History of Philosophy," in J. T. Fraser, ed., *The Voices of Time,* pp. 3–31. For selection of texts on philosophy and theory of time see Charles M. Sherower, ed., *The Human Experience of Time: The Development of its Philosophical Meaning* (New York: New York University Press, 1975).

15.   Joseph Needham, "Time and Knowledge in China and the West," in Fraser, *The Voices of Time,* p. 128.

16.   Ibid., pp. 133 ff.

17.   Ibid., p. 130, quoting from Heinrich Zimmer, *Philosophies of India* (New York: Meridian Books, 1958), "Myths and Symbols," pp. 11, 16, 19, and M. Eliade, *The Myth of the Eternal Return* (London: Routledge & Kegan Paul, 1955), p. 169.

18.   Zimmer, *Philosophies of India,* p. 450.

19.   Hajiume Nakamura, "Time in Indian and Japanese Thought," in Fraser, *The Voices of Time,* pp. 77 ff., 81 ff., 99 ff., 106 ff.

20.   Needham, "Time and Knowledge," pp. 99 ff.

21.   Ibid., pp. 106 ff.

22.   Gimbel, *Medieval Machine,* pp. 150–70. Also quoted by him is J. Needham, W. Ling, and D. J. de Solla Price, *Heavenly Clockwork* (Cambridge: Cambridge University Press, 1960), p. 6, n. 3; p. 141.

23.   Karl Bücher, *Arbeit und Rhythmus* (Leipzig; Hirzel, 1897).

24.   This section appeared in a somewhat different text in Italian in *Saggi Su Valori Socialie Struttura* (Rome: Università di Roma, 1966), p. 91 ff.

25.   English Edition, New York: Dover Publications, 1952, p. 6.

26.   H. Poincaré, *Science and Hypothesis,* English Edition, New York: Dover Publications, 1952, p. xxi.

27.   English translation of parts of Condorcet in Frederick J. Teggard, revised by G. H. Hildebrand, (University of California Press), 1949 p. 321. Excellent review and anthology of concepts of change and progress.

28.   Ibid. p. 433.

29.   B. Malinowski, *Coral Gardens and Their Magic,* New York: American Book Co., 1935, Vol. 1, p. 175.

30.   "In the Trobriands, marriage put the wife's matrilineal kinsmen under a permanent tributary obligation to the husband, to whom they have to pay yearly gifts of

urigubu for as long as the marriage lasts. The marriage contract is affected by the exchange of reciprocated gifts the balance of which is not the whole favourable to the husband. ... This is packed into decorative, oblong, prism-shaped receptacles which are erected by the brother in the front of the freshly constructed yam house of the new household. This gift ... is the first installment of the urigubu contributions.'' Malinowski, *Coral Gardens*, p. 199.

Part III
VALUES

14

Hierarchies of Values: Vertical Structure

In this part of our study we shall limit our inquiry to the static or vertical structure of values, to the hierarchies of values. The horizontal approach corresponds to a dynamic approach, to the dynamic function of goals, to the relationship between goals and individual and group actions.

The vertical structure corresponds to the hierarchy of norms. This hierarchy in turn suggests the morphology, the static relationship of norms.

Empirical and Declaratory Data

There is always a risk of reification of values and norms in our theories, our discussions, even our observations and experimentations (should the latter be feasible at all). Values are not separate entities, independent of man and society. They are symbolic articulations of man's goals or norms of conduct, as well as theoretical constructs. They do appear, however, in our actions and behavior since they may, in certain areas of human activities, set the direction and regulate our actions. It is here, in our action and behavior, as well as in institutions, that their relevance is witnessed.

The ideal norms can be also "registered" rather than "observed" when they appear in the form of an essay, statement, declaration, sermon, or admonition or in the concise style of imperatives and commandments. We may call such data "declaratory data." It is in this declaratory form that we may register at times the real as well as the ideal norms.

The learned books of Newton of Galileo are not the declaratory data of physics. They are findings, theories, oriented toward the relationship of nondeclaratory data, but facts, extraneous to man and to his observations. But how can we observe values? What we can observe in action (not a form of declaration) is relations between individuals and groups. Values appear as well in an empirical sense of observation and experimentation in a context of actions or behavior.

Otherwise their existence appears in statements and declarations, or we may discover them by means of introspection. In this sense values are relative, since they appear when related to a person, group, or object. A distinction has to be made between *relative* in this sense and *relativistic*. Values, esthetic and otherwise, may appear in our relations to nature, to art, to animals; in this sense they are relative. When the evaluation varies with culture or individuals or groups, we may call them relativistic. (We shall return to this theme below.)

The Static Approach: Vertical Structure

What was called the horizontal goal and value structure is simply a sequence of independent or interdependent goals and values related to actions. In addition to this dynamic approach we may also study the morphology of values, their hierarchy, what was called the vertical structure. To compare this with natural science: We do study anatomy, a universe of interrelated elements, as a static system of subsystem. Here again the concepts of system and structure are only theoretical constructs. The world does not stop for the moment. The human body is active as long as we live, and the anatomy of a living person is in a sense an abstraction, since it does not present the physiological processes that are at work all the time. But morphology, the static approach, presents the structure, the system within which the process is moving.

The vertical structure concerns intensity of values, their subordination and superordination, preferences—in a word, the hierarchy of values.

The vertical goal structure can be presented in the form of a triangle (or pyramid), which corresponds to a concept of a hierarchy of values (see figure 14.1). This entire pattern is an abstraction, a theoretical construction of a reality. On the lateral lines values are placed according to their relevance and intensity from the top down.

In both approaches, horizontal and vertical, the universe of data is identical. It is the vantage point that is different. The same universe of data suggest not a single but several realities, and they lend themselves to different analysis. Each different approach to the same universe of data correspond to viewing the facts from a different vantage point—to put it again in visual terms. Such a pluralistic approach is, of course, not unusual. In photography the reality can be presented in a static and dynamic way. A conventional photographic picture corresponds to a static presentation or a replica of reality. A moving picture presents the same reality extended in time and in a dynamic way. In a photograph of a military formation we shall see its structures, order, position of soldiers, noncoms, officers in rank order. A moving picture presents the same universe of data in action, in a dynamic way (for example, a military parade). The reality in this case is replicated in two different ways.

The same universe of data is also subject to different types of analysis. An art historian may analyze a picture in terms of form, style, color, or subject

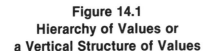

Figure 14.1
Hierarchy of Values or
a Vertical Structure of Values

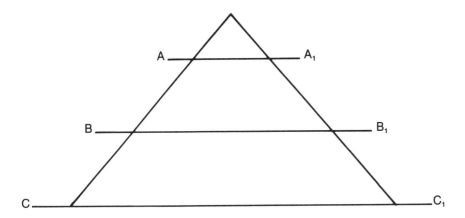

A   dominant values
B   subordinated
C   lower level of subordination

matter. Still, during all the time that he looks at the same picture, the universe of data is the same.

How to Identify Values, Norms, and Ranks

We have to begin with this elementary question: How do we find, how do we identify, our data of values, norms, and or that form the vertical structure, the hierarchy of norms? This question has been already discussed, but we shall return to it, shall broaden the question.

A philosopher considers values above all in terms of what ought to be done, what is right and what is wrong. A judge as an actor makes the choice between right and wrong. His decision-making process and ordering of norms are the subjects of our study. We are concerned here above all with what is, with the descriptive-empirical nature of data, of norms, with their rank in man's effort to order his norms in terms of relevance and situation.

We may roughly divide the way we make such findings into objective and subjective approaches. The latter is the way of introspection.

In an objective approach we discover data by observation, even experimentation. But we may also observe, notice, register norms simply in our language; furthermore in our documents, declarations, statements we describe their meaning, their articulation in conduct.

The process of hierarchization, the process of ordering of norms, appears in dialogues, in discussions, and in the decision making of groups and individuals.

We may identify such value orders by asking or interviewing, here belongs also the quantitative gathering of data by means of questionnaires or schedules, scales. Interviewing or questioning may involve substantial representative samples, and this type of polling is generally used. Another way of ascertaining a hierarchy of norms is this most human and natural way of gaining an understanding of man: conversation and dialogue.

We can also ascertain the stucture and relevance of norms by observing individual and group actions, social relations.

Language and Values

To begin, we may observe and notice norms, their strength and rank, simply in our language. Aschenbrenner, in an original and fresh approach to the problem of values, devotes an entire volume to a linguistic analysis of this issue. Aschenbrenner begins with this well-established distinction between fact and value, and his study is dedicated to the vocabulary of appraisal. "One of the principal purposes behind our investigation of the language of evaluation is to show its vast subtlety and complexity, but note only that it is also that investigations of values have shown unpardonable neglect of this vocabulary of concepts in their zeal to come to a decisive analysis of good and to settle victoriously for one side or another the conflicts over ethical naturalism and its alternatives," wrote Aschenbrenner. He found, however, a study of appraising terms as far back as antiquity, beginning with Plato.[1]

His study is, however, broader: It is devoted to the "actual employment of the vocabulary by means of which we appraise, regard, accept, etc." The appraisal, is not the end of the matter, continued Aschenbrenner: "We also dedicate ourselves to certain values, purposes, or destinies, and we ordain the observance of them.... If we are skilled at self-observation, we can discern the shape of our body of values, or our ideology; this may be a part of a religious system of thought and practice. But matters do not stop there, for ideologies may not be deliberately constructed, nor, if they simply grow, do they grow in order to entertain and edify us. Decisions are taken on the basis of them, and as a result, we are in the thick of accusation, correction, condemnation and even vengeance."[2]

Hence the process of evaluation or decision making in consequence of choice and judgment can be noticed, observed in our language. The process of judgment can be observed; in this sense, it is a datum, a fact. Moreover, the norms appear in documents, statements, declarations, oratory, sermons, dialogues. They do appear as directives, imperatives, or commands. They do appear in the Ten Commandments as well as in the Declaration of the Rights of Man of the French

Revolution, in the Declaration of Independence, or in the Universal Declaration of Human Rights of the United Nations. Those are, of course, ideal norms, but they are stated as guides for desirable—moreover, mandatory—behavior. They may not be followed, true. But they are indicative of man's equipment, intellectual and verbal, to make such decision. They are articulations of an essential capacity of man to understand and make judgments. We have called such data, which in a written or oral form state or declare normative directives or guidelines, declaratory data.

The process of judging, appraising, or evaluating appears in human behavior, in relations between man and man, man and objects, man and environment. All this can be observed, of course, and the purpose of this action, or absence of any purpose, can be inferred from relationships of facts.

However, the nature of our facts and data is not the same as that in natural sciences, especially in physics, nor is the universe of facts, the nature of realities within which we move and act. *Mutatis mutandis*. Voltaire put this clearly and in his own way:"... il n'y a point de secte de géomètres, d'algèbristes, d'arithméticiens, parce que toutes les propositions de géometrie, d'àlgèbre, d'arithmétique sont vraies. Dans toutes les autres sciences on peut se tromper. Quel théologien thomiste ou scottiste oserait dire sérieusement qu'il est sûr de son fair?''

Social sciences are not akin to religion. Nonetheless, one should not forget the different nature of facts in social sciences, of our definitions, hypotheses, ways of validation. It is a different field of inquiry, and in consequence it calls for modification of our methods and approaches.[3]

Those qualifications of our data and inferences extend beyond the empirical-inductive ways of research, applied in social sciences. But here belongs above all the process of ranking of norms (hierarchization), introspection.

The next question is this: How are the hierarchies of norms formed? How do individuals and groups proceed in discovering and ordering norms? The process of hierarchization of norms, the process of ordering norms in ranks, is perceived in discussion, dialogue. It appears in decision making, when the choice is resolved in a group by means of conversation.

As was said before, hierarchization of norms can be well established by statistical methods, by assigning values to norms plotted on a scale. For example, we may ask a respondent to assign scores—from 1 to 5—to values that are listed. His preferences will appear in numbers—1 to 5 assigned to values on this scale. Of course this is a rough simplification. Sophisticated quantitative studies of values have been carried out, and there is an extensive discipline, but it is not included in our present study.

However, we may gain an understanding of this process also by way of introspection. Introspection does not conform to the inductive and empirical techniques of gathering data and validation that are applied in natural sciences. It does not fit tightly within the boundaries of empirical and inductive inquiry. Still, introspection was and is widely used in psychology and also in sociological analysis of ethos. Dilthey's and Weber's concepts of *Verstehen* (understanding), imply introspection.

We may take as an example an attempt at the reconstruction of ordering and ranking norms in an imaginary court case of assassination in Sicily. A young man assassinated a boyfriend of his sister, who did not keep his word, dishonored the young lady, and refused to marry her. Not many years ago the delinquent would have been considered as a hero who followed centuries' old customs, respected in his village. In his community this act would be considered not as murder, but as an act of popular justice. The judge who considers the sentence is guided by legal norms. Legal norms form the boundaries of his options. Within those boundaries, we shall assume, the judge exercises his independent judgment. He can qualify the case in different ways, impose shorter or longer sentences, suspend the enforcement of the sentence. Within those legal boundaries the sentence will reflect the ethos and the attitudes; and should he be an opportunist, then it will reflect a practical, perhaps personal, consideration on the judge. But our judge is a dedicated one; he may begin with three orientations, three norms; justice, mercy, public interest. At this point the judge does not attempt to define what justice is or should be. He has a general sense of direction, an appraisal of the case. Let us postulate that he has a general sense of justice. In the view of justice as our judge perceives it, the delinquent deserves a severe punishment: An innocent person was killed. Then he looks at this case with compassion, from the vantage point of mercy: The delinquent is a young, otherwise honest person who followed a centuries' old custom. He follows now his emotions of mercy. A young life may be utterly destroyed. Mercy dictates a mild sentence. The judge has sympathy for the predicament of a young man, and perhaps he is also affected by customs of his native Sicily. But now he considers again this case as a problem of public interest. This type of delinquency, common and accepted as a custom, must be discontinued. It is in the public interest, in the interest of life and safety of citizens, that "private justice" should be stopped. Our judge chooses public interest as a dominant norm, next to his concept of justice, and qualifies by a subordinated norm of mercy, again as he experiences it. The legal precepts *in dubio mitius* (milder in a dubious case) supplies a normative support for his decision, based on a certain order, a ranking of norms.

At the beginning of his thinking and evaluating all three norms were at the same level. As the process of choices and decisions advanced, he kept changing his views, shifting between the norms. At the beginning he had considered spontaneously the three "aspects" of the case, the three norms that at this time were at the same level. In time, while the case was considered, the ordering of norms took place. Public interest in our case became the dominant one and justice the next one, immediately subordinated. Mercy was subordinated, but it still affected the dominant one.

What is the dominant value? It is the norm that sets the "strategy" of the behavior, action, or decision, sets the general direction of evaluation and choice. In a given limited case or occurrence norms that are consummatory and ends in themselves are dominant. In this case the subordinated norms affected the dominant ones; they were correctives, qualifications. The increase or decrease of the intensity of values is articulated in this hierarchy of norms.

In that way the hierarchy of norms was formed in this imaginary case. Out of the same "inventory" of norms a variety of hierarchies can be formed. A hierarchy of values does not necessarily consist of single, dominant guiding norms while all others are subordinated. The entire structure, at least in theory, may be guided by two or more dominant values. An increase in the intensity of one may affect the others, however, and may reduce them to a lower, less intensive level.

The process of judging and appraising is, of course, far more spontaneous, less conscious in the ranking of norms. The value judgment is there, while the judge does not necessarily relate consciously the case to an a priori ranking. As deficient as my attempt is, it illustrates the process and the effort of structuring norms in a hierarchy and relating to the case.

A spontaneous process of hierarchization takes place whenever decisions in complex cases have to be made. This interplay of values, a spontaneous one, appears in many areas. Consider a business deal in which the businessman may expect a high profit on the expense of principles of honesty or in violation of accepted principles of fair trade. He had to choose between the principles of honesty and the temptation of profit, the paramount value in business. Should preference be given to the profit, then our businessman will surrender the other norms and principles, pay a bribe, or take a kickback. Should he choose the norms of conduct guided by honesty and fair trade, he may land with a less profitable deal or lose the opportunity, but he will conform to the norms.

Similar ranking may also appear in an esthetic evaluation, for example, in an evaluation of the merits of form, color, and theme of a painting. A judge of a painting may subordinate the value of the theme and consider form and color as superior guiding norms. In a propaganda approach, which Stalin has baptized as "socialist realism," it was the theme that was considered as dominant; all others were subordinated, or dependent. In such an appraisal—or, rather, a kind of illustrative form and color, an illustrative-naturalistic style, again subordinated to the political theme of the picture—was essential. Most of the American and European art historians would dissent with this type of aesthetic judgment.

The General Ethos, the Megaethos

The process of ranking is again an exercise of choice, of appraisal and decision. Nonetheless, man is guided by or states and recognizes definite, already established hierarchies of values, which we may visualize in terms of vertical structures. We are guided by a number of "codes," stated, established normative orders that are accepted by some and questioned by others. Those stated, already established orders have their dominant and subordinated norms. The dominant norms are consummatory in their nature; they form the ends. Subordinated norms may be either of similar, consummatory nature, or—more often than not—they may be derived from the latter, and in such a case they are usually instrumental; they form the means toward the dominant ones, toward the ends.

Those established orders can be found in a general ethos that we shall also call a megaethos or super ethos. We have called a general ethos a normative system, the directive-regulatory orientation of major ideologies or belief systems that integrate vast social collectives, a culture, a civilization, or a wide religious community. The general code is a supreme regulatory and directive apparatus that in turn controls other subsystems. (We shall return to this theme in chapters 16 and 17.)

A great civilization that marks an entire historical period has a complex set of values, norms, and orientations, some complementary, others contradictory, conflicting, continuously adjusted, changing, reinterpreted, discussed. Hence within this general code we may visualize a number of subsystems affected directly by the latter. The various subsystems have diverse norms, often contradictory. It is still the general ethos, the megasystem, that integrates them all and supplies a general sense of direction, sets the limits of choice and boundaries of a civilization.

In spite of the fact that a modern society consists of a variety of groups of diverse political, religious, and generally normative orientations—in spite of those inner differences—there is a unity, supplied by the comprehensive ethos. Furthermore, in spite of the fact that a world outlook may form a quite extensive philosophy of complex norms, the entire culture or civilization is integrated and hangs on few norms. One may challenge their existence, dispute or argue the relativistic nature of its meaning. Still, in a moment of crisis those few norms, articulated as symbols, are invoked and displayed since the survival of culture depends on their continuation. Breakdown of those norms is tantamount to the breakdown of social control—more, at times, of a civilization. Change in dominant norms may also be tantamount to changes in a historical period.

In spite of vagueness and generalities, the dominant values of a political system, its philosophy, its general code sets the directions when institutions and public policies are considered.

One may argue of course over what is the dominant or core value in a given culture or in a given case. But, nonetheless, dominant values have been identified by ancient philosophers as well as by historians and political and social scientists for two millennia. Their relevance has been tested in debates, arguments, and struggles. They are not "complete fantasies"; the ideal concepts, ideal norms, have their practical effects. This was the meaning of Montesquieu's argument, in his introduction to *The Spirit of Laws*, when he wrote: "les hommes, et j'ai crus, dans cette infinite diversité de lois et de moeurs, ils n'étaient pas uniquement conduits par leur fantaisies."

He begins his magnum opus, *The Spirit of Laws*, with a separate "Notice of the Author" (*Avertissement de l'Auteur*), where he states the basic, dominant virtues or core values. In this "notice" he discusses the basic political values;

more, he writes that his four initial books deal with "virtues" tantamount to what we call now values. It is not, he argues, a moral or a Christian virtue; it is a political virtue—*vertu politique*. The political virtue of a republic, he continues, is the love of equality and the love of fatherland, In fact, for Montesquieu, love of fatherland is tantamount to the love of equality: "ce que j'appelle la *vertu* dans la république est l'amour de patrie, c'est-à-dire l'amour d'égalité." Honor is the basic norm of monarchy, he argues: "l'honneur est le resort qui fait mouvoir la monarchie." Montesquieu, further, makes a distinction: General virtues, virtues of the general ethos, he calls Christian good (*bien chrétien*), while honor is a political good (*bien politique*). Hence he follows in distinguishing those two separate sets of norms. Those fundamental political virtues are values, norms that move the entire institution, that motivate the people (et celle-ci est le ressort qui fait mouvoir le gouvernement républicain, comme l'honneur est le ressort qui fait mouvoir la monarchie."

Montesquieu suggests here the fundamental nature of his virtues. The entire political system is built on them. We may argue about definitions. What is seminal is his identification of values as one of those forces that on one hand move man to action and on the other supply legitimacy to his exercise of power. Those are of course ideal norms. They may serve as well as rationalization, and nothing more, of domination and the privilege of a few at the expense of many, oppression of the weak and defenseless. This was indeed a rationalization of the legitimacy of the French Monarchy. Montesquieu may have inserted this statement to protect himself and his work, which fostered political freedom and advocated superiority of a representative even republican rule. Nonetheless, the nature of his argument, the *virtue*, the norm is of interest.

Codification of the Megaethos: Ranking of Ideal Norms

The general ethos is sometimes codified in major statements, declarations, manifestos. Man usually states at the beginning of his major declarations those interests or guidelines he considers as most relevant or dominant. This sequence of norms, within the document, which begins with those most comprehensive and relevant and ends with what we may call less rigorous norms, establishes a certain hierarchy. Even in contracts, the Romans distinguished the *essentiale* and *accidentale negotii*, the essentials and the accidentals or subordinated elements. The ranking of guidelines, norms, precepts in terms of their relevance is a consequence of our logic, our process of reasoning. In the contents of such documents the structuring of norms according to their relevance and strength is sometimes noticeable, clear. Structuring of norms in such cases has its particular logic.

By means of conversation, discussion, and dialogue as well as introspection, we perceive and follow processes of ranking (hierarchization), of making or ordering a normative, vertical structure. Analysis of ideal norms (declaratory data), of statements and codes, of what might be called fundamental documents, suggests an order of already established and shared hierarchies of ideal norms. In that way we may identify the order and ranking of the latter, for even the paramount, core norms have a ranking of their own.

We may begin with the Ten Commandments, a major fundamental document, binding a vast cultural as well as religious community. Its normative impact extends over three great religious systems, a vast number of sects and denominations, although its original text is controversial, dubious.

We may identify a rather clear ranking or hierarchization of values in this major declaration of norms. Sacred is the supreme value, since the Ten Commandments constitute a religious act, a pronouncement. The initial four commandments direct man's behavior toward the supreme being. They are clearly related to the sacred (in Durkheim's terms). They are *par excellence* religious. The fifth commandment conducts toward the collective, the family. The five latter commandments are directives of conduct toward individuals and objects of commerce. There we find again an additional ranking of those norms, as respect for human life (Thou shall nor kill) begins this third set of norms. It seems that the intensity of norms diminishes with descending orders.

The hierarchy of norms of the Ten Commandments suggests four levels of intensity of norms: (1) sacred, strictly religious; (2) subordinated to the religious: the family, the collective; (3) describing conduct toward persons; (4) describing conduct toward objects of commerce, considered as "things." The document in itself articulates a hierarchy.

The megaethos, like any ethos, can be presented as a vertical model on a triangular graph. The dominant, most intense norms are few; the lower the level, the more extensive the inventory of norms. Thus the dominant, guiding directives are comprehensive; at least in most cases they integrate the entire idea system, supply the elements of synthesis.

To return to our graphic presentation: It is a device for our logical convenience. It harbors some logical perils. The graphic form may impose a kind of a straitjacket on our thinking. It may prompt us to force data into an a priori designed model. Nonetheless, as long as we remember the perils and shortcomings, the graphic form is a useful device in organizing our thinking and inferences.

We may postulate that the dominant directives or norms cannot be reduced all the time to a single imperative or commandment, although there is a tendency or search for a single, unifying norm or concept such as utility, interest, summum bonum, freedom, equality, justice.

Eighteenth-century revolutions produced a number of important normative documents that set the direction of political and social development. Those declaratory data were and are, of course, ideal norms. Still, they have their impact and in some way are translated into pragmatic laws or policies. Here belong the two great documents of the eighteenth-century revolutions and of the Enlightenment: the American Declaration of Independence and the French Revolution Declaration of the Rights of Man. Both begin with the dominant norms.

The United Nations Universal Declaration of Human Rights, a major declaration of universal norms of our times, begins with dominant norms that set the direction of the entire document. The very concept of "universal...human rights" is, of course, a set of values in itself, and it is correctly defined as a "common standard" by this very document. The preamble begins with a statement on dominant or core values—freedom, justice, peace—and, furthermore, refers to this paramount value: the dignity and worth of human beings. The document proclaims as guiding principles norms that derive from the general principle of universal human rights: "equality of man and woman, social progress, freedom."

All this sounds like another document of the eighteenth century, of the age of Enlightenment. No doubt, eighteenth-century documents, have more beauty, are far better written, and, one feels, spontaneous sincerity in those documents written by political activists and thinkers. The United Nations document is a result of compromise and diplomatic penmanship. And one feels it. It derives its strength from those earlier documents.

It is, of course, easy to argue that the United Nations document has been an instrument of double standards. Moreover, this is to a large extent true. Still, the Declaration of Human Rights sets the general direction, and the very contradictions between practice and ideal norms prompt criticism—more, opposition—and legitimize the struggle for change.

The structure of those various documents may vary; so does, of course, the content. What is common to all is the identification of dominant, supreme norms and the hierarchy, the vertical structure: listing norms derived from the dominant and subordinated.

Even a radical variance of norms follows a hierarchy, emphasizing the dominant and indicating others, derived from the former, as subordinated.

Interestingly enough, in a revolutionary ethos the division of norms into dominant and subordinated may be at times more limpid than in sectarian, religious idea systems, with their emphasis or ritual and piety.

The modern history of revolutionary movements gives us a singular case of a revolutionary moral catechism. The appellation alone suggests the influence of religion as an idea system and mode of thought on modern revolutionary development, even if such movements were at times opposed, even antagonistic, to the established creed and institutions.

More than a century ago a "Catechism of a Revolutionary" was written by a theoretician of a particular ideological orientation, akin to an anarchistic creed. It is still an unresolved controversy whether this declaration of political ethos was written by Nechayev or by Bakunin.[4] The dominant values of this ethos are clearly expressed, and the goal is limpid: destruction of the tsarist system, emancipation of the working classes, and establishment of socialism as it was understood by the authors of this catechism.

The strategic goal of this catechism is the destruction of the existing political and social system and the establishment of a new one, rooted in the dominant, supreme values of social justice, equality, and freedom. Those are the dominant values; all the others are subordinated and ancillary. Assassination of political enemies, fraud, and lies are ethical in a subordinated sense, if they are performed in the service of this supreme norm, if they serve the revolution and the destruction of the oppressive system. Hence all values but the dominant are in this case instrumental. They are positive as long as they serve the dominant. In consequence the subordinated values of various ranks are clearly dependent on the supreme one. Killing—in terms of this ethos—is an ethical act only in a case when it serves the revolution; so is robbery or fraud. If, however, killing is a means to personal glory, power, or enrichment, then it is an evil; it is negative, a violation of the highest norms also in terms of the revolutionaries or of the author of the catechism. The lower, subordinated norms are weak, moreover, flexible. They can be changed if such change is necessary or advisable in terms of service to the supreme values of the revolutionary ethos.

In a dynamic approach in a horizontal model the dominant part of this revolutionary ethos represents the strategic goals; the subordinated values and goals related to the latter are tactical and stage goals. In this document the normative boundaries of political actions are entirely lifted, displaced by considerations of pragmatic effectiveness of actions.

To be sure, this catechism was embraced by a small group of revolutionary anarchosocialists of the time. It was considered, by a wider group of revolutionaries knows as Narodniki, later the S.R. (Social Revolutionaries), as well as by the Social Democrats, as negation of ethics or a moral deviance, called later Nechayevshchyna. Dostoevski, in his famous novel *Biesy* (The Obsessed), gave a vivid, as well as a partial, account of a young group of radicals who were guided by such an ethical code. In terms of such ethos all acts are moral that serve the advancement of the dominant values and goals or what is considered as advancement by the holders of power in this revolutionary group. In fact, Lenin and his faction adopted Nachayev's ethos. On a vertical model of values this conflict between the normative and the pragmatic appears in a static form. In such an approach a single norm—social justice, articulated in the revolution— is paramount, while all the others are derived from and entirely dependent on the former. Furthermore, they derive all their strength only from this dominant imperative.

Nechayevshchyna did not disappear even in our times. It reappeared again in the modern postindustrial societies with the contemporary terrorists. The terroristic act, to be understood, has to be perceived in terms of the terrorist perception of the situation, not in terms of the judge or in terms of our society, our approach to public policies. The act in this case has to be perceived in terms of the actor and not in terms of a witness who believes in a different ethos than the terrorist does. Moreover, the terrorist constructs the image of reality applying his values, his analytical method. His perceptions and modes of thinking, in this case, are different. He acts according to the ways he thinks, analyzes, understands the situation, perceives the reality. His directive and regulatory apparatus is different.

This does not mean that we have to condone his act. That is a different matter. What we try, indeed, is to understand the other.

The goal of a terrorist from the Red Brigade is a perfect society—a society that *he* perceives and constructs as perfect. It is his image. And this image of society forms the supreme values that supplies, in his beliefs, legitimacy to his act. All the other norms of conduct are related to this dominant norm and to his strategic goal. They are entirely subordinated to this paramount value. Their meaning and understanding derive solely from the former. They are flexible. They can be changed any time, as long as they serve the dominant one. The subordinated norms of conduct are in this case clearly derived from the dominant. Furthermore, the vertical model, the hierarchy of values of this terrorist can be rather easily translated into a horizontal structure of actions and goals. The dominant, it was already indicated, represents the strategic goal; the subordinated norms are tactical and stage goals. Not all revolutionaries, of course, did or do share this kind of an ethos. We are dealing here with a specific group. In our case this example is relevant, since the ranking and order of norms are clear and their function quite evident. The example shows more: In a general outline the ethos of the contemporary terrorist in Italy or West Germany corresponds to the old Nechayevshchyna. The continuation of this ethos in a revived form, its perhaps independent reappearance, is striking. Terror is a highly complex phenomenon. There is not a single type of a terrorist. For some, absolute power is a consummatory goal. The power hungry terrorist may not realize fully his own desires and urges. A perfect society, or freedom and justice in his interpretation, of course, are indeed rationalizations. They supply symbols and legitimacy for his own quest for total power. But some are guided by the search for a perfect society, a utopian ideal, or simply for liberation from oppression. Violence for those is only an instrument, a strategy in a political struggle. Next to an idealist we may find a power hungry man of politics. At times, goals and motives are fused.

In our times the term "revolutionary" has many and contradictory meanings. The victory of some of the movements called "revolutionary" means displacement of one dictatorship by another one usually even more oppressive. The very term "revolutionary," gives them legitimacy to outrageous acts. However, this does not necessarily mean that all revolutionary movements have appropriated solely symbols.

To conclude, the ranking of norms in a revolutionary ethos of this type is distinct. This clear ranking of norms is not the case with equally orthodox ideologies of a religious nature. Here the difference between the dominant and subordinated norms cannot be so easily established. A ritual symbolic movement of hands, or a repetition of prayers, may be considered of equal relevance as the very creed and moral precepts. The concept of piety may be reduced to repetition of those rituals, repetition of sayings, prayers, fasting, movements. All this may have a powerful psychological or religious effect, true.

The concept of sin, on the other hand, establishes a hierarchy and ranking of norms. The stronger norms, dominant in terms of the believer, are connected with an equally forceful concept of sin, which forms a religious sanction. Breaking of a stronger, dominant religious norm is considered as heavy sin (mortal sin) and as connected with heavier religious punishments than breaking of a subordinated or ancillary norm. Breaking of a simple ritual may be considered as a heavy sin—simple, of course, in our terms. The way of moving the hand—the sign of the cross—at the prayer was of a major relevance in the Greek Orthodox religion. The old believers refused to accept the innovation in rituals and in the holy sign and insisted on moving their hands and fingers the old way. The Russian government, at times, when the Renaissance and the Enlightenment were making their inroads in the West, enforced the new ways of crossing the breast in prayer. Persecutions were cruel. The history of the Inquisition is also instructive of how much significance man has attached to the exercise of rituals.

Excursus: Hartmann's and Scheler's Theory of Value Rank and Order

Major philosophical schools answered the questions of values and their ranks by applying methods and ways germane to their disciplines, in terms of utility, interest, intuition, or reason, or by assuming an absolute existence and rank of such order. Some theologians answered by means of a dogma and interpretation of the latter by a single authority. Most of those schools approached the problems of values and hierarchy in a rather a priori fashion, assuming a single premise for their ranks and order. Discussion of and polemics with those many and prominent historical schools are beyond the scope of this modest volume. Moreover, literature in this area is so extensive that it is almost impossible to condense in a single chapter the variety of approaches to this problem so closely related to the fundamental area of ethics, a discipline with a history almost as ancient as our alphabet and writing. Social theorists who made such substantial contributions in this area, to mention Max Weber, Tawney, Parsons, Sorokin, and Martindale, seldom if ever referred to the philosophical works on values. Znaniecki in one of his last works referred to them in footnotes. One of the reasons was perhaps that an excursus in the philosophical direction could have easily frustrated their own scholarly goals. By overextension of the scope their own important contribution would have been lost in polemics, quotations, and digressions.

It seems to me, however, that a short excursus into one of the major contributions in his field, related in its theme to the problem of hierarchy of values, not only is illuminating but also is very fruitful and contributes to a broader perspective. It brings a different view and also an outlook from a different vantage point. We shall limit ourselves solely to the work of Nicolai Hartmann and Max Scheler, the latter in Hartmann's interpretation.

Hartmann argued (and this is logical and intuitive) that the realm of values presupposes preferences and gradations. Moreover, he spoke about "consciousness of values and consciousness of its gradation." However, Hartmann pointed to the difficulties in problems of gradation. It is neither a clear nor a simple way. "All that can be shown is the existence of certain more or less evidently connected groups which cluster about single dominant and fundamental value," wrote Hartmann, but the grade or the position of other norms in relation to the dominant one cannot be clearly or permanently established. Paramount is the search for a unifying principle, indeed, not easy to locate. In consequence, to follow Hartmann, the procedure must be of "loose and tentative character."[5] Still he advanced a detailed theory of rank and grade of values. The highest values, in his view, are those which are comprehensive, those which form a synthesis of the lower values. This synthesis might be composed of antithetic elements: "With the Aristotelian virtues it became clear that in every antithetic the synthesis is higher than the factors which are united in it." This principle suggests, of course, a certain order, a structure. In consequence, the higher the norm, the more antithetical content has to be fused into a synthesis; and "more firm the fusion, so much higher does it stand in the order and rank."[6] Thus the rank in this hierarchy of values is determined by the level of complexity. The higher the synthesis, the broader the complexity, the more dominant in rank are the values, the higher the norms. At the same time, the higher the synthesis, the more dialectical or more antithetical it is. Thus the lower values are elemental and their strength, argued Hartmann, lies in their simplicity, in their elemental nature. The strength of the value is not identical with its height in the hierarchy. Stronger values, in Hartmann's theory, are the most elementary and in the lower rank of the hierarchy. He suggested a "law of strength" in ranking values: "The higher principles are dependent upon the lower but the converse is not true." Hence the higher norm is always more dependent and weaker. Furthermore, the fulfillment of the higher value depends entirely on the fulfillment of the lower values.[7] A sin against a lower value, according to Hartmann, is generally considered as more grave than a sin against a higher one. Hartmann's examples are, however, not convincing: Property is of lower value than benevolence, and violation of property is much more reprehensible than malevolence. This is, of course, his own arbitrary judgment. He followed this with a number of similar examples.[8] Order and ranking in those cases are personal and elusive; he admits this in his further discussion of rank.

Hartmann considered also Max Scheler's theory of value grade. Scheler suggested distinctive marks as ranks in a system of values. Scheler's theory was based not on mutual relationships between the values but rather on relations of a norm to the entire "realm" of values. Here is a summary of Scheler's views.

1. Values are higher, the more permanent, enduring, and timeless they are.
2. Values are higher, the less they increase or decrease with their division or extension. The higher the values, the less *their quality* increases or decreases with their division and/or extension: "Spiritual values are not in themselves capable of being divided."

Material goods can be shared or divided, but their value for an individual declines with each division.

3. A distinguishing mark of the lower values is that they are dependent on the higher.

4. The higher the value, the more profound the satisfaction. Scheler wrote about the depth of satisfaction, which is not identical with the strength. Here he compares satisfaction in material good and in arts. The latter has more depth than the former.

5. The less the values are relative, the higher their grade. Values of pleasure are meaningful for certain personalities, certain dispositions. In a sense they can be related to persons and their enjoyment. Moral values are broader, approach absoluteness; their existence is not relative to particular individuals or groups. They are of general quality.[9]

Scheler's gradation reflects his philosophy; its meaning derives from his general outlook. He did not make an effort to validate his hierarchy. Nonetheless, on a normative and logical level his ranking is convincing.

Hartmann's answer to Scheler's gradation is rather brief: Scheler's distinguishing marks are not a sufficient device; they do not permit one to assign grades beyond general outlines. Scheler's criteria indicate that moral values are higher than material. But, argued Hartmann, this is quite evident without those five principles.

A discussion of ranks and hierarchies of values leads of course, to a paramount question: Is there a single, supreme value or virtue?

The Greeks had a comprehensive concept of virtue as a supreme value (*arete*) and supreme values of good (*agathos*) and beautiful (*kalos*). But even those supreme concepts have to be related to a changing situation and historical condition. Their meaning is reinterpreted with changing times.[10] This question today, however, seems to be far more complex, and we shall return to this argument in a section on universal values (see chapter 16). But we may follow here some of Hartmann's attempts.

The philosophical issue is different from an empirical and sociological one. Hartmann answers this issue in terms of inner logic of ethics and his intuition. First, there is a question whether such values do exist and, if they do, whether they are elemental or complex: a result of a synthesis. In their search for unity and in an attempt to establish a supreme value, philosophical schools followed both directions. Here come the values of happiness, pleasure, self-preservation, justice, utility. An unknown supreme value may be also assumed. The supreme core value may not be identified, but still the multiplicity of norms in itself reflects a tendency or a need for unity, a need for a supreme concept that would create a synthesis and organize the norms, reconcile the antinomies and dialectics.

This supreme value must encompass both oppositions and harmonies, and it must resolve the contradictions. Even a plurality of values calls for some kind of a unifying principle.[11]

There is no need to go any further into details of Hartmann's and Scheler's ideas. Moreover, it may be fruitless to embark here on a lengthy and involved discussion of these two prominent philosophers. Ours is a pragmatic issue of the applicability of a value theory to social change, to social actions, to practical issues of the day. Ours is a matter of understanding individuals and society; it is largely, although not solely of course, an empirical or close to an empirical approach.

General Outline of Ranking Norms

Therefore, we shall limit ourselves to a kind of hypothesis, or only to what Henri Poincaré in his *Science and Hypothesis* called the fixing of ideas on the nature of ranking and order of norms.

First, we assume that (in a static hierarchical approach) the directive and regulatory orientations are, or may be, governed by a set or supreme or core values. Those supreme or core values we have called the megaethos; this general code may control a number of subordinated, at times conflicting subsystems. What we mean by "a normative subsystem" of course is that we postulate the existence of a group or groups of persons who share those values. Furthermore, we assume a general ethos or a megaethos of a culture or of a civilization. This set of values unifies or coordinates the various orientations of an entire civilization. The general code, the megaethos, of a civilization is recognized by a variety of differing groups. The medieval Christian societies formed a civilization integrated by a belief system and values. Various sects and churches practiced what was considered by Rome as a heresy. Differing creeds did not share in common institutions. Still, there was shared a minimum set of values and beliefs.

This general ethos is the source of the ultimate legitimation of power. We speak, of course, about ideal norms. They may, and as a rule do, deviate even substantially from the realities of life. Here belong such norms and values as freedom, equality, justice, primacy of the individual and person vis-à-vis the state or the reverse primacy of the state vis-à-vis the person. A partisan of apartheid may believe that he follows Christian ideas of the brotherhood of man, and he reinterprets his concepts and his norms by means of appropriate biblical commentaries that serve his interests and his views. In his perception he recognizes this supreme ethos and finds in it legitimation for his privilege.

The general ethos may be broader than a single set of values of a culture within a nation or a state. It embraces a number of otherwise differing cultures: It is a broad collective of persons unified by a set of values, traditions, and identification. We call such a collective a *civilization*.

At the same time, a civilization is expressed in typical skills and material products, artifacts. In this sense we speak about the Hellenic as well as the Hellenistic civilization, the latter embracing a number of nations, differing in language, customs, and religion but still united by a community of certain values, interests, and material culture.

Second, we assume that higher values are comprehensive since they integrate various subordinated and ancillary values, some of which are antithetical, conflicting.

Third, the lower values in the hierarchy of norms are dependent on the higher ones, or they are interdependent.

Fourth, in an empirical, descriptive approach, the strength of the values has to be identified in a social context, within the context of reality and not out of it. In every case, by means of observation or experimentation, the strength of values has to be established. Their strength is discovered in their resistance to change or by sanctions attached to such norms. Some of the norms may yield more easily than the others. In fact, here is one of the keys to social change strategy. Strong resistance to change indicates that those norms have been well integrated into the present social fabric, social institutions, customs, mores.

This statement calls for clarification. The intent may be easily misunderstood. The initial distinction between actor and observer has to be repeated here. When I act as a judge, when *I* judge my own or somebody's conduct, I know or sense the strength of the norms. I know or I must at the end decide what is right and wrong. I follow my ethical order, my intuition or education, my sense of justice. However, when I evaluate the strength of norms of *others*—especially in a different culture—my task is to discover the strength of *their*—not my—norms, to determine what *they*—not I—consider a relevant or as a core value. This is of course a difference between descriptive and prescriptive approaches. When I judge, I follow norms, imperatives. When I describe the conduct of *others*, I make an attempt to discover the strength of the norms of *others*. In this sense the strength of the norms has to be established and discovered.

Fifth, ranking of values can be established by quantitative methods, of course, by means of questionnaires, tests, scales, or other instruments. Numerous quantitative studies have been made, and it would take a volume to discuss the methods and findings of opinion polls and similar extensive and complex inquiries. Frequent polls, popular and generally accepted today as an adequate measurement of public opinion, articulate value ranks as well as normative orientations.

Our definition of values, however, is limited to the directive and regulative functions. Interests explored by quantitative studies are far wider. Furthermore, in a quantitative inquiry the norms, or quantified values, are out of a particular context. They are separated from the situations of various groups of respondents. Since the data are precoded, they may reflect perceptions and interests of the researchers. No doubt, however, the public opinion polls do express value orientations of large groups. They reflect also value preferences in spite of limitations due to the very nature of the field of the study and the nature of the data.

Sixth, in a descriptive and empirical approach the strength of norms may be identified a priori only as an initial hypothesis. The strength and intensity may change with the changing situation. The hierarchization of norms, emergence of ranks of norms, is frequently a dynamic process. Ranking is formed while choice is exercised and decisions are made. Experience suggests the evidence of strength. The strength of norms has to be tested *in situ* in the context of a social situation.

Seventh, values may appear in sets (that is, an individual or a group) considering a choice, and a decision may begin not with one but with a set of interrelated value-goals. At the beginning (of a process of ranking) all are of equal priority or relevance.

Maximizing one of the value-goals may, and usually does, argues Irani affect the others, diminishing their strength or chances of achievement or setting lower levels of achievement for the latter.[12]

Broadening of opportunities in education may decrease the very quality of education, at least at the initial stage. Open admission to a university, necessary as it may be, does increase the fulfillment of a value-goal of equality and democratic education. At the same time the level of excellence of education and the requirements and subject matter or curriculum are affected and lowered, since broadening encompasses students who had lesser opportunities in their preparatory schooling and also those who did not take their duties seriously enough and did not develop the necessary, even elementary skills. In consequence a university, maximizing the value-goal of equality in education, must at the same time minimize the value-goal of excellence. As a rule, it is difficult, if possible at all, to maximize two conflicting or competitive value-goals at the same time.

A planner or decision maker, in terms of rational planning and action, may search for an optimum answer that would reconcile the competing values and secure an outcome considered as desirable within the limitations imposed by these competitive or conflicting goals. What a planner establishes as optimum will set a hierarchy of goals.

Eighth, a general ethos, shared in some way by a whole society, does not preclude existence of a number of particular groups sharing specific normative systems, groups frequently antagonistic in their outlooks, antithetical in their normative subsystems. No modern, complex society can be reduced to a single monistic ethos. Attempts were and are made by totalitarian states and religions to impose a single ideology and at the same time a single normative system, exclusive of subsystems or competitive ethos. In spite of those attempts, different and opposed ideologies, philosophies, or religious creeds did survive. When we speak here about normative systems or ideologies, it is of course understood that we mean groups sharing a set of norms or ideas.

However, no pluralistic system can function unless a minimum set of norms and a common procedure are at least de facto shared. An individual or a group who desires a society that permits him to practice a political or religious creed of his own, even if it is strange and bizarre in terms of majorities, has to recognize the right of others to practice their own creeds. In the absence of the latter, pluralism cannot be practiced (more in chapter 17).

And ninth, in the past the general ethical code appeared in a codified form. It may be argued that at that time, however, societies were simple, forms of social organization were well established and stable, and norms were homogeneous and generally shared. The basic principles of legitimacy of power were few, even monistic, and were generally accepted. It may be further argued that in modern, rapidly changing times, when stability in many parts of the world has been affected and rapid changes have brought some societies to the brink of disintegration, a codified normative ethical system may be difficult to establish.

Moreover—to continue the same argument—in the past the binding ethos embraced a single nation, culture, or in a broader sense civilization. Now, the problem is to establish a universal general code.

However, in a sense, the United Nations Declaration of Human Rights is an attempt toward a codified system of a megaethos. At this point a question can be asked: Is codification of a general ethos necessary? In fact this question has been asked by some contemporary philosophers.

However, in some great religions norms were codified. They were also codified in fundamental documents in times of historical change. Moreover, when institutions broke down, the codified norms suggested a sense of direction and supplied means of social reconstruction.

So we shall leave, at this point, this question unanswered.

It seems, however, that modern conditions call for norms that are broad enough to be able to supply the necessary flexibility and that still maintain a vigorous sense of direction and normative limits.

In our century—in spite of wars, conflicts, organized hostilities of various kinds—mankind has been bound together more tightly by common interests and needs than anytime in history. We know more about peoples who live on continents and islands very, very distant from our home. Many, while not all, are sincerely concerned about miseries and sufferings, famines and oppressions, expulsions of entire nations. The very survival of this planet in our age suggests a paramount and universal public interest. Thus, the present world calls for a common denominator.

There are common positive sentiments, elementary in their nature—such as friendship, mutual aid, willingness to cooperate—that in one form or another appear in all societies. They can be articulated in moral orders of a universal nature, supported also be compelling needs imposed by life on this planet.

In the presence of those needs and sentiments advanced ethical orders of universal nature can be also constructed (more about this in chapter 16).

Hierarchy of Values of Subsystems

But does an analysis of a hierarchy of values, of a vertical structure of norms, have any pragmatic relevance? It seems to me that it does and that an analysis of norms is essential in any planned social change. The structural analysis of norms permits understanding how groups and societies work, how they act.

The general ethos, megaethos, encompasses the entire society or large majorities of a society. But within a single nation or society we shall find a number of groups of differing normative subsystems. In a modern, industrialized society a person belongs usually to several groups of differing normative subsystems, and his behavior may vary in their different roles and within different groups.

It is the general ethos that helps an individual to integrate his different roles and differences in behavior related to those different normative subsystems (more about this below in chapter 16). But not only religious and political groups have differing normative subsystems or their own. Professions have differing and particular ethos. The norms of professional ethos may, of course, correspond primarily to the pecuniary interests of a profession. However, such a total dedication to economic gain and advantage (for example, by medical doctors) shall or may also be considered by consumers as ruthless exploitation (and it is in fact) and may be challenged by majorities as a violation of public interest. Strong departure from a recognized professional ethos in favor of gain and economic interest is considered as not professional or as detrimental to the interests of others, to the public interest in general. Of course such departures and exploitative practices are common. The simple evidence of it is the cost of health services in the United States and the excessive, even shocking annual income of physicians as compared with other intellectual professions such as engineers, college professors, teachers, or public servants. Nonetheless, the critics of such development point to the ideal code of the medical profession, to those codes idealized in images of family and country doctors.

The vertical structure of those subsystems is not necessarily fully compatible with the hierarchical order of the general code of ethics. The dominant values of certain subsystems are usually evident, known, accepted, and in some cases achievable within a definite and limited time span in terms of a "project". Here belongs, for example, the concept of profit. Profit as a general norm is a continuous, even infinite value. It is never fully achieved; it is a moving target. But within a definite time span a stockbroker makes a profit on a definite deal.

In order to achieve or approach the dominant value-goal of the subsystem the actor must follow norms of conduct that would secure success. Those norms, of a regulatory nature, are necessary to achieve the consummatory value; in this sense they can be considered as means or as instrumental. Those regulatory norms, norms of conduct of major relevance, are called subordinated, since they are subordinated to the dominant value-goal. While they are articulations of the dominant ones (of the subsystem), they are also interdependent. However, realization of dominant value-goals depends on proper working of the subordinated norms, which set the path of conduct. Regulatory or instrumental norms of relevance lower than the subordinated shall be called ancillary.

The subordinated norms are a necessary condition of success, whereas the ancillary are not.

The ancillary norms of conduct facilitate and enhance; the achievement does not necessarily fully depend on the latter, however. Their absence may, however, lower the chances of success.

We may visualize this subsystem in the form of a triangle (see figure 14.2). On the very top we can observe the dominant values (*A*); below are the derived subordinated or dependent values (*B*); and still loosely connected are the ancillary values (*C*), values that are only indirectly connected with the entire value structure.

Figure 14.2
A Vertical Approach to Values

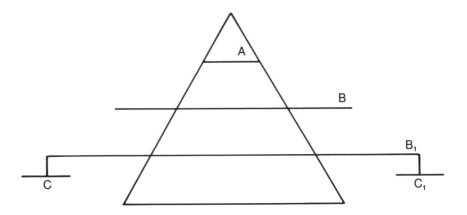

A$_1$ — Dominant Values

B, B$_1$ — Derived Values; subordinated

C, C$_1$ — Ancillary Values

Now let us try to identify the vertical value structure of such a complex institution as Wall Street, or the financial district of New York. We may limit ourselves to the financial companies that operate on the stock exchange. The actual, not the ideal, values of these companies are reflected in the economic behavior of those who are employed by or who are the decision makers of the companies. The dominant value is, of course, profit (*A* on our figure 14.2). Profit—success in profit making and the accumulation of money—and financial skills, an expertise, give status on Wall Street. But a number of values are subordinated to this dominant one (*B* and *B$_1$* on figure 14.2) and the entire vertical value structure gives us a general picture of the ethos of the Wall Street financial community. One of the relevant subordinated values is dependability "keeping one's promise." Orders are given on the telephone, decisions are made quickly, and stipulations and promises are definite. Dependability or reliability in those operations is striking for an outsider. Much of the business is performed simply by means of an unwritten telephone order. There are other values that are dependent or subordinated, such a punctuality. The great emphasis is put on time. Promises have to be kept or executed on time. Meetings and appointments are kept to the minute. A clerk or broker who is not punctual will not be kept by his employer. These two values, dependability and punctuality, are related to the very nature of profit making on Wall Street. Business of this type cannot be efficiently transacted without these two values.

Wall Street, of course, is highly competitive, but between the companies there are certain limits imposed on the competitive process: "You compete, but you do not destroy your competitor." These are, of course, unwritten rules. Competition, free competition, is again another subordinated norm of conduct. However, on the other hand, this one is balanced by another one, also subordinate one: fairness in competition, rules of fair trade (our normative parameter).

What are the ancillary values? How can they be identified? They appear is such details as taste in dress or even taste in drinks. And though the business might be fast, shrewd, speculative, and risky, the appearance is solid, punctual, honorable, and conservative (C, C_1 on figure 14.2). Nevertheless, the whole value structure is highly functional. Profit making, as well as an efficient operation, requires an elaborate value pattern. Even the ancillary values, though not as essential, have function and meaning. A customer trusts his money and business willingly to a conservative, restrained, and calm officer of a company.

In consequence, ancillary and subordinate values are instrumental; they work like tools that help to achieve an end—profit. The ancillary values in this case derive from the subordinate. The broker may have his own preferences, different from the style of the Wall Street imperatives of conservative fashion, but he cannot work effectively in his milieu and in his Wall Street office dressed in red pants and fancy shirts. He can do it on Sunday in his home, somewhere in Westchester. Submission to those unwritten norms that govern daily behavior in the Wall Street district is a condition of his financial success, and his financial success is tantamount to the dominant value—profit.

Value Hierarchy and Strategy of Planning

Understanding and analysis of value hierarchies may have a wide area of application in the planning of revolutionary or nonviolent social change.

In large sections of the world, social planning and social change have been carried out with extensive use of force and violence. No doubt, in our historical past basic social changes necessitated or resulted in various patterns of mass coercion. This is not, however, the universal and the sole pattern of innovation. Innovation was and is carried out with limited or no coercion, especially when such innovative processes agree with culture and major values of groups and communities affected or initiating such changes. In the latter type of innovation and change we may say that social engineering, the structure and relative strength of norms, has to be carefully considered, studied, and understood before a change is initiated. We may call such innovation nonviolent.

Central in any culture is the ethos, the set of values that integrates the entire culture. A nonviolent introduction of a new technology or basic policy may be carried out by two related, but different means.

We may adjust our policies as well as technology to the dominant features of a society, to their culture, to fundamental values of a community. Instead of adjusting the society to the new technology, we may—in certain cases at least—adjust the type of technology to the community. Such a policy may call, for example, for improving the efficiency of tools accepted and used by the community rather than for introducing entirely new and difficult technologies.

However, a basic change may be also introduced in a different way. The first method may be inadequate. Introduction of a new technology or policy may necessitate or result in substantial changes in values, institutions, and social structure as well. Introduction of new crops in a traditional agricultural society, even new fertilizers, new tools and skills, new policies such as planned parenthood or population control involve changes in norms of conduct and perhaps in the entire configuration of values. Such changes in the long run will usually affect institutions and social structure, will contribute to emergence of new classes and decline of traditional ones. The change in certain values in such a process is of a strategic nature; it is fundamental. Of course, in the long run, those changes will probably also affect and modify the belief systems.

In a planning process there are two parties; those who plan and those for whom it is planned, the planners and the planned. Of course, the most desirable process, a fully democratic one, is one in which the planners plan for themselves. However, large-scale policies are not simple. Population control may involve outside planning, as do some of the technical changes that call for a substantial expertise and control of economic and political power. It is important, even imperative, to include the decision and will of the planned into the entire process; hence understanding of their culture, society, and—in terms of our theme—values is essential.

Understanding of the latter is a condition of a social change of this type, a social change that may have some chance of voluntary cooperation and acceptance. Not all planning of such type will be successful, of course. It may end with a failure, and in the past some of the most humane projects did indeed fail.

In a strategic, initial approach to such a project the strategic issues are (a) of configuration, a hierarchy of values; (b) the strength of norms and their nature, and (c) the location of political, social, and economic power. To consider the first, the planners have to anticipate the values that will be affected or the changes in values that are essential to secure success of the project. Certain norms may be weaker and may yield to persuasion or to the offer of aid to pressing needs of individuals and the community. Those attitudes may be less resistant to the new options. Advantages of innovation and alternatives to the painful and urgent problems may be convincing. Other norms might be deeply anchored in a culture and might lead a strong resistance to innovative processes. A community may prefer to continue with their miseries than abandon the dominant value or religious tenets. Understanding of the strength of norms, of the hierarchies, may assist the planner in designing proper strategies. He may consider where to direct the action, where to start, what values to affect, where to "knock." In an effort to find those elements that may yield to innovation the planner considers carefully the culture, values, customs that the planned-for may be willing to abandon, where neither pain will be suffered nor resentment felt. It is a strategy where to direct our action, how and where to push the reform, the change, how to do it with due respect for the views and culture of the community. This may affect the way the innovators present their alternative options to the leadership and to the community. Some of the subordinate, or ancillary norms of conduct (*B* and *C* in figure 14.2) may yield more easily than the others and may pave the road to change. Or, to put it in reverse, changes that at the onset will not affect the basic value hierarchy may be more easily accepted.

Of course, a general question can be asked here, a general question of our own moral commitment: Do we have the right to advise changes, to impose changes on weaker communities, weaker nations, even by means of persuasion? Do the stronger have the right to impose changes on the weaker by means of social engineering? Do the planners have the right to impose or advise changes they consider as beneficial, even though those for whom the changes are planned consider them as harmful or unattractive?

There are, however, areas that suggest definitely the moral legitimacy of social change. This is the wide area of health, hunger, and those concerns of all mankind. Take such a case as securing clear and healthy water, control of pests and epidemics. There might be, in some cases, strong resistance to acceptance of any necessary changes related to improvement in those areas. Or problems of overpopulation and food. We shall only register problems that have prompted a large literature in the past decades.

We may conclude that a rational and humane project of social change may begin with a careful study of values, institutions, and social structure, the culture of the community. And such a planning has to be carried out with a primary scope of the benefit and interest of the community and, moreover, with an effort so that changes are planned and made with participation of those who are affected by them.

Notes

1.   Karl Aschenbrenner, *The Concept of Values* (Dodrecht; D. Reidel, 1971), pp. 9ff.

2.   Ibid., pp. 5, 13, 16.

3.   Alfred McClung Lee in *Multivalent Man* (New York: Braziller, 1965) made penetrating comments on this difference in the nature of facts and studies in social sciences, especially in these areas: (1) Much of the useful data is complex and impressionistic. (2) Much of the data is uncomparable. (3) Some of the data is from not dependable sources. (4) Criteria for selecting among the conclusions of disagreeing clinical sociologists tend to be relative rather than conclusive.

4.   See Max Nomad, *Apostles of Revolution* (Boston: Little, Brown and Company,

1939), pp. 211 ff.—his essay on Nechayev ("The Fanatic"). Translation of the "Catechism" begins on p. 228.

5.   Nicolai Hartmann, *Ethics*, vol. 2, *Values*, part 2, "The Realm of Ethical Values" (London; Allen & Unwin, 1963), pp. 44, 45.

6.   Ibid., pp. 445, 446.

7.   Ibid., pp. 447–51.

8.   Ibid., p. 53.

9.   Max Scheler, *Der Formalismus in der Ethik und Die Materiale Wertethik* (Halle: M. Niemeyer, 1921), p. 88, quoted by Hartmann, "The Realm of Ethical Values," chap. 4, "The Criteria of the Grade of a Value," p. 54. Karol Wojtyla, later elected Pope John Paul II, in an important attempt applied Max Scheler's value theory toward a construction of Christian ethics. (see Bibliography).

10.   A. W. H. Adkins, *Moral Values and Political Behavior in Ancient Greece* (New York: W. W. Norton, 1972), pp. 6, 7, 10, on range and strength of norms, meaning of terms, and problems of their translation. The entire volume is pertinent to our discussion.

11.   Hartmann, "The Realm of Ethical Values", chap. 5, "The Problem of the Supreme Value," pp. 65 ff.

12.   See also K. D. Irani, "Values and Rights Underlying Social Justice," in Randolph L. Braham, ed., *Social Justice* (Boston and the Hague: Nijhoff, 1981), pp. 29ff.

15

Multiple Sets of Values: Parallel Hierarchies

Dual Ethics

While continuing our discussion on normative subsystems, let us begin with a theme of the previous chapter that postulates a normative superethos (megaethos) shared in various degrees by the entire society, a kind of a global system, that in turn does not preclude existence of a number of particular cultural and social groups, sharing particular normative subsystems.

The logic of social evolution may suggest a simple and rather idyllic society, perfect in its pristine morality. Such were the pictures advanced for at least three centuries, if not more by philosophers of natural law. Philosophers of the Enlightenment popularized this attractive lore with their wit and talents. Rousseau won his first glories with an intelligent essay on the illusion of progress, on happiness of the primitives. Voltaire and, above all, Diderot, with his witty dialogue on the ''Supplement to the Voyage of Bougainville,'' presented the ideal morals of the ''primitives''—unspoiled by the advanced civilization. Today we know well that those beautiful images were not necessarily true, useful as they were in terms of historical struggles against prejudice.

Of course, we have no records of normative codes of the very early societies; the only way left to us is a hypothesis, supported by our information about contemporary or past, less advanced, tribal societies, those we have called ''primitive.''

An idealized image of an early society suggests a well-integrated group, controlled by a single normative code shared by all members of the group. There is some truth in this image. However, even among those early societies the normative code was split: one moral code guided relationships with outsiders, with other tribes or peoples, and a different one controlled conduct toward insiders. Already at the early stages of mankind the same persons followed two different normative codes (or subcodes)—codes, moreover, that were not complementary, but contradictory. Many if not most of the outgroups, the different tribes, were considered as adversaries, even enemies. The norms toward them were dictated in terms of aggression and defense. Contrariwise, cooperation and mutual aid guided the conduct toward one's own group. Hence an ethical dualism appeared quite early in man's history. Early man operated not on a single system, but on two normative systems that were antithetical. To kill an enemy is a virtue; to kill a member of one' own group is a crime. This ethical dialectics has affected our general, normative code from the early days and continues till today.

Hence already in a primitive society (and we use the term *primitive* in want of a better one) the general code (superethics) may have had two dimensions, two different hierarchies of norms of behavior toward the in-group on one hand and toward the out-group on the other. This difference grew in intensity when a tribal society faced an enemy outgroup.

Spencer's Theory of Ethical Dichotomy

More than a century ago, Herbert Spencer pointed to this dichotomy, to the two different roots of our ethics.

The presence of antagonistic societies affects our entire ethical system, argued Spencer. It affects the subordination of personal to social welfare. Survival of the group becomes paramount—since an individual cannot survive alone. Once the group is conquered, subjugated, destroyed, he suffers the fate of all others.

The life of the social organism must, as an end, rank above the lives of its units. The conduct toward the alien group at this stage is guided by enmity, while amity dominates the conduct toward the same society. Hence, the ethical system is inconsistent.

At present the individual man has to carry on his life with due regard to lives of others belonging to the same society; while he is sometimes called to be regardless of lives of those belonging to other societies. The same mental constitution, having to fulfill both these requirements, is necessarily incongruous; and the correlative conduct, adjusted first to the one need and then to the other, cannot be brought within any consistent ethical system.

Hate and destroy your fellow man is now the command; and then the command is, love and aid your fellow man.[1]

At every level of social evolution, ethics is determined by this conflict of external and internal norms of conduct, "between the moral code of enmity and moral code of amity." A consequence of this conflict is a compromise "not indeed a consistent and definable compromise, but a compromise fairly well understood."[2]

The highest form of life, of a completely evolved conduct, Spencer argued further, is guided by a code and actual behavior that exclude all forms of aggression: "not only murder, assault, robbery, and the major offenses generally, but minor offenses such as libel, injury to property and so forth."[3]

Gradually, as wars disappear, Spencer continued, the inner conflict between these two subsystems of conduct will decline. The conflict between the interest of an individual and that of society or the state will decline, too; at this point a final, permanent code of conduct will be formulated, "so constituting ethics as a science in contrast with empirical ethics."[4]

Man and his society, argued Spencer, subject to those two conflicting codes of conduct, arrive in time at some kind of a temporary compromise between two codes. Moreover, in advanced civilizations an attempt to reconcile both may be noticed.

Spencer, a utilitarian, stressed the function of the inner ethics, the ethics of the in-group in terms of survival. Since the major end and function are survival of the species, of the nation, then survival of the group becomes paramount. But the individual survives only thanks to the association, thanks to the group. Outside of a human community, alone and in isolation, he cannot exist and survive. In consequence the individual must at times surrender his welfare to the welfare of the group. Hence the inner dialectics within the group and at times the conflict between individual and group interest.[5] This inner conflict affects the inner code of behavior.

Spencer's Augury: Dual Ethics and the "Militant" State

That human society is guided by those two different ethical codes, or subcodes, is not difficult to verify. History offers vast evidence for Spencer's theories and findings. The abundance of data—more, the vast experience shared by many millions—makes this theory commonplace.

But Spencer applied this theory of two codes to the study of the evolution of human society and arrived at rather prophetic conclusions. More than a century ago this father of English sociology anticipated a totalitarian state. One can read moreover in those lines, in those carefully guarded words, an apprehension that it was coming, that this was the future, since the totalitarian state may win. He did not call it *totalitarian*; the word, I suppose, was not coined as yet, He called it a militant state.

The defense against aggressors involves organization and institutions structured differently from those geared toward peaceful and productive pursuits. He called such activities "industrial" as opposed to "militant." Hence human society, since its beginning, is guided by two types of conduct governing the two major activities: aggression or defense on one hand and peaceful industrial activities on the other; the external of aggression or defense, the internal of production and cooperation; the regulative system of the former is guided by enmity, as opposed to amity, which guides the latter. The need of an effective organization of defense, accompanied at times by greed for power, leads to emergence of powerful militant institutions. The militant organizations developed for defense have a tendency to grow and extend their control. Coercive in their nature, they are guided by rules of subordination and command.[6] Since they are efficient in their major function—defense—they are slowly extended into the civil society.

Wrote Spencer:

A further trait of the militant type, naturally accompanying the last, is that organizations other than those forming the part of state organization are wholly or partially repressed. The public combination occupying all fields excludes private combinations.... Any structures which are not portions of state structure serve more or less as limitations to it, and stand in the way of the required unlimited subordination.... Their governments are coercive; in some cases, even to an extent of killing those of their members who are disobedient....

The process of militant organization is a process of regimentation, which primarily takes place in the army, secondarily affects the whole community.... Labor is carried on under coercion; and supervision spreads everywhere.[7]

Spencer used this term *regimentation* quite early. The term and the practice of regimentation had a wide application and use in the fascist, the German National-Socialist, and other totalitarian states (Stalinist Soviet Union, Mao's China). The militant (totalitarian) type of control extends over the entire society; it takes hold of the regulative system, the directive and regulatory apparatus of the nation. The entire regulative system is now as the service of the militant (totalitarian) state. "The nature of the military form of government will be further elucidated," continued Spencer, "that it is both positively and negatively regulative. It does not simply restrain; it also enforces. Besides telling the individual that he shall not do, it tells him what he shall do.... Under the militant type this positively regulative action is widespread and preemptory. The civilian is in a condition as much like that of a soldier as difference in occupation permits."[8]

An Inference and a Question

We may conclude this discussion with an inference and a question. Since the early times of mankind, the normative code that controls the conduct of the group and of the individuals has two orientations: one governing the conduct of aggression and the other one, the conduct of solidarity; the latter toward the in-group and the former toward the out-group. In consequence we may speak about two normative subcodes: one internal, and the other external. Even within this internal code or subcode we shall find a further differentiation with the development of societies. Some of those subsystems are contradictory, even antithetical, to mention the external and the internal ones; others are complementary or indifferent. We have called them multiple or parallel because they appear within the same society or group. But to this theme we shall return later.

Since the internal and external patterns of contradictory, a question has to be asked: Is there indeed a single normative code, a superethos, a single directive, regulatory apparatus that encompasses both codes? Or is man controlled from the very beginning by two or more entirely independent codes of conduct? Till we return to this question of megaethos or superethos, the nature of those parallel or multiple subsystems, those subhierarchies of conduct, calls for more discussion and inquiry.

We shall limit our discussion now to what has been called the internal normative subsystem or code of conduct.

Internal Ethos and Subsystems

We were using two terms, *system* and *subsystem* (superethos and subethos) interchangeably. Should we assume that there is a general code of conduct, which embraces both the internal and external patterns of conduct—and this I postulate—then, of course, the two latter are subsystems of the general code that we have called superethos or megaethos. Furthermore, should we limit our analysis of structure to the internal code only, then again we may consider the latter as a general system and the particular, subordinated or parallel structures as subsystems. It is, in fact, a matter of general concept, of outlook, and also of simple semantics. We may consider the internal system as a general one, limit our discussion to the latter one, before we come to the issue of a certain unity of both.

The early human societies were rather tightly controlled by a single regulative system (what we have called a normative code or ethos). Such an ethos was shared by a vast majority, probably by all members of those early associations. A single religious creed and magical outlook integrated the early social organizations. The codes of behavior were generally accepted; and when violated, they were backed by customary sanctions. We may still notice this type of ethos among preliterate societies (we have called them primitive), among more advanced tribal associations, and moreover among traditional rural communities. In nineteenth-century Europe this single and effective ethos was still common in rural communities. It continued in many parts of eastern and southern Europe even a few decades ago; it still survived in some, needless to say, in many parts of the world. The belief system is strong in those cases; usually it is a religious outlook, at times integrated with magical beliefs, different as the latter are in their basic concept, as it was already pointed out in the classic studies of James G. Frazer (*The Golden Bough*). At this stage already, the ethos is affected by its external and internal dichotomy. All members of the group or the majorities share the internal and external normative valuations; they share the solidarity as well as the enmity. In this sense the code is unitary, integrated, composed of two subsystems—the external and internal ones. Nonetheless, a closer scrutiny of the early societies indicates already a differentiation of the internal normative system (in other words, the beginnings of subsystems) within this internal code, for no society that we know today, or that we have some knowledge of their past, is or was unstructured. The early Australians or Veddas or Fueggians had their generational structures and elementary institutions, the family. When we speak about the status of children or women in a primitive society, we mean of course also the set of norms by which relations are regulated. There are particular sets of norms of conduct that govern relations with and between men and women, men and children, men within the same age group, generations, old and young. Sex and age are setting the principle as well as the limits of those specific subsystems. However, those particular subsystems control only specific areas of activities and social relations. They are both articulations and consequences of the general belief system and of the general ethos. For this reason we may consider such a normative structure as consisting of a major, general hierarchy of norms (a superethos) that controls the entire community but also extends the control to particular subsystems, subordinated to the former. This general code and subordinated parallel ones form a basic structure of social control. They form the boundaries of what is permitted and what is prohibited to those who belong to the same cultural community. The general code and those differing subsystems are, however, integrated by individuals and by the community. Their beliefs integrate them all, since they are shared. And, we may remember from previous discussion, the norms are in this case no more than articulations of religion and general world outlook. However, belief systems vary, as do the family structures, norms governing status in the community due to sex and age. Hence the value structures, the general normative hierarchies, differ greatly not only in more advanced societies but also at the early levels of development.

Urban Community and Differentiation of Ethos

Development of urban communities resulted in further differentiation of ethos. Class and occupational differentiation appeared in the early cities and resulted in a new status and class structure, in addition to the more ancient structure based on sex and age. This in turn was associated with new subsystems of conduct. Soon the norms of conduct governing the crafts and classes became customs or were codified, at times in a written form.

Slavery effected a major change in the general ethos. It appeared, however, early in the cities. Here the internal and external subethos met in a historical contradiction. Slavery was a consequence of war, conquest of a foreign tribe or nation. The norms governing the conduct of masters and slaves were quite different from all the other subsystems of the community, of the internal ethics. A particular subethos developed, in part akin to one toward domesticated animals, dogs and horses, even cattle, and in part still human, in terms of communication or even physical contact. Now a slave, who was still an object of the external ethos, became a part of the household, also a part of a subservient class. The ethos of hostility met here with an internal ethos of solidarity. The two subsystems clashed continuously. They were contradictory. Those contradictions affected religion and philosophy, where philosophy had been created. In some religions and philosophies an effort was made to reconcile those two contradictory aspects.

Aristotle in his *Politics* (chapters 2 and 3) wrote about the three distinct relations in a Greek city: master and slave, husband and wife, parent and child. What this meant also was three distinct patterns of conduct, three different codes of norms. However, argued Aristotle, among the barbarians slaves and females share the same lot; they are subject to the same rules of conduct. Therefore, he agreed with the poet who said that the barbarous people should be ruled by Greeks. But slavery called for legitimation, for a set of values that justify the institution; and Aristotle found the reasons for slavery in the very nature of man, in the quality of the master to rule and the slave to serve.

The Sermon and the Dialogue

We can identify here a number of particular subsystems, subhierarchies of norms, particular regulative subsystems, but can we identify clearly a single system, or what we have called superethos, megaethos, the general code? In some cases, yes, we may and we do. This is, for example, the case of the Israelites. In the case of the ancient Israelites the general code was clear and powerful: the Ten Commandments. It was codified, it had a religious sanction and legitimacy, and it overruled all the other subsystems. And the Greeks? In a different way, there since the time of Socrates, also earlier, we shall find an intense search for a universal ethos and unviersal values, even those of absolute nature.

The Greeks were pluralists; they did not codify the norms in the form of short imperatives. Their general ethos reflected the general culture of dialogue. The Israelite culture is prophetic in form. The prophet in his sermon gives the message, and this message is accepted as ultimate truth or binding interpretation of the Holy Scripture. Here one single man speaks; the nation listens and obeys. What he says becomes a matter of revealed message and faith.

The Greeks built a culture of a dialogue. Greeks had no prophets. Socrates (who comes close to such stature only because we, the readers of Platonic dialogues, were trained and educated on prophetic messages and project the image of a prophet on Socrates) appeared always in a dialogue, never as a sole, unique prophet-philosopher. For the Greeks, there was not one but more than one truth in those matters. The dialogue expressed the ways to state those different viewpoints. Hence, views on basic norms were open to discussion. They were not codified, but they were discussed all the time, analyzed and formulated by Socrates, Plato, Isocrates, Artistotle, to mention only a few, and this continued into the Hellenistic period. In both those traditions the general ethos, the megaethos, was sensed, searched, and rediscovered in various ways. But it was there, in their beliefs and philosophies (see also chapter 2).

Religion, Ideologies, and Proliferation of Normative Subsystems

Even the Holy Scriptures, the book of the only and ultimate truth for the faithful, becomes a source of disagreements and heresies that foster new differentiations and interpretation of the religious norms.

Most Western idea systems, once developed, display a tendency toward ideological splits and heresies. They harbor inner contradictions. Few, if any, belief systems or ideologies are consistent to a point that no contradictions can be identified.

Contradictions and group antagonisms appear sooner or later in advanced societies. Those divisions appear along class or interest lines, and they are reflected in attempts to reinterpret the religion, ideology, world outlook, and values.

What is, however, more seminal for our discussion at this point are the contradictions that appear within ideologies and are of an ideological nature. No ideology or creed is free from inconsistencies, even opposites. And those inner contradictions of the idea system itself—above all, the contradictions between ideal norms and real behavior of the faithful, discussed and reinterpreted by believers and followers—lead to splits and heresies, to the emergence of new reinterpretations of norms of conduct, of further differentiation of the general ethos. Hence, again, new subsystems appear, referring to the earlier codes. The same scriptures, the same ethos, is now claimed and reinterpreted not by one, but by several groups, which share now a new or reinterpreted ethos. What we get in fact with what was once hatefully and contemptuously called heresy is a number of normative subsystems that are united, in spite of wars and struggles, by the same original scriptures. Christianity is, indeed, a broad concept of many deeply dissenting groups that claim the veracity of the same creed and share the same early tradition, which they interpret in a different way (see chapter 2).

Those inner ideological contradictions and reinterpretations lead to the emergence of new subsystems, new ''subethos.''

With the great religious and ideological changes the number of parallel subsystems increased too. They were in part complementary and in part contradictory.

This normative differentiation can be traced in histories, historical documents, and ancient philosophical treatises.

In the history of the Israelites the religious bond was traditionally very strong. Moreover, the religion supplied a well-developed system of norms of conduct, a detailed and very specific code of rules of behavior. This code imposed limits on permissible daily behavior and divided days and the year by prayer, fasting, and penitence. Here was a normative system that survived millennia. Moreover, in times of crisis and persecutions the entire regulatory and directive apparatus of the community, the ethos, was rather stronger than in times of relative peace. The sense of direction and sentiments of duty appeared at such time with clarity and dramatic strength.

Still, deviations from this general ethos, tendencies to reinterpret in a variety of ways, trends of orthodoxy and of a more independent outlook within this religious community appeared again and again throughout history. It is simply not true that the religion of Israelites does not know heresies or sectarian movements. The fact that a religious community that considers itself as a true and faithful one expels the dissidents, those who differ, does not change the fact that those expelled are or were only a new sect or a religious community related, akin to the first. Christianity was and still is a powerful innovative religion, a synthesis of Hebrew and Hellenic ethics and philosophy and of Oriental rites.

The various sects recognized the same general code, the same Bible and Ten Commandments, which were differently interpreted. Hence within the same nation and state a number of parallel normative subsystems was shared by various groups, which still recognized some of the basic superethos, the same general code.

Throughout history the sermons of the prophets seemed to indicate continuous deviations from the normative code and, above all, the hiatus between ideal norms and real conduct, which prompted the prophetic movements and at times, the reinterpretation of ethos. Hence what seems to appear is on one hand a reinterpretation of the superethos and on the other an emergence of new, parallel religous and normative subsystems, sects, and congregations. The general ethos, the megaethos, in various interpretations remains as a powerful, what Durkheim would call a "collective" representation, binding the various dissenting tribes and sects, affecting the sense of direction.

Neither inquisition nor the anathemas were able to arrest the natural process of revision, the consequence of contradictions or of new ideas and views, of changes within the society. There were, of course, large, passive societies in history and orthodox ideologies of long duration. However, the history of what we call Western civilization evidenced this unusual tendency of reinterpretation and splits of ideological groups, which could not be arrested forever and at times even for long. Those changes resulted in continuous emergence of new subcodes that affected religious communities or at times declined and disappeared, as the Manicheans or Jansenists did, while the old creed continued to exist.

Religion and Ethics: The Jewish and Hellenic Pattern

This process of differentiation of ideologies and value subsystems appeared in Greek history rather early, in those various philosophical schools, discussing and arguing about goals and values, about their relevance and intensity.

The Greeks were different in this respect from the Israelites, however. The religion, this central belief system of antiquity, was separated from the ethos, from the normative systems. Greek gods were free of moral restraints. They enjoyed their life in a way mortals would consider not proper; only gods enjoyed such complete license all the time. Gods were not necessarily examples of virtue, nor were they fond of moderation, so strongly advocated by the philosophers. Some were incestuous, Leda practiced sodomy, most of them indulged in sex, and Mercury might have even patronized the pickpockets. Hence the belief system of an educated Greek of antiquity consisted of the religious lore on one hand and of a particular philosophy he cherished on the other. Ethos, separated from religion, was to become a realm of philosophy. It seems that ancient Greeks developed philosophy also due to the fact that their ethics was separate, separated from religion, not chained to religious sanctions. This was not the only cause of course, but a contributing factor. In consequence the difference in views was not subject to excommunication or bodily punishment. There were, of course, exceptions. Nor were the dividing lines clear for the general populace, and a philosophical argument might have been and sometimes was considered as offense of the gods. But those sentiments, although they were expressed in the literature and history, were probably not as common and as strong as among the Israelites and later in the Christian culture.

A variety of philosophical schools advanced various interpretations of ethics, assigning a dominant or secondary status to different norms. In times of Thucydides' Athens or Cicero's Rome, ancient Greeks and Romans had various philosophical schools instead of various religious sects or denominations. This came later and from the Orient. It was not Hellenic. In consequence, Greeks developed a multiplicity of ethical subsystems, at times contradictory. Partisans of different philosophical schools did not kill each other. Here we had a number of parallel normative subsystems.

To gather from such writings as Plato's or from such orations as Cicero's, or even more so, from the dramas and tragedies, the fundamentals of norms and values were intensely studied and discussed. But this was not a consequence of interpretation of one single sacred book or holy scripture of ultimate truth. Among the Israelites the new subsystems developed in consequence of interpretation of a single bible. Not among the Greeks. They did not produce any single bible, a book of ultimate verity and belief; what they were producing all the time were books, not a book, subject to continuous discussion and inquiry.

Codified and Not Codified Superethos

The Hebrews of antiquity did not produce lay philosophies. Once the Hellenic and Judaic traditions and cultures were fused, in Alexandria, the Jewish intellectual creativity appeared also in philosophy. Contrariwise, Greeks were a nation of many books of different ethical philosophies developed freely, as did the inquiry later called scientific. The Greeks can be credited with the very term of *ethics*. Ethos had at the begining a much wider meaning: customs, manners, character, habits. In its later development it assumed this general, contemporary meaning. Hence the general ethos, the superethos, appears in both, in the Hebrew and Greek tradition. There is, however, a difference. The ethos of the Israelites is codified, well established, and patiently shared. It is known; it has been found or given. The Hellenic way is different. The Greek ethos is not codified; it is not definite as among the Jews; it is neither given nor yet found. It is continuously discovered in discussions and philosophical writings. Among the Israelites the truth has been already revealed and discovered; among the Greeks there is only a continuous search for truth. In the Hebrew tradition the codified norms are defined and specific. They are norms of conduct. They tell you what to do or, rather, what not to do. The Greeks did not even try to establish a codified system, a list of specific prescribed commandments. The search above all was for the principle; they tried to discover the roots of man, the ends (Cicero wrote a volume entitled *De Finibus [About Ends]*, what is good or what is justice, and how justice differs from equity).

In both cultures one can discover a longing for a general ethos, a need for a supreme kind of rule of conduct or for an ideal yardstick of conduct, and an uneasy search for direction. The two cultures established, however, two different traditions and two different styles or methods: the Israelites, a tradition of codified supreme norms; the Greeks, noncodified ethos, an ethos in continuous debate of many viewpoints. The Decalogue of the Israelites established a firm base, eliminated doubt, forever. It was a beginning of absolutes. Not so for the Greeks and their Hellenic and Hellenistic tradition. The Israelites fathered the dogma; the Greeks fathered the hypothesis and axiom.

Multiplicity of Values and National Character

We may follow a development of multiplicity of normative subsystems, or rules of conduct, from the early beginnings. The general ethos is affected at first by sex and generational structure of the early society, later by the class and occupational divisions, and furthermore by ideological trends, religious dissent. This long process results in the growth of normative subsystems, continuously integrated or subject to attempts of integration by a megaethos. It is man and his society who long for such integration and search for a paramount sense of direction. This long historical development could not remain without effect on the development of modern nationality.

Plurality of normative orientations appears in what is called the "national character" of contemporary as well as historical nations. It appears, of course, in various degrees, with various frequencies. Some nations make an impression of being monolithic in their ethos, attitudes, values, and institutions. At closer scrutiny, however, we may discover a number of normative patterns (value orientations). And we do not mean here solely ethnic subcultures.

What a national character is may be generally said: It is a culture. But this is too broad. More distinctly, by national character we mean specific "national" institutions, values, customs, behavioral patterns. We shall limit our theme solely to values, to the ethos.

There, in the values, the national character is strongly articulated indeed.

Since the turn of the eighteenth century, humanities and later social sciences have been influenced by a myth rather than a reality of a homogeneous nation-state, composed of one single nationality and of a single and unique national character later called a "culture pattern." This traditional approach goes, of course, back to the Greek and Roman historians, to Tacitus and his surprisingly accurate image of the Germans of his time. During the time of the Renaissance this view, which permitted easy generalizations and—we must admit—also penetrating insights, continued; we may mention here as an example Machiavelli's essay on French national psychology, *De Natura Gallorum*. Again, in the times of the Enlightenment, Johann von Herder and Madame de Staël continued this trend. In *De L'Allemagne* Madame de Staël gave us an eighteenth-century image of the humane and noble quality of German personality, without a trace of suspicion that other types of national character were feasible. And let us consider Ruth Benedict's *Patterns of Culture*, where the image of the culture of the Zuni and Hopi Indians and their national character is clear and homogeneous. Then a series of interesting volumes continued up to almost the present about the Germans, the Italians, the "authoritarian personality" and similar traits of a given national character.

In such a viewpoint most if not all Germans have definite cultural traits and follow a definite political tradition and culture, and so do the French or the British.

Is there, then, a complete absence of veracity in all those generalizations?

Of course, many of those images or stereotypes of a single national character are strongly affected by prejudice, and the most common error is that they integrate some verifiable, true qualities with others that are projections of unique experiences or acquired prejudices and are far from general characteristics. The fusion of truth and untruth into a single category has a psychological appeal and a semblance of veracity.

In a small, rather simple structure of an Indian tribe, true, a single cultural pattern may indeed prevail. But otherwise the nationality is by no means a homogeneous one, nor is a single, exclusive cultural pattern the only one within one state or one nationality. In the same nation-state two or more culture patterns, two national characters, may coexist.

But let me suggest here that in some of those works that deal with national character and limit the argument to a single cultural or political pattern there is sometimes some or even a good deal of truth. Where, then, is the error? The basic error is in a fact: That within the same nation or nation-state not one but many cultural-political patterns, even contradictory ones, coexist; or, to put it perhaps better, there is not one but several value structures or national characters of the Germans, French, and British. In consequence of these differences in national characters and values an unusual phenomenon occurred in our history: The same nation produced both a Goethe and a Hitler. Of course, historical changes have their effect. The reality, the total picture of a society or of a nation, is, however, even far more complex, since in addition to the diverse patterns reflected in norms of conduct, personality differences should also be considered.

And as we well know, personality types differ substantially, although here too the ethnic values are significant.

Nonetheless, within the same historical period and within the same nation-state one finds authoritarian and permissive fathers, authoritarian families and permissive ones.

An early theoretical approach to this problem was advanced by David Hume in his essay *Of National Character*, published in 1748; perhaps it was Hume who introduced this term. Hume argued in a convincing way indeed that the national character is formed above all by political institutions and political rule. The more powerful the government, the greater the uniformity of national character: "We may observe that, where a very extensive government has been established for many centuries, it spreads the national character of the entire empire."[9] But the same Hume, although his essay attempts to advance a theory of a major and uniform national character, qualifies his views. There are variations and differences within this pattern, Hume tells us: "We may often remark" a wonderful mixture of manners and characters in the same nation, speaking the same language and subject to the same government."

Most of those writers, however, assumed generally a single value system, which controls the conduct of a national community. Furthermore, those theories suggested a single, typical set of institutions and behavior. In that way they created a uniform image of a nationality. This kind of approach postulates a single directive-regulatory apparatus, an exclusive ethos for every nationality. There is, of course, a good deal of veracity in those often brilliant comments and observations. Today, students of ethnicity make an evident and noticeable effort to avoid stereotypes, and that is done above all by the avoidance of negative characteristics or critical comments, as well as by the awareness of bias and prejudice in this area, a bias that is responsible for discrimination and persecutions. But veracity is not necessarily produced by omission of negatives and by stress on positive qualities.

Advanced modern nations, with a differentiated occupational and class structure, an extensive urban civilization, and a variety of ideological trends and religions, harbors not one but several directive and regulatory normative orientations or subsystems. There are several national ethos or subethos, integrated by some kind of general rules and dominant norms. The differences are substantial; the subsystems are not only complementary but more often contradictory. Of course, we may find certain similarities in taste or behavior, a sharing of certain customs. However, the normative substructures are different. Those are not ethnic "subcultures," regional or ethnic differences reflected in dialects, customs, and folklore. Here the difference appeared above all in the directive-regulatory system, in terms of the concept of collective goals and norms of conduct.

At this point the determinants of those differences are not our subject matter. What is seminal is that in the same nation, tied together by major institutions and traditional unity, by some elements of a general normative code, a number of groups of different normative-ethical subsystems can be identified, that instead of a single national character and a single national ethos we can usually identify two or more at times contradictory national or ethnic value structures.

Mexico has two dialectical traditions, one of the native conquered Indians and the other of the Spanish conquerors. Those traditions affect the normative, national ethos. A Mexican whose ancestry is Indian as well as Spanish harbors traditions of the conquerors and of the conquered, of Cortez and of Guatemoc, who revolted against the Spanish rule. Bohemia's historical traditional is Protestant. Jan Huss, the Hussite, Protestant movement, and its liberalizing effects are a part of the historical tradition a young Czech learns in his elementary schools; it is a part of a lore that appears in literature as well as even in music. But a large part of the Czech population is Catholic. Jan Huss died at the stake; it was a judgment and order of the Roman Catholic and imperial authority. The day of his suffering is a Czech national holiday. Counterreformation marks the end of free Bohemia. There is also a basic, normative contradiction between orthodox Catholicism of the Counterreformation and the Protestant Hussite creed. A Czech Catholic has two dialectical, opposed traditions—the Hussite and the Catholic, his ethos is affected by both.

The difference of norms may often serve as rationalization of different interests and rationalization of conflict and privilege. What we are concerned with at this point, however, is the difference in normative or value hierarchies, in differences in what we have called the vertical value structures, in fundamental differences in norms of conduct and value-goals.

Two differing cultural patterns or normative subsystems within the same nation—patterns that meet in certain areas and differ diametrically, even oppose, in other areas—may be presented graphically as two vertical normative structures, hierarchies, in parts mutually overlapping (see figure 15.1).

What, then, keeps the entire modern nation together? Above all, the state, which controls political power. But this is not all and not above all in all cases. The nation is held together also by voluntary social control, by some of paramount and shared values and accepted rules of conduct even if divided into many normative subsystems. In a modern, civilized and democratic state, what is seminal is an acceptance of common political and social procedures; we may call them rules of the game (*B* in figure 15.1). The rules of the game are well known and applied in sports, where two contending parties, in a contest that should as a rule end with the defeat of one, agree to follow and obey common rules and in consequence form a unity in an orderly conflict (more about this in chapter 17).

But this is not all. In addition, there is a superior and not codified superethos, a normative commitment and acceptance of some core values. What happens when the rules of the game break down on the basic norms, the core values, are violated or abandoned, even by a minority?

Then, of course, the entire unity breaks down, and the integration of society

Figure 15.1
National and Multiple Value Subsystems

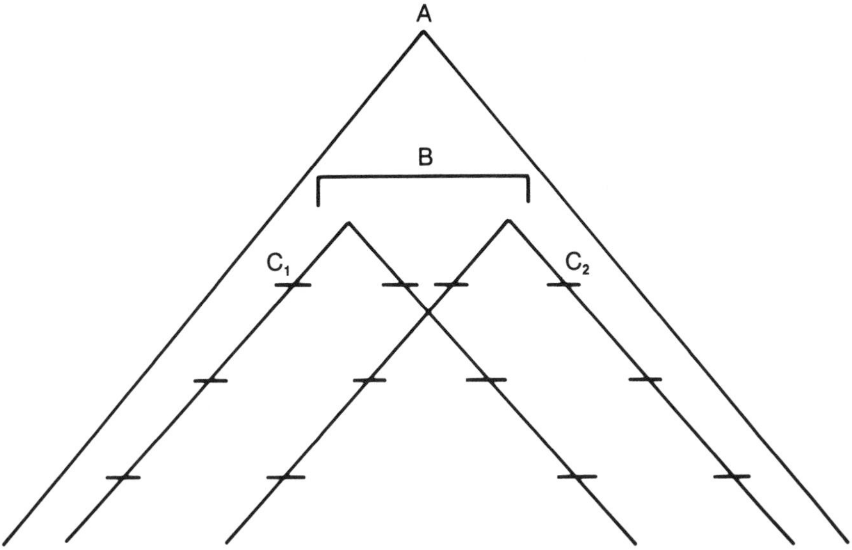

A — General code (megaethos)
B — Rules of the game
C — Parallel or partially overlapping normative systems (Ethos)

is accomplished by control of the means of coercion while reintegration is usually enforced by violence.

This is the time of sudden ideological shifts.

The strength of a nation, however, appears in its spontaneous ability to unite and act together in times of a crisis, to reduce at such moments the differences, to emphasize the common values and interest, and to marshal the voluntary discipline to act together.

The Multiplicity of National Values and Shifts in Value Orientations

This duality or multiplicity of ethos appears not only within a nation or within a society that is integrated by some core values but is still differentiated by subsystems. It appears also at times within ourselves. An individual too harbors contradictory emotions and also contradictory values. He may shift as the situation changes and, in many personalities, as the interest and need change. Changes in situations, when combined with a skillful appeal, may effect sudden shifts in value orientation and loyalties. An effective emotional appeal may trigger and carry massive ideological changes and shifts in value hierarchies when it appeals to vital interest or needs.

This plurality of ethos within the nation and within a substantial part of society may result during political and social crisis situations in those sudden shifts in political orientation and movements. It is not a simple matter of political parties and platforms; it is, in terms of norms and emotions, a far more elementary, profound issue of value orientations, of our ethos, which have historical roots, appear and reappear in the same society, and are transmitted from generation to generation by early socialization, informal and formal learning. Its elements are in our lore and even in scholarly disciplines of history, philosophy, or literature. This plurality or multiplicity of values is not the only sufficient cause, but it is far more than a contributing one; it is a necessary if not a sufficient one.

A society has a number of stratification and divisions. The class division is a major one, but not the sole one. Moreover, the different stratification and divisions may or may not coincide.

Normative Divisions of a Society

One of those divisions is the ideological division. There is a still more seminal division, into those of different normative commitments, different ethos, or differing subethos in terms of our classifications. This is, of course, reflected in ideological-political divisions but not solely so, for those divisions are even more fundamental.

The political-ideological divisions are consequences or articulations of class position, but also of other needs and determinants, which at times may be stronger than the class one, even dominant.

For the next few pages, however, let us focus our attention not on class but on normative and ideological divisions, which may not coincide with the superior and inferior, dominant and subordinated status of the class structure.

Within such divisions we may identify those definitely committed to their ideology or ethos and dominant values of the latter. In political movements, which may reflect such divisions, we shall find them on the right as well as on the left. Those committed to a given ideology or ethos, those who really identify themselves with the latter, with the ideal norms, form the core group of an ethos or a political or religious group. Even substantial changes in social and economic situations may not affect their value orientations; to the contrary, they will perceive and respond to the situation in terms of their values.

There is, however, a normative and ideological periphery—and a substantial one. A substantial part of people have their own traditions or are familiar with the two traditions and ideological orientations, but they are not committed firmly to either of the prevailing ethos; their views and orientations shift and change with the situation. They are hesitant and ambivalent. Some are flexible, others are simply opportunistic, and still others are sensitive to threat, real or imaginary, to which they respond by submission. Whatever the determinants, we shall find the firm and the hesitant and ambivalent, the in-between.

We speak here about ambivalence between fundamentally different normative, ideological systems, for example, democracy and fascism, personalism and totalitarianism, an aristocratic world outlook and a democratic one. Those are opposed ideological systems of mutually opposed core values. Such basic differences, which are associated with political or ideological ambivalence, should not be confused with an independent voter, who simply refuses to join any camp, has his own views, exercises his judgment in every single case. His weight is of course felt in elections, and his votes shift. But this is different from individuals and groups susceptible to strong appeals and pressures and shifting to the extremes.

This ambivalence appears clearly in times of sudden political crisis, such as the decisive moments of a revolution. There are visible in times of crisis situations, manmade disasters, such as postrevolutionary or extended terror. Those are times when political power, control of weapons and means of physical coercion, shifts to an ideologically definite group, which is visible and can be identified by symbols and the display of power in the form of armed detachments, uniformed persons, prisons, concentration camps. Those are also times when ideas and programs in a simplified form guide powerful social movements and make history. At this point the extremes of reward or punishment appear clearly, and news of persecution of opponents and dissenters are diffused by press, radio, television and also by gossip and conversations. Threats of persecution, present dangers, and imperatives of survival are now of primary concern to those who are not yet directly associated with the advancing and winning movement or with the opposition.

This threat results in continuous fears and anxieties, not unlike a chronic and destructive fever. At such a time, far more than in times of peace and what might be called normalcy (in want of a better term), the ambivalent marginals, the in-betweens move to the winning side.

Fear, collective and individual, grows in its intensity, since terror in various forms, intimidation, becomes at such time a major instrument of power, and direct coercion is used as a paramount means of social control. Fear is individual and collective, since it appears also in group behavior. At times fear is also a warning system (true or false) of an oncoming danger.

In such times of disasterlike crisis, social divisions grow deeper. Now the ambivalent and hesitant shifts rapidly in search of advantage or avoidance of threat at times not fully conscious of his break with his past. He had internalized, as most people had, two ethos in a variety of intensities: in the case of Iran, for example, the Islamic one and the Western. Identification with the winning side is rationalized by choice of an appropriate ideology; its ethos and loyalty are displayed by visible trimming of dress, insignia, slogans, songs. Rationalization is tantamount to legitimization of an act; the show of symbols, to practical action.

This ideological shift and identification with symbols of the winning side also (and above all) constitute an identification with those in power, those who control access to economic and political resources and to the entire reward system.

Now a few qualifications are still necessary. Not all move with the winning party. Many of the noncommitted or independent go into hiding or try to survive by a display of outward indifference, although their sentiments of opposition are strong. When the situation changes, in a new crisis, they may reappear as active partisans of the new opposition, of the new party of change.

Thus the situation and response are functionally interrelated. Changes in situation affect the response. Second, the nature of this ambivalent mass of people varies, and it is difficult to evaluate and describe their sensitiveness, volatility, proneness to those sudden shifts. The shifts are sudden, rapid, unexpected, it seems, where cultural differences are deep, where different cultures and largely conflicting, contradictory normative orientations meet.

We speak in such cases about volatile "masses," since those changes and shifts move suddenly and in a variety of ways. Social control, as well as collapsing governments, in those cases was usually based on excessive coercion and fear, and once the coercive system broke, the emotional appeals and variety of interests facilitated sudden shifts.

Multiplicity of Values and Hitler's Germany

The phenomenon of those sudden shifts and of political ambivalence is not limited solely to the nonwestern or westernized cultures although volatility in the Islamic areas seems to be striking today. Only a few decades ago, the advent of National Socialism in Germany, the victory of Adolph Hitler suggests a similar event, similar to those observed today in Iran, and of Khomeini and his fundamentalist followers.

Two major different normative and ideological systems have dominated Germany since the middle of the nineteenth century. One of racial or national superiority combined with nascent social Darwinism, the other one humanitarian, democratic, and federalist. The major orientations appeared with various intensities and different interpretations in various ideological movements. Many who witnessed Hitler's advent to power and lent their support to his cohorts, remembered World War I and the nationalistic appeal of that period. Many served in the army, dominated by the creed of extreme nationalism, and German superiority. Many shared their leisure between associations of diverse ideologies and were affected by and internalized, contradictory world outlooks.

The shift of orientations did not arrive suddenly, however; it could be observed on the streets of Berlin or major German cities, since various political movements were associated with political armies and, militias which appeared on the streets of those cities. In fact, they cherished their uniforms and displayed them not solely during the political parades.

Men and women, but above all men, in political uniforms were visible everywhere. They were the visible symbols of various orientations: the Republican *Reichsbanner*, the Communist *Rothe Front*, the monarchist *Stahlhelm*, the National-Socialist, Hilter's *SA* and *SS*. During the late 1920s and early 1930s, leftists, the Republican and largely Social Democratic *Reichsbanner* and the Communist *Rothe Front* dominated the streets. Soon the landscape changed toward the Right. Monarchist *Stalhelm* disappeared, absorbed by the *SS* and *SA*. The polarity typical in such times made its appearance.

But the change could have moved in several directions. Hitler struck above all against the general rules of political conduct that we have called the rules of the game: the democratic procedure of political action and change. The use of violence in political action, combined with mass support eroded rather rapidly the democratic institutions. At the same time he struck at the basic ethical norms—the megaethos—displacing the Judeo-Christian ethics by a worship of strength and violence. His victory, the seizure of the instruments of power and his use of violence, prompted further symbolic and ideological shifts and the identification of groups and individuals with the ideology and creed of racial superiority.

For a visitor, who traveled through Germany annually, this change of the human landscape was rather striking. The reader may forgive a personal note. A few months after Hitler's victory, I was traveling in a train across Germany. Arriving on the *Schlesischer Banhof* of Berlin, I could see from my coach the broad streets of Berlin's midtown. The street was filled with a mass of uniformed men, marching in cohorts in their ugly yellow-brown uniforms, heavily belted, with plenty of various brass insignia of caps and shirts, and flags, party eagles carried like the Roman legions in those Cecil B. deMille movies did. We remembered well not only the democratic Weimar Republic, but also the times of humane Enlightenment. Were those two different nations, or a nation of two different ethos?

Those sudden shifts are to be related to changing situations. They do not take place in a social-economic void. Ideas and norms gain support when they appeal to a variety of interests and needs. Their presence permits integration of unstructured masses of people into organized groups. They not only supply an essential means for integration but also suggest goals and actions.

Ambivalence

Plurality of normative systems within the same society affects individuals and groups. This is not solely a matter of a specific personality structure or of a specific sensitivity and is not necessarily one of an undecided person. It is a problem and a reality of a complex society.

Aristotle pointed to this social and individual nature in his simple, already quoted sentences about the differences in relations with, or conduct toward, a slave and a member of the family, differences in rules of conduct when a man acts as a father on one hand and as a master of slaves on the other, furthermore when he carries out his duties as a political man, a citizen. Almost two and a half millennia later, the nascent modern social sciences had to return to this theme independently and with a new theoretical approach. The presence of a number of normative subsystems is easily observable; it is open to a frequent and general experience. Hence it is not accidental that both a rather early modern sociologist and a prominent psychologist and philosopher returned to this theme.

Herbert Spencer, with his obvious theory of split ethics, of enmity toward the outsider and amity toward the insider, stressed the social nature of the plurality of ethos. About thirty years later, William James, in *Principles of Psychology* and *Psychology* pointed to the individual and social but, above all, individual quality of this plurality:

[Man] has as many different social selves as there are distinct groups of persons....From this there results what originally is a division of the man into several selves; and this may be a discordant splitting, as where one is afraid to let one set of his acquaintances know him as he is elsewhere; or it may be a perfectly harmonious division of labor, as where one tender to his children is stern to the soldiers and prisoners under his command.... Thus a layman may abandon a city infected with cholera, but a priest or a doctor would think such an act incompatible with his honor. A soldier's honor requires him to fight or to die under circumstances where another man can apologize or run away with no stain upon his social self.

Those well-known sentences of James were quoted many times. Moreover, James's theory of self implies at times contradictions of the material, social, and spiritual self.[10]

Somewhat later perhaps, if not concurrently, the Swiss psychiatrist Paul Bleuler advanced his notion of ambivalence, while young Sigmund Freud suggested an original theory of ego and of inner conflicts. It is Bleuler who is credited for the concept and term *ambivalence*. Did Bleuler and Freud know about James's work? Or James about Spencer's?

Since that time, the theory of ambivalence has been widely discussed and advanced. It is beyond the the scope and major theme of this volume to extend this digression. We may solely note that since James this theme of multiplicity of self has become an important area of American psychology and sociology. It appears in the concepts of self, social situation, and role in the works of G. H. Mead, C. H. Cooley, W. I. Thomas, and Gordon W. Allport, to mention the major and early contributions in this field.

In European scholarship, emotional conflicts became a major subject of psychiatry and psychology.

However, it was Alfred McClung Lee who made a major study of normative ambivalence and originated the appropriate term of *multivalence*. This multiplicity of values is the central theme of his work; he reviews also critically the major, earlier, primarily American theories.[11]

Ambivalence is the early term. Today it expresses an individual's attitude of indecision, of shifting loyalties and emotions.

A study of the history of ideas may probably reveal that this theme of ambivalence appears among other, earlier writers, above all those French essayist-philosophers, although there seems to be little of it in Montaigne. Ambivalence was, however, a theme of poets and writers before the term appeared or became a part of our daily parlance. This insight into the ambivalent nature of man strikes a reader of Dostoevsky's novels. His novels are well understood by the readers in many countries and of many languages, since the problem of ambivalence seems to be sensed. We may respond to the latter in different ways in different cultures, but it is a part of a complex, modern society. Moreover, some readers may discover some kind of ambivalence in themselves.

Ambivalence was discussed long before the term was introduced. The introduction of the term is, however, relevant, since it makes us far more concious of its presence. The term makes the concept visible; the reality is articulated in the latter. The term so it seems, appeared in psychiatry and later in psychology shortly after 1910. It was probably used casually before then. The prominent Swiss psychiatrist Paul Eugene Bleuler is credited with the introduction of this term, and perhaps he coined it. It was also Bleuler who introduced the term *schizophrenia* and made a major contribution by identifying this major mental disorder, a mental disharmony, a state of mind of contradicting tendencies.[12]

Ambivalence, at this beginning, denoted two contradictory emotions that a person experiences or expresses toward others; later on, it came to mean the presence in a judgment of two contradictory values or of two opposing attitudes, positive and negative. Ambivalence, two judgments, "bijudgment," is contrasted with equivalency, a single value judgment, corresponding to a situation. At first, the term was used above all for identification of contradictory emotions experienced by the same person.

Alfred McClung Lee introduced with his theories a new, more adequate term with broader application—*multivalence*—and a term to use instead of *equivalency*—*monovalence*.[13] Lee, in an incisive way, put the issue at the very beginning of his contribution: "Society has a multiplicity of conflicting moral values. It is multivalent and its members who become more or less normal part of it are also multivalent".[14]

Multivalence: Alfred McClung Lee's Theory

The major theme of Lee's volume is the ramifications of "many-valueness," particularly of a conflicting multiplicity of values or, to use his term, a multivalence in society. The individual faces the multiplicity of values, has to respond to it. But his response affects also the society, the way those norms are applied. Since a person belongs to many groups of contradictory values, such as class, ethnicity, religion, he acts within those groups according to norms of conduct of the particular one.

The world of ours is one of many interchangeable roles, continued Lee, and daily life necessitates changing of roles. Roles are, of course, associated with various status, class, and ethnic groups. Changing of roles implies at the same time shifting to different values. Hence, a person who is integrated, consistent all the time, argued Lee, is simply a fiction. Changing the role means changing from one to another set of values that might be quite different.

But here a question arises: Do we have an integrated sense of direction, a regulative system, an orientation in society, or is man only a bundle of responses to situations, moving his actions on attitudinal channels? Is man only a somewhat incoherent apparatus reacting to situations, integrated solely by his physical personality, by the fact that the forms a somatic entity, or does he have and follow an organized normative system? In the first case, there is no general ethos, at all, no superethos that would suggest a direction, no integration of our conduct.

Ambivalence and Integration: Gordon Allport and Others

However, the clarification of this problem calls for a brief perusal of at least a few viewpoints before we resume our own arguments.

Gordon Allport in his earlier work took a critical view of James's theory of multiple personality: ''the case for existence of separate and distinct selves is easy to exaggerate,'' wrote Allport, further, ''James is responsible for his exaggeration because of his quotable aphorism.'' Allport argued further that the extreme cases of full integration on one hand and of dual personality on the other are also extremely rare. A dual personality like Dr. Jekyll and Mr. Hyde is a clinical case. But a completely integrated personality that follows one single philosophy and is dominated by a single passion is also unreal. It is perhaps a quality of a hero of a novel. Such perfect integration may be tantamount to rigidity. He concluded that a well-integrated personality is a flexible rather than a rigid one and that flexibility is not contradictory with integration. He recorded, however, the viewpoint of other scholars (Wertheimer) who argued that in a well-integrated personality one always finds a single dominant pattern, passion, or *radix*.[15] (Wertheimer's argument is convincing indeed).

However, in his later work (discussed also in Lee's volume) Allport argued that personality may be versatile, but still it is consistent. There is a pattern of consistency, he argued, and personality is not simple a bundle of *n* roles and *n* selves. The theory of roles may be a risky simplification, since it reduces a consistent personality to a loose bundle of disconnected roles. In the type of response to various situations one can still find a certain consistency of behavior.[16] For A. Maslow an individual is an integrated entity, and in spite of inconsistencies, a person operates in various situations because he is coordinated and integrated.[17]

There seems to be an agreement, however, that a person may be stable, normal, and still follow different patterns of conduct in different group situation. Moreover, there seems to be agreement that this type of stable personality is a consequence of flexibility rather than rigidity.

Superethos and Flexibility of Norms

The problem we are concerned, however, is the relationship of multiple patterns of conduct or subethos to a general code, what we have called superethos or megaethos. How are those hierarchies of norms shared by various groups? How are they structured and mutually related? Is this plurality of norms of conduct an inconsistent and uncoordinated set of orders of behavior or are those subsystems related to a superordinated order of normative directions, of values that we have called a mega- or superethos? We are back at the problem of a general code, of a basic ethos, a problem that escapes an ultimate answer. We understand by this question a problem of a broad and flexible moral, normative system of core values that sets the ultimate boundaries of actions, of do and don't.

What the social scientists and science in general overlook today are the simple terms of good and bad, honest and dishonest, cruel and humane. And even in those times, when the concentration and extermination camps became a part of public administration and method of government, use of such purely normative terms was embarrassing, since they are not scientific. True, we do become better human beings by trying to understand others, not by preaching. But we do avoid cruel and bad people just the same. Although all those norms are difficult to define, they are most vital for everyone in our daily life. Moreover, a person may be very honest in one situation and dishonest in another. If everyone in a sense is to an extent multivalent, still there are honest and dishonest persons, persons who stick to their principles and opportunists who will serve for a price. Our daily life has to do with those rather simple valuations. It is not accidental that Aristotle devotes much space in his *Nicomachean Ethics* to a single inquiry of what is "good," what this term means. It is, of course, difficult to identify, to define; perhaps it is not even possible to do it, at least without a margin of flexibility. Without such flexibility one may easily move toward bigotry. What is good is not necessarily useful. One could well argue that the ethical commitment appears clearly at the point where utility and reward end, where man chooses punishment instead of reward for the sake of moral commitments.[18]

Here we are back at problems philosophers have debated for more than two millennia. To return to our experience, to society and the individual, the basic concepts of conduct are considered generally as of primary relevance. The boundaries of what is decent, if not clearly drawn, are still considered and often violated, of course, but it is realized by individuals and groups that they were violated. At this point we are not arguing whether those norms are universal. The general code, the superethos, is a code of a society, a nation perhaps, a culture. They are setting the boundaries of choices within the subsystems, within this multiple structure of rules of conduct. Man expresses through the centuries a need for some coordinating value system, a supreme code of conduct in a number of fundamental documents. Those documents indicate the uninterrupted need for some kind of ethical direction, for a system of established rules of conduct. Moreover, it may be as well suggested that a general code is being constructed today by a complex social mechanism, and it is, above all a changing, flexible, and unwritten one.

What those documents (or unwritten, not codified sets of principles) do represent is the supreme set of values that sets the boundaries of our choices. There is, of course, the difference between ideal norms and real behavior, between the morals and the mores and folkways. Nonetheless, the ideal norms set the sense of direction and the ultimate boundaries of our actions. The fact that man in his historical vicissitudes has formulated again and again his principles indicates that he felt the need of such principles, the need of such guidance. Of course, the multiplicity of values and rules of conduct is a reality that calls for flexibility. But while one follows the various codes of behavior, he is aware of those limits and contradictions. We do realize how far we can go in this flexibility before the Hegelian quantity changes into quality and we hit the threshold of complete departure from our philosophy of life, morals, or religious principles, whatever one senses his dominant commitments.

There are, however, many interpretations of those boundaries of positive norms, of what is honesty, fairness, or equity.

Various groups and various individuals display different levels of flexibility as well as rigidity. Moreover, the boundaries of superethos are flexible or are interpreted with various levels of intensity. What some individuals will consider as *still* fair, others may evaluate as definitely *unfair*. Again, situations and personality, a group ethos determines the limits and nature of flexibility. The ethos of the Amish, humane as it is, is rigid, as is the ethos of the Hassidim. But a Hassidic rabbi may stretch his rules by means of interpretation and may adjust them to the new conditions.

Man relates to his subethos and superethos in a variety ways. Those ways of interpretation and response have, however, a certain individual and group pattern. We may say a person has his style. Style is the way a person responds to a situation, chooses and applies the norms of conduct in various group situations.

A Well Integrated Value Structure

Groups and individuals vary of course. Stable communities have a well integrated ethos, others are "volatile," shifting from one extreme to another. With a weak integration by general directive view and sentiments, we have called "super ethos," they display intensive ambivalent tendencies.

Stable communities as well as individuals display a definite, strong super ethos which integrates the multiple, parallel subsystems. We may identify the latter rather in their general sense—such as respect for human life, humanity, rectitude, mercy, sense of justice, mutual aid, fairness, freedom, but this inner meaning for the actors escapes description or empirical data. Here are the "impondera-bles," the province of the sacred principles, supreme in moral guidance for those who sense it—they are the absolutes. What happens, when the sanctity of those principles is challenged—we saw in the holocaust when Hitler and his associates, as well as large sections of a nation, for a decade or more did. In fact—here are the "absolutes" of those who are called "just;" they give to them the strength to oppose vast majorities.

After discussing ambivalence, multivalence, and theories which negate inte-gration, let us move to a concrete case, of a vigorous, well working super ethos, which controlls two parallel, different subsystems, one of communal value of solidarity and friendship, the other, the competitive one of trade and commerce. Such is the ethos of fishermen and lobstermen of the islands of Northeastern Maine, we have called Yankee Islands.

In spite of changes, the mores and values of this group are probably close to those of the original American settlers. Due to specific economic conditions, partial isolation, the basic way of life seems to have survived. Perhaps the values of those fishermen and sea captains, most of whom carry the names of original settlers and trace their ancestry back to those times, reflect the old ethos of late eighteen-century New England colonists.

What "you do" and "you don't" seems to be generally shared without any further discussion. Those common standards begin already at the mainland har-bors. Still in 1965, a stranger could cash a personal check in a local bank without being asked for identification. Many of the residents and summer visitors on the island do not lock their house, day or night. As for the island-substantial con-tracts, such as drilling an artesian well, rebuilding and restoring a house, are made without any written documents, often without any advance.

The dominant norms of the communal-social values are mutual aid, solidarity-cooperation ("give a hand"). Contrariwise, the emphasis of the economic value subsystem is on independence and profit-gain ("to be my own boss"). While in community affairs, in the Grange and town, as well as in times of emergency, such as hurricanes, cooperation and solidarity are spontaneous, in lobstering—competition, risk, (chance-gamble) profit and personal independence are the dominant norms.

"We give always a hand to each other, but will not work together. If some one needs a hand to pull a boat, help out with traps, find them on a shore after a storm, we will always help. But we never show each other a place where you can catch more lobsters, we shall never work together on a boat, form a company. Fishing and lobstering are two different things. Two fishermen will work to-gether, you may need two fellows to fish. Usually you have a friend to work with. Lobstering—you go alone."

Economic values (values of the trade) are different from social-communal ones: you "give a hand" and never pay. Paying for it would be regarded as an offense. When a boat arrives, everyone helps in unloading. For services which are considered as economic, professional, the customer pays promptly. The price is not discussed. Should the craftsman charge high, the price is paid without comment, but the customer goes to someone else with his next job.

There is in lobstering and fishing another element—the element of gamble, the chance. Chance is an important motive. The unknown outcome, expectation of success if not a personal one, then for those we favor, has its roots in the element of risk. It is one of the earliest virtues of man when his daily food was dependent on hunting, his survival often determined by his ability to take risk, hence courage, to which the concept of risk and chance is related. In sport, the gamble is a kind of ritualized risk. The element of gamble and game element is there in lobstering. Your catch today may bring you even a thousand dollars.

The trade ethos of work and commerce is not limited to a single, though dominant industry, lobstering. This is the ethos of the entire community, an ethos one can sense and observe also in the neighborhood, on the mainland. Lobstermen in their ethos follow traditional, normative patterns, the ethos of those early colonial communities. Their type of work and ways of trade reinforce and maintain the pattern. However, the dominant norms of independence and individualism operate in this particular case due to the fact that the entire regulatory system, Spencer's regulative system, works. All those norms are mutually interdependent.

Business and friendship are separate areas governed by two different sub-ethos. The same persons: friends, neighbors, and family form the market and the community; it is a primary group. The business sub-ethos and the market relations within this primary community are the same as toward the outsiders.

These two separate ethical sub-systems are not contradictory, they do not result into a conflicting situation, into individual inner conflicts or ambivalence. They form two separate value scales, consistent within the general code. The differences are more visible, perhaps plastic, due to the fact that the trade ethos of this community is dominated by individualism and personal independence while the communal-social ethos of interpersonal relations, cooperation by consensus and solidarity. But the communal sub-ethos does not influence the economic attitudes.

The communal sub-ethos can be defined in a single term of solidarity, and to narrow it down, solidarity of consensus. Consensus solidarity may be defined as a) ability and skills in exchanging views in a rational way, b) skills and ability in arriving at a decision and resolution acceptable not only to the majority, but also at one which does not offend the minority. In brief, the ability to agree and accept a disagreement, c) to act jointly as well as express to the outside groups the views of majority, "with a single voice" as a single answer and act accordingly, d) skills and ability to act and work together in problem solving, e) a general pattern of assisting and helping, especially in times of crisis and disaster. Hence, solidarity means ability to carry out a dialogue, agree and disagree in a rational way, qualities of cooperation and mutual aid. It is a general norm of conduct, articulated in two major areas of activity: cooperation and mutual aid, especially in times of disaster.

The skills of voluntary cooperation appear in the ability of the entire community to solve common problems, act together practically without a mechanism of law enforcement and punishment.

The parallel value configuration of the island community, as was already indicated, consists of two separate systems of valuation, integrated under one roof of a "general code" or super ethos. The "general code" (super ethos) is a normative, regulatory social mechanism which sets the limits of "do" and "don't" for the entire island community, and wider social aggregates. This general ethos is dominated by standards of respect for person and human, life, freedom, simple decency, friendliness, humanity, mutual aid, and fair behavior. Within this general code, the two different sub ethos's are consistent and parallel. They are consistent in terms of the general ethos of the islander, although for a stranger they may appear as contradictory.

The tensions within the community are weak and skillfully reduced by mores and cooperative techniques, perhaps at the end repressed by individuals. Moreover, one sub-ethos touches the other, but the communal cooperation in matters of government does not foster or even facilitate economic association. The latter may appear as a consequence of changes in the economic situation and with a new generation. Such change came in the mid 1970s when old fishermen retired and the young formed a kind of a cartel in a form of a cooperative. But individualism and independence continued in its primary relevance, the same other values-risk and profit. The latter even increased.

Ambivalent Environment

Let us return again to this quasi-laboratory situation, to the manmade disaster or crisis situation when personality and conduct are subject to a difficult and severe test, in war and conquest.

It is a crisis situation when this diversity of responses of choice appears. Not every foreign occupation creates such a test situation. Foreign rule may be far more humane than rule by so-called national government such as Idi Amin's in Uganda. But the occupation of Eastern Europe in 1939, particularly of Poland by the German and Soviet armies, created such a test situation, especially since the two regimes were different. The Soviet one created possibilities of survival for the price of ideological submission. The German one left as an alternative only the lowest forms of submission and participation in criminal activities. In the Soviet occupation the deportation of an estimated million Polish citizens to the labor camps in Siberia and political persecutions created an expectation of punishment for those who chose to resist. In the German-occupied part, mass executions and death camps and torture implied an alternative of total submission, but even the latter did not offer security. It was indeed a situation akin to a disaster situation. It was a laboratory case for a study of the emergence of different behavioral patterns and the vitality of different normative orientations. What happened in Poland at that time, instead of total submission, was an almost immediate emergence of a nationally wide and popular resistance movement.

The elementary strategy of the resistance movement, the first stage, is the establishment of a new power center, a power center now called an informal one. It is a strategy of diarchy, of two power centers. Diarchy emerges by the very fact of organization of a second power center, supported by an active part, even a minority, of the population. Hence on the same territory two power centers, the formal and the informal ones, exercise or attempt to exercise social control. The formal one is established by the conquerors, with their symbols of power, administration, army, police force, visible on the streets of the cities by this display of uniforms and variety of symbols and, above all, by exercise of force and legalized although illegitimate violence. The informal power center, represented by an underground government or committee, avoids this type of visibility. The informal power center is unable to display its symbols all the time, but it has its own ways of visibility, of asserting its presence and actions. Underground publications, radio, posters that appear suddenly on the streets of the city, graffiti testify to its presence and vigor. Moreover, people learn from undergound papers, radio, or gossip about actions. In terms of virtual influence and social control the informal power center may be even stronger than the formal one. Both centers proclaim their codes of political behavior; both claim exclusive loyalty of the population. The conquerors proclaim the rules of conduct, the binding norms, by public announcement, official and unofficial press, mass media; The resistance, by their underground means and radio, usually located abroad. In certain countries, for example, Poland, those rules of conduct for the civilian population were even written in a prescriptive form—in a sense, codified. The situation thus created can be called a situation of normative ambivalence. A citizen moves continuously between two codes of conduct; his behavior has to adjust to both. It is an ambivalent situation, and he, in his choice, must consider both. Both, at least in the case of Poland, control sanctions. The conqueror threatens resisters with cruel responses, often summary executions; the resistance movement on the other hand promises an opportunist a severe punishment after the victory, or, in cases considered as treason, the potential traitor realizes that he might be shot by the resistance military organization.

Now the citizen must choose between the two loyalties: one to the conqueror, the other one to his own underground government. Who knows, today's persecuted men and women of the resistance may win tomorrow. An individual has to find his way in this environment of normative ambivalence. To certain extent he must follow the rules of conduct imposed by the conquerors; otherwise he will perish. On the other hand, he is aware that he should not move beyond the boundaries that are established by the informal power center. Those are the boundaries between the permissible or acceptable and treason.

The choice is difficult, oppressive. Different personalities respond in different ways to this situation. The entire population in the conquered territories has to take a stand vis-à-vis the two power centers, two sets of norms, and two loyalties. A normative-political stratification appears now within the nation.

Now the flexibility of norms is tested in a peculiar way. The population breaks into three major political-normative classes: (1) opportunists; (2) positivists; (3) resisters.

The opportunists accept without reservation the norms of conduct of the conquerors and serve their objectives. Their major motivation is self-interest, individual utilitarianism, personal advantage. Opportunism is a kind of unprincipled, utilitarian flexibility.

The positivist is a realist; He considers in a realistic way the present situation of his nation and his fellow country people, the fact that his country is controlled by a foreign power. Hence he attempts to advance and support a "positive" policy, a policy possible and relatively advantageous under the existing conditions. Since politics is a choice of evils, since there is no ideal solution, the positivist evaluates a political task as choosing the lesser evil. In fact, his is a kind of *realpolitik* of the conquered. The term *positivist* has, however, its historical tradition.[19] The positivist looks for the best compromise he can get, not for himself but for the society he identifies himself with, a compromise, however, within the boundaries he and his party consider as permissible under circumstances of such an uneven distribution of power. A positivist does not necessarily look for his own personal advantage or for advantages of his family and friends. An honest, dedicated positivist considers the interest of his nation or society in terms of immediate, present utility. He is a utilitarian, yes, but in terms of his community, not in terms of his own narrow interest. (This is, of course, an ideal type.) A positivist practices a principled flexibility of norms within the boundaries of a principled utilitarianism. His choice considers the boundaries of basic norms, of what is still considered as permissible. He attempts to choose an honest response within means that are open, possible. Contrariwise, the opportunist sets no such limits.

The resister rejects entirely any form of cooperation with the conquering power. He follows the norms established by the underground committee or government. He opposes and fights the conquerors in a variety of organized ways. His flexibility appears above all in his tactics of struggle. Thus, three patterns of rules of conduct, three normative subsystems, emerge after a time. Those are different responses to the same situation.

The formation of those divisions, support for one or another group, depends largely on the nature of conquest and occupation. The German conquest of Poland did not offer any conditions for a positivist policy. The systematic destruction of the national, cultural heritage that was associated with slave labor and mass executions divided the nation into a large mass of those who supported the resistance and a narrow margin of collaborating opportunists.

The history and political culture of a nation, the dominant national character, affect the behavior. Since a nation has usually not one but more cultural patterns, the attitudes and political programs may also develop in a variety of ways. This is a matter of flexibility of tactics. In Czechoslovakia, which has different traditions and where some of the values vary from the Polish, the pattern of resistance was different, passive rather than active. The size of a nation plays a role, too. A powerful conqueror may rather easily eliminate, destroy, or transfer to a distant territory a small resisting nation. The policy of deportation of the Crimean Tatars and other ethnic groups was practiced under Stalin's rule. The Gypsy nation in Eastern Europe was exterminated on Hitler's orders or on orders of his party. The fate of the Jewish population under German rule during World War II is well known. Hence the size of the group, its dominant values, its historical traditions and diverse subsystems on one hand and the nature of foreign conquest, the policies of the conquerors on the other shape the attitudes. A new situation is created. Now various groups respond to this new, at times disasterlike situation.

In this type of a situation, a number of patterns of conduct develop. As already indicated, a modern nation is not reduced to a single value system, a monolithic "national character." Usually a number of value orientation are present at the same time. A number of patterns of conduct appear within the same nation which reflect the multiplicity of normative subsystems of various groups, different political styles of behavior, as well as different personality types.

Slowly there are established boundaries of what is permissible and what is not in terms of the formal power center, in terms of the resistance. But those boundaries are neither sharp nor obvious. Within those boundaries an individual finds a labyrinth of conflicting values, and he has to choose his way to survive. The conquerors establish their boundaries of permissible behavior, the underground, the conflicting one.

At times, those are deadly divides. Here flexible norms mean a potentiality, at times skills to act within those boundaries. An individual tests his behavior against the rules of conduct of the opponents, but also against some basic principles of his belief system. Since the norms are in continuous conflict, psychological stress, combined with the fears and anxieties associated with a resister's life, is quite oppressive. Within such a complex situation an individual makes his choice, and in this he follows usually his own life style, guided by his philosophy, his ideology, and his principles adjusted to the situation. Hence in many cases his choice can be anticipated. In fact, early recruitment in the resistance is guided by this type of anticipation of an attitude, of choice of a code of conduct in a new situation. The leadership anticipates who will choose the ways of an opportunist and who the ways of resistance. It is the past history, the political style, the personality that supply the elements of a future behavioral forecast. However the attitudes change in such an oppressive situation, the pressure is of such a magnitude that some cannot bear to carry the risk. One has at times an impression that those are matters of psychological strength. Of course, when the resistance is popular and carries large groups, then the choice is easier, since an individual feels also more secure within a resistance group.

Still, within such a situation, a flexibility of norms can be noticed or even observed in actual events.

In 1940 this writer observed in Vilna, under Soviet rule, the celebration of the October revolution. It was an official parade and manifestation. Students from the *gymnasia*, the advanced high schools, marched in their uniforms, and many carried appropriate signs with inscriptions and portraits of the Soviet leaders. Stalin's in the front, while portraits of lesser commissars with Molotov and Woroshilow followed. Students marched silently and turned the boards with the giant pictures of Communist leaders backward. They were followed by a group of workers from the local sawmills. When the workers approached, a *zapievala*, a crier, a member of the directing team who initiated the slogans, songs, and exclamations through a loud speaker, appealed in vain to hail the leaders and the Soviet Union. The workers marched silently with no response.

The students and the workers were ordered to march in this parade, so they went to keep their jobs or to follow the school regulations and orders. They followed the rules of conduct of the formal power center of the new government of the victors. However, the presence of onlookers, and there was quite a crowd, called for a symbolic expression of their attitudes, of their will to resist or protest in some way. This was demonstrated by turning backward the pictures and by silence. These were expressions of true sentiments and called for courage. The norms of conduct were articulated in their behavior. In the same parade the conflicting rules of conduct of the conquering power and of the resistance were articulated at the same time.

With this multiplicity of contradictory rules of conduct emerges also a multiplicity of contradictory behavior. A resister may display submission to the rules of conduct imposed by the conqueror by paying taxes, but his basic creed, his sentiments, his principles may remain unaffected, even be strengthened. Once the strength of the enforced social control breaks, once the sign of weakness of his enemies appears, the values that are the core of his ideology may determine his choice of appropriate actions.

But is there any integration of those conflicting sets of norms?

Integration of Norms

An extreme opportunist does not feel the need of any other integration but his own utility and advantage. But there is a difference between him and the two other categories. Integration depends of course on the nature of personality. But in a moment of stress and continuous inner conflict, when a positivist or a noncommitted is forced on one hand to collaborate and on the other to hear or witness suffering of his neighbors, to hear about mass deportation, extermination, and concentration camps, he tries to seek his guidance in the supreme values, which cannot be overstepped, the *imponderabilia*, the core values, the norms and sentiments one cannot define, but senses in such times of suffering and mass oppression. Those are the core values, the dominant ones, the threshold one should not cross. Beyond that begins total submission, even negation of fundamental principles. He finds that he is not alone, that others face a similar choice. What counts is the moral threshold, the loyalty to elementary human values. This is the superethos, which integrates those men and women.

However, not all choose that way or sense this responsibility. Many are guided by a single and supreme goal-value: survival. Yes, survival, but in what way? In a disaster situation of a cruel rule there is little choice indeed. But some will keep their dividing lines, find an existence that permits them to escape from complete submission. For those the core values will outline the boundaries of permissible norms of conduct.

In a normal situation, problems of choice between a multiplicity of rules of conduct is, of course, more simple and less painful. We do it by means of compromise or by preference.[20] Here, with far less stress and danger, our conduct is kept within boundaries established by our life style and core values, our dominant philosophy, and regulatory-directive orientations.

Double Standards

What we call a *double standard* is the case of an absence of coordination by a superior ethos of the various normative systems or subsystems. In a nutshell, it is a case when for the same type of deeds one person is punished while another is not punished or is actually rewarded. This extreme type of ambivalence takes place in those cases when a universe of persons, for example, delegates to an international association, apply in a similar situation two different sets of norms or rules toward two sections of the same group. Similarly, it occurs in cases when a set of rules is applied to one but not to another one. In this case "the same group" means one integrated with the others by the same institutions, rules of the game, procedures, and basic normative commitments considered as supreme, a true megaethos—for example, the United Nations or, in the past, the League of Nations.

Traditionally, double standards were practiced in international politics, this area of dual ethics where the norms of an "external" ethics never disappeared (see above). Herbert Spencer hoped that the evolution of human society would move toward elimination of war, and at the time when defense and aggression disappeared, the double ethics would disappear, too, and internal ethics of amity would prevail in relations between nations. We are still far away, although we had hopes with the old League of Nations and still have with the United Nations.

However, at present, the United Nations General Assembly is at times an interesting double-standard community, a community that has a supreme set of values, codified indeed in major documents (Universal Declaration of Human Rights and others), but applies these values to selective cases and groups only, judging the other members by different types of rationalizations or standards.

What *A* does is wrong. *B* does the same but it is right. An act of violence or the violation of an international convention by *A* is a crime and constitutes racism.

The same, or worse, done by *B* is a custom of a traditional society, a necessary act in a transitory stage of a developing society, a revolutionary act. Or, simply, the violation by *B* is not mentioned; it is covered with silence, a silence devoid even of embarrassment.

The case of the Republic of South Africa compared with Uganda, Mauritania, or some of the Arab states may serve as an example. The racial policy of South Africa, particularly, the institution of apartheid, is an obvious violation of the Universal Declaration of Human Rights. In consequence, the government of South Africa deserves a censure, and sanctions might be applied to this country. They are indeed. The Republic of South Africa was expelled from the United Nations. All this granted censure against the South African republic is in order, in accord with the basic norms of the United Nations.

At the time of the expulsion of South Africa, Idi Amin's Uganda practiced the genocide of its own nation, mass murder of Ugandans. The Cambodian government of Pol Pot practiced a massive genocide of Cambodians. Somewhat earlier some of the Arab kingdoms practiced slavery; so did Mali and so does Mauritania today. There is ample documentation about the slave trade and slavery in the Arabian peninsula prior to 1962 and even later. There is also 1981 adequate documentation about slavery in Mauritania.[21] Neither Cambodia nor Uganda nor Mauritania has been subject to sanctions or censure. Moreover, Idi Amin presided over the Organization of African States, a regional organization of states that are members of the United Nations, states whose representatives signed the Declaration of Human Rights.

Interestingly enough, the United Nations report on slavery of May 27, 1965, does not mention any violations or any practice of slavery with the exception of a minor nine-line notice on Mali. In 1957 the *New York Times* reported the execution of twelve fugitive slaves in Saudi Arabia. Three were beheaded in the square before the king's palace in Riyadh as an example to other escapers. At this time, a conservative estimate suggested 500,000 slaves in Arab countries.[22] French authorities took a stand in matters of slave traffic, and the French Assembly in its report stated clearly a case of selling persons into slavery and mentioned in a rather guarded way the perils of travelers of "pious intentions" on their pilgrimage to Mecca in Saudi Arabia. In another document concerning slave traffic between Saudi Arabia and French Africa (*Arabie Saudienne et l'Afrique noire française*), urgent measures of the French government were suggested to reassure protection and safeguard of French citizens making pilgrimages to Mecca.[23] Again, representatives of the London-based Anti-Slavery Society issued in 1967 a statement about the increase of slave traffic in Arab countries. Detailed information about routes and markets of the Saudi Arabian slave trade were published in the *Manchester Guardian*.[24] In 1981 the slave population of Mauritania was estimated at about 100,000. Virtual slavery in the form of forced labor is practiced in Ethiopia; 14,000 were estimated in a transport to the provinces of Tigre in 1981.[25]

The cases of Idi Amin of Uganda and Pol Pot of Cambodia are notorious;

documentation is easily available. Rough estimates suggest that one-third of the Cambodian population has been slaughtered or otherwise destroyed by Pol Pot and his partisans. Schools and hospitals have been closed. We may assume even more conservative data: only 5 percent of the entire population. For the United States this would mean a million victims.

No sanction or censure was applied to those states. Most recently no such steps were taken against Mauritania. The sole culprit in the past and present, so it seems, is the Republic of South Africa.

The relevance, and for many of us the existence, of shared supreme core values appears in those cases of extreme ambivalence and double standards. This type of extreme ethical relativism is tantamount to ethical nihilism.

What is ethics after all? It is a set of constant, ethical principles that a person considers, obeys, follows, and adjusts to while the social situation varies.

Ethics in a collective, shared form is a set of constant principles, core values, in a changing situation. Flexible, of course, but within definite limits.

Now we may return to the problems of flexibility of norms and integration. Those cases may be considered as extreme forms of flexibility, ambivalence, with no integration whatsoever. We still feel that this type of conduct is in violation of basic principles of our times. But if there is no integration, no superior ethical code, no core values—if multivalence is total—then, of course, a double-standard policy is the only one notable for its superior flexibility. The need and search for a supreme and universal directive and regulatory system for all of mankind, which sets boundaries to human actions, reappear again in this case. We are returning all the time to this basic but difficult, even obsessive problem of the universal and supreme or superior norms of conduct which are constant.

Notes

1. Herbert Spencer, *The Data of Ethics* (New York: Hurst, n.d. Introduction dated June 1879), pp. 165 ff.

2. Ibid., p. 167.

3. Ibid., p. 169.

4. Ibid., p. 181.

5. Ibid., pp. 168–81.

6. Herbert Spencer, *The Principles of Sociology* [1886], 2d ed. (New York: Appleton & Company, 1899) vol. 2, chap. 12 "Militant Type of Society," p. 568.

7. Ibid., pp. 573, 574, 576–77.

8. Ibid., vol. 3, pp. 588 ff.

9. Since David Hume, the impact of the state on the formation of national culture and "national character" has been widely discussed. The national culture, however, did continue for centuries without a state, for example, the Balkan nations, Greeks, Serbs, Bulgarians, under Turkish rule, which continued for five hundred years. Florian Zna-niecki's penetrating volume on the state and national culture explored the relationship

between political power and formation of national culture. Znaniecki, *Modern Nationalities* (Urbana: University of Illinois Press, 1952).

10. William James, *Psychology* (New York: Henry Holt, 1907), pp. 179ff. James makes a distinction of material, social, and spiritual self.

11. Alfred McClung Lee, *Multivalent Man* (New York: Braziller, 1965.).

12. The *Oxford English Dictionary* (1933), Supplement p. 73) credited Bleuler's articles of 1910-1911 (*Psychiatr. neurol. Wochenschrift*, nos. 18–21) for the early use of term. The term is used a year later in *Lancet* (Dec. 21, 1912) as "a condition, which gives at the same time two contrary feelings and "invests the same thought simultaneously with both a positive and negative character." The *Oxford Dictionary* lists a third publication, again a year later, *The American Journal of Insanity* (1913) (880), with finding that "ambivalency leads, even with normal people, to difficulties in decision and inner conflicts." It seems that the term *ambivalence* was used by Bleuler in conjunction with his study of schizophrenia. He called it "affective ambivalence" when the same stimulus or concept results simultaneously in pleasant and unpleasant feelings, and he made further a distinction of ambivalence of the will (a patient who wishes to eat and does not wish to eat) and intellectual ambivalence (when a thought is accompanied by a counterthought). See Eugene Bleuler, *Dementia Praecox or the Group of Schizophrenias* (New York: International Universities Press, 1966), p. 53. However, at that time the term was not associated with group behavior or values. The term *ambivalence* was at the beginning applied primarily to the conflict of emotions, inner split of sentiments, manifestations of schizophrenia. Today, it is generally applied to the conflict of values.

13. Lee, *Multivalent Man*. However, the concept appeared also in his earlier work, dating back to 1949: "A Sociological Discussion of Consistency and Inconsistency in Intergroup Relations," *Journal of Social Issues* (1949), pp. 12–18; and "Attitudinal Multivalence in Relation to Culture and Personality," *American Journal of Sociology* 60 (1954–1955), pp. 294–95).

14. Lee, *Multivalent Man*, p. vii.

15. Gordon Allport, *Personality* (New York: Henry Holt, 1937), pp. 146 ff. This volume had a number of editions, but later editions (for example, 1950) carried the same text on integration.

16. Gordon Allport, *Personality and Social Encounter* (Boston: Beacon Press, 1960), pp. 22 ff., quoted also by Lee *Multivalent Man*, p. 84, n. 22.

17. Abraham Maslow, *Motivation and Personality* (New York: Harper and Brothers, 1954), pp. 63, 75, quoted by Lee, *Multivalent Man*, p. 92.

18. Even the broad, humanitarian standard of John Stuart Mill's utilitarianism—"the happiness of all concerned" (defined in "What Is Utilitarianism" [1861])—is not sufficient as the only supreme moral standard. However, I may admit that the utilitarian principle has contributed to the happiness of the *"Greatest Number"* in Great Britain and America.

19. The term *positivist* as tantamount to a realist and at the same time favoring constructive economic and educational policy, appeared in Poland after the Insurrection of 1863. The insurrection resulted in mass deportation of young and active people to Siberia, mass imprisonment of participants, political immigration, and even more oppressive rule. A new political camp and philosophy advanced an "organic" policy of developing economically and culturally the country within the existing conditions rather than mounting a new armed resistance. The other camp, the partisans of political liberation and independence, continued. Even before the insurrection the political classes of the

nation were divided into the "reds," partisans of armed resistance, and "whites," the advocates of a realistic, positivistic orientation. In the Austrian part, however, where a constitutional monarchy secured autonomy and political rights, especially after 1867, not a single political group advanced a policy of armed resistance against the Austrians after the Cracow uprising of 1846.

20.   The choice of preferable values is the usual mechanism of decision. The actor selects what in a given situation is possible and "preferable" rather than "preferred," if the latter cannot or is difficult to be achieved. Charles Morris discussed extensively the process of appraising and choosing. "Organisms, given certain needs," wrote Morris, "prefer certain objects to others. Such preferential behavior is widespread and perhaps universal characteristics of living systems". Morris, *Signs, Language and Behavior* (New York: Prentice-Hall, 1950), section 8, "Appraisors and Appraisive Ascriptors, pp. 79 ff.

21.   *Slavery*, Report of the Special Rapporteur on Slavery Appointed Under Council Resolution 960 (XXXV), United Nations Economic and Social Council, 27 May 1965. This report has 224 pages, mentions slavery only in Mali, and devotes to it nine lines. Slavery in Mauritania was reported by the London Anti-Slavery Society to the subgroup of the United Nations Human Rights Commission in 1981: *Economist* (September 19, 1981). See also: Greenidge C.W.W. *Slavery and the United Nations* (London: The Anti-slavery Society, 1954).

22.   Leslie Housden, "About Slavery" *New York Times Magazine* (January 20, 1957).

23.   *Assemblée de l'Union Française, 14 Fevrier 1957, no. 234; Assemblée de l'Union Française, Session de 1955–1956*; MM. La Gravier et Le Brun Kris and other conseillers de l'Union Française urged the French government to gather immediately information and witnesses concerning black slave traffic.

A letter from the French embassy in Djidda reported a sale of five slaves, among them two women. *Assemblée de l'Union Française: Annexe au Procès Verbal de la Séance du 17 Novembre 1956*.

24.   *New York Times* (April 7, 1967), p. 13; also *New York Times* (March 8, 1967, and February 21, 1956); *Manchester Guardian* (August 16, 1956).

25.   *Economist* (September 19, 1981; "Slavery 1981," Intercom, (December 1981), vol. 9.

16

In Search of Universal Values

The Question of Universal Norms: The Megaethos

In previous chapters, we have at times identified—or only postulated—the existence of a controlling normative system, a superior set of values that exercises some control over related subsystems. It has been argued, however, that in terms of validation such controlling supersystems appear in particular cultures or societies.

Now a question has to be asked: Do we have, or can we identify, elements of a megaethos, of a worldwide universal ethos, a system that is sensed, expressed, if not recognized by all, sensed by an entire mankind? There are of course codified systems of supreme norms, and the United Nations Charter and Declaration of Human Rights is a more recent expression of such sentiments, evidence of a tendency.

The search for a supreme ethical system, shared by all mankind, was of course a central theme of philosophy and theology for centuries. In this search contradictory ideas appeared. The ancient Greeks, beginning with Pythagoras, saw a harmony, a perfect structure in those highest principles directing the destiny and conduct of mankind. Others, however, discovered dialectics.

A vision of an almost scientific ethical system, a system of perfect proportions, was designed by Spinoza. On the other extreme, philosophers perceived early mankind as marked by the absence of any ethical code, as a complete ethical chaos—*bellum omnium contra omnes*, guided by egoistic interest, greed, and the will to dominate, but harnessed eventually by institutions and a legal order of a society that developed the state in the interest of survival and as protection against those destructive forces inherent in man.

Hence, in their longing for a better, even perfect humanity as well as for legitimacy of a better society, philosophers tried to discover natural laws common to all persons, all societies, inherent in the very nature of things, rights inborn and inalienable. They were also in search of eternal principles, external truth. This school of natural law spanned centuries and our Declaration of Independence is an articulation of this philosophy and of our political, secular faith.

This is a continuous, unending search, in itself an expression of sentiments and longings for a permanent and secure moral order. At this point it is not even seminal whether such values do exist. The longing is here; it is a historical reality if only limited to parts of mankind, to certain civilization. It is a long debate indeed.

But do we have an evidence of such a universal community of norms?

The Absolute Norms

In this long history of the search for a universal, worldwide ethics, three major views have been advanced: absolute, relativistic, and universal.

In an extreme expression of the absolute view, ideas have their own existence, independent of space and time. In such an outlook the ethical system is permanent, absolute, and definitive. Right and wrong are clearly defined. In such a view we are endowed with the necessary knowledge of what is good and bad, and in dogmatic religions questions in dubious cases are referred to an authority that in turn are endowed with such an ultimate judgment. For those whose viewpoint is orthodox, all divisions are clear red and green. For the rigid and dogmatic, there is but little yellow in between. Those clearly established norms are considered as self-evident, sometimes obvious. Their discovery is a matter of our insight or intuition. They supply the ultimate guidance for our conduct.

An absolute viewpoint appears of course in various gradations. Even an absolute outlook may be rigid or flexible. It is frequently related to personalities: Some are rigid while others are flexible, reflective. Such a viewpoint may be also a part of a secular or religious outlook.

Like other sets of values, the absolutes are articulations of an idea system.

With the separation of philosophy from religion or rules of conduct, the general field of ethics called for rational interpretation, for logical explanation, understanding, and evidence. The concept of hypothesis, exploration by means of dialogue, does not favor absolutes. Separation of ethics from religion has weakened indeed the philosophical basis of absolute norms. Still, the evidence for absolutes has been suggested by philosophers in terms of our sentiments, especially of our intuition.

And indeed, in times of war, invasion, persecutions, and deportations, this feeling of destruction of a moral order, of absolutes, is almost an instant reflex. Their destruction becomes a reality. When an ideology of equality and social justice serves as legitimation and rationalization of absolute power, oppression of the weaker, and conquest, then sooner or later the idea system breaks down under the impact of those contradictions. Then it is abandoned or revised by many partisans of such ideologies. It breaks down as their belief system. They do not believe anymore in its original veracity or workability, since it contradicts the paramount values of social justice, equality, and freedom. But what remains is a sense, often a vigorous belief, in those supreme values that have been violated. Ideologies decline but values continue, and those values form again a core of future reconstruction of ideas.

Even the utilitarian viewpoint may become an absolute. The happiness of the largest number, of the majorities, whatever *happiness* may mean, is also an absolute, an axiom in this case, not a dogma—an axiom, true or false, since it is suggested as an obvious truth rather than a revealed one.

However, it is faith, religion, or revealed truth that supplies a firm basis for an absolute viewpoint. Here the norms are a consequence and articulation of a world outlook, of the broad idea system. It is a truth that has been revealed, and the norms are simply a part of this faith.

In a secular acceptance of absolute values they do remain, in spite of all, in a certain void. Absolute values call for certainty. Their very nature is an ultimate one. Science has no certainty, only hypotheses and findings. Its advance is prompted by doubt and rejection, or at least by criticism, of once accepted verities. Sciences call for scientific validation. Only axioms are self-evident. But are they? And with all our attempts, attempts at challenging the validity of absolutes, men and women who have a moral sense know and speak out when human beings are abused, harmed, and mistreated. They sense the absolute moral imperatives and sooner or later realize that those moral commitments are close to the very spiritual roots of our existence.

The Relativistic Viewpoint

With the advance of science as a modern idea system, the ideology of our century, the realm of values and moral norms became a subject of scientific inquiry. The weakening of religious beliefs and separation of philosophy from theology, the dominant position of science and scientists, the diffusion of a scientific outlook affected now the search for an inquiry into ethical principles and concepts as well as theory. In a religious outlook, values were a matter of faith and revelation. But in a society educated with a scientific approach to life, human conduct and norms called for scientific interpretation and evidence. Norms were not accepted solely as a matter of faith. Their meaning called now for facts, data, causes, mutual relationship of causes for meaning and function. The certainty about the rights and wrongs was gone, since science cannot provide us with an ultimate truth.

But the longing for discovery of universal, immutable principles continued. This trend of an ancient origin, the search for a scientific-philosophical basis for the universal and immutable reappeared again in the sixteenth century. It was the search for "uniform or natural not variable or positive elements" in law and political institutions, the search for permanent norms and rules governing man and society, as Gierke put it.[1] This search for natural law was guided by principles of philosophical methods. It was a consequence of nascent and winning rationalism. This was largely a deductive exercise, an inquiry guided by scientific fantasy and also by political wisdom, careful reflections on nature of human society. The contribution of this period toward a better society, toward humanization of society and law, is fundamental. We are still guided by and profit from those humane teachings of the Renaissance, Reformation, and Enlightenment.

With the growth of inductive and empirical methods and advances in natural sciences due to the effectiveness of empirical techniques and methods, man turned to those methods in the social sciences, even in the humanities, as well. The basis for norms and their validity had to be found now in relationship of data and facts. So did the scholars turn to data gathering on unity and difference in mankind. They discovered or rediscovered both unity and difference.

At first the prevalent interest was in this striking difference in norms of conduct, in customs and manners (here the interest goes back to antiquity). This difference in norms or development of ethos was discovered or rediscovered in the works of William E. H. Lecky, Herbert Spencer, and, later, Edward Westermarck.[2] Even here this trend can be traced back to the Enlightenment and numerous reports that appeared at this time and were later used by French philosophers who fathered the French Revolution. They translated those reports into bucolic, at times naive, images of primitive life.

However, methodological, anthropological, or ethnographical studies of diverse cultures all over the globe revealed differences not only in customs but also in rules of conduct and norms, even the basic values.

The discovery or emphasis on ethical relativism (which came later) was neither accidental nor solely a result of anthropological studies. Development in science affects our world outlook, not only sciences but also humanities, above all our philosophy and social sciences. Eventually those developments affect the world outlook of sections of society, sections who control education as well as cultural activities. The twentieth century concepts and theories of relativism were not confined to physics. The very idea of relativism as a principle had an impact on social sciences and humanities and reinforced a relativistic viewpoint. It challenged once firmly established rules and set a direction of thought and inquiry. Differences in norms and values had an adequate, scientific concept, an important and fashionable term. Of course, the very matter of humanities and social sciences is different from hard sciences, especially physics and mathematics. Concepts that are applicable in the latter cannot be projected directly or literally into humanities and social sciences. True, but this is done all the time, and development in sciences has its impact on humanities as well.

That cultures are different and values relative was of course known before, although the terms used in those times were different too. In the sixteenth century Montaigne broadened our outlook and humanized our views by his kind of ethical relativism. In his *Essays* Montaigne pointed with candor and courage to the differences and similarities in norms; he taught us to understand and respect cultural and moral differences, differences in moral judgment. He commented on the conduct of the natives of the New World: "I finde (as farre as I have been informed) there is nothing in that nation that is either barbarous or savage, unless men call that barbarism which is not common to them. As indeed we have no other ayme of truth and reason, than the example and idea of the opinions and customs of the countrie we live in. It is ever perfect religion, perfect policie, perfect and compleat use of all things'' (John Florio translation, 1603). He discusses the customs and religion of those peoples to conclude, ''I find that there is nothing I could call barbarous in this nation.''

Moreover, commenting further on cannibals, he found them more reasonable, even humane, than contemporary Europeans and Frenchmen. It is less barbarous, he wrote, to roast and eat human beings once they are not anymore alive than to torture, draw by horses, break, and burn because they differ in religion. The cannibals compare well with the Inquisition, although the latter is not mentioned for obvious reasons. Montaigne discovered the common norms, yes, but also— and that is his contribution—the relative nature of norms and above all of our judgment.

To return to modern ethical relativism, relativism in its extreme may suggest that all norms of conduct, all values, are relative. What is right and wrong cannot be validated in terms of absolute values since existence of the latter cannot be scientifically validated. In terms of function and utility, norms that are functional in one culture may be dysfunctional in others. No values, a radical relativist may argue, are valid for all cultures; even incest was practiced and was accepted, especially in ruling classes, of some societies. The French historian Jules Michelet suggested that incest was not absent in French medieval peasant communities. Oppressive and cruel conditions of life in medieval France, argued Michelet, prompted incest.[3]

Extreme relativism suggests that there are no common norms, no common values, for all mankind. Values are relative to perceptions, viewpoints, cultures. What is right for *A* might be considered as wrong by *B*, who belongs to a different society or different group and cherishes different beliefs. Historical and anthropological data, carefully chosen, may supply as well an ample evidence of this relativity.

Historians discovered the diachronic difference and change in values, anthropologists, the synchronic one. The norms differ indeed in terms of historical periods and changes, and in the same historical stage the differences in norms appear among various cultures. The anthropological and historical data indicated that what is considered right in one culture, in a given historical period, was wrong in another one. The rights and wrongs of the preachers were not necessarily the practiced norms of the community, moreover of the preachers themselves.

The norms, the evidence seemed to suggest, vary; they are relative to cultures and situations.

Belief in absolute values derived its strength from faith, from religion, and later from philosophical speculations. Partisans of relativistic views found their arguments in scientific evidence.

The modern inquiry into the nature of society and human conduct, however, supplied two types of data: those on cultural difference, which fed the relativistic arguments, and those which pointed to similarities in norms of all mankind. The empirical evidence has not been solely limited to the relativistic hypothesis of ethos. The issue in itself is dialectical, since on one hand the difference in norms and the relative meaning of norms are discovered all the time and on the other hand one finds at the same time some basic norms, as well as social structures, that bear similarity; moreover, they are identical. We do rediscover humanity all the time in the vast mankind of the world. After all, the basic needs and drives are common to all mankind; they must be met.

While Lecky, Spencer, and Westermarck, among others, pointed to the variations of morals and customs, their argument did not necessarily suggest the total absence of universal norms. Spencer, in *The Data of Ethics*, pointed to altruism as a universal principle a generation before Kropotkin. Kropotkin's theory suggested mutual aid as a basic and common principle. Moreover, Darwin's theory had also two contradictory impacts. On one hand social Darwinism advanced the theory of selection and survival of the fittest. This type of interpretation suggested an ethos with the primacy of the strong and ruthless, an ethos that gave legitimacy to the nineteenth-century industrial philosophy of expanding capitalism. The sociology and philosophy of social Darwinism supplied legitimacy to exploitation of the working class. On the other hand, the concept of evolution and progress pointed toward the hopeful development of ethics. Here belongs Spencer with his hopes and augury of the future decline of the external ethics. The emphasis, the major interest of scholars, however, pointed to the differences in norms, to the relativistic nature of rules of conduct, to their variability rather than to unity.

Universal Norms of Conduct: Altruism and Mutual Aid

This extensive inquiry into ethics, norms of conduct and customs, was dialectic, led to contradictions. Studies and volumes pointed to differences and variations of human conduct and customs. At times, however, the same authors discovered not only differences but also a community of norms of conduct, which seemed to appear in all human societies. Such norms could be interpreted in terms of utility and functions; nonetheless, they were there. Perhaps those common norms were now discovered and emphasized because of this longing for the unity of mankind, longing for common, shared values of all mankind, for a foundation for our creed, our belief in equality of man. The interest in universal values, the search for universals, was also an expression of our views and ideologies as well as our perceptions. Spencer discovered this unity in altruism; Kropotkin, in mutual aid.

Nonetheless, Spencer's utilitarian argument on altruism is convincing indeed. Altruism, argued Spencer, in its elementary function secures a child's survival. Moreover, self-sacrifice and altruism are a condition of child's survival. In mother's love, self-sacrifice, and altruism Spencer discovered the roots if not the beginnings of our ethics.

If we define altruism as being all action which, in normal course of things, benefits others instead of benefiting self, then, from the dawn of life, altruism has been no less essential than egoism. Though primarily it is dependent on egoism, yet, secondarily, egoism is dependent on it.
Under altruism, in this comprehensive sense, I take in the acts by which offspring are preserved and the species maintained.

Altruism, in Spencer's utilitarian philosophy, is only an articulation of individual and collective self-interest and another aspect of egoism. Egoism and altruism in Spencer's views are closely interrelated:

From the dawn of life, their egoism has been dependent upon altruism and in the course of evolution the reciprocal services of the two have been increasing.
As there has been an advance by degrees from unconscious parental altruism to conscious parental altruism of the highest kind, so has there been an advance by degrees from altruism of the family to social altruism.

From there, Spencer continued, evolution moves toward a universal set of altruistic norms.[4]

Furthermore, Spencer commented critically on and reinterpreted the utilitarian doctrine of Bentham and Mill in terms of altruism and egoism. He rejected a utilitarianism of pure altruism: "Statement ... of pure altruism ... involves the belief that it is possible for happiness, or the means of happiness, or the conditions of happiness to be transferred. Without any specified limitation the proposition taken for granted is that happiness in general admits detachment from one and attachment to another. But a moment's thought shows this to be far from truth.[5]

A forthright theory of universal norms, as a basis for scientific ethics, has been advanced by the anarchist philosopher, geographer, and social scientist Peter Kropotkin, a generation after Spencer's work. Mutual aid, argued Kropotkin, is the fundamental and universal principle of society, of its evolution and survival. The theory of mutual aid originated also with other Russian sociologists, to mention especially M. Mikhailovsky and perhaps other theoreticians of the early Populist (Social Revolutionary) movement. Kropotkin, however, took the initial theory from the work of a Russian zoologist, Karl Kessler, from his lecture "The Law of Mutual Aid" delivered at the congress of Russian natural scientists in 1880.[6] Kropotkin's view on mutual aid as a fundamental principle of evolution may also be traced to his earlier experience and observations made during his journeys and forays in Siberia and Manchuria. Young Kropotkin, serving at this time in a Cossack regiment, noticed mutual aid and cooperation among animals, especially before and during the seasonal migrations. Perhaps his earlier recollections and ideas were only reinforced and organized by Kessler's lectures. However, Kropotkin's views were made famous with his series of articles on mutual aid published between 1890 and 1896 in a well-known English review. The articles appeared later in a single volume.[7] Nonetheless, the idea was not new: It was discussed and supported by observations, by the early animal sociologists (for example, the then well-known and today forgotten book by A. Espinas on animal societies [1877]).

Kropotkin, who returned to Russia at his old age to take part in the building of a new society, takes a definite stand on ethics. His last book is prompted by his experience, by the need he feels to answer the crucial issue of morals. He rejects any kind of moral relativism, any separate "bourgeois" and "proletarian ethics." To the argument that there cannot be any single ethics in a class society, divided by strong antagonisms, he pointed to the fact that first of all we are human beings, and a part of mankind, and that the basic moral commitments have their roots at this elementary level, which bind us toward all, whether Europeans or Bushmen.[8]

Spencer and Kropotkin differed of course greatly in their general approach, method, and above all general philosophy. Common to both was an argument that definite norms of conduct, altruism and mutual aid, are universal qualities, part of human nature and present in all societies.

Kropotkin's ideas were not confined solely to the narrow circle of his political friends and to those in London and New York who, though they disagreed with his anarchism, still were attracted by his humanity and by his serene, warm personality. Leading anthropologists found his theory an important and valid one; it concurred with their own findings based on years of careful field work. Bronislaw Malinowski considered mutual aid and cooperation as universal conduct in all societies. Ashley Montagu followed the footsteps of this search for universals of mutual aid.[9] The universal values are dominant in their quality; they control the entire normative system and integrate particular subsystems. Today, identification of such universal orientations has been established also in anthropological studies.

This sense of dominant universal norms appears in a detailed statistical study of value orientations carried out by Florence R. Kluckhohn and Fred I. Strodtbeck. Kluckhohn and Strodtbeck studied dominant and variant values in five carefully selected communities: Spanish American, Mormon, Texan, Zuni, and Rimrock Navaho. Their findings did not depart far from their assumptions. They began with a general assumption that there is a limited number of problems that all societies must meet and respond, problems for which they "must find formulae," to use the terms of two anthropologists. While variations in those formulae exist, they are not limitless. Furthermore, "all variants, all the major values appear in all cultures" but receive from one society to another ... "varying degrees of emphasis." True, they discovered important differences in rankings and also important similarities in two pairings of the five cultures.[10]

The problems were, however, a priori selected by the authors; in a sense they were precodified and reflect also the interests of the authors of this extensive study.

Kluckhohn and Strodtbeck identified the normative structures of affective, cognitive, and directive nature. In all those cultures they identified dominant, directive values. What has been identified in particular case studies appears in great and complex civilizations as well as in specific political systems.

Some Findings

The basic tenets of those findings and philosophy postulate that some norms of conduct, such as mutual aid and altruism, are universal. Moreover, they are a necessary condition without which no society can exist or survive. Those norms can be identified, observed in all societies. Unlike the absolute acceptance of values, universals are empirically verified. The findings are derived from data and are not revealed or taken as a matter of faith. Their existence is a matter of a hypothesis or findings. Although they are not prescriptive per se, they may form a scientific and universal basis of ethics, a supreme norm for all societies, a megaethos.

Attempts to create a scientific basis of ethics continues of course. Modern psychology made its contribution too. Here the universal norms, or rather the basic values, were linked to human needs, and since elementary needs of man are of the same or similar nature, corresponding norms and values can be identified that way.[11]

Identification of universal norms of conduct, of elements of a megaethos, of norms of conduct shared by all mankind, departs of course from an extreme relativistic viewpoint. The extreme relativist may argue that (at least in theory) there are no shared values, that our norms of conduct are relative, valid only within the context of a single or related culture.

However, the existence of universal norms is not contradictory with a qualified relativistic viewpoint. To the contrary, both are complementary. The universal norms suggest that in all cultures we may find some identical elements, or some elements are common since certain elementary needs are identical. The ways, however, man responds to those needs differ. Although the nature of those conditions of life and survival differ, man must respond to them in terms of his existence. In empirical terms, the argument of universal values is limited in its content by rules of validation. A higher ethical order also has, however, an ancient religious and philosophical base.

The Altruistic Expression

The identification of universal values, whatever the motives of the authors, is not prescriptive per se. It is primarily descriptive; the essence of the findings are data that say what is, not what ought to be done. When we identify altruism as universal, for example, the altruism of a mother toward an infant, it is a generalization based on data. It tells you about the conduct of a mother, but at this point it is not yet a commandment: "You should behave in an altruistic way because such is the nature of things." No doubt it has normative qualities, too. But, it tells you, mutual aid or altruism in a variety of forms is a part of a regulatory and directive system; those are the ways people behave; those are the norms. The statement must be qualified: Not all behave that way; some do.

Nonetheless, the effort and research toward identification of universal values were more often than not guided by a desire to establish a scientific and secular basis, a scientific philosophy for our morals. Universal norms suggest an answer to the extreme expressions of relativistic philosophy and to moral disorientation, to a moral anarchy due to the absence of a definite and firm moral commitment.

The argument that sociability and mutual aid is an instinct (as Darwin in the *Descent of Man* or Kropotkin in his work suggested), that altruism is simply an expression of human nature, serves in its logical consequence as rationalization, legitimation of ethics. Here is an independent, scientific basis for morals, one may argue.

Attempts of a naturalistic scientific approach to our ethics have reappeared today, it seems independently, in a number of etiological contributions, as well as in new attempts to apply biological findings to sociology.[12]

Maternal or parental altruism and sociability, however, are not the only pattern of conduct that appears in nature. The basic principle of our ethics is protection of and assistance to the weaker. The laws of selection do not work that way, even if mutual aid among animals appears in their group behavior. Darwin's observations and findings initiated after all social Darwinism, a philosophy that equated the survival of the fittest with the survival of the strongest and ruthless. On the other hand, far less known and less influential was the philosophical inspiration that some have derived from Darwin and other naturalists for their theories of moral evolution.

Observation of nature resulted in two contradictory philosophies: one, a philosophy of relentless struggle and of the supreme right of the fittest, that is, the strongest, in practice usually the ruthless one. His is the right of survival and well-being at the expense of the weaker and unprotected. Such are the unpardoning laws of selection. The other philosophy is one of altruism and mutual aid, a promise of our moral evolution. Both do appear in nature.

Nature does not supply us an adequate and an exclusive foundation for our morals. Nor does primitive custom. The fact that Calibans act as they do does not create an imperative that I should follow Caliban's example because he is closer to the nature of things. To the contrary, my moral acts might conflict with what I may observe in nature. We do not kill or reject newborn children when they are weak and not promising. Some animals and some tribal societies do, and the Eskimo did it until recently, in fact (it was reported by Nansem).

Nor do the utility of our actions and the happiness of the greatest number form a complete and always sufficient foundation for individual ethical acts, although many times they may and they do. Ex post facto, we may interpret the act, its function, in terms of social utility. The actor, however, acts for different reasons. His motives are quite often quite different from our interpretations.

And now happiness of the greatest number?

The survivors of Hitler and the twentieth-century mass folly in Germany may give us examples of happiness of large majorities at the expense of small, helpless minorities, men, women and children expelled from towns and communities, later tormented, with the approval of those vast majorities.

And statistics—the fact that a majority does it, that it is the conduct of the majority, is this an evidence of right at a given time? A single person who opposes the evil doings of an overwhelming mass of people shows indeed moral strength. French President Mitterand abolished capital punishment. Polls may suggest Mitterand did it against a general attitude, against a statistical majority of the voters. Does this make Mitterand's position unethical and that of the partisans of capital punishment ethical?

The philosophy of ethics has its own normative basis. We sense at times quite clearly our moral commitments, though we are unable to explain where their roots are. True, we may discover them ex post facto in class position; true, the utilitarian and naturalistic school may explain a large area of our dominant norms; but it does not encompass the totality. Moreover, we may understand and interpret in a plausible way why a person acts as he does. We may comment in terms of social conditions, psychology, nature. But the subjective process and a personal, individual act of choice, the choice of ethical action in a given situation, constitute a different problem. A pragmatic act is different, too. Here my action and an understanding of preference for the latter coincide clearly. Its workability, utility, and efficiency are obvious.

A choice of a "purely" or spontaneous altruistic act has different antecedents, unless it is an institutionalized act of an association, an agency. The actor might be guided by reason, but in a spontaneous altruistic act ethical motivation, sentiments, and inner commitment affect the decision.

In many cases we do follow and we "should" follow the altruistic principles because "they are right," because we sense that we should do it that way and feel empathy for the person. At this moment of choice, not ex post facto, there is no other explanation than this inner commitment and ethical urge.

Altruism, however, appears in a variety of intentions and types of conduct. It appears as a simple, spontaneous response and as a consequence of a philosophical, rational concept, as individual spontaneous acts and as pragmatic, institutionalized actions.

The spontaneous response gives some insight into the origin of an altruistic act, into its earliest, even natural roots. In this spontaneous response we rediscover the origin or the beginnings of what we call today humanity.

We shall review some of the types of altruistic conduct, beginning with the natural spontaneous response.

Spontaneous Altruistic Conduct

A rare insight into expressions of altruism was given us by a British surgeon, Mungo Park, in a calm report of an African explorer of the late eighteenth century (1795–1797) at the time of a thriving slave trade on the west coast of the African continent. On the coast Europeans traded with the Africans. In the interior the slave trade was in the hands of native rulers and traders. Slavery was practiced in a variety of ways, beginning with simple kidnapping of women and children at the borders of a village and extending to large-scale armed raids on peaceful and hard-working agricultural populations, wars with the sole purpose of getting slaves. Violence and brutality made up the daily routine. In a wide area of Africa at that time children and women, and even men, could not move safely beyond the narrow limits of their tribal villages.

In many of those villages and tribes Mungo Park noticed altruistic feelings, moreover friendliness or compassion toward a stranger, who otherwise was an object of hostility and open hatred. But even among some slave traders he found a multiple standard, compassion to a stranger, different toward the slave and different toward a person he considers as a friend. What is, however, more interesting is the altruism of slaves toward their fellow man.

This expression of altruism appeared, so it seems, clearly among women, slaves and free (whatever freedom women had in those tribes). This volume, written long before Spencer's work, seems to support his argument about the female roots of altruism.[13]

Park's account tells us about both the predatory and the altruistic behavior in Senegal or farther in the interior in those relatively advanced societies still thriving on slavery and robbery.

Those are examples of a spontaneous response to a situation, a response Darwin or Kropotkin may call instinctive. The present-day biosociologists may even argue that norms are programmed in our genes, but there is no evidence of it. It is sufficient for us to state simply that there is a spontaneous response of human altruism.

Let us assume compassion as part of human nature. Then the way it is expressed is also culturally determined; it is at least in part a consequence of learning and also of reflection. It is emotive in many cases, but it may also be a consequence of reflection and reasoning. The very concepts of altruism may be articulated in a variety of ways and its very concept may also vary.

The African response, quoted above, was simple and humane. In the ancient Greek, Roman, and Hebrew concepts and expressions it was far more subtle, subtle in philosophical terms (not in emotional) and complex as well. It is far more institutionalized, a matter of culture and prescribed behavior.

The Greek and Hebrew Concept of Altruism

Altruism played a major role in Greek society. The Greeks coined a term for a broad philosophical concept: *philanthropy*. They did create a broad term and diverse philosophical orientations as well as philanthropic institutions. This already is indicative of the relevance of altruism and philanthropy in the Hellenic and later in the Hellenistic culture. The Jews, too, had concepts of their own altruism and humanity, although not as broad nor as universal as the Hellenic. The fusion of Hellenic and Hebrew ideas and norms opened the road for Christian altruistic values. Two Greek terms are associated with the concept we call now altruism: *philanthropia* and *agape*. *Philanthropia* in general terms means love for mankind, benevolence, humanity, clemency, liberality. It meant also the king's benevolence toward his subjects, the city's assistance and concern toward orphans, toward the sick and strangers, toward any kind of misfortunate, toward the captives. In its later meaning, according to Constantelos, *philanthropia* is a Byzantine norm, a fusion of Christian and Greek idea systems, is tantamount to *agape* or love, and suggests an active attitude and sentiments toward a person, qua human being, "irrespective of this person's identity and actions.[14] Hence it is a concept that corresponds to a broad idea we call today "humanity"; it has a universal orientation and an active quality, a "purposeful expression of love and compassion," to quote again Constantelos.

Greek altruism was institutionalized in a variety of forms. The Greek philanthropy was active; this was not a passive pity and compassion. They built *xenones*, hospices for the strangers, and supplied the strangers with food and shelter. Brotherhoods of hospitality, *xenoi*, maintained those institutions, looked after the needs of strangers. Cities had brotherhoods of *xenoi* and special chests, as well as a patron—Apollo. Temples had hospices called *katagogia*, which served as resting places and clinics. Epidaurus, a town known for its unusual theater, which is admired and still active today, had also its *katagogion* and was known for its physicians.[15]

This active nature of philanthropy appeared in the development of altruistic activities and institutions. In addition, it was also reflected in language: *Philanthropos* means a humane person, benevolent and kind. *Agape* generates a term, *agapoi*, for Christian festivals. Perhaps it was an early, if not the earliest, defined universal concept of an active friendship toward mankind, the beginning of the very idea of mankind, in times of strong identification with your own tribe and nation and your tribal or national deities.

But the Greeks had many differing philosophical schools. The same terms— *benevolence, altruism*—were probably differently interpreted by differing philosophical orientations.

The Greek concept of philanthropy and altruism as well as the Roman, which derived from the Hellenic, was rational rather than emotional, according to Hands. It could be summed up in a dictum of a stoic philosopher: "If I being a man do not aid man's lot, how shall I appear of right mind." A concept of altruism was rather a separate one, separated from pity. Pity or compassion had a different meaning than in Hebrew or in the older Egyptian tradition, continued Hands. The Greek, stoic concept of altruism was *zuhelfen* and not *mitzuleiden* (as Hands suggested), to use the German expressions, to help actively rather than to suffer together. Morality for the Greeks was a matter of reason not emotion. However, Hands continued, the concept began to change about the first century A.D. It was reflected in Seneca's writings. One may sense in his work "greater allowance for human feelings.[16] At the time of Seneca, Jewish Hellenistic influence and the nascent Christianity affected the philosophical thinking and the norms of sections of the empire.

The attitude toward the poor varied too. The general attitude toward the poor and destitute in ancient Greece and Rome, argued Hands, was one of contempt and not one of empathy and compassion. This showed rather clearly in Cicero's writings when he questioned the right to Roman citizenship of those who worked for pay: "Do you suppose that body of men to be the Roman people which consists of those whose services are hired out for pay? . . . a mass of men, of hired men, of rogues and destitutes?" He called the poverty-stricken *sordes et faecus urbis*, filth and dregs of the city. There was also little evidence among the Roman historians of compassion and humane sentiments toward the working poor, the slaves, and those working in the mines. It did appear at the beginning of the Christian era in the writings of the historian Diodorus. The general attitude toward beggars did not indicate any compassion and understanding, rather contempt. Hands contrasted this attitude with the Hebrew and Egyptian. In the Jewish texts, continued Hands, the poor were often equated with the pious and deserving.[17]

The classic scholars examined the basic norms and concepts in terms of the written sources, of course, the writings of philosophers, poets, statesmen, or historians. The content of those values and norms could vary substantially in time and among different classes; the interpretation as well as the conduct could have been different. The class division did after all exist, and what *philanthropia* or *philanthropos* meant among the craftsmen, sailors, or slaves of Greece might have been different than the meaning of those terms among the intellectuals, above all the philosophers and historians. The terms were not entirely relative, of course; the core, the essence, might have been the same. However, the attitudes and conduct, the real behavior, might have differed. This can hardly be discovered in a linguistic interpretation. But still the linguistic interpretation is highly illuminative and, under certain circumstances, a fruitful method of historical reconstruction. We have no other ways of reconstructing the meaning of those terms. Professor Hands has done it with skill and insight, in a penetrating way.

Let us, however, return to the study by Professor Hands, who, unlike Constantinelos, suggested that the Greek term for friendship and altruism, *philanthropia*, was coldly logical and devoid of the broader sympathy expressed in the Latin concept of *humanitas*, associated with a broad human charity. *Humanitas* was a fruit of Roman universalism; it was an expression of Rome's wide relations with nations and peoples of different races and cultures. Its content was humane and universalistic.[18] Was it then Hellas or Rome that gave us a concept of universal friendship and benevolence, the concept of humanity and mankind? We shall leave this matter to the linguists and historians for further discussion.

However, one is struck with the vast number of terms commencing with the adjective *philo* in the Greek language, an adjective that stands for friendliness, benevolence, interest, humanity, concepts and ideas related to altruism rather than to egoism. A further linguistic analysis may challenge Hands's hypothesis.

Altruism and Sensitivity

Are the altruistic response and conduct relative? Is this a universal quality, or does this conduct, this set of norms, have a different meaning in different cultures, considered in one as a virtue and in others as a foible?

First, a distinction has to be made between individual, especially spontaneous, expressions of altruism, such as one described by Mungo Park, and the altruistic norm and conduct in collective behavior, a set of cultural norms and institutions.

To begin with cultures and groups, the collective and institutional response toward the weaker and helpless varies indeed with cultures.

The difference in altruistic behavior between two different groups may appear due to the breakdown of the norms in one of the groups, the lifting of legal and normative imperatives, or due to the absence or weakness of the altruistic value in one of the cultures when compared with the other one. In the first case, once the normative (ethical) boundaries are lifted, the pent-up hostilities are released toward the target. Past history tells us that cruelty and brutality are associated with such situations. Holocaust is only one of the many examples that history supplies, testifying to the extremes man is prone to when the ethical system breaks down or the legal and normative imperatives are lifted. Such was the case of Saint Bartholomew's night, this holocaust of the Protestants in Paris on Sunday, 24, 1572, or the sack of Rome in 1572.

However, in times of relative stability, in one society, altruism and mutual aid are institutionalized, form a part of formal and informal learning, approved by society and voluntarily supported, while in other societies the altruistic norms may be weaker or limited solely to a narrow in-group. In some modern societies the idea of mankind is well advanced and the mutual aid and altruistic norms are considered as universal, or universally binding, while other societies are tribal or narrowly national. The solidarity in the latter case is narrow and limited. Those differences in ethos and in behavior can be noticed, even studied.

The difference in response to what might be called an altruistic situation (predicament of the weaker, less protected) appeared clearly during the post-Vietnam period and the mass escape of Vietnamese by land and boat from their country. The fate of the boat people—people who belonged to various social strata—testifies to this cultural relativism in ethical conduct.

The difference in collective altruistic behavior appeared again on two levels: formal, institutionalized and informal, voluntaristic.

Aid given by various governments in admitting the unfortunate refugees, saved from unseaworthy boats and miseries, varied, as evidenced in figures of boat people admitted to those countries, as shown in Table 16.1.

Table 16.1
Boat People Admitted to Various Countries as of September 1978

British Colony of Hongkong	3,354
Thailand	1,544
Japan, Singapore, and others	1,484
Australia	9,784
France	2,238
U.S.A.	19,867

Source: *Economist*, (London), October 7, 1978, p. 49.

We have selected a few data solely as an example. The United States had a special responsibility as an ally. Still the difference between the numbers of admitted is striking, comparing only the tiny British colony of Hongkong and "Japan, Singapore, and others" (how many others?). Here normative relativity appears again. Nonetheless, the governments of English-speaking countries, members of the British Commonwealth, and France were more generous than the close Asian neighbors.

Furthermore, the Vietnamese refugees were subject to piracy, robbery, and rape by some of their close neighbors, some of the Thai fishermen. (Others, of course, were helpful or indifferent.) On the high seas some ships assisted the shipwrecks and boat people, rescued them, or gave them food, while others did not. When they landed, there was seldom a friendly reception.

On one of the Thai islands, Ko Kra, 167 boat people were killed. A month earlier, according to the *New York Times* in December 1980, 80 boat people were murdered. Thai fishermen were arrested in a case in which 17 refugees were killed. "The survivors were held on the uninhabited island for several weeks and asserted that they were continually sexually assaulted by about 500 fishermen who ply the waters around the island.[19]

Reading such reports, one questions indeed the universality of altruistic norms. A relativistic interpretation is here on the winning side. But this is not the sole and only behavioral pattern. The response to the situation varied too.[20]

There are variations in collective behavior, that are determined by normative differences in culture and social situation of a given time.

There are also, however, differences in personal reactions toward a needy person, and those are differences in personality. Nonetheless, expressions of individual altruism appear in many cultures. They are *universal*, although culturally determined. In their collective and institutional expressions they are *relative*. We shall return to the problem of this relationship between absolute and relative norms as well.

Sensitivity toward the fate of one's fellow man varies. This individual sensitivity is not unlike a talent, an inborn ability, an esthetic talent in music or painting. Some are endowed with such subtle emotions and feelings; others are not. Some perceive in a subtle way; others are not sensitive.

Types of Altruistic Response

Moreover, there is not one single form or pattern of altruistic behavior but a number of them, some types appearing more frequently than others.

Comte suggested two major human tendencies or, some may argue, instincts: egoism and altruism. Between extreme expressions of each, there is a vast number of variations.

First, a distinction must be made between altruistic and mutualistic conduct, although both are closely related and partially overlapping. In a spontaneous altruistic act a person does not expect reward or reciprocity in the future. There is no advantage for the actor. It is a spontaneous act or a response in terms of a commitment, sentiments, or duty. Altruistic conduct is guided by duty; mutualistic by its utility—at times, direct, pragmatic utility.

Duty meant and means a moral imperative with no rewards in most cases. It is a one-sided act of a person toward other individuals or society, legitimized by the very concept of duty, not by utility, not by reward or advantage for the actor.

The utilitarian and pragmatic philosophy, which explains human objectives in terms of happiness, utility, and efficiency; social Darwinism of a specific kind, with its emphasis on the paramount right of the stronger, the fittest, to win and dominate the weaker; a narrow interpretation of historical materialism, with its emphasis on class position and ethics; furthermore, extreme behavioristic interpretation of personality—all those modern trends have little use for the moral concept of duty. Still, without this essential norm society hardly can function. The very meaning of altruism, as well as of humanity, is closely associated with the imperatives of duty.

By contrast, mutual aid by definition is related to reciprocity, to an actor's response toward the community, which will assist him and reward him tomorrow, as he helps the others today. But let us list some of the major types of altruistic conduct, and let us encompass both altruistic and mutualistic. This is of course a theoretical division, for life is not divided into tight compartments.

Within this wide family of individual and collective responses we may distinguish the following major types:

1. spontaneous altruistic acts

2. mutual aid and related mutualistic responses

3. rational cognitive responses

4. institutional responses

Those divisions, to repeat, are not tight; they are often overlapping and also appear fused together. Classifications are theoretical; they are always generalizations and to a degree abstractions. Nonetheless, this classification is necessary for our general discussion of the major theme.

First, the spontaneous altruistic response is universal; that is, it appears with various intensities in known societies. It appears as a response to a predicament of man or animal with no expectation of a reward. In most cases this response involves a personal sacrifice of a various quantity and quality.

This personal sacrifice may be at times as irrelevant as the refusal of minor comfort to oneself or as the voluntary deprivation of pleasure. But in far-reaching cases it is an act of true sacrifice, of personal well-being, and of self-sacrifice. The altruistic act of a Catholic prostitute in the City of Lwow during the German occupation of Poland, a prostitute who voluntarily hid and fed persecuted and destitute Jews at the risk of her life, and the spontaneous act of a slave woman in Africa toward Mungo Park, one and a half centuries before, are closely related.[21] Both are articulations of the same sentiment and spontaneity. And a passerby who gives a sandwich or a coin to a derelict in a New York City subway does not risk his life or well-being, but articulates the same sort of sentiments. Those acts are a response to our ethical needs, needs akin to the esthetic rather than to the biological, although all those needs are integrated by a person, by the very nature of man. In those simple, spontaneous acts, our directive-regulatory system appears in an intuitive response and also in a limpid way. However, an altruistic response appears also in a more complex form, already affected by customs and institutions. Here it may be mentioned that all those acts to a degree are affected by culture, since they are also affected by the social situation to which an actor responds.

The second type is mutual aid conduct. To return to our earlier argument, mutual aid belongs to a broader family of social relations, determined by the principle of reciprocity. In an ideal type of an altruistic act the act is "complete"; that is, there is not an expectation of any rewarding response or future assistance or service. In a mutualistic act the actor expects a reciprocal service, sometimes in the future or as a reward. Mutual aid, however, appears as an immediate and spontaneous response. It is articulated in customs or in set, accepted "routine" conduct. Routine is an accepted performance in similar, repetitive situations.

In 1958 such a mutualistic routine conduct could be observed in the Sicilian fishing village of Trapetto. Fishermen were working one evening onshore. They did the usual chores, common in times prior to introduction of nylon nets, repairing the nets, a tiresome and rather dull occupation. Later in the evening, boats, Sicilian *barcas*, began to arrive. The water in Trapetto is shallow; those are not the deep harbors of northern Maine. Those on the shore put their work away, rolled up their trousers, and moved slowly into the water. Lines were thrown to them from the boats, and now they hauled the boats silently, along with parts of the crew, and beached them on the *spiaggia*. This was a routine, repeated every working evening. The actors changed. Those who fixed their gear yesterday went into the sea fishing today; the next day upon their return the crews of yesterday, now fixing their nets helped them out. This was both spontaneous and mutualistic conduct, a matter of routine and customary cooperation. No reward is expected, but a Trapettino knows that he will be helped tomorrow or another day when, tired after a day long fishing, he steers his boat back to the village. I observed these daily labors from the beach carefully. The work was strikingly spontaneous, at times silently done, while conversation and laughter usually accompany a friendly Sicilian meeting. It was a routine that one simply does, although those villages are not free from intense, at times violent, dissension and quarrels. The borderline between a spontaneous altruistic act and spontaneous mutual aid is of course very thin, at times overlapping. Aid to a neighbor whose house is on fire, even if such act involves the risk of one's life— is this an altruistic act or mutual aid? Or does it really matter in the end? What matters is the act, a sincere expression of humane sentiments.

However, mutualism *sensu largo* is a large area of human relations. It is a vast continuum of diverse intensities, which at a point changes, its very altruistic quality becomes contractual. Mutuality and reciprocity are an articulation of our sociability. This is a basic relationship between persons and groups, an elementary principle of society and also an elementary bond. This mutuality of sentiments and services is also articulated in a variety of expressions. We may imagine a continuum of mutualism as a line that begins with altruistic responses and, at a point, changes into contractual. Commerce begins at this point. Hence from an exchange of gifts (mutualistic relationship) what follows is barter, purchase, and loan.

Roman law encompassed a vast category of mutualistic relationships under a general heading called "obligations". It is not accidental that the term for *loan* in Latin is *mutuum*, a reciprocal, mutual act.

The third type of altruism is rational and cognitive conduct.

Can altruism in the form of charity become purely rational and cognitive conduct, free of sentiments? Hands, who made careful distinctions in types of altruism, seemed to suggest that such was a nature of a stoic, whether Greek or Roman, concept of altruistic conduct.[22]

Unless institutionalized, and a part of an institutionalized routine, altruistic conduct is often a combination of sentiments and reflection, of rational thinking. Even the stoics, who attempted to reduce charity to a logical and rational act, were prompted by human sentiments, so it seems.

The fourth type is institutional conduct. In advanced societies altruism and its articulation, charity, are institutionalized in a variety of customs and laws. Once it is institutionalized, it develops routines of its own. Such institutions are of course articulations of idea systems, reflecting social-economic conditions and the general culture.

Ancient Greece, Byzantium, medieval Christian Europe, Islamic societies— all have created charitable institutions in the form of foundations, shelters, or hospitals, although they differed in their structures, organizations, and specific objectives. Ancient Byzantium had an advanced system of social welfare. Fifteen hundred years ago, they had already *xenones*, hospices for strangers; *gerocom-exea*, homes for the aged; orphanages; *ptocheia*, houses for the poor; reformatories for the prostitutes, *xenotapheia*; cemetery institutions; homes for the blind.[23] The extensive Byzantine charities may have influenced the Islamic institution. The routine sets into any institutional conduct. A philanthropic institution, after a time, might be just a job for some, but a source of enrichment for others.

The continuation of altruistic functions of those institutions may depend on their ability to conserve those original sentiments of empathy, the spontaneous sentiments of an altruistic act.

With time the institutional conduct of those organizations may become entirely a matter of routine, at best a matter of bureaucratic efficiency, measured by the number of cases attended and terminated. With institutionalization the conduct moves from individual to collective. In their institutional form altruism and mutualism become culturebound.

Altruistic conduct is complex and diversified. There is not a single, unique type of altruism, but many set patterns of altruistic and mutualistic behavior. Both are affected by processes of informal and formal learning and socialization. The informal process of learning altruistic behavior begins in the family, and it moves later to the peer group and, farther, to the influence of the entire complex social experience. This process of learning is also affected by the unique experience—for example, war, flood, famine—a child was exposed to. The perception of what may be called an "altruistic situation" is eventually affected by the world outlook or idea system a person acquired in his process of socialization or was converted to later.

Three ideal types of conduct of man are elementary: egoistic, mutualistic, and altruistic. They are "ideal types" of behavior, at times overlapping. Seldom does a person have a single motive; more often than not, motives are mixed, combined. All three types of conduct appear in human societies, and all are modified by learning and culture. Hence the norms of altruistic and mutualistic conduct are universal but at the same time modified by culture.

Survival

A single norm is obviously universal, clearly pragmatic and utilitarian: the survival of mankind. This is an extension of the basic, supreme value of a person, his life, and his community. Today, however, this norm has a new, although obvious relevance.

The discovery of nuclear energy, the introduction of nuclear weapons, makes the issue of survival different, very different indeed than in the entire past history of mankind. Our survival may now depend on our rational behavior and ability to control emotions, on skills in cooperation, on our will to apply rational thinking to our actions and to select rational goals. The times call for rational behavior, alertness of our reason, virtues advanced by the age of Enlightenment, perhaps for a revival of rationalism in this age. Decision in this matter belongs above all to the governments; they have the power to decide. Hence the future of mankind depends on sane and rational government.

The discovery of nuclear energy, progress in science, came too early in history and development of mankind. We have not yet matured to a point that would warrant a safe and careful use of those energies, immense and difficult to control (shall we ever?) Nor did we learn to conduct the business of government and relations with other societies and nations without the use of excessive force and violence.

World political challenge and international politics are closely associated with this threat of the use of nuclear weapons or protection against such threat. Last, but not least, we do not even fully know how to dispose safely of the growing accumulation of nuclear waste. To a certain limit, yes, but what will happen with further production of nuclear waste? Past history does not give us any experience with this type of materials, with a deadly toxicity and intense social risks spreading over centuries and millennia. In the past there is hardly an example of a large accumulation of materials that may destroy human and animal life within such a vast radius.

And at the same time we face the emergence of volatile mass movements of intense uncontrolled emotions, no different from those of past centuries. They are guided by intense hostility and hatred toward other nations and persons. Iran alerts us to the dangers mankind may face, once this kind of fanatic, hostility-driven leadership assumes power over a nation that has nuclear capacities.

The survival of mankind—an obvious, utilitarian goal, articulated as a norm, a principle—becomes supreme. It is shared by responsible leaders, whatever the differences and contradictions between the United States and the Soviet Union. With all its ideological dogmatism, the Soviet government is still a rational one, a government that represents a modicum of responsibility. Its leaders are cognizant of the dangers.

Whatever the differences and antagonism, it is the issue of survival that compels both powers to act with highest responsibility and seek adequate means in cooperation, in control of the weapons, and in prevention of their use. Highly rational ways in thinking, in choosing goals and actions, are now essential.

And here the concept of mutualism, of mutual aid and cooperation in international relations, becomes conscious and rational. Now mutual aid and cooperation as a conduct for survival are interdependent; the former is a condition of the latter. They are rational and utilitarian.

Such is the universal sense of those values, and here are the building blocks of a political unity of mankind.

Complementarity of Value Orientations

The universal approach suggests solely identification and description of what is. The utilitarian or functional interpretation suggests why or how norms work and why they are relevant. It is both descriptive and prescriptive. The relativistic approach describes the nature of norms, tells us that they are different and relative. The concept of absolute norms is prescriptive and tells what ought to be done in terms of past, present, and future.

The concepts of absolute and relative norms can also be evaluated in historical and sociological terms, in terms of their effect on society. A distinction has to be made between a rigid, dogmatic and a flexible, common-sense concept of absolute and relative value orientation. A total approach suggests a dogma, a rigid and closed belief in the veracity of the doctrine and intolerant practice of policies derived from such beliefs. A common-sense approach suggests flexibility, an element of creative doubt, and consideration of social acts and relations not as abstract principles. Instead, an attempt is made to relate actions and relations, conduct and norms, to the personality of the actor, to the nature of the act and to the social conditions of time of the act, as well as to social effects of each action. At this point we shall discuss both absolute and relative norms in their prescriptive quality. Those two viewpoints, absolute and relative, which in a total approach are contradictory and exclusive, are in fact complementary rather than contradictory in a common-sense understanding. It is in this latter sense that they have made their contribution to the advancement of a civilized society.

Absolutes in their total, extreme interpretation, belief in dogmatic and ultimate verities of faith and political ideas, the ultimate knowledge of good and bad, right and wrong, with an absolute certainty, moreover, with a condemnation of any differing view as sin or crime, led to religious and political persecutions, to religious and political intolerance.

But a common-sense absolute ingredient, acceptance of basic though limited core values, impedes opportunism, an eventual consequence of radical utilitarianism. Moreover, it supplies a firm sense of commitment and moral direction and counters the moral nihilism of an extreme relativistic evaluation of norms.

This constant quality of supreme norms supplies a sense of direction in times of rapid social change. While subordinated and ancillary norms change, the dominant value, with their absolute quality, supply the necessary element of stability and direction.

The core values are also the building blocks of reintegration of a humanitarian idea system, of a constructive revision in times of strong contradictions between ideology and practical action, or in times when ideological movements of mass oppression—like fascism or Nazism—are on the winning side. Then the core values legitimize and direct the protest, even the use of force and violence of the resistance.

During those times, when varieties of tyrannies covered the nations from the Atlantic Coast to the Pacific, the question "What really matters?" became paramount. That the basic humanitarian commitments matter more than advanced political theories, uncommitted to ethical principles and values, was a simple inference in evaluation of the time we lived in. That ethical principles are not necessarily reflected in actions of majorities became obvious when Hitler led the German nation and won a majority in most communities of a powerful state. At such a time, the core values, akin to or equal with absolutes, established a threshold, a borderline. Here were the limits of integrity, self-respect, and humanity.

A relativist viewpoint faces different perils than the absolute does. A total relativistic evaluation leads to moral nihilism, to a loss of sense of direction. If all norms are relative, and there is no supreme moral code of conduct, then Hitler should be judged only in terms of his ethos; and within his ideology and his ethos he was right, not wrong. Since there is no scientific basis for ethical judgments, since our evaluations cannot be validated in a scientific way, any ethical system should be recognized as equally valid, a relativist may argue. In consequence in an extreme relativistic view Hitler's ethos is as valid as Gandhi's. Relativism in such a case could well serve as rationalization of support for the Nazi party and legitimation of its power, since one ethos is as good as another one. We may read in the Marquis de Sade's philosophy an approval of murder and an argument that, after all, a populous state loses little, even if it is a murder for amusement.

However, relativism in flexible, common-sense terms is the basic philosophy of toleration. It is a corner-stone of modern toleration and pluralism. Relativism tells us that values have to be related to culture, cultures are different, and so are their normative systems, fundamental sentiments and core values. Different values imply different judgment and decision and different needs. Next comes the relativisitic imperative: Since people are different, and they have the same rights as you have, do not impose your values on others, learn to live with people who have a different ethos, provided there exist an agreement on and acceptance of fundamental norms. You have no right to impose your norms on others. Relativism in such a sense is a philosophy of respect for cultural differ-ence, for different ways of life. A pluralistic, multiethnic, multireligious, and multiparty society calls for a strong, relativistic ingredient.

In turn, a common-sense utilitarianism supplies today in a nuclear age a paramount value-goal: survival.

In their prescriptive quality, all three, even four approaches—absolute, rela-tivistic, utilitarian, and universal—are at one time contradictory and other times complementary.

In our modern, complex society our sense of direction is affected by all four orientations. None is sufficient, and all are necessary components of a modern megaethos.

We arrive indeed at the first step in our very tentative answer to the initial question: Do we have a megaethos, a supreme normative system of mankind, of humanity?

This megaethos, it may be suggested, is sensed by many. It is a general binding concept of supreme and elementary principles, necessary for the survival of mankind, essential for individual and social well-being, and above all essential as a guideline of our moral conduct and relations. A supreme directive and regulatory system can be and in a sense is constructed from elements supplied by the four major value orientations. Construction of such a system of principles is formed by means of complementarity of those orientations and at a point where those orientations are complementary rather than contradictory.

At least in terms of theory and hypothesis, the dominant or core values are the constant, relatively permanent. Subordinated and ancillary values are subject to frequent changes. The absolute quality, though flexible and tolerant, appears in dominant or core values; the relativistic, in subordinated and ancillary.

Reconstruction and Dialogue

But even the core values, the absolutes or dominant, are not petrified concepts. The human society is changing all the time, and even the constant and permanent call for interpretation and redefinition. Redefinition of norms marks cultural periods. This does not mean that there is no permanency in our basic values. Stability calls for change and reinterpretation for rigid concepts break down in times of the rapid transformation of society.

The end of the eighteenth century was a distinct period of redefinition and revision of values. It was a conscious and constructive attempt at liberation of the human mind from dogma and prejudice and clarification of basic norms and concepts in terms of reason and a rational inquiry.

The norms were revised and reinterpreted. This appears clearly in Diderot's *Encyclopedia* and in its origins. This was not an isolated effort, as it was a time of proliferation of philosophical dictionaries that defined the new meaning of norms and concepts. It was not accidental. There was a need for redefinition.

We find in the *Encyclopedia* a redefinition of some basic concepts: freedom, equality, tolerance, humanity, man, to mention a few. Or take Voltaire's *Philosophical Dictionary* and his redefinitions of dogma. Two hundred years later, after this work of the Enlightenment, a philosopher in Poland found it necessary to define and restore to its true meaning the very basic concept of ethics in a new dictionary, *The Ethics of Solidarity*. A young philosopher defined again those essentials concepts and norms: solidarity, dialogue, work, adversary, and others.[24]

The need for rational reinterpretation of our norms, of those which are constant or permanent and those which are changing, continues. The terms of our norms, our values, appear in daily parlance. What do they mean in reality today, in a context of the present situation and change? One of the ways of demystification of symbols is clarification, definition of their meaning.

Contradictions and conflicts, contradictions within ideas and society, this entire social process, affects our norms, and in turn our values affect this process. Values are formed and reinterpreted in those conflicts, which may end with a tyranny over the minds of men or may continue in a dialogue and calm exchange of ideas.

A rational construction and reconstruction of values is accomplished in a continuous exchange of ideas, in a dialogue, which at times culminates in an agreement expressed in codification of norms, in those declaratory documents. Those declarations are ideal guidelines of our conduct. The way of dialogues and guidelines is the way of rational reconstruction of our ethics, ideas, and norms.

The megaethos is a postulate for some, a common bond for others, a result of a sense of values and goals. It is or it should be today a dialogue between individuals and cultures, a never-ending conversation, with its contradictions, sometimes exploding in conflicts. It has its constants, the core values, and its variables, the relative norms. The dynamic nature of a society calls for flexibility and continuous reconstruction. It is perhaps an emerging directive and regulatory apparatus of humanity. It is a general, overall guideline, which may integrate and coordinate the diversity mankind is displaying. But it may not encompass all cultures, all political parties. Not all societies, nations, and peoples desire such a unity.

The very idea of humanity, of mankind, is not necessarily universal. However, universal is the recognition and acceptance of norms, rules or conduct, customs, of mutuality or reciprocity, cooperation and mutual aid. Altruism is not limited to a single culture and civilization. We do have propensities, capacities to form and accept a normative order.

Notes

1. Otto Gierke, *Natural Law and the Theory of Society: 1500–1800*, with a lecture, "The Ideas of Natural Law and Humanity," by Ernest Troeltch (Boston: Beacon Press, 1957), p. 39.

2. William E. H. Lecky, *History of European Morals from Augustus to Charlemagne* [1869] (London: Watts & Co., 1946); Herbert Spencer, *The Principles of Sociology* [1886] (New York: Appleton & Company, 1899); Edward Westermarck, *The Origin and Development of Moral Ideas* [1908] (New York: Books for Libraries, 1971), and *Ethical Relativity* (New York: Harcourt, Brace, 1932).

3. Jules Michelet, *Satanism and Witchcraft: A Study in Medieval Superstition*, trans. by A. R. Allinson (New York: Citadel Press, 1939), pp. 113 ff. Michelet used extensive medieval documentation.

4. Herbert Spencer, *The Data of Ethics* (New York: Hurst & Co., n.d., Introduction dated June 1879), chap. 12, "Altruism versus Egoism," pp. 241 ff., 258–60, 244.

5. Ibid., chap. 13, "Trial and Compromise," pp. 261 ff., 275.

6. Karl Kessler's lecture appeared in *Trudi*, Memoirs of the Saint Petersburg Society of Naturalists (vol. 2, 1880). Kessler was professor of zoology and also dean at the University of Saint Petersburg.

7. Peter Kropotkin, *Mutual Aid: A Factor of Evolution* (New York: New York University Press, 1972). See also his *Memoirs of a Revolutionist* (Boston and New York: Houghton Mifflin, 1899).

8. Peter Kropotkin, *Ethics, Origin and Development* [1924] (New York: Tudor Publishing, 1947), pp. 5 and xiv (Introduction by the Russian editor, N. Lebedev). See

also Kropotkin, *Mutual Aid*, N. Lebedev in the Introduction to *Ethics*, Paul Avrich in the Introduction to the 1972 edition of *Mutual Aid*, and Kropotkin in his own 1914 Introduction discussed the origin of his theory and Kessler's influence.

9. Malinowski commented on Kropotkin's theory in an unpublished lecture delivered in New York in 1942. Ashley Montagu's viewpoint appears in many of his contributions. See, for example, *The Humanization of Man* (Cleveland: World Publishing Co., 1962), and *On Being Human* (London: Abelard-Schuman, 1957).

10. Florence R. Kluckhohn, Fred L. Strodtbeck, *Variations in Value Orientations* (Westport, Conn.: Greenwood Press, 1975) pp. 10 ff., 341 ff., 353 ff.

11. Among psychologists A. Maslow in his major contributions suggested a scientific frame of reference based on human needs. See, for example, *Motivation and Personality* (New York: Harper and Brothers, 1954), and *New Knowledge in Human Values* (New York: Harper, 1959).

12. George E. Pugh, *The Biological Origin of Human Values* (New York: Basic Books, 1977). See also an interesting (although not convincing) sociobiological argument in a debate on altruism of Marvin Harris and E. D. Wilson, "Encounter" in *Sciences* (October 1978). Wilson advances a sociobiological viewpoint; Harris, a cultural-anthropological. For an etiological approach see Irenaus Eibl-Eibensfeld, *Love and Hate: The Natural History of Behavioral Patterns* (New York: Holt, Rinehart & Winston, 1971); T. Eibl-Eisensfeld, *The Biology of War and Peace* (New York: Viking Press, 1979); Robert Ardrey, *Social Contract* (New York: Atheneum, 1970). For informative, general readings in etiological approach see Claire H. Schiller, ed., *Instinctive Behavior* (New York: International Universities Press, 1975).

13. Mungo Park, Surgeon, *Travels in the Interior Districts of Africa: Performed under the Direction and Patronage of the African Association in the Years 1795, 1796 and 1797* [1799], reprint ed. (New York: Arno Press, 1971), pp. 69 ff., 197 ff.

14. For the meaning of the term *philanthropia* in ancient Greece and Byzantium see Demetrios J. Constantelos, *Byzantine Philanthropy and Social Welfare* (New Brunswick, N.J.: Rutgers University Press, 1968), pp. 1–12. Constantelos discusses extensively the meaning of this term. Follow also the informative footnotes in chap. 1, "Hellenic and Christian Background," pp. 3–18. In fact, the entire first part of this excellent study is dedicated to the very meaning of philanthropy in Greece and Byzantium: "Philanthropia in Thought World of Byzantium," pp. 3–61. The Greek concept of *philanthropia* has an extensive literature and wide research devoted to its interpretation. Footnotes in Constantelos' first chapter give an extensive bibliography and comments.

15. Ibid., pp. 7 ff.

16. A. R. Hands, *Charities and Social Aid in Greece and Rome* (Ithaca, N.Y.: Cornell University Press, 1968), pp. 82–85.

17. Ibid., chapter 5 "The Poor," pp. 61–76, but especially pp. 63–65.

18. Ibid., pp. 63, 87 ff.

19. "Thai Pirates Kill 70 'Boat People,' " dispatch by Henry Kamm, *New York Times* (January 11, 1980); "200 Vietnamese Die off Malaya Coast," by Henry Kamm, *New York Times* (November 23, 1978); "Refugees Depict a Grim Cambodia," by Daivd A. Andelman, *New York Times* (May 2, 1977), and other dispatches.

20. Canadian authorities were generous: see: "First Vietnamese Refugees from Ship Land in Canada," by Henry Ginger, *New York Times* (November 27, 1978).

21. This was related in detail to this writer by one of the survivors.

22.   Hands, *Charities*, pp. 81 ff., especially on concept of pity.

23.   For detailed data see Constantelos *Byzantine Philanthropy*, part III, "Philanthropic Institutions," pp. 145–279, and Hands, *Charities*, chaps. 7–9, pp. 89–145.

24.   Jósef Tischler, *Etyka Solidarnosci* [Ethics of Solidarity] (Crakow: Znak, 1981).

17

Toleration and Pluralism

Questions Asked

After discussion of universal values and the search for unity, we shall return to the obvious reality of mankind: to its difference in values. It is the difference that primarily attracted the attention of ancient historians and scholars, and the discord nascent from this diversity prompted medieval and Renaissance philosophers to search for the unity. The unity had to be discovered, but the difference was and is visible and obvious.

The question that we ask in this chapter is this: How do groups of various, differing value orientation live in a single society? What kind of political and social systems were practiced by the ruling classes or by the people in order to maintain a unity, cohesion within diversity? What modes of coercion or consensus were applied? Furthermore, considering past experience, what kind of system can be outlined or postulated for the future?

We have postulated a universal, superior megaethos, an overall value orientation, a regulatory directive apparatus or system of mankind. But such a system—fundamental as it is—is limited, reduced to the basic core values. It represents a tendency and a dialogue. The difference of other values continues. Moreover, this difference is not contradictory with the idea of the unity of mankind. The dynamic qualities of change and revision of values appear in these continuous dialectics between difference and unity. The changing values of various cultures affect the overall ethos and result in new interpretations. It is the modern doctrine of democracy and toleration, also relativism, that commands respect for this difference and the right of man to cherish his own culture and follow his code of conduct.

The question is asked now whether groups of fundamentally different normative systems, which profess different, even antagonistic ethical codes, can live within the same community or states or whether a state of such strong normative disagreements will disintegrate. We shall narrow our problems to values, although ideologies and values may correspond—in such a political context—to less or more definite interests.

For millennia, of course, people of various commitments and values lived together within the confines of a single state. The states, however, differed in their nature and in their relations to the dissidents. They differed also in ways that power or authority was exercised, differed in laws that imposed or did not impose controls over dissidents and groups that differed within a single polity.

Building of a state calls for a minimum set of common values and common interests and furthermore, a certain level of identification. In the absence of the latter, unity can be imposed by force, even by a minority. Hence a unity can be created either by consensus on basic norms and rules, as well as common interest, or by command and coercion. But even a coercive system over a large territory inhabited by diverse, often opposing groups requires the realization of a common interest and the acceptance of some common norms by the ruling groups.

In the past, various states applied diverse types of social control. Those controls varied from extreme forms of coercion to moderate, even extensive consensus. In all cases, however, the state had to impose a minimum or maximum set of rules and legal norms, which were considered by the political classes that controlled the state as supreme and necessary for continuation of the political order they did practice. Political classes of some nations, consciously and with candor, tried to reduce such norms to a bare minimum set of norms. The ruling classes of other nations extended such norms by means of legal codes to all corners of private life.

The differences in values, differences in ideologies, religions, general or even sexual ethos, were either suppressed or permitted in various degrees.

In this history of mankind various social systems, articulated in the political form of a state, could be plotted or evaluated on this continuum of coercion and consensus. The systems of coercion coincide with rules of political or theocratic classes that legitimated their total power by means of ideological absolutes, intolerant toward other political or religious creeds. The tolerant and pluralistic states adopted a measure of relativism, relativism that admits the existence of not a single one but a number of religious and ideological systems and that recognizes the difference of norms of conduct. Such states did not impose rigid absolutes.

Many types of states appeared in this continuum of tolerance and intolerance. History does not suggest a simple, evolutionary process, a proud progress from intolerance to higher forms of toleration of difference. Ancient Rome—until the second or third century—was far more tolerant than medieval Christian states, which were built on the ruins of this empire. Catholic and imperial, the postfeudal Austro-Hungarian monarchy at the turn of the century was a tolerant state. Hitler's Austria and Germany, which followed after twenty years of an interlude, was an oppressive one, with an antiethics elevated to a dominant ethos, imposed by force. A tolerant Netherlands of free cities was conquered by intolerant Spanish rulers.

Four Major Types of States

Within those varieties of regimes four major types may be distinguished:

1. An inquisitorial state, a state that imposes an ideological or religious monopoly, a single creed, and enforces it, developing specialized institutions to control groups of different creeds and values. In such a state the legal system is integrated with the ideological one. Church or political parties in those states are not separated from the state. The earlier forms of integration of church and state have been now displaced by integration of the state with a single political-ideological creed or party.

2. An intolerant state. Not all intolerant states are, however, of such an inquisitorial, totalitarian nature. States that do not practice a wide measure of toleration may still maintain political power and primacy of the dominant creeds with various levels of moderation.

3. A tolerant state. It permits difference of creeds and ideologies, but a primacy is given to those who identify themselves with the dominant creed.

4. A Pluralistic state, a state that accepts a variety of ideological and normative orientations and activities. Such a state does not only tolerate the difference but recognizes equal rights of all different religious, ideological, or ethnic groups under conditions of voluntary acceptance of a limited set of rules and principles.

The Inquisitorial State

The inquisitorial state imposes a single creed, religion, or ideology, establishes hierarchies of ideological or religious norms, and imposes them on subjects by all the means the government has at its disposal. Such a state is a total instrument of political or theocratic classes in power. The administrative apparatus and armed guards or political police cannot control the minds of citizens. But they can control the public, even private, activities and articulations of their creed or beliefs by controlling the press or education, by prohibiting meetings, associations, and expressions of freedom of speech. The ruling classes in such case proclaim a single ideology and ethos and a single rigid and orthodox hierarchy of values. No deviations from the religious or political ethos are tolerated. Any divergent expression or interpretation is called heresy or deviation. The hierarchy of values is fused with political power. Control of the ethos as well as of the entire belief system is usually exercised by a specialized institution or agency. The decisions of the latter are enforced by the government and its organs, organizations that have the legal authority to use force and violence. The Inquisition, which lasted about six hundred years, epitomizes the system we have called inquisitorial.

The Inquisition originated a historical pattern of an agency dedicated to the supervision of idea systems and religious conduct as well as of the entire field of cultural activities. Its function was to impose a single ideological-normative as well as religious pattern in all areas of cultural activity, to persecute the dissidents to the point of extermination.

This institutionalized pattern has survived to our times, but the content has changed. The system has been projected into political life, in the form of ideological monopoly and dictatorship. Its tradition continued—it may seem paradoxical—even during the French Revolution, when Jacobins instituted special committees of public salvation and administered mass terror against dissidents and what they called "enemies of the people." In our times totalitarian political parties have displaced religious hierarchies. Specialized political police—organs of repressions—displaced the Inquisition. (Incidentally, the inquisitorial political police had little if anything in common with police and its function in democratic states, for example, England.) Now the political world outlook, the political ideology, supplied a new hierarchy of values, a new ethos. The function of the new organizations of ideological "correctness" was enforcement of a new creed. The ideological content was different, of course, from the religious content of the past, but the basic social function of the institutions was not.

Tolerant and Plural State

A tolerant state secures a dominant position for a single religious or political denomination and tolerates the others. The tolerated are called "minorities." However, "majority" is tantamount above all to dominance; "minority," to subordination. The majority may in fact represent a small section of the population, governing over large numbers of a variety of ethnic and cultural groups. The political meaning of those terms is quite different from the statistical one.[1] The difference between ethnic, religious, and political toleration and pluralism is analogous to one of toleration and full religious liberty. Historically, origins of pluralism can be traced to this historical process of development (not necessarily an evolution) of religious toleration and pluralism.

Toleration here means securing conditions of existence and continuation of a minority creed, within definite limits. The dominant position is still a privilege of a single religious or political denomination. A state that requires identification with a dominant religion for admission to positions of political power, or even to administrative office, may still practice toleration toward the others.

Closely related to the tolerant state are plural states. The term *plural* can be easily confused with *pluralistic*, still both terms have been introduced and are widely used. True, it is easy to confuse the meanings, but once-accepted terms should continue.

We have defined pluralism, or pluralistic state, as a state that secures to all different cultural or ethnic groups, as well as to groups professing different normative systems, an equal access to opportunities, beginning with access to representation.

A specific kind of colonial and postcolonial societies, now states, are and were called plural. In such colonies—for example, at one time, India and Dutch Indonesia—the colonial government practiced a policy of noninterference in religious, social, and even tribal political relations. At the same time, however, the government monopolized political power. In addition, major economic resources as much as the general political power were in the hands of the ruling classes of the mother country and in control of the colonists identified with the latter. The beginnings of the plural system may be traced as far back as to the seventeenth-century Dutch colonies.[2] Here a system of relative cultural toleration was associated with a system of colonial rule and exploitation as well as social subordination.

Toleration escapes a single definition. There are various types, moreover various degrees of toleration. The state, the same group or persons, might be tolerant toward one religion or political orientation and intolerant toward others. At certain points the borderline between a tolerant state and a state that practices intolerance with restraint is rather subtle.

Ottoman Turkey was intolerant and oppressive indeed toward Armenians or Serbs, but still it practiced a modicum of toleration toward others. The Greek Orthodox church, even the office of the patriarch in Constantinople, survived half a millennium, while in Spain, Moslems and Jews were expelled or exterminated, and their once-flourishing communities disappeared. Jews in the Turkish state cherished even a measure of toleration, far more than in fifteenth- or sixteenth-century Western Europe. There was no Moslem inquisition. Still, Turkey was not a tolerant state; it was *relatively* tolerant to some and in many areas very intolerant, cruel, and oppressive. Armenians suffered persecutions and humiliation under Turkish rule; they had a full share of Ottoman intolerance and experienced not one but many holocausts.

The government may tolerate one of the dissident religions and persecute members of another one. The state may as well grant various degrees of toleration to its subjects or citizens. The Catholic Act of Toleration of the Colony of Maryland of 1649, known as the first enactment of toleration by a legislative body, granted religious freedom to all Christians who professed the faith in the Holy Trinity. Blasphemy and any offense of the Holy Trinity came, however, under the death penalty. Toleration was limited indeed. Protestants who moved to Maryland from Virginia replaced the Catholic Act of Toleration by a new one of 1654—excluding from privileges of religious toleration all the "Papists and Praelatists." The Declaration of Rights of Man of the French Revolution of 1789, a great, historical landmark of freedom, promulgated a general toleration of religious opinions; nonetheless, Catholicism was recognized as a dominant religion. Mirabeau protested against the concept of tolerance and domination and called for unlimited liberty of religion.

Thus the doctrine of religious liberty goes farther; it is a doctrine broader than toleration. According to such a doctrine, none are dominant, and members of all creeds enjoy equality, believers as well as unbelievers. All citizens enjoy equal rights, deserve equal freedom, and share equal responsibilities. Partisans of religious liberty, a doctrine of the Enlightenment, considered tolerance as an opposite of religious liberty. Those inner contradictions of the doctrine of toleration and the meaning of religious liberty were clearly expressed by Thomas Paine in his *Rights of Man*: "Toleration is not the opposite of intolerance; it is the counterfeit of it. Both are despotisms. The one assumes itself the right of withholding liberty; the other of granting it."[3]

The very concept of toleration is a historical one; it is a consequence of a long history of persecutions interrupted by short pauses of toleration, evolving at the end in the initial concept of religious liberty. Its meaning changes in this historical context. The history of the term and concept in Western civilization can be traced to periods of virtual toleration in the Roman empire, to cessation of persecutions by edicts of religious liberty.

Development of the contemporary meaning of toleration took centuries. It is rather paradoxical that the term and policy of toleration are associated with long periods of persecution. Since toleration was selective and was applied at times to some creeds, while others suffered discrimination, the dividing line between tolerance and intolerance is not necessarily always clear and sharp; to the contrary the dividing line is frequently blurred.

The idea of religious toleration and liberty is closely associated not only with political freedom but also with the general area of human rights. Hence toleration, which at the beginning was a religious doctrine and a policy of interreligious relations, has been extended to the realm of ideologies and value systems, as well as to ethnicity and race. From this broad concept of religious liberty leads the historical path to the modern doctrine of political and general pluralism.

Indifference

Indifference or neutrality toward groups of differing values is tantamount to a measure, however moderate, of toleration. Indifference means here that every group lives its own life, without interfering in the life styles of others, with no attempt to convince the neighbor that he is deadly wrong, while the group, the true believers, are absolutely right. Indifference—in its abstract definition a pattern of no relations—is a part of plural society and an ingredient of a pluralistic one. It means that we do not evaluate nor do we participate; we simply respect the right to difference.

Indifference is a general way for in- and out-groups of differing cultures to live on the same territory with little face-to-face relations, still relatively peaceful. Such is the case of American Indians sharing the same reservations—for example, Arapahoes and Shoshones on the Wind River of Wyoming, or Hopi and Navajo. In those, but not all, cases each group lives its own life within the state, and the state respects their aloofness. However, those are rather rare examples.

Religious communal conflicts in India, to mention only one example, tell a different story.

Let us add that complete self-containment of neighboring groups with no contact and relationship between them is hardly possible today.

Pluralism—General Comments

Pluralism suggests a more active and constructive answer than toleration or only passive indifference. In our inquiry into various ways the state governs societies of different cultures, norms, and ethnicity, pluralism ranks high for those who profess democratic and humanitarian values. This preference for a political system is of course a consequence of our ideological values; it is subjective.

The pluralistic pattern envisages a complementarity of major value orientations: relativistic, universal, utilitarian, and absolute. Since its major function is to integrate individuals and groups of differing ideologies, norms, ethnicity, and culture into one community or state, it carries a wide application of the relativistic view: recognition of different, even conflicting values.

In a relativistic view, values that are different than mine are not necessarily right or wrong, but they are different and related to major dominant norms of another—not my—ethos.

A society calls, however, for a set of shared norms; this is a condition of integration of the vastly different groups. Those shared values, which we have called the superethos or megaethos, are of utilitarian quality, such as the survival of mankind, or of universal, even absolute, quality, such as individual freedom and justice.

Pluralism today is primarily a cultural and political plan of complex societies of diversified ideological, cultural, ethnic, and racial groups. It means more, however. It suggests continuous choice of alternative ways. It is tantamount to social reconstruction and continuous change and experimentation with various ways and methods. It is an attitude not hesitant to commit but also to recognize an error. Hence economic pluralism means that diverse economic systems or ways have to be applied in order to attain a variety of goals. Merit and deficiency of such a method are tested by results, by efficiency in attainment of those goals.

In terms of our major theme, the various types of states could be compared and scaled not only by humanitarian and democratic values but also by levels of coercion and reduction of the latter. This scaling follows, of course, a subjective evaluation. In those terms the pluralistic state would rank highest. The inquisitorial state is ranked lowest and is followed by other patterns, as indicated in figure 17.1. The dividing line (0) runs between the tolerant state and the plural societies. The oppressive and highly coercive systems are marked with a minus sign, those permissive and liberal systems, with a plus sign.

The Origins of a Doctrine

The wider idea and concept of pluralism has been developed almost *ad oculos* during the past thirty or forty years. The doctrine originated from three major sources:

1. the democratic tradition of freedom of expression, the traditions of religious liberty and democratic society
2. pragmatic policies and problem solving of interracial and interethnic relations
3. contrast of and opposition to totalitarian systems

It was by contrast and practice, by problem solving, that the pluralistic system was tested and described, even discovered, and that later a term was attached to it. It grew from a broad and historical experience and from struggles in those large American cities, where people spoke many languages and still did not repeat the biblical story of Babylon. In spite of conflicts and differences, workers of many languages and many races built the skyscrapers of New York City and Chicago, turned out cars in Detroit, and worked together, agreed on goals and rules of conduct. The term *pluralism* was at first associated with the idea of ethnic and racial relations. It was the policy of ethnic and racial pluralism that was advocated by liberals in American cities.[4]

The practice of democratic ethnic and race relations met with historical traditions and the experience of religious liberty and toleration. Here was a well-established and accepted tradition. Attitudes were shaped in school, if not at home; the mind was trained to respect the difference or at least to respond to it with indifference. A well-established doctrine and practice in a related area of

Figure 17.1
Types of Multicultural States

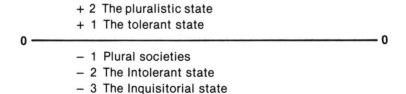

+ 2 The pluralistic state
+ 1 The tolerant state

0 ——————————————————————— 0

− 1 Plural societies
− 2 The Intolerant state
− 3 The Inquisitorial state

human relations met with new needs and responses to situations. But it was far more than practice and problem solving alone. The values, well-established norms, supplied the guiding principles, the directive-regulatory social apparatus.

At its very roots we may find a search for and a need, indeed a paramount need, for a system that would permit people of different values—creeds, views, races, nationalities, and philosophies—to keep and cultivate their identity and to live together in the same town without continuous violent confrontations. It was also a need for a system that would at least reduce discrimination against the weaker, against minorities. At the same time various ethnic and cultural groups were strong enough to claim and fight for their rights and access to political power and economic opportunities.

There is of course also a different tradition in the United States, a heritage of prejudice, discrimination, superiority and dominance of a race, and religious bigotry. But the latter does not form, at least in our times, a powerful historical current, a current of strong support of parties, government, churches, or unions.

It was the tradition of toleration and liberty that was the guiding principle.

The continuity and strength of this broad tradition appeared in the 1960s, in the civil rights movement, as well as in an ancillary and symbolic way, expressed by large sections of the population in toleration for or indifference to (without sympathy, perhaps) various cults, among them hippies and yippies, rather unusual movements of bizarre and confused young people.

The political culture of democracy, within which the concept of pluralism advanced, affected the entire doctrine. Doctrines and ideas do not advance in a vacuum. The concept and the term applied to race and ethnic relations have been extended and encompass today the entire realm of cultural, intellectual, religious, and political intergroup relations. Pluralism denotes freedom of choice of ideas and goals in politics, humanities, science, economics as well as freedom in choice of life style and values. It is tantamount to respect for difference in race, ethnicity, religion, more, to equal opportunities and rights of all.

It is in a sense an extension of democracy, but it is not necessarily identical. Freedom of choice of methods in science does not necessarily indicate that all methods and all research are equal in efficiency or relevance. Some may lead to failure; others, to discovery. Freedom of choice of life styles does not suggest that all have made an equal contribution to the common welfare. Nor does difference necessarily suggest that different things and activities are of equal social, esthetic, cultural, or scientific value.

What pluralism means is that one can practice different styles, choose different roads. On the other hand, it means also that people of different views and different religion, different race or ethnicity, should have the same rights and same opportunities, should enjoy the same respect. Minorities in such a view are not only tolerated, but are equal partners in a great social and political enterprise; they are partners as well as architects of a common national or universal culture. And indeed the great civilizations, such as the Eastern Mediterranean and the Hellenic or Hellenistic, were the fruit of meeting of many cultures, races, and ethnic groups. The originality of American civilization, witnessed in New York, is a product of the meeting of many of ethnic, racial, and cultural groups and styles. The product is not necessarily perfect, but it is creative, dynamic.

What is suggested here is a general, integral doctrine of pluralism. We have called it integral in want of a better term and in distinction of particular types of pluralism, such as ethnic or racial pluralism, which is a part of the general concept but is not identical. *Pluralism* today is an accepted term. But it encompasses a number of concepts or doctrines. Hence this distinction has to be made.

In contrast to pluralism an authoritarian ideology and its practice eliminate free intellectual choice, impose a single doctrine and at times even a single method of inquiry. Free choice and competition of ideas, life styles, cultural development, scientific inquiry, and literary and artistic creativity are displaced by a single doctrine imposed by the ruling group or political party.

The Three Related Meanings: The Doctrine

The general concept of pluralism has three related meanings. It involves doctrine, policy, and state.

All three aspects—doctrine, policy, state—are of course related and interdependent. They should be, however, distinguished. The doctrine forms the general theory, the philosophy of pluralism. Policy is concerned with courses of action and with its application in concrete problem solving, in workings of public and private institutions. Furthermore, a pluralistic state is a state in which the exercise of political power is guided by the principles of pluralistic doctrines and which has a share of institutions that make a pluralistic social system workable. (This definition will be extended later.)

The vision, the plan of a pluralistic state, and the general philosophy of pluralism correspond to a set of ideal norms, while the policies and working of the state correspond to the real, to practical expressions of the doctrine. There is of course a dichotomy between the ideal and the real, between theory and practice. The ideal is never fully expressed in actions. Theory cannot meet in all its detail the practical needs of life. Moreover, the government in its exercise of the doctrine meets with conflicting interests of groups and classes. It is also an instrument of those in power. The doctrine supplies legitimacy to their actions and interests.

At this point, however, our discussion is limited to the doctrine, not to its application and results. In its logical consequence the doctrine of pluralism leads to ethical pluralism, at least to full recognition of plurality of normative hierarchies, as we have called them, multiple vertical structures of values. There is, however, always a substantial community of shared values in a workable, pluralistic society.

The historical and philosophical roots of the doctrine reach still farther into the past, farther than our democratic traditions, and there we shall find its ancient beginnings and deeper roots, long before the term and practice appeared in our times. The history of political thought, since the early Hellenic times, moves between the dilemma of the individual and the collective, the person and the state. At times the two ends seem to be opposed, while in interpretation of other philosophers they are complementary.[5] Theories shifted at one time toward a higher value of the individual, then moved again in assigning the supreme values to the collective. "The sense of the value of the individual," argued Barker, "was the primary condition of development of political thought in Greece."[6] It is in this concern for the right and position of the individual, for the person, which appears in Western political thinking, that the supreme values and ancient origins of pluralism (at least the philosophical origins) can be identified. This preoccupation with the place and the rights of the person, not only with the exercise of power of the ruler or the state, follows the entire history of the idea and philosophy of natural law, branches off in many directions, sooner or later serves as legitimation or rationalization of limitation of power of the king, eventually of any government.

The centrality of an individual appears also as a later development of the political and philosophical perception of ends and means. In the Oriental theories the ruler and the state, his welfare and power, appear as a prevailing end. The subjects are means toward this end. However, another, even more powerful orientation appears especially in the Anglo-American political tradition and philosophy. In such a perception the state becomes a means; a person and his associations, his society, are the end. In organistic sociological theories as well as in philosophies of totalitarianism, the state, the collective, continues to be a supreme end.

A good society, or what we call one, is built on the proper balance of those two seemingly polar values.

Doctrine: Privacy and the Limitation of Power

Pluralism—with its theme of the right of the individual to be different, to cherish ideas of his own, to make his own choice, and (what was paramount later in the struggle for religious liberty) the right to an honest error—is just a continuous tradition, dialogue, and struggle. All those expressions of freedom are related to this sense of the value of individuals.

But this freedom of choice and difference is also a consequence of the limitation of political power of the state and government. Without the latter the full dignity of the person and his freedom of choice cannot be expressed. It is not accidental that the idea and practice of political freedom and of political, ethnic, religious, and cultural pluralism have advanced primarily among those nations that originally developed the concepts and tradition of the limitation of power.

The limitation of power reduces the area within which the state can exercise coercion. This in turn leads to the development of the concept of privacy. The recognition of privacy is tantamount to the recognition of the right to difference. Privacy means that not only is a definite area of activities of an individual or group exempt from state interference, but also a certain space is private, that is, controlled solely by an individual and his associations. The state can interfere in this area only in case of violation of laws. Individuals and associations are otherwise free to follow their life styles, to cherish their values.

Pluralism calls not only for social proximity but also for a measure of social distance. This is expressed in a modicum of benign indifference toward the out-group and in respect for individual and group privacy. The idea, the norm, of privacy protects a person and a group from interference not only of the state but also of other individuals and groups in their capacity as private persons. This protection and exemption extend to the entire private space or territory. No private person, group, or public agency can intrude into space protected by the norms of privacy. In a despotic state laws do not secure any area of privacy or limits to exercise of power by the ruler.

Doctrine: State and Society

According to Barker, the state is legally organized in assuming "aspects of a single association ... for the single purpose of making and enforcing a permanent system of law and order." The society, however, is socially organized, in groups and associations that follow different social goals, different impulses.[7]

Those associations have many goals and, as we have already argued, many normative systems. Here the distinction has to be made between the state and society. Pluralism postulates the right of the individual and his association to difference, to different normative systems, life styles, and goals.

A democratic state divides the space of activities into public and private. The public space is defined, and all the rest belongs to free exercise of the right of persons and free associations. Here, of course, pluralism is only an expression of a rational, democratic state.

Pluralism is not a plan for a society free of conflicts. To the contrary, tensions and non-violent conflicts or oppositions of goals and conduct are a normal social experience. However, the problem of resolution and reduction of such tensions is paramount—and the way they are managed is subject to the rules of the game, to the procedures accepted by vast majorities.

Without a spontaneous acceptance of rules of procedure and without common core or paramount values a pluralistic society is unable to function. It is reduced to a paralyzed or disorderly state. Historical experience tells us, however, that many nations did not display in the past a capacity for such a spontaneous agreement on goals, values, procedures, rights, and issues.

Doctrine: Conditions of a Working Pluralism

The doctrine, however, extends beyond the vision or the plan of a pluralistic state. It is both wider and narrower, for pluralism can be practiced by a city, by a province, by a state. But it can also be supernational, and a vision of a pluralistic community may as well encompass large sections, even all, of mankind.

The size of the group, what we may call horizontal dimensions, both in terms of territory as well as of society, affects the doctrine and practice. The shared and different norms call for flexibility. They have to be adjusted to different realities, since they respond to different needs and are articulations of different cultural associations.

Pluralism calls for a proper balance between difference and unity, between norms that differ and those which are shared; in practice, between groups whose conduct and norms are different and those broader associations within which they have to share common rules and norms. Without a set of shared norms and rules of procedures a pluralistic system will not work.

Hence the working of a pluralistic system on any level, city, state, or supernational, calls for:

1. recognition of the right to and respect for different norms, culture, and goals
2. a set of accepted and shared norms (a superethos or megaethos)
3. acceptance of the rules of the game and of proper procedure
4. legitimacy of norms of a pluralistic state

What we discuss first is a doctrine of integral pluralism. At the very beginning particular types of pluralism were differentiated from the integral one. We shall return to the particular types later. However, the integral pluralism encompasses a wide area of individual and group activities and conduct. One of its attributes, a major attribute, is the right to difference, the right to cherish values and norms of one's own choosing, to follow a way of life one prefers within the limits of public order. It can be also expressed in positive ways.

Pluralism postulates political equality of all members of a community or society, of all creeds, political orientations, philosophies, ethic and racial groups. Furthermore, at least as an ideal norm, it postulates equal access to opportunities and power. Pluralism is articulated in the right of an individual to choose his own way of life, the right to enjoy the freedom of his views, to cherish a culture, religion, or a philosophy of his own choosing, to form associations and communities of those who have similar needs and views. Hence pluralism is expressed in the right of individuals and groups to form communities of different value systems, different normative orientations, as long as they do not harm or affect the rights of others. America of the mid-nineteenth century had its Catholic monastic communities next to Shakers, Amish, and Hutterites; it had its socialist utopian colonies next to lodges of all kinds, including the Ku Klux Klan.

Second, a pluralistic society, on the other hand, cannot exist without a set of common norms of conduct and common rules shared and accepted by vast majorities of individuals and groups. Without such collective symbols, ideas, goals, and rules society cannot be simply formed; it is a condition of social cohesion and of a minimum of social control, without which no social group nor society can operate, save a utopia.

A pluralistic state has a certain, even limited, set of common norms, an ethos. In a wider pluralistic society, or a community of nations, the set of common values megaethos is more limited than in a nation; it is solely elementary, basic, but at the same time it embraces wider areas and larger groups. We have called such an ethos a megaethos, as distinct from a superethos of a more limited general code of a nation.

In a pluralistic society the size of the group determines not only the nature of shared values but also the extent of social control, the extent of conduct subject to such common norms. A hypothesis may be suggested that the larger the group within such a pluralistic system, the narrower and more limited is the set of shared values, the more limited and less effective is the voluntary (informal) social control within such a system. The number and extent of norms of a megaethos, of a value system that embraces several nations or is planned for the mankind (for example, the United Nations charter) are less extensive than a set of shared norms necessary to keep working effectively a state that practices pluralistic policies.

The norms of a megaethos that is universal, that embraces many cultures and nations, are above all basic, elementary. This may be noticed in major declaratory statements of norms, whether of universal religions, such as Christianity, or in a secular sense, in the various international declarations of human rights.

Third, next to an accepted general code of norms (a superethos or a megaethos) a pluralistic pattern calls for a common set of rules of procedure, the rules of the game, which are accepted and observed by individuals and groups. Those rules deal with a vast area of individual and group activities. Relevant, however, are rules pertaining to resolution of tension and conflict. The rules of the game are not necessarily laws, as the procedures are, but they may be customs and usages such as negotiations, arbitrations, and mediations of conflicts, general principles of fact finding, and, above all, acceptance of a dialogue and exchange of views and opinions, respect for disagreement.

Relations and conflicts between differing interest groups, different parties and ideological movements, are channelled through those nonviolent procedures.

In sports the rules of the game are explicit. They form a condition of a successful game. Two competing teams are in a quasi-conflict. Still they follow the rules, and without the latter there is no game.

A pluralistic plan can be played the same, and it works only when the rules and usages are acknowledged and followed.

Pluralism has its limits, its boundaries. The normative boundaries that separate this system from others are established by the core values, the superethos or megaethos, and by the procedures and rules of the game. Not all can be defined, indeed. A wide freedom in expression of difference is an essential condition of pluralism; in fact it defines pluralism. The question, however, is how wide? It is not unlimited as far as *action* is concerned. Groups organized with the single purpose of destruction of the elementary freedoms of a pluralistic society hardly fit within such boundaries of pluralism. They may express their view, but a pluralistic state cannot tolerate or submit to their attacks and subjugation. A world association that professes a modicum of pluralism can hardly tolerate membership of a nation that practices genocide of those who profess a different religion or simply of those who disagree with the ideas of the government.

Extreme egoistic and libertarian ideas, such as Max Stirner's individualistic anarchism expressed in his *Ego and His Own*, can be expressed but hardly practiced. When Stirner argues "I do not want the liberty of men nor their equality. I want only my power over them. I want to make them my property, material for enjoyment," then of course someone must pay with his total submission for Stirner's unlimited freedom, which becomes a license.[8]

No society can function without some kind of social control, and thus far no man can survive unprotected by the state. The Marquis de Sade suggested a society entirely free from social control and laws, a utopia of unlimited freedom and license for some and of total submission for others. His utopia suggested a society with laws "so mild and few, that all men, whatever their character might easily obey them."[9] Only one of his reforms deserved respect: abolition of the death penalty. However, in de Sade's utopian society murder, theft, and rape were permitted, even enjoyed. Special provision, suggested de Sade, should be made to force the women to submit to the will and whim of citizens of this paradise republic. De Sade's utopia is in fact a vision of a tyranny of few.

A distinction between word and action is seminal. In a democratic society, and a pluralistic one belongs in this category, the word is free unless it directs criminal action in a concrete, present situation, unless it directs others to kill and enslave, as Amin did.

Fourth, a pluralistic community, whether a state or a larger association of nations, is a free community. In consequence, the exercise of power calls for a spontaneous or voluntary acceptance of legitimacy of those norms by large majorities, not solely by the ruling classes. This legitimacy is at first formulated by the representatives of the community. Legitimacy is a set of values, a doctrine that forms the real basis or only rationalization of the exercise of power.

A pluralistic state, at least a state of integral pluralism, cannot be imposed from above by a minority, a ruling group, by force and coercion. This contradicts its very nature. Pluralism calls for voluntary or spontaneous acceptance from below, by large sections of citizens. It calls for an honest legitimacy, principles which on one hand bind the power of the government and on the other values exercised by the latter in practice, in everyday life.

In absence of such an agreement a pluralistic state cannot function. Not all societies have values and institutions favoring pluralism. But values and institutions can be constructed. This is, however, a new and a difficult theme.

Particular Ethnic and Religious Pluralisms

We have outlined a doctrine of what was called integral pluralism. Particular types of pluralism differ, however, from the former. Ethnic pluralism, even in its affirmative form, does not necessarily secure a broad freedom of choice and expression of different political, ideological, or religious orientations. Stalin's nationality policy was a combination of ruthless persecutions and a modicum of ethic pluralism, paradoxical as it may seem. Ancient Tatar tribes, as well as other nationalities, were torn from their ancestral lands and deported to distant provinces during and after World War II. Stalin's was an inquisitorial state that did not tolerate any departure, any deviation from the set party line. In such a political climate there was still some sort of ethnic pluralism and equality in this inequality, since Russians have suffered too or even more. Ethnic cultures and folklore were tolerated and supported, alphabets for various languages developed, and literature in native languages supported, as long as the authors and actors were in agreement with the official policy and doctrine. But anything, even innovative trends in music considered as different, not in accord with the official doctrine of socialist realism, were not only risky, but subject to repression. Ethnic pluralism, narrowed solely to a bare ethnicity reduced to language and folklore, is not tantamount to a broad freedom of choice, the right to difference. It may be practiced even in a tyranny.

A certain measure of religious pluralism may be practiced by a military dictatorship or by an autocratic ruler. Some of the Latin American dictatorships tolerated a modicum of religious freedom. Somosa in Nicaragua did not persecute religious dissidents; Protestants could practice their religion. The shah of Iran and his regime practiced religious toleration, secured freedom of worship for various denominations, did not persecute Christians or Jews, employed the Bahais in his government. The same governments, however, did not respect political freedoms and human rights, norms essential in an integral pluralistic doctrine and practice.

Pluralistic Policies

Seldom do the ideal norms merge with the real. What ought to be is near to or distant from what is. However, the distance between the two orders of norms—the ideal and the real—varies; the practice might be closer to the ideal plan or to solely a distant social myth. Policies bring down a theoretical plan for a society to the practical level; they form the bridge.

During the past decade the quest for ethnic and racial pluralism in the United States has been articulated in what was called affirmative action. By means of affirmative action an attempt was made to close the distance between the ideal norm and reality, to bridge the hiatus between declarations—rhetorics—and facts.

Policies were applied in order to affirm by hard facts the principle of equality of opportunity and equal representation. The practice of equal opportunities is affirmed by employment of minorities in various fields and by securing for the latter participation and representation, especially in those branches of industry and government where they were not equally represented before, where they were even excluded or at best tolerated. An effort was made to close the gap between the normative and pragmatic boundaries of policies, to apply the normative imperatives, the values of equality of opportunity.

The policy of affirmative action led to inner contradictions as well as to contradictions between the normative and pragmatic imperatives: ideological, political principles on one hand and efficiency and practical imperatives on the other.

The Pluralistic State

After discussion of the doctrine and the policies, we are arriving at the problem of a pluralistic state by the back door. Major premises or conditions of such a polity were already outlined. The elements for definition are here. However, at this point a question has to be asked again: What are the major objectives of a pluralistic plan, of a pluralistic society and state? The pluralistic state today is above all a democratic state, a state of the basic representative institutions, with the elementary safeguards of the rights of citizens and, in consequence, provisions for limitation of power. Pluralism is an articulation of democracy, we may suggest here but it is in itself a broadening of the democratic system. A democratic state may well function within the limits of toleration. A pluralistic state is broader than a tolerant one. The legitimacy of its power is based on an assumption that the state consists of many different groups, different in ethnicity, race, values, creeds, and ideologies, and that all of them are equal partners; they are not simply tolerated by the majority. This is of course a set of ideal values. This is a simple answer to the question: How should various cultures and ethnic groups relate to each other, and what are conditions of management of a multicultural state?

Hence the pluralistic state is one that applies such a doctrine by means of policies and meets the four conditions necessary for its working: respect for different norms and cultures; a set of shared values, a superethos accepted by large sections of the citizen; shared rules of procedures and rules of the game; and last but not least, proper legitimacy.

Here pluralism calls for recognition of a set of norms that has an absolute or universal quality in a democracy: human rights, freedom of expression and association, to mention only some; on the other hand, a pluralistic state follows a substantial share of a relativistic doctrine, since those who administer the state recognize vast cultural differences, differences in conduct of the citizen, the right to be different. The government exercises authority in a way that those various groups can cherish their cultures, can safely practice their way of life.

Is then a pluralistic state necessarily one of very limited areas of activity, since a wide area of activity is left uncontrolled and is a domain of privacy of citizens? The state has, however, many functions. We have limited our discussion to problems concerning a multicultural state, the problem of its relations to this multitude of groups and multiplicity of value orientations and needs. This does not mean at all that the state should withdraw from those activities that contribute to the well-being of its citizens, that are necessary to maintain a viable and working economy that could meet the needs of the citizen. Since the superethos of a pluralistic state is founded on democratic and humanitarian principles, it is its prerogative to assist and protect its citizens if such a need arises. Whenever the representatives of the voters agree that there is a need for public intervention or planning action, the state is of course an instrument that will be used for such objectives.

Nonetheless, it is a state of many goals. Therefore, in terms of economic activity the state provides conditions within which a variety of alternative economic systems or methods can operate, a variety of economic goals can be met.

Universal Pluralism

Pluralism is a plan for a variety of levels: a city, a state, or far wider areas, which may encompass sections or all of mankind as a universal principle or doctrine. Perhaps it never will be as broad. Nonetheless, in terms of a vision, a plan, there is the problem of a vast mankind of many cultures, value orientations, ideologies, interests, and goals and the imperative of living together and, today, of preserving the very nature of this globe. All those levels bear a certain similarity; in all cases the problem is one of unity and difference.

Although mankind consists of this great variety of cultures, there is a unity of mankind. There are needs and corresponding sentiments and values that create this unity.

Here we have to return to our discussion of the complementarity of the four value orientations.

Universal pluralism, which embraces many nations, many cultures, calls for a minimum set of common norms, a megaethos that could integrate or associate the variety, the multiplicity of ideological and cultural orientations. This megaethos, which consists of core values, generalized symbols universally known and shared by large sections of the population, forms this minimum set of norms, of a working pluralistic system. The quality of this general code depends on its ability to adjust to and reinterpret within the continuously changing situation. Hence flexibility is its major merit: flexibility and sensitivity toward difference, toward a different outlook.

The first question to be asked concerning the dominant, core values of a megaethos of mankind is, of course, this: What is the central value of such a wide directive and regulatory system?

Today in this nuclear age the paramount norm of mankind, the top priority, is obvious—a realistic and radically utilitarian one: survival of mankind and preservation of our earth and nature. But survival as a central norm harbors other values of equal relevance: human life and welfare. Because of our concern for human life and our concern for welfare, survival is this major issue. Our concern for human life and welfare, in a universal sense, is not limited to a single group or ethnicity. It is a wide concept of everybody's life. And welfare, on the world scale, suggests active assistance, active help, not compassion alone. Welfare is not solely an abstract concept; it has a practical meaning, expressed in active mutual aid and altruism. Hence altruism in a broad sense, in terms of mankind, in terms of helping those who are needy in distant continents, becomes a derived norm, derived from the utilitarian. However, altruism by itself has both absolute and universal qualities. And this assistance to distant nations, people who suffer hunger or persecution, is not necessarily utilitarian. Helping the hungry and destitute in Somali has no immediate utilitarian meaning for those young men and women from England, the United States, Germany, or other countries who volunteer and work in adverse, often dangerous conditions. This disinterested, sincere idealism should not be underestimated or ignored, simply because it cannot be interpreted in terms of a recognized theory. But are those concepts of such a universal altruism shared or even accepted by all?

I cannot prove in a scientific way their veracity. Moreover, veracity is not a proper term in this case. At this point my views were normative; in a sense, prescriptive. I do accept those core values of altruism—freedom and justice, respect for life—as absolute; without such acceptance no general directive and regulatory system of such broad dimensions, no ethics, can be constructed. Hence the absolute viewpoint, with its flexibility is complemented by a relativistic and universal viewpoint.

Conflicts of Interests and Values

Not all political orientations and ideologies lend themselves to a pluralistic society, which after all works by means of dialogue, negotiations, compromise, and agreement which resolves conflicts possibly by nonviolent means.

Interests of groups, class interests, differences in ideologies and norms can be clear and sharp to the point that a common ethos and procedures, conditions of pluralism, are neither accepted nor workable. Polarization of values and interests may lead to separatism or conflict.

Social and economic inequality, profound class divisions, and strong disparity of income are incompatible with a working democracy and with a pluralistic society. Pluralism calls for a measure of economic democracy and social justice.

Conflict and conflicting goals are a part of modern and working society. They reflect different values, different interests, different orientations. Conflicts are not necessarily destructive. Social conflicts today and in past history were also processes of constructive change, of emancipation of slaves and serves, of advancement of the working class. They will not disappear; moreover, their total disappearance suggests a passive society or a totalitarian one, which quells all symptoms of opposition by means of violence.

A working democracy as well as a working pluralistic society calls, however, for skills in conflict resolution, skills in rational and peaceful articulation of disagreements as well in arriving at an agreement. Hence it calls for a continuous and calm dialogue.

There is no perfect society. Still, without a distant image mankind does not move. A vision of a perfect pluralistic and democratic society is an ideal, a vision and an image of a perfect pluralism that has utopian qualities. But not solely.

Pluralism is also and above all a guideline for policies that were after all expressed so many times in practical reforms and projects in this and other countries. It is a guideline for a society that respects the differences but still can share common interests and values, and one that is able with all its disagreements and conflicts to work and prosper together.

Notes

1. For more about political power and ethnic minorities see F. Gross, *Ethnics in a Borderland* (Westport, Conn. and London: Greenwood Press, 1978), pp. 133 ff.; also Anna Maria Boileau and Emidio Sussi, *Dominanza e Minorzanze* (Udine: Editrice Grillo, 1981), "Dominanza e Minoranze: L'Assimetria del Potere," pp. 23 ff.

2. J. S. Furnivall in his study of Burma and Netherlands India introduced the term and concept of plural societies. See *Colonial Policy and Practice* (New York: New York University Press, 1956), pp. 303 ff., 313 ff.

It seems to me that the very nature of colonial economy of the sixteenth- and seventeenth-century trading companies favored a plural economy and a plural society. First, those traders were too weak at that time to force full domination on the native peoples. But Protestant and democratic traditions of the Dutch way have contributed to a plural philosophy.

A "dual economy," coexistence of capitalistic and noncapitalistic, was already introduced into Netherlands India by Jan Pieterszoon Coen (seventeenth century). George Masselmann, *The Cradle of Colonialism* (New Haven: Yale University Press, 1961), p. 412. Once a pattern is set, it guides the development of social relations and institutions. A dual economy is, after all, a base of a plural society.

For a discussion of plural societies and pluralism see Leo Kuper and M. G. Smith, *Pluralism in Africa* (Berkeley and Los Angeles: University of California Press, 1971), "Plural Societies," pp. 7 ff., and "Institutional and Political Conditions of Pluralism," pp. 27 ff. Also see Crawford Young, *The Politics of Cultural Pluralism* (Madison: University of Wisconsin Press, 1979).

3. J. B. Bury, *A History of Freedom of Thought* (London: Williams & Norgate, 1925), pp. 97, 111, 113 ff., on the concept and history of toleration, see chap. 5, "Religious Toleration," pp. 92–127.

4. Literature on ethnic pluralism is quite extensive in American sociology and anthropology. However, the two different concepts of plural societies and pluralism are at times blurred, sometimes confused.

5. It seems to me that Ernest Barker mentions in his work the opposed concepts of individual and collective and that it is his view that the history of Greek political philosophy moves between those two values. I was, however, unable to locate the correct source, although I have retraced my reading. It might have been in his *Greek Political Theory* [1918] (New York: Barnes & Noble, 1960) or in *Principles of Social and Political Theory* [1952] (Oxford: Oxford University Press, 1967).

6. Barker, *Greek Political Theory*, p. 2.

7.   Barker, *Principles of Political Theory*, pp. 40 ff.

8.   Max Stirner, *The Ego and His Own*, ed. and introduced by John Cazzoll (New York: Harper & Row, 1971), p. ii.

9. De Sade, ''A Bedroom Discourse,'' in Frank E. Manuel and Fritzie P. Manuel, eds. *French Utopias and Ideal Societies: An Anthology* (New York: Free Press, 1968), pp. 220 ff.

Bibliography

Note

If one should see in a bibliography only a careful listing of books and other publications that were directly quoted or used in this volume, then this is definitely not the case or only part of it.

Many of the publications listed here were not consulted for this volume; some may advance views and theories to some extent indifferent or even adverse to those suggested by the author. Conversely, many sources used by the author and quoted in the footnotes are not listed in this bibliography.

Then what was the purpose of this bibliography?

To begin with, this list is focused primarily on values and ideologies. Most of historical sources or documents used in this volume and referred to in footnotes—concerning, for example, time span or architectural projects—are not listed. Furthermore, in spite of the fact that specific chapters deal with planning and strategy, this literature, quoted in footnotes has not been included, with the sole exception of the last book by Liddell-Hartt, a worthy representative of this field indeed.

Those fields have their own and extensive literature, and planning and strategy have been considered in this study in terms of goals and norms. To include even some of the literature of those disciplines would expand the size of this list beyond the intentions of the publishers and the author. The major problem was to keep the bibliography within manageable limits.

The purpose of this bibliography is in part to list publications and sources consulted or referred to but also to indicate the range of interest as well as type of contributions in sociological and related studies of values and ideologies.

It was not the purpose of the author to present a survey of theories; a bibliography—so I hope—reflects this wide range of interest in the field of values.

Some of the publications could not be located in libraries I have been working in, but were mentioned or quoted, and I have considered them as relevant for such bibliography. Others I could locate in *Sociological Abstracts* or in similar sources. Still others I found in bibliographies and catalogues. My European colleague wrote me about titles that I could not find in New York libraries, but I trust Dr. Friedrichs's judgment. His own bibliography was an important and useful guide.

The literature of the subject is very extensive. It was not an easy choice. The first bibliography was revised, extended, and again reduced. This is a third version. The bibliography had to be kept within the limits.

The concept of values and related theories crosses the disciplinary boundaries. In spite of the sociological focus of this study, at times the boundaries had to be crossed too. Disciplinary, dividing lines are not tight. Furthermore, a rigid approach is neither possible nor productive.

Hence this related literature had to be reflected in a bibliography, since the purpose of the latter was also to give a sense of the broad ramifications. There is a certain contradiction, I admit, between the purposes of narrowing the field and at the same time relating to other areas. Space imposes further limitation. An adequate, comprehensive bibliography of this subject matter would necessitate a small volume. Choice had to be exercised in a specific way. Hence at times a relevant trend and work of a school had to be reduced to two or three representatives: for example, the Viennese school of values has been reduced to works of Brentano and Ehrenfels; the positivists, to Schlick. The work of those schools has not been directly applied in this volume. On the other hand, an anthropological field study of a subarctic fishing community, although seemingly distant, has been included. The findings, that the value system and not solely the environment affects the entire economy of the natives, concur with my earlier study of a fisherman community in Maine.

In consequence, by including some rather specialized monographs this bibliography may omit some of the major contributions that shall appear, however, in some of the quoted volumes.

Preference was given to the theoretical work. While the wide field of quantitative and public opinion studies has been greatly reduced, again it is a field of its own.

The choice as always is arbitrary to a point. The reader may excuse the omissions and shortcomings of judgment.

It was indeed difficult to drop a title of a known work. I looked at the worn-out index cards at the New York Public Library, pondering how much work was behind those few lines, behind those terse and modest titles of volumes. Thus productive authors of many volumes and monographs are represented only with one or very few entries.

Then, the reader may ask, why has this writer listed so many of his own contributions?

This volume is based on work that stretches over decades and is reflected in those listed publications, which were either used in or even incorporated into this volume. It is a matter of integrity to indicate that sections of this volume and ideas of once-published work appear here in an organized and revised way.

No one realizes more than the author the shortcomings. But after four or more months of choice and revisions, one has to stop and simply say, We have to stop here. Dates of available or recent editions are given.

Abel, Theodore. *"Verstehen I and Verstehen II." Theory and Decision*, February 1975.

Adams, G. P.; Loewenberg, J.; and Pepper, S. C., eds. *Studies in the Problem of Norms.* Berkeley: University of California Press, 1925.

Adkins, A. W. H. *Moral Values and Political Behavior in Ancient Greece.* New York: W. W. Norton, 1972.

Adler, Franz. "The Value Concept in Sociology." *American Journal of Sociology*, November 1956.

Adler, Mortimer. *The Time of Our Lives.* New York: Holt & Rinehart, 1970.

Albert, Ethel M., and Kluckhohn, C. *A Selected Bibliography on Values, Ethics and Esthetics*. Glencoe, Ill.: Free Press, 1959.

Albert, Hans. "Theodor Geiger's Wert Nihilismus." *Kölner Zeitschrift für Soziologie und Sozialpsychologie*, 1955.

Allport, Gordon. *Personality*. New York: Henry Holt, 1937.

Allport, Gordon; Vernon, P. E.; and Lindzey, G. *A Study of Value*, [1951]. Rev. ed. Boston: 1960.

Apter, David E., ed. *Ideology and Discontent*. New York: Free Press, 1964.

Aquaviva, Sabino S. "Crise des Valeurs et des Significations de l'Existence dans la Société Italienne Contemporaine." *Cahiers Internationeaux de Sociologie*, July–December, 1977.

Aron, Raymond. "L'Idéologie, Support Nécessaire de l'Action." *Res Publica*, 1960.

Aschenbrenner, Karl. *The Concept of Values*. Dodrecht: D. Reidel, 1971.

Ashley, Montagu, Francis M. *The Humanization of Man*. Cleveland: World Publishing Co, 1962.

———. *On Being Human*. London: Abelard-Schuman, 1957.

Ashmore, Jerome. "Three Aspects of *Weltanschauung*." *Sociological Quarterly*, 1966.

Ayab, Eliezer B. "Value Systems and Economic Development in Japan and Thailand." *Journal of Social Issues*, January 1963.

Baier, Kurt, and Rescher, Nicholas, eds. *Values and the Future: The Impact of Technological Change on American Values*. New York: Free Press, 1971.

Bandini, Luigi. *Uomo e Valore*. Turin: Einaudi, 1949.

Bandis, Panos, "Absolute Values in a Changing Universe." *Social Science*, Spring 1977.

Barker, Ernest. *Greek Political Theory*. New York: Barnes & Noble, 1960.

Barnsley, John H. "On the Sociology of Values: Patterns of Research." *American Sociological Review*, May 1972.

Baum, Reiner. "Values and Democracy in Imperial Germany." *Sociological Inquiry*, September 1968.

Beck, Ulrich. "Soziologische Normativität." *Kölner Zeitschrift für Soziologie und Sozialpsychologie*, June 1972.

Becker, Howard. *Through Values to Social Interpretation*. Durham, N.C.: Duke University Press, 1950.

Bell, Daniel. *The End of Ideology*. Glencoe, Ill.: Free Press, 1960.

Belshaw, Cyril S. "The Identification of Values in Anthropology." *American Journal of Sociology*, May 1959.

Bendix, Reinhard. "The Age of Ideology: Persistent and Changing." In David E. Apter, ed., *Ideology and Discontent*. New York: Free Press, 1964.

———. "Industrialization, Ideologies and Social Structure." *American Sociological Review*, October 1959.

Benedict, Ruth. *Patterns of Culture*. New York: Houghton Mifflin, 1934.

Berger, Peter, and Luckman, Thomas. *The Social Construction of Reality*. Garden City, N.Y.: Doubleday, 1966.

Berket, Fikret. "Fishery Resource Use in a Subarctic Indian Community." *Human Ecology*, 1977.

Beteille, André. "Ideologies: Commitment and Partisanship." *L'Homme*, July–December 1978.

Bidwell, Charles E. "Norms and Integration of Complex Social Systems." *Sociological Quarterly*, 1966.

Boodin, J. E. "Value and Social Interpretations." *American Journal of Sociology*, vol. 24, 1915.

Bouglé, Celestin Ch. A. *The Evolution of Values*. New York: Holt, 1926.

Brentano, Franz. *The Foundation and Construction of Ethics*. New York: Humanities Press, 1973.

Brown, D. Mackenzie. *The White Umbrella: Indian Political Thought from Manu to Gandhi*. Berkeley: University of California Press, 1959.

Bryson, Lyman; Finkelstein, Louis; Hoagland, Hudson; and MacIver, R. M., eds. *Symbols and Society*. New York: Harper, 1955.

Bücher, Karl. *Arbeit und Rhythmus*. Leipzig: Hirzel, 1897.

Bukharin, Nikolai T. *Historical Materialism*. New York: International Publishers, 1925.

Bulateo, Rev. Jaime. "Philippine Values: The Manileno's Mainsprings." *Philippine Sociological Review*, January–April 1962.

Bury, J. B. *A History of Freedom of Thought*. London: Williams & Norgate, 1925.

————. *The Idea of Progress*. New York: Dover, 1952.

Calegari, Paolo. "Problemi Umani Comuni E Funzione dei Valori." *Critica Sociologica*, Autumn 1975.

Calogero, Guido. *Filosofia del Dialogo*. Milan: Edizioni Di Communità, 1962.

Candill, William, and Scarr, Harry. "Japanese Value Orientation and Culture Change." *Ethnology*, January 1962.

Carter, Roy E., Jr. "An Experiment in Value Measurement." *American Sociological Review*, April 1956.

Cassirer, Ernst. *The Philosophy of Enlightenment*. Princeton: Princeton University Press, 1951.

Castel Franchi, Christiano. "Scopi Externi" [External Goals]. *Rassegna Italiana di Sociologia*. July–September 1981.

Catton, W. R., Jr. "A Retest of Measurability of Certain Human Values." *American Sociological Review*, June 1956.

————. "A Theory of Value." *American Sociological Review*, June 1959.

Cesari, Paul. *La Valeur*. Paris: Presses Universitaires de France, 1957.

Chevalier, J. J. "La Naissance des Idéologies." *Res Publica*, 1960.

Cicero. *De Finibus Bonorum et Malorum*. trans. H. Rakham. Cambridge: Harvard University Press, 1967.

Connor, John W. "Value Continuities and Change in Three Generations of Japanese Americans." *Ethos*, 1974.

————. "Persistence and Change in Japanese American Value Orientation." *Ethos*, 1976.

Constantelos, Demetrios J. *Byzantine Philanthropy and Social Welfare*. New Brunswick, N.J.: Rutgers University Press, 1968.

Cowell, F. R. *Values in Human Society*. New York: Horizon Books, 1970.

Cuber, John Kenkel, William F.; and Harper, Robert A. *Problems of American Society: Values in Conflict*. New York: Holt, Rinehart & Winston: 1964.

Cunov, Heinrich. *Die Marxsche Geschichts, Gesellschafts und Staatstheorie: Grundzüge der Marxchen Soziologie*. Berlin: Vorwärts, 1920–1921.

Dewey, John. *Theory of Valuation*. Chicago: University of Chicago Press, 1939.

Dilthey, Wilhelm. *Weltanschauungslehre, Abhandlungen für Philosophie der Philosophie*. Góttingen: Teubner, 1960.

————. *Gesammelte Schriften*. 10 vols. Stuttgart: Teubner, 1965–1973.

Diquatro, Arthur W. "*Verstehen* as an Empirical Concept." *Sociology and Social Research*, October 1972.

Diwald, Helmut. *Wilhelm Dilthey Erkenntnistheorie und Philosophie der Geschichte.* Göttingen: Musterschmidt, 1963.

Dodd, S. C. "How to Measure Values." *Research Studies of the State College of Washington*, vol. 18, 1950.

————. "On Classifying Human Values; A Step in the Prediction of Human Valuing." *American Sociological Review*, vol. 16, 1951.

Domanski, Juliusz. *Poczatki Humanizmu* [Beginnings of Humanism]. Wroclaw-Warsaw: Polska Akademia Nauk, 1982.

Du Bois, Cora. "The Dominant Value Profile of American Culture." *American Anthropologist*, December 1955.

Durkheim, Emile. *The Elementary Forms of Religious Life.* New York: Collier, 1961.

Dworak, Max. *Idealism and Naturalism in Gothic Art.* Notre Dame, Ind.: University of Notre Dame Press, 1967.

Edel, Abraham. *Ethical Judgment: The Use of Science in Ethics.* New York: Free Press of Glencoe, 1955.

Ehrenfels, Christian von. *System der Werttheorie.* Vol. 1, *Allgemeing Werttheorie, Psychologie des Begehrens*; vol. 2, *Grundzuge Einer Ethik.* Leipzig: O. R. Reisland, 1897, 1898.

Elbing, Alvar O. *The Value Issue of Ethics.* New York: McGraw-Hill, 1967.

Engels, Friedrich. *Dialectics of Nature.* Moscow: Foreign Languages Publishing House, 1954.

Fallding, H. "A Proposal for the Empirical Study of Value." *American Sociological Review*, vol. 30, 1965.

Farrington, Benjamin. *Greek Science.* Harmondsworth, England: Penguin, 1949.

Febleman, J. K. "Toward an Analysis of the Basic Value Systems." *American Anthropologist*, vol. 56, 1954.

Ferrarotti, Franco. "L'Ideologia del Progresso e la Prospectiva Individualistica." *Rassegna Italiana di Sociologia*, April–June 1962.

————. *Max Weber e il Destino della Ragione.* Bari: Laterza, 1971.

————. *Una Teologia Per Atei.* Bari: Laterza, 1984.

Feuer, Lewis. "The Sociology of Philosophic Ideas." *Pacific Sociological Review*, Fall 1958.

Findlay, John W. *Values and Intentions.* London: Allen & Unwin, 1961.

Fischer, Claude S. "The Effect of Urban Life on Traditional Values." *Social Forces*, 1975.

Fischer, Joseph, "Die Philosophie der Werte Bei Wilhelm Windelband und Heinrich Rickert." *Beitrage zur Geschichte der Philosophie des Mittelalters*, Supplementband, Münster, 1913. No. 1, p. 449–66.

Foss, Jeffrey. "A Rule of Minimal Rationality: The Logical Link between Beliefs and Values." *Inquiry*, Autumn 1976.

Fotia, Manzo. "Ideologies et Elites Contemporaines." *L'Homme et la Société*, July–September 1967.

Fouillée, Alfred. *L'Evolutionisme des Idées-Forces.* Paris, Alcan: 1890.

————. *Le Socialisme et La Sociologie Reformiste.* Paris: Alcan, 1930.

Fraser, J. T. *Of Time, Passion and Knowledge.* New York: Braziller, 1975.

Fraser, J. T., ed. *The Voices of Time.* New York: Braziller, 1968.

Freisitzer, Kurt. "Soziale Normen und Rechts Normen; zum Problem Soziologischen und Juristischen Rechtsdenkens." *Sociologia Internationalis*, 1972.

Fried, Charles. *An Anatomy of Values.* Cambridge: Harvard University Press, 1970.

Friedrichs, Jurgen. *Werte und Soziales Handeln.* Tűbingen: Mohr, 1968.

Frondizi, Risieri. *What Is Value?* Translated by Salomon Lipp. LaSalle, Ill.: Open Court, 1963.

Fustel de Coulanges. *La Cité Antique.* Paris: Hachette, 1947. English translation, *The Ancient City.* Garden City, N.Y.: Doubleday, Anchor Books, 1956.

Geiger, Theodor. "Evaluational Nihilism." *Acta Sociologica*, 1955.

Gibbs, J. P. "Norms: The Problem of Definition and Classification." *American Journal of Sociology*, 1965.

Gini, Corrado. "Occidental and Oriental Conceptions of Economic Progress." *International Social Science Bulletin*, 1954.

Glansdorff, Maxime. *Les Déterminants de la Théorie Générale de la Valeur.* Brussels: Université Libre, 1966.

Goldman, Alvin I., and Dordrecht, Jaegwon Kim, eds. *Values and Morals: Essays in Honor of William Frankena, Charles Stevenson and Richard Brandt.* Boston: D. Reidel, 1978.

Goldschmidt, Walter. "Values and the Field of Comparative Sociology." *American Sociological Review*, June 1953.

Goffman, Erwing. *Strategic Interaction.* Philadelphia: University of Pennsylvania Press, 1969.

Goodman, Mary Ellen. "Values, Attitudes, and Social Concepts of Japanese and American Children." *American Anthropologist*, December 1957.

Graff Piotr. *O Procesie Wartósciowania i Wartósciach Estetycznych* In Polish, *On the process of valuation and esthetic values.* Warsaw: Panstwowe Wydawnictwo Naukowe, 1970.

Gross, Feliks. "Language and Value Changes Among the Arapaho." *International Journal of American Linguistics*, vol. 17, Jan. 1951.

———. "Soziologie und Ethik: Grenzen Wissenschaftlicher Wertmasstabe in der Sozialen Forschung." *Kolner Zeitschrift für Soziologie*, 1953/54.

———. "Valores y el Cambio Social." *Revista Mexicana de Sociologia*, January–April 1963.

———. "Infinite Value and Social Change." *Transactions of the New York Academy of Sciences*, June 1964.

———. *Saggi Su Valori e Struttura.* Rome: Istituto di Statistica C. Gini, Universitá di Roma, 1966.

———. *Il Paese: Values and Social Change in an Italian Village* New York and Rome: New York University Press and Istituto di Statistica C. Gini, Universitá di Roma, 1973.

———. "Origins of an Ideology." *International Journal of Contemporary Sociology*, October 1974.

———. "Yankee Islands: Social Values of Fishermen of the Islands of Northern Maine." *Revue Internationale de Sociologie*, April 1974.

Gross, Feliks. Ed. *European Ideologies.* New York: Philosophical Library, 1948.

Guthrie, W. K. C. *The Greeks and Their Gods.* Boston: Beacon Press, 1954.

Hagea, Everett E. "How Economic Growth Begins: A General Theory Applied to Japan." *Public Opinion Quarterly*, Fall 1958.

Hall, Everett W. *Our Knowledge of Fact and Value*. Chapel Hill: University of North Carolina Press, 1961.

Hands, A. R. *Charities and Social Aid in Greece and Rome*. Ithaca, N.Y.: Cornell University Press, 1968.

Handy, Rollo. *The Measurement of Values*. Saint Louis: 1970.

Hardy, Jean. *Values in Social Policy: Nine Contradictions*. London and Boston: Routledge & Kegan Paul, 1981.

Hare, R. M. *The Language of Morals*. Oxford: Oxford University Press, 1952.

Hart, Hornell. "A Reliable Scale of Value Judgements." *American Sociological Review*, vol. 10, 1945.

Hart, Samuel. *Treatise on Values*. New York: Philosophical Library, 1949.

Hartman, Robert S. *The Structure of Value*. Carbondale: Southern Illinois University Press, 1967.

Hartmann, Nicolai. "Das Wert Problem in der Philosophie der Gegenwart." *Actes du Huitième Congrès Internationale de Philosophie*, 1934. Reprinted in English translation in Dagobert Runes, ed., *Treasury of Philosophy*. New York: Philosophical Library, 1955.

———. *The Realm of Ethical Values*. London: Allen & Unwin, 1963. Vol. II. Values.

Hatcher, Harlan H. *The Persistent Quest for Value*. Columbia: University of Missouri Press, 1966.

Hayes, E. C. "Social Values." *American Journal of Sociology*, vol. 18, 1913.

Heisenberg, Werner. *Across the Frontiers*. New York: Harper & Row, 1974.

Herman, Robert D. "A Social Welfare Approach to the Value Issue in Social Problems Theory." *Humanity and Society*, August 1978.

Herz, Thomas. "Der Wandel von Wertvorstellungen in Westlichen Industriegesellschaften." *Kölner Zeitschrift für Soziologie und Sozialpsychologie*, July 1979.

Hines, Joseph S. "Value Analysis in the Theory of Social Problems." *Social Forces*, March 1955.

Hofman, Werner. "Wissenschschaft und Ideologie." *Archiv fur Rechts und Sozial Philosophie*, 1967.

Honeycutt, James M. "Altruism and Social Exchange Theory: The Vicarious Rewards of the Altruism." *Mid-American Review of Sociology*, Spring 1981.

Hook, Sidney, ed. *Human Values and Economic Policy*. New York: New York University Press, 1967.

Hutchins, Patrick. *Kant on Absolute Value*. Detroit: Wayne State University Press, 1972.

Ingarden, Roman. *Erlebnis, Kunstwerk und Wert*. Tübingen: Niemeyer, 1969.

Ingelhart, Ronald. *The Silent Revolution: Changing Values and Political Styles Among Western Public*. Princeton: Princeton University Press, 1977.

International Conference on the Unity of Sciences (Boston, 1978). Proceedings. *The Reevaluation of Existing Values and the Search for Absolute Values*. New York: International Foundation Press, 1979.

International Congress of Philosophy (11th, Brussels, 1953.) Proceedings, vol. 10. *Philosophy of Values*.

Irani, K. D. "Rationality in Thought and Action." Manuscript courtesy of the author, 1981.

James, William. *Psychology*. New York: Henry Holt, 1907.

Johnson, Allison H. *Modes of Values*. New York: Philosophical Library, 1978.

Kalleberg, Arne L. "Work Value and Job Rewards: A Theory of Job Satisfaction." *American Sociological Review*, February 1977.

Kallen, Horace M. *Cultural Pluralism and the American Idea*. Philadelphia: University of Pennsylvania Press, 1956.

Kaplan, Morton. "Freedom in History and Politics." *Ethics*, July 1969.

Kautsky, Karl. *Materialistische Geschichtsauffassung*. Berlin: J. H. W. Dietz, 1927.

Kecskemeti, Paul. *Meaning, Communication and Value*. Chicago: University of Chicago Press, 1952.

Klages, H., and Kmieciak, P., eds. *Wertwandel und Gesellschafts Wandel*. Frankfurt-New York Campus, 1979.

Kluckhohn, C. *Culture and Behavior*. Edited by Richard Kluckhohn. New York: Free Press of Glencoe, 1962.

Kluckhohn, C., and H. A. Murray, eds. *Personality in Nature, Society and Culture*. New York: Knopf, 1953.

Kluckhohn, Florence R., and Strodtbeck, Fred L. *Variations in Value Orientations*. Westport, Conn.: Greenwood Press, 1961.

König, René, "Einige Ueberlegungen zur Frage der Werturteilsfreicheit." *Kölner Zeitschrift fur Soziologie*, 1964.

Kohler, Wolfgang. *The Place of Value in a World of Facts*. New York: Liveright, 1938.

Kolari, Risto. "Uber Ideologische und Nationale Werte." *Transactions of the Westermarck Society*, 1969.

Kolb, William. "Values, Positivism and the Functional Theory of Religion: The Growth of a Moral Dilemma." *Social Forces*, 1953.

Konwitz, Milton R. *On the Nature of Value: The Philosophy of Samuel Alexander*. New York: King's Crown Press, 1946.

Kraft, Victor. *Die Grundlagen Einer Wissenschaftlichen Wertlehze*. Vienna: Springer, 1937.

Krober, A. L. *Anthropology: Culture Patterns and Processes*. New York: Harcourt, Brace, 1963.

———. *Style and Civilizations*. Berkeley: University of California Press, 1963.

Kropotkin, Peter. *Ethics, Origin and Development*. New York: Tudor Publishing, 1947.

———. *Mutual Aid: A Factor of Evolution*. New York: New York University Press, 1972.

Kumata, Hideya, and Schramm, Wilbur. "A Pilot Study of Cross-Cultural Meaning." *Public Opinion Quarterly*, Spring 1956.

Kutschera, Franz von. *Einfuhrung in die Logik der Normen, Werte und Entscheidungen*. Freiburg, Munich, 1973.

Labriola, Antonio. *Saggi sul Materialismo Storico*. Rome: Editori Riuniti, 1964.

Lafferty, Theodore Thomas. *Nature and Values*. New York: Columbia University Press, 1976.

Laird, J. *The Idea of Value*. Cambridge: Cambridge University Press, 1929.

Lang, Kurt, and Lang, Gladys Engel. "Experience and Ideology: The Influence of the Sixties on the Intellectual Elite." *Research in Social Movements, Conflict and Change*, 1978.

La Palombara, Joseph. "Decadencia de la Ideologia: Una Discrepanzia y una Interpretacion." *Revista de Ciencias Sociales*, September 1967.

Larson, Richard F. "Measuring 'Infinite' Values." *American Catholic Sociological Review*, Fall 1959.

Laswell, Harold; Lerner, Daniel; and Montgomery, John D., eds., "Values and Development" in *Appraising Asian Experience*. Cambridge: M.I.T. Press, 1976.

Lautman, Rudiger. *Wert und Norm*. Cologne: Westdeutscher Verlag, 1971.

Lavelle, Louis. *Traité des Valeurs*. Paris: Presses Universitaires, 1951.

Lecky, William E. H. *History of the Rise and Influence of the Spirit of Rationalism in Europe*. New York: Appleton & Company, 1906.

Lee, Alfred McClung. "Levels of Culture as Levels of Social Generalization." *American Sociological Review*, vol. 10, 1945.

———. *Multivalent Man*. New York: Braziller, 1965.

———. "Il Persistere Delle Ideologie." *Critica Sociologica*, Spring 1967.

Leeds, Ruth. "Altruism and the Norm of Giving." *Merrill-Palmer Quarterly*, 1963.

Leonardi, Franco. "Sociologia dell' Ideologia e Ideologia Sociologica." *Rassegna Italiana di Sociologia*, April-June 1962.

Lepley, Ray. *The Verifiability of Value*. New York: Columbia University Press, 1944.

Lepley, Ray. ed. *Value: A Cooperative Inquiry*. New York: Columbia University Press, 1949.

———. *The Language of Value*. New York: Columbia University Press, 1957.

Lessing, Theodor. *Studien zur Wertaxiomate*. Leipzig: Meiner, 1914.

Levine, Hillel. "Prolegomenon to a Sociology of Evil." *Humanity and Society*, August 1978.

Levy-Bruhl. L. *La Morale et la Science des Moeurs*. Paris: Alcan, 1910.

Lewis, Clarence Irwing. *Values and Imperatives*. Stanford: Stanford University Press, 1969.

Lichtheim, George. *The Concept of Ideology*. New York: Random House, 1967.

Liddell-Hart, B. H. *Why Don't We Learn from History?* New York: Hawthorne Books, 1971.

Linton, Ralph. *The Cultural Background of Personality*. New York: Appleton-Century, 1945.

Loevenstein, L. "Üeber die Verbreitung der Politischen Ideologien." *Zeitschrift fur Politik*, December 1956.

Ludz, Peter, ed. *Spengler Heute*. Munich: H. Beck, 1980.

Lundberg, George A. "Human Values: A Research Program." *Research Studies of the State College of Washington*, vol. 18, 1950.

———. "Science, Scientists and Values." *Social Forces*, 1952.

Lynch, Frank, ed. *Four Readings in Philippine Values*. Quezon City: Ateneo de Manila, University Press, 1964.

McGreal, Alan P. *The Art of Making Choices*. Dallas: Southern Methodist University Press, 1953.

Mackenzie, John S. *Ultimate Values in the Light of Contemporary Thought*. London: Hodder, 1924.

McShea, Robert J. "Biology and Ethics." *Ethics*, January 1978.

Malinowski, Bronislaw. *A Scientific Theory of Culture*. Chapel Hill: University of North Carolina Press, 1944.

———. *Freedom and Civilization*. New York: Roy Publishers, 1944.

Mannheim, Karl. *Ideology and Utopia*. New York: Harcourt, Brace, 1936.

———. *Man and Society in an Age of Reconstruction*. New York: Harcourt & Brace, 1948.

Margolis, Joseph. *Values and Conduct*. Oxford: Oxford University Press, 1971.

Marshall, Thomas H. "Value Problems of Welfare-Capitalism." *Journal of Social Policy*, January 1972.

Martindale, Don A. *Limits of and Alternatives to Functionalism in Sociology*. Philadelphia: American Academy of Political and Social Sciences, 1965.

———. *Sociological Theory of Culture and Problems of Values*. Columbus, Ohio: Merrill, 1974.

———. "Aesthetic Theory and Sociology of Art." *Research in Sociology of Knowledge, Sciences and Art*, vol. 1, 1978.

Marx, Karl, and Engels, Friedrich. *The German Ideology*. New York: International Publishers, 1947.

Masci, F. "La Filosofia dei Valori." *Reale Academia dei Lincei Rendisconti Classe di Scienze Morali*, ser. 5, vol. 22, 1913.

Maslow, Abraham. *Motivation and Personality*. New York: Harper and Brothers, 1954.

———. *New Knowledge in Human Values*. New York: Harper, 1959.

Mbiti, John. "African Concept of Time." *MaKarere Sociological Journal*, February 1965.

Mead, George Herbert. *The Philosophy of the Act*. Edited by Clark W. Harris. Chicago: University of Chicago Press, 1972.

Meehan, Eugene J. *Value Judgement and Social Science: Structures and Processes*. Dorsey Press: Homewood, Ill. 1969.

Meinecke, Friedrich. *Historism: The Rise of a New Historical Outlook*. New York: Herder & Herder, 1972.

Meinong, Alexius. *Psychologisch-Ethische Untersuchungen zur Wert Theorie*. Graz: Leuschner & Lubensky, 1894.

Mering, Otto. *A Grammar of Human Values*. Pittsburgh: University of Pittsburgh Press, 1961.

Merton, R. K. *Social Theory and Social Structure*. Glencoe, Ill.: Free Press, 1957.

Meynaud, M. *Destin des Ideologies*. Lausanne, 1961.

Mill, John Stuart. "What Is Utilitarianism." Reprinted in John Stuart Mill, *On Politics and Society*, edited by Geraint L. Williams. New York: International Publications Service, 1976.

Montoya Briones, Jose de Jesus. "Valores y la Teoria Social." *Revista Mexicana de Sociologia*, 1964.

Moore, Charles A., ed. *The Status of the Individual in East and West*. Honolulu: University of Hawaii Press, 1968.

Moore, Wilbert E. "The Utility of Utopias." *American Sociological Review*, December 1966.

Morris, Charles W. *Signs, Language and Behavior*. New York: Prentice-Hall, 1950.

———. *Varieties of Human Value*. Chicago: University of Chicago Press, 1956.

———. *Signification and Significance: A Study of Relations of Signs and Values*. Cambridge: M.I.T. Press, 1964.

Morris, Charles, and Jones, L. V. "Value Scales and Dimensions." *Journal of Abnormal and Social Problems*, vol. 51, 1955.

Morris, Richard T. "A Typology of Norms." *American Sociological Review*, October 1956.

Moser, Shia. *Absolutism and Relativism in Ethics*. Springfield, Ill.: Thomas, 1968.

Muensterberg, Hugo. *Philosophie der Werte*. Leipzig: Barth, 1903.

Mukerjee, Radhakamal. *Social Function of Art*. New York: Philosophical Library, 1958.

————. *The Dimensions of Values: A Unified Theory*. London: Allen & Unwin, 1964.

————. "Humanism, East and West." *Indian Journal of Social Research*, December 1966.

Mumford, Lewis. *Technics and Civilization*. New York: Harcourt, Brace, 1963.

Murphy, Arthur D., and Stepick, Alex. "Economic and Social Integration Among Peasants." *Human Organization*, Winter 1978.

Mussacchio, Enrico. "Utilitarismo edonismo e calcola della felicità." *De Homine*, September 1972.

Myrdal, Gunnar. *Value in Social Theory: A Selection of Essays on Methodology*, Edited by Paul Streeten. London: Routledge & Kegan Paul, 1958.

————. "The Place of Values in Social Policy." *Journal of Social Policy*, 1972.

Nahirny, Vladimir C. "Some Observations on Ideological Groups." *American Journal of Sociology*, January 1962.

Najder, Zdzislaw. *Values and Evaluations*. Oxford: Oxford University Press, 1975.

Needham, Joseph. *Science and Civilization in China*. Cambridge: Cambridge University Press, 1954.

————. "History and Human Value: A Chinese Perspective for World Science and Technology." *Centennial Review*, Winter 1976.

Nielsen, Kai. "Taking Human Nature as the Basis of Morality." *Social Research*, Summer 1962.

Nietzsche, Friedrich. *Genealogy of Morals: Beyond Good and Evil*. New York: Tudor Publishing, 1931.

Nieuwenhuize. C. A. O. van, "Social Development: Concept and Policy." *Humanity and Society*, May 1979.

Nilson, Sam, and Tiselius, Arne, eds. *The Place of Value in a World of Facts*. 14th Nobel Symposium. Stockholm, 1968. New York: Wiley Interscience Division, 1970.

Northrop F.S.C. *The Meeting of East and West*. New York: The Macmillan Company, 1960.

Oates, Whitney Jennings. *Aristotle and the Problem of Value*. Princeton: Princeton University Press, 1963.

Oliver, W. Donald. "Rational Choice and Political Control." *Ethics*, January 1956.

Olkinuora, Erkki. "Socialization, Structure of Personal Norms and Norm Alienation." *Acta Sociologica*, 1972.

Ormsby, Eaton Howard. *The Austrian Philosophy of Values*. Norman: University of Oklahoma Press, 1930.

Osborne, Harold. *Foundations of the Philosophy of Value: Examination of Value and Value Theories*. Cambridge: Cambridge University Press, 1933.

Ossowska, Maria. *Podstawy Nauki o Moralnosci* Warsaw: Czytelnik, 1947.

————. "The Problem of Universal Ethical Standards." *Studia Filozoficzn*. 1962.

Ostwald, Wilhelm. *Die Philosophie der Werte*. Leipzig: Kroner, 1913.

Otero, Lenēro Luis. *Valores Ideologicos y las Politicas de Poblacion en Mexico*. Mexico: 1979.

Panoff, Michel. "The Notion of Time among the Maenge Peoples of New Britain." *Ethnology*, April 1969.

Parker, De Witt Henry. *The Philosophy of Value*. Ann Arbor: University of Michigan Press, 1957.

Parsons, Talcott. *The Structure of Social Action*. Glencoe, Ill.: Free Press, 1949.

————. *The Social System*. Glencoe, Ill.: Free Press, 1951.

————*Essays in Sociological Theory*. Glencoe, Ill.: Free Press, 1964.

Parsons, Talcott; Bales, R. F.; and Shils, E. A. *Working Papers in the Theory of Action*. Glencoe, Ill.: Free Press, 1953.

Parsons, Talcott, and Shils, E., eds. *Toward a General Theory of Action*. Cambridge: Harvard University Press, 1962.

Peel, J. D. R. "Understanding Alien Belief-Systems." *British Journal of Sociology*, March 1969.

Peirce, Charles S. *Philosophical Writings of Charles Peirce* [1940]. Selected and edited with an introduction by Justus Buchler. New York: Dover, 1955.

————. *Values in a Universe of Chance*. Edited by Philip P. Wiener. Garden City, N.Y.: Doubleday, 1958.

Pellicani, Luigi. *Introduzione a Ortega y Gasset*. Naples: Liquori editore, 1978.

Pellizzi, Camillo. "Alcuni Appunti di Epistomologia e di Etica Sociologica." *Rassegna Italiana di Sociologia*. January–March 1963.

————. "Sulla Viscosita delle Idee." *Rassegna Italiana di Sociologia*, January–March 1973.

Pepper, Stephen C. *The Sources of Value*. Berkeley: University of California Press, 1958.

Perry, Ralph Barton. *General Theory of Value: Its Meaning and Basic Principles Constructed in Terms of Interest*. New York: Longmans, Green, 1926.

————. *Realm of Values* [1954]. Westport, Conn.: Greenwood Press, 1968.

Pfordtem, Otto V. *Konformismus: Eine Philosophie der Normativen Werte*. 3 vols. Heidelberg: C. Winter, 1910–1913.

Picard, Maurice. *Values Immediate and Contributory*. New York: New York University Press, 1920.

Plekhanov, George. *Essays in Historical Materialism*. New York: International Publishers, 1940.

————. *The Development of the Monist View of History*. Moscow: Foreign Languages Publishing House, 1956.

Polin, Raymond. *La Création des Valeurs*. Paris: Presses Universitaires de France, 1952.

Pugh, George E. *The Biological Origin of Human Values*. New York: Basic Books, 1977.

Ravis-Giordani, Georges. "Alta Politica e la Bassa Politica: Valeurs et Comportements Politiques dans les Communautes Villageoises Corses." *Etudes Rurales*, July–December 1976.

Rawls, John. *A Theory of Justice*. Cambridge: Harvard University Press, 1971.

Reid, John Robert. *A Theory of Value*. New York: Scribner's Sons, 1938.

Reininger, Robert. *Wertphilosophie und Ethik*. Vienna and Leipzig: Braumuller, 1947.

Rescher, Nicholas. *Introduction to Value Theory*. Englewood Cliffs, N.J.: Prentice-Hall, 1969.

Rickert, Heinrich. "Lebenswerte und Kulturwerte." *Logos Int. Zeitschrift für Philosophie und Kultur*. 1911.

————. "Psychologie der Weltanschauung und Philosophie der Werte. *Logos.*, 1920, v. 9.

Rickert, Heinrich. *Kulturwissenschaft und Naturwissenschaft*. Tübingen: J. C. B. Mohr, 1926.

Rickman, H. P., ed. *Dilthey Wilhelm: Pattern and Meaning in History: Thoughts on History and Society*. New York: Harper & Row, 1961.

Rivière, P. G. "The Honor of Sanchez." *Man*, December 1967.

Rokeach, Milton. *Beliefs, Attitudes and Values: A Theory of Organization and Change.* San Francisco: Jossey-Bass, 1968.

————. *The Nature of Human Values.* New York: Free Press, 1973.

Rose, Arnold M. "Sociology and the Study of Values." *British Journal of Sociology*, March 1956.

Rose, Arnold M., ed. *Human Behavior and Social Processes.* Boston: Houghton Mifflin, 1962.

Ross, Alsworth. *Social Control,* New York: Macmillan, 1924.

Roucek, Joseph S. "The Component Parts of Ideological Forces." *Sociologia*, September 1960.

————. "Historia del Concepto de Ideologia." *Revista Mexicana de Sociologia*, May–August 1963.

Roucek, Joseph, ed. *Social Control for 1980.* Westport, Conn.: Greenwood Press, 1980.

Roura, Parella Juan. "El Pensiamento Politico Del Nicolai Hartmann." *Revista Mexicana de Sociologia*, May–August 1956.

Royez, Penn J. "Measuring Intergenerational Value Differences." *Social Science Quarterly*, September 1977.

Rozsohazy, Rudolf. "The Concept of Social Time." *International Social Science Journal*, 1972.

Rubin, Vitaly A. *Individual and State in Ancient China.* New York: Columbia University Press, 1976.

Ruyer, Raymond. *Le Monde des Valeurs; Etudes Systematiques.* Paris: Aubier, 1948.

Sachs, R. "Wandlungen des Ziel und Wertsystems." *Sociologia Ruralis*, 1965.

Sahakian, William S. *Systems of Ethics and Value Theory.* New York: Philosophical Library, 1963.

Sano, Chiye. *Changing Values of the Japanese Family.* Washington, D.C.: Catholic University of America Press, 1958.

Sartori, G. "Politics, Ideology and Belief Systems." *American Political Science Review*, June 1969.

Saussure, Ferdinand de. *Course in General Linguistics.* New York: Philosophical Library, 1959.

Scheibe, Karl E. *Beliefs and Value.* New York: Holt, Rinehart & Winston, 1971.

Scheler, Max. *Vom Umsturz der Werte.* Leipzig: Neŭe R. Geist, 1919.

————. *Der Formalimus in der Ethik und Die Materiale Wertethik.* Halle: M. Niemeyer, 1921.

Schellenberg, James A. "Social Choice and Similarity of Personal Values." *Sociology and Social Research*, March–April 1957.

Schlick, Moritz. *Problems of Ethics.* New York: Dover, 1962.

Schmidkunz, Hans. "Neŭes von den Werten Psychologische Grundlegung. Eines Systems der Wert Theorie." *Kritik.* Leipzig, 1904.

Scott, William. A. "Empirical Assessment of Values and Ideologies." *American Sociological Review*, June 1959.

Shepard, Herbert. "The Value System of a University Research Group." *American Sociological Review*, August 1954.

Shepardson, Mary. "Value Theory in the Prediction of Political Behavior: Navajo Case." *American Anthropologist*, 1962.

Sherif, Musafer. *The Psychology of Social Norms.* New York: Farrer & Straus, 1973.

Sherover, Charles M. *The Human Experience of Time: The Development of its Philosophical Meaning*. New York: New York University Press, 1975.

Shiller, Robert E. *New Methods of Knowledge and Value*. New York: Philosophical Library, 1967.

Sidgwick, Henry. *Outlines of the History of Ethics*. Boston: Beacon Press, 1968.

Sills, Milton, and Holmes, Ernest S. *Values: A Philosophy of Human Needs*. Chicago: University of Chicago Press, 1939.

Simey, T. S. "Weber's Sociological Theory of Value: An Appraisal in Midcentury." *Sociological Review*, March 1965.

Simpson, R. L., and Simpson, I. H. "Values, Personal Influence and Occupational Choice." *Social Forces*, vol. 39, 1960.

Smelser, Neil J. *Theory of Collective Behavior*. London: Routledge & Kegan Paul, 1962.

Smelser, N. J., and Smelser, W. T. *Personality and Social System*. New York: Wiley, 1970.

Smith, Brewster M. "Psychology and Values." *Journal of Social Issues*, 1978.

Smolicz, J. J. *Culture and Education in a Plural Society* Canberra: Curriculum Development Centre, 1979.

Smith, Nicholas. "A Calculus of Ethics: A Theory of the Structure of Values." *Behavioral Sciences*, April and July 1956.

Sombart, Werner. *Die Vorkapitalistische Wirtschaft*. Munich and Leipzig: Duncker and Humblot, 1928.

Sorel, Georges. *Réflexions sur la Violence*. 10th ed. Paris: Rivière, 1940.

Sorokin, Pitirim. *Social and Cultural Dynamics*. New York: American Book Company, 1937–1941.

———. *Society, Culture and Personality: Their Structure and Dynamics: A System of General Sociology*. New York: Harper & Brothers, 1947.

———. *Altruistic Love*. Boston: Beacon Press, 1950.

Spencer, Herbert. *The Principles of Sociology* [1886]. New York: Appleton & Company, 1899.

———. *The Data of Ethics*. New York: Hurst & Company, 1879.

Spiegelberg, Herbert. *Antirelativismus*. Zurich and Leipzig: Niehans, 1935.

Stern, Alfred. *Philosophy of History and the Problem of Value*. The Hague: Mouton, 1962.

Stevenson, Charles L. *Facts and Values*. New Haven: Yale University Press, 1963.

Straus, Roger. "The Theoretical Frame of Symbolic Interactionism." *Symbolic Interaction*, Fall 1981.

Stuart, Henry W. *Valuation as a Logical Process*. Chicago: 1918.

———. *Human Value: An Ethical Essay*. Cambridge: Cambridge University Press, 1923.

Sufin, Zbigniew, and Wesolowski, Wlodzimierz. "Work in Hierarchy of Values." *Polish Sociological Bulletin,* 1963.

Tatarkiewicz, Wladyslaw. *Estetyka Sredniowieczna* [Medieval Esthetics]. Wroclaw: Ossolinski, 1960.

Tawney, R. H. *Religion and Rise of Capitalism*. New York: New American Library, 1954.

Taylor, Paul W. *Normative Discourse*. Englewood Cliffs, N.J.: Prentice-Hall, 1961.

Thirtha, N. V. "Dharma: A Sociological Analysis of a Dominant Theme in a Telangana Village." *Eastern Anthropologist*, September–December 1963.

Thomas, William I. ed. Volkart, Edmund H., *Social Behavior and Personality: Contri-*

butions of William I. Thomas to Theory and Social Research. New York: Social Science Research Council, 1951.

Thomas, William I., and Znaniecki, Florian. *The Polish Peasant in Europe and America.* Vols. 1–5. Boston: Richard G. Badger, Gorham Press, 1918–1920.

Tischler, Joseph. *Etyka Solidarnosci* [Ethics of Solidarity]. Crakow: Znak, 1981.

Treves, Renato. *Spirito Critico e Spirito Dogmatico.* Milan: Istituto Editoriale Cisalpino.

Tullio-Altan, Carlo. *Valori, Classi Sociali, Scelte Politiche.* Milan: 1976.

Tzu, Chuang. *Basic Writings.* New York: Columbia University Press, 1964.

Van Dyke, V. "Values and Interests." *American Political Science Review,* September 1962.

Vernon, Glenn M. "Locating Values." *Humanity and Society,* Summer 1977.

Vickers, Sir Geoffrey. *Value Systems and Social Process.* New York: Basic Books, 1968.

———. *Value Systems and Social Planning.* Harmondsworth, England: Penguin, 1970.

Villegas, Uribe. "El Progresso: Una Exploracion Lexica y una Exploracion Sociologica." *Revista Mexicana de Sociologia,* January–March 1972.

Visalberghi, Aldo. *Esperienza e Valutazione.* Turin: Taylor, 1958.

Vogt, Evon. *Modern Homesteaders.* Cambridge: Harvard University Press, 1955.

Vogt, Evon, and O'Dea, Thomas F. "A Comparative Study of the Role of Values in Social Action in Two Southwestern Communities." *American Sociological Review,* December 1953.

Ward, Leo R. *Values and Reality.* London: Sheed and Ward, 1935.

Ward, Lester. *Dynamic Sociology.* Westport, Conn.: Greenwood Press, 1968.

Weber, Alfred. *Kulturgeschichte als Kultur Soziologie.* Leiden: Nijthoff's, 1935.

———*Prinzipien der Geschichts und Kultur Soziologie.* Munich: Piper & Co., 1951.

———. *Das Tragische in der Geschichte.* Munich: Piper & Co., 1959.

Weber, Max. *Essays in Sociology.* Translated and edited with an introduction by H. H. Gerth and C. Wright Mills. New York: Oxford University Press, 1946.

———. *Gesammelte Aufsatze zur Religions Soziologie.* Tübingen: A. Mohr, 1947.

Werkmeister, William H. *Man and His Values.* Lincoln: University of Nebraska Press, 1967.

Westermarck, Edward. *Ethical Relativity.* New York: Harcourt, Brace, 1932.

———. *The Origin and Development of Moral Ideas.* New York: Books for Libraries, 1971.

White, Irwing H., ed., in collaboration with George B. Franklin et al. *Essays in Value.* New York: Appleton-Century, 1938.

Whitehead, Alfred North. *Science and the Modern World.* New York: Macmillan, 1925.

———. *Symbolism.* New York: Macmillan, 1927.

———. *Modes of Thought.* New York: Putnam Sons or Capricorn Books, 1958.

Whittemore, Robert. "Positivistic Path to Value." *Tulane Studies in Philosophie,* 1972.

Wiederhold, Konrad. *Wertbegrief und Wertphilosophie.* Berlin: Reuther & Reichard, 1920.

Wiener, Martin J. *English Culture and the Decline of Industrial Spirit.* New York: Cambridge University Press, 1981.

Wilding, Paul, and Vic, George. "Social Values and Social Policy." *Journal of Social Policy.* October 1975.

Willi, Victor Joseph. *Grundlagen Einer Empirischer Soziologie der Werte und Wertsysteme.* Zurich: Orell, Fussli, 1966.

Williams, B. "Democracy and Ideology." *Political Quarterly,* 1961.

Williams, Robin. "Unity and Diversity in Modern America." *Social Forces*, October 1957.

Windelband, Wilhelm. *An Introduction to Philosophy*. London: Unwin, 1923.

Wolf, Kurt H. "For a Sociology of Evil." *Journal of Social Issues*, January 1969.

Wolfgang, Rudolph. "Die Amerikanische 'cultural anthropology' und das Wertproblem." *Forschungen zur Ethnologie und Sozialpsychologie*, 1959.

Wojtyla, Karol. *Miłość i Odpowiedzialność [Love and Responsibility]*. Lublin: Towarzystwo Naukowe Katolickiego Uniwersytetu Lubelskiego, 1960.

―――. *Ocena Mozliwości Zbudowania Etyki Chrześcijanskiej przy Zalozeniach Maxa Schelera*. [Evaluation of a Possibility of Construction of Christian Ethics on Premises of Max Scheler]. Lublin: Towarzystwo Naukowe Katolickiego Uniwersytetu Lubelskiego, 1960.

Wright, Wiliam K. "The Evolution of Values from Instincts." *Philosophical Review*, vol. 24, 1915.

Zecha, Gerhard. "Wie laut das 'Prinzip der Wertfreicheit'?" *Kölner Zeitschrift fur Sociologie und Sozialpsychologie*. December 1976.

Zetterberg, H. "On Axiomatic Theories in Sociology." In P. P. Lazarsfeld and M. Rosenberg, eds. *The Language of Social Research*. Glencoe, Ill.: Free Press, 1955.

Zimmer, Heinrich. *Philosophies of India*. New York: Meridian Books, 1958.

Zimmerman, Carle C. "The Proper Study of Mankind." *International Journal of Contemporary Sociology*, July–October 1976.

Zito, George V. *Systems of Discourse: Structures and Semiotics in Social Sciences*. Westport, Conn.: Greenwood Press, 1984.

Znaniecki, Florian. *Zagadnienie Wartości w Filozofii* [Problem of Values in Philosophy]. Warsaw: Wende, 1910.

―――. *Humanizm i Poznanie* [Humanism and Knowledge]. Warsaw: Wende, 1912.

―――. *Cultural Sciences: Their Origin and Development*. Urbana: University of Illinois Press, 1952.

―――. *Social Relations and Social Roles*. San Francisco: Chandler, 1965.

―――. *Social Actions*. New York: Russel & Russel, 1967.

Zwolinski, Zbigniew, *Byt i Wartość u Nicolais Hartmana* In Polish: Existence and Value in Nicolai Hartmann. Warsaw, 1974.

Index

Abel, Theodore, 42 n.2
Absolute norms, 244-45, 294
Abstract time and goals, 191, 198-202
Actions, 152
Acton Lord, 61
Agape, 285
Ambivalence, 253, 257-67
Adler, F., 23
Aleatory, nonpredictive behavior, 78
Allport, Gordon, 256, 258-59
Alternative goals, 155-56
Alternatives. *See* Options; Alternative goals
Altruism, 278-92, 318
American Revolution, 220
Ancillary norms, 231-35
Apache, 63
Arapaho, 63, 96, 185-86, 205, 305
Aristotle, 9, 81, 93, 195-96, 243, 259
Aschenbrenner, Karl, 214
Asian societies, 35
Attention span social-historical, 177, 178-80

Bakunin, Mikhail, 221
Barker, Ernest, 311
Basic needs. *See* Biological needs
Becker, Carl, 26
Behavior, 5
Benedict, Ruth, 23, 248
Benedictine order, 28

Beneficient social planning, 131-32
Bentham, 279
Biological needs, 92, 111-12
Blanc, Louis, 130
Bleuler, P. E., 256-57
Boat people, 288
Bohemia, 250
Bonaparte, Napoleon, 194
Brentano, Franz, 21
Bridge building, goals and time range, 165, 173, 175
Bücher, Karl, 199
Byzantium, 291-92

Calculatory sense, 176
Calendars, medieval, 188-89
Cambodia, 260
Catechism of a revolutionary, 221-22
Cathedrals, time-span, 161-67, 174
Catholic church and clocks, 198
Charitable institutions, 285, 291-92
Chiliastic movements, 105
Choice, 6, 87-89
Cicero, 81, 92, 246, 247, 286
Civilization, goals and values, 180, 227
Clausewitz, Karl von, 122
Clocks, 192
Clocks: in Catholic church, 198; in China, 198
Codification of norms, 219
Communist vision, 137

Complementary values, 293-96
Comte, A., 27, 37, 73
Condorcet, M.J. de Carital, 37, 204
Conrad, Joseph, 7, 92
Consensus solidarity, 262
Constantelos, Demetrios J., 285
Contradictions, 38-41, 54, 244, 318
Cooley, C. H., 256
Core, value, *See* Dominant values
Cortez, Hernan, 250
Counter Reformation, 250
Counter-strategies, 155
Crisis situation, 253
Culture and goals, 158
Cunov, Heinrich, 32
Cyclical goals, 158, 183
Czech historical tradition, 250

Darwin, Charles, 278, 282
Death penalty, 280
Decalogue. *See* Ten Commandments
Decision, 88-90, 173
Declaratory data, 211-12
Declaration of Human Rights, United Nations, 220-21, 230
De Sade Marquis, 314
De Saussure, Ferdinand, 59-60
De Stael, Madame, 248
Dewey, John, 22, 37, 138
Dialectics, 41
Dialogue, 296-97
Diarchy, 264
Dichotomy, ethical, 238-39
Dictatorship, 137
Diderot, Denis, 237, 296
Dilthey, Wilhelm, 21 n.6, 27, 41-42 n.1, 216
Diodorus, 286
Directive and regulatory system, 3-9
Disagreement, 16-20
Disagreement resolution, 151-53
Disaster situation, 88
Discipline, 117-18
Distant goals, time range, 158-82
Dogma, 153
Dominant values, 216, 218, 226
Dostoyevski, Feodor, 222
Double standards, 268-70

Dual ethics, 237, 239-40
Durkheim, Emile, 8
Duty, 113
Dworak, Max, 42 n.3

Eastern Europe, German and Soviet occupation, 263-67
Egyptian religion, projects and time range, 162-63
Egyptian tradition, 285-86
Ehrenfels, Christian, 21 n.6
Eiffel, Alexandre-Gustave, 176-77
Eight hours working day, 200-201
Elementary goal structure, 83
Empedocles, 64
Empire State building, 177-78
Empirical data, 211
Enforcement of goals, 139
Engels, Friedrich, 30-33, 35, 40
Environment, 64, 263
Epidaurus, 285
Error, 141
Eskimo, 282
Espinas, A., 280
Ethical dicotomy, 237-40
Ethics, 64, 92, 128-44, 238-39, 246
Ethnic pluralism, 314-15
Ethos, 227-230, 242, 245, 285-87
External norms, 238

Fecamp calendar, 188-89
Fibonacci da Pisa, Leonardo, 24
Finite goals, 203
Five year plan, 130, 134
Flavius, Josephus, 90
Fletcher, Banister, 161
Flexibility of norms, 259-260
Frazer, J. G., 241
French revolution, 123, 130, 140, 193, 220, 304
Freud, Sigmund, 256
Friedrichs, Jurgen, 24, 321
Forced labor, Soviet camps, 115, 138
Forecasting, strategic, 124-25
Forecasting in planning, 147, 179
Functional theories, 29
Futurology, 179

Germany, 283
Gierke, Otto, 275
Gimbel, Jean, 161, 198
Gladiators sequence, 116
Goals, 80; agriculture, 183-85; alternative, 87, 155; basic, 79-90; and civilization, 180; consumatory, 81-82; cyclical, 158, 183-202; distant, 94, 104, 155-182; enforcement, 139; finite, 203; formation, 94; generalized-ideological, 105-8; horizontal sequence and structure, 73, 103-18; immediate, 104; in an Italian village, 109; incentives, 110; independent and interdependent, 105, 109-10; infinite open, 203-5; instrumental, 81-82, 104, 168; intermediate, 104; irrational, 79, 121-22, 131; linear horizontal goals, 194; in a medieval society, 187-93; messianistic, 197; normative, 82-83, 97; in planning, 154; pragmatic, 82-83, 98-101, 175-78; preferential, 87, 108; religious, 117, 160-68, 174-75; seasonal, 184; secular, 168; social, 200; strategic, 81, 119-127; structure oriented behavior, 79, 117; substitute, 155, 195; tactical, 81-82; and time, 191, 195-97; vertical structure, 212-13
Great depression, 130
Greek architectural projects, time range, 162-63, 166, 172
Guatemoc, 250

Hands, A. R., 285-86, 291
Hartmann, Nicolai, 22 n.6, 224-27
Hebrews, 285-86. *See also* Jews
Hegel, G. W. F., 40
Hellenic ethos, 245, 285-87
Heraclitus, 195, 196
Herculean value, 176
Herder, Johann, 248
Heresy, 244
Herodotus, 196
Hesiod, 196
Hierarchies of values, 211-35
Historical memory, 178-79
Historical materialism, 30-33, 49
Historicism, 178

Hitler, Adolf, 136, 254, 283
Holidays, in Bavarian mines, 190
Holy scriptures, 244
Horary divisions of time, 199
Horizontal structure, 73, 103-18, 194
Huizinga, J., 21, n.6
Hume, David, 249
Huss, Jan, 250
Huxley, Thomas, 154

Ideal and real, 116
Ideational culture, 166-67
Ideology, 26, 29-30, 33-56, 177, 180
Ideological test, 150
Imagination, 95-100, 189
Immediate, intermediate, distant goals, 104, 105, 109-10, 155-82
Incentives, 110-18, 140
Incest, 277
Indifference, 305-6
Industrial ideology, 176-78
Industrial revolution, time-goals, 186, 194-95
Infinite value-goals, 203-7
Inquisitorial state, 302-3
Institutions, totalitarian, 139
Integration of norms, 258-63
Internal norms, 238
Intolerance, 301-2
Inventions, and goals, 197
Iran, 108
Irani, K. D., 101, 229
Irrational goals, 121; means and ends, 131
Islam, 8, 291
Isocrates, 243
Israelites, 244-45, 247, 266, 285-86
Italian village, 109
Iter, path of actions, and goals, 82, 95-101, 121

James, Wiliam, 94, 256
Jews, 244, 245, 247, 266, 285-86
Judaic tradition, 37-38, 285-86

Kautsky, Karl, 32
Kessler, Karl, 279
Kluchohn, F. R., 280

Kropotkin, Peter, 14, 218, 279, 280
Kuhn, Thomas J., 40

Labriola, Antonio, 32
Language and value, 214-15
Laplace, P. S., 203
Lecky, William E. H., 64, 276
Lee McClung, Alfred, 23, 236, 256-58
Legitimacy, 66-68, 135, 314
Lenin, 138
Liddel-Hart, B. H., 122
Limitation of power, 310-11
Long range projects, 162-75

Machiavelli, 124, 248
Maenge (tribe) time concept, 185
Maine, Yankee Islands, 261-63
Mahdi, 107
Malinowski, Bronislaw, 4, 91-92, 97,
    184, 204-5, 280
Manichean values, 7-8
Mannheim, Karl, 52
Martindale, Don, 21 n.6, 224
Maryland Act of Toleration, 304
Marx, K. 30-33, 35, 37, 40
Maslow, A., 258
Means and ends, 132-33
Medieval society, 28, 187-93
Megaethos, 217-224, 227, 237, 243,
    273, 295, 297, 313, 317
Meinong, Alexius, 21 n.6
Meliorism, 135-36
Messianistic goal, 197
Method, 49
Mexico, 250
Michelet, Jules, 277
Mikhailovsky, Mikhail, 279
Militant state, 239-40
Military strategy, 124
Mill, J. S., 271, 279
Mirabeau, Comte de, 304
Minimum program, 107
Mitterand, F., 283
Modes of thought, 47
Monistic doctrine, 140-42, 152-54
Monocausal theories, 29
Montaigne, Michel Eyguem de, 64, 257,
    276-77

Montesquieu, Charles Louis de, 218-19
Morris, Charles, 23, 272
Mukerjee, R., 24
Multicausal theories, 29
Multilinear change, 34-36
Multiple sets of values, 237-267
Multivalence, 257-58
Münsterberg, Hugo, 22
Mutual aid, 278-92, 318
Mutuality, 291

Nansen, F., 282
National character, 247-52
National socialism, 254
Navaho, 280
Nechayev, Sergey, 221
Needs and goals, 91-93; ethical, 92
Needham, Joseph, 196-98
New York, time span of projects, 173
Nietsche, F., 8
Night of Saint Bartholomew, 287
Norms: of conduct, 5, 62-64, 273-76;
    flexibility of, 259-60; integration of,
    258-63; internal, 238; reconstruction
    of, 296
Nye, J. F., 24

Open admission, 229
Optimum, 229
Options, 84, 87-90, 152-54, 148-55
Orthodox church and clocks, 198

Paine, Thomas, 305
Parallel values, 237
Parameters, ethical, legal, moral, norma-
    tive and pragmatic, 85, 120, 121, 128-
    29, 132-40; of planning, 146
Pareto, Vilfredo, 34, 84, 101
Park, Mungo, 284, 287, 290
Parsons, Tallcott, 9, 23, 71, 195, 224
Path of pragmatic goals, 82, 98-101, 121
Peace strategy, 122
Peirce, S. Charles, 21 n.6
Perfectionism, 135-36
Personalist principle, 136
Peruggia, 188
Philanthropy, 284. *See also* Charitable
    institutions

Planning, social, 128-32, 140, 229, 233-35; beneficial, 131-32; coercive, 138-39; forecasting in, 147, 149; logic of, 145; monistic, 140-42; pluralistic, 140-42; pragmatic, 132; scientific, 154-55; total, 132-40, 143; two meanings, 131-32

Plato, 243, 246

Plekhanov, G., 30-33

Pluralism, 224, 300, 306-19

Pluralistic doctrine, 140-42, 153

Pluralistic state, 302-3

Plutarch, 64

Poincarè, H., 203, 227

Poland, 264

Political strategy, 124-27

Polls, 228

Pol Pot, 139

Post-industrial society, change of goals, 179-80

Power, political, 126

Pragmatic architectural, goals, and projects. *See* Goals

Predictive behavior, 77-79; predictive predictable, 78

Preferable, 272

Priorities, 108, 111

Privacy, 310-11

Probability, 203

Procopius, 174

Progress, 37

Prophet, 56-57

Public interest, 179

Pythagoras, 64

Quantification, 176-78, 228

Ranking, ranks of norms, values, 213, 219-230

Rashdall, Hastings, 9

Rational actions, 152; behavior, 87-89, 93, 101-2; means, 131; planning, 141, 154; unit of time, 191; work, 187

Rationalization of time units and goals, 193

Reconstruction of norms, 296

Record as a value, 176-77

Regimentation, 240

Regulatory system, 126, 137

Relative and relativistic, 212

Relativism, 275, 280, 294-95, 301

Religious pluralism, 314-5

Religious projects, time range, 161-65

Revolutions, 107, 138, 140, 221-23; American, 220; French, 123, 130, 140, 193, 220, 304; Russian, 61, 139-40

Rewards, 110-18, 140

Roads, time-span, 173

Roman law, 291

Roman long range projects, 172-73

Roman temple building, time range, 163-64

Rousseau, J. J., 237

Ruskin, John, 26

Russian Revolution, 61, 139-40

Sack of Rome, 287

Saint Celestino, 28

Saudi Arabia, 269

Scheler, Max, 224-27

Science, scientific outlook, 179

Seasonal goals, 184-87

Secular goals in architecture, 168

Senegal, 284

Sequence of goal formation, 95

Sermon, 36, 56-57

Shoshone, 63, 305

Sign, 59-60

Sin, 224

Slavery, 242, 269-70, 284

Social attention span, 160

Social control, 8, 67-68, 140, 301, 313

Social myth, 52, 135

Social product, 129

Social security, 88

Socialist pragmatism, 18

Socialist theory and planning, 130, 135

Socrates, 243

Sombart, Werner, 176, 190

Sonification of time, 199

Sorel, Georges, 135

Sorokin, Pitirim, 22, 166-67, 224

South Africa, 269

Soviet camps, incentives, 115; planning, 137-40

Spanish-Americans, 280

Spencer, Herbert, 8, 14, 22, 37, 204, 238-40, 256, 277-78
Spinoza, Benedict, 274
Stages, 103, 138
Stalin, J., 130, 137-39, 266, 315
Stirner, Max, 314
Strategy, 54, 119-127
Strodtbeck, F. J., 280-81
Subordinated norms, 231-235
Substitute goals, 155
Subsystems, 230, 241
Sun dance, 96
Superethos, 246-47, 259-60, 268. *See also* Megaethos
Superstructure, 30, 33
Survival, 392
Symbols, 48, 58-62

Tacitus, 248
Tactics, 54, 119
Targets, 82, 105-8, 201
Tarn, W. W., 61
Tatar tribes, 315
Tawney, R. H., 29, 224
Technology and ideology, 176-78, 180
Telic behavior, 78, 80-81
Ten Commandments, 15, 220-21, 243, 247
Terror, 223
Test: ideological, pragmatic, scientific, 150
Texans, 281
Thai, 288
Theater building, time range, 166, 169, 175
Thomas, W. J., 256
Thucidides, 246
Time division, French Revolution, 193; in China, 197; horary division, 199; in India, 196; sonification, 199
Time and goals, 191-202; time, linear-horizontal, 194; time range of goals, 159-82; time schedule-leisure, 201-2
Tischner, J., 296
Tolerant state, 302, 303-5
Toleration, 300, 303-5
Totalitarian planning, 133-42; state, 239
Triobrand Islands, 204

Trotsky, L., 138
Turkey, Ottoman, 304

Uganda, 269
Unilinear change, 34-36
United Nations, 220, 230, 268-70
Universal norms, 273-96, 278-81
Urban communities, 242
Ure, Andrew, 194
Utilitarianism, 275, 279
Utopias, 52

Vacations, 201-2
Validation, 12-13, 19, 149
Values, 9-16, 64-66; absolute, 294; ancillary, 231-35; complementary, 293-96; core, 73, 216, 218, 226, 270, 294, 313; dominant, 45, 216, 226, 231-35; hierarchies, 211-35; infinite, 74, 203-7; multiple, 238; national, 247-52; parallel hierarchies, 237; polar, 6; universal, 273-76 *See also* Symbols
Values, valuation, scientific pragmatic normative, 149
Verification, 19. *See also* Validation
Vertical structure, 73, 211-13
Verstehen, 27, 42
Vietnam, 287-88
Vinci, Leonardo da, 98
Visualization of time, 199
Vital routine, 186
Vitruvius, 172
Voltaire, 215, 237, 296

Wall Street, values and norms, 233
War strategy, 122-24
Weber, Max, 9, 21 n.6, 195, 216, 224
Weekend, 201
Welfare state, 130
Weltanschauung. *See* World outlook
Westermarck, Edward, 276
Whitehead, Alfred North, 154
White Sea Canal, 137
Will, 94, 111
Wilson Coach, 96
Wilson, W. J., 24
Wittfogel, Karl, 35
Wojtyła, Karol, 236

Working day, 200-201
World outlook, 26, 29, 44-45, 63-64,
142

Yankee Islands, Maine, 261-63

Zimmer, Heinrich, 196
Znaniecki, Florian, 10, 21-22 n.6, 72,
224, 270
Zuni, 281

ABOUT THE AUTHOR

FELIKS GROSS is Emeritus Professor at Brooklyn College and President of the City University of New York Academy for Humanities and Sciences. He is the author of *Ethics in the Borderland* (Greenwood Press, 1978); *The Revolutionary Party* (Greenwood Press, 1974); *Violence in Politics*; and many other studies. His numerous contributions have appeared widely in international publications.